SOLANO COMMUNITY COLLEGE
3 7045 00030 1285

D0389326

# The Electoral Politics Dictionary

# THE ELECTORAL POLITICS DICTIONARY

Peter G. Renstrom
Chester B. Rogers
Western Michigan University

ABC-CLIO
Santa Barbara, California
Oxford, England

**Library of Congress Cataloging-in-Publication Data**

Renstrom, Peter G., 1943–
The electoral politics dictionary.
(Clio dictionaries in political science)
Includes index.
1. Elections—United States—Dictionaries.
2. Electioneering—United States—Dictionaries.
3. Political participation—United States
—Dictionaries. I. Rogers, Chester B., 1939–
II. Title. III. Series.
JK1971.R46 1989 324.7′0973 88-34440

ISBN 0-87436-517-1 (alk. paper)
ISBN 0-87436-518-X (pbk.: alk. paper)

96 95 94 93 92 91 90 89 10 9 8 7 6 5 4 3 2 1 (cloth)
96 95 94 93 92 91 90 89 10 9 8 7 6 5 4 3 2 1 (paper)

ABC-CLIO, Inc.
130 Cremona, P.O. Box 1911
Santa Barbara, California 93116-1911

Clio Press Ltd.
55 St. Thomas' Street
Oxford, OX1 1JG, England

This book is Smyth-sewn and printed on acid-free paper ♾.
Manufactured in the United States of America

*To Bobbi, Dan, and Joey,*
*for their loving support*

*To my new family—*
*Elise, Jeff, Cat, and Lis*

*Clio Dictionaries in Political Science*

*The African Political Dictionary*
Claude S. Phillips

*The Arms Control, Disarmament, and Military Security Dictionary*
Jeffrey M. Elliot and Robert Reginald

*The Asian Political Dictionary*
Lawrence Ziring and C. I. Eugene Kim

*The Constitutional Law Dictionary,* Volume 1: *Individual Rights*
Ralph C. Chandler, Richard A. Enslen, and Peter G. Renstrom

*The Constitutional Law Dictionary,* Volume 1: *Individual Rights*
Supplement 1
Ralph C. Chandler, Richard A. Enslen, and Peter G. Renstrom

*The Constitutional Law Dictionary,* Volume 2: *Governmental Powers*
Ralph C. Chandler, Richard A. Enslen, and Peter G. Renstrom

*The Dictionary of Political Analysis,* Second Edition
Jack C. Plano, Robert E. Riggs, and Helenan S. Robin

*The Electoral Politics Dictionary*
Peter G. Renstrom and Chester B. Rogers

*The European Political Dictionary*
Ernest E. Rossi and Barbara P. McCrea

*The International Law Dictionary*
Robert L. Bledsoe and Boleslaw A. Boczek

*The International Relations Dictionary,* Fourth Edition
Jack C. Plano and Roy Olton

*The Latin American Political Dictionary*
Ernest E. Rossi and Jack C. Plano

*The Middle East Political Dictionary*
Lawrence Ziring

*The Presidential-Congressional Political Dictionary*
Jeffrey M. Elliot and Sheikh R. Ali

*The Public Administration Dictionary,* Second Edition
Ralph C. Chandler and Jack C. Plano

*The Public Policy Dictionary*
Earl R. Kruschke and Byron M. Jackson

*The Soviet and East European Political Dictionary*
Barbara P. McCrea, Jack C. Plano, and George Klein

*The State and Local Government Political Dictionary*
Jeffrey M. Elliot and Sheikh R. Ali

Forthcoming

*The International Development Dictionary,* 1991
Gerald W. Fry and Galen R. Martin

*The Judicial Political Dictionary,* 1991
Peter G. Renstrom

*The Peace and Nuclear War Dictionary,* 1989
Sheikh R. Ali

*The Urban Politics Dictionary,* 1990
John W. Smith and John S. Klemanski

# *SERIES STATEMENT*

Language precision is the primary tool of every scientific discipline. That aphorism serves as the guideline for this series of political dictionaries. Although each book in the series relates to a specific topical or regional area in the discipline of political science, entries in the dictionaries also emphasize history, geography, economics, sociology, philosophy, and religion.

This dictionary series incorporates special features designed to help the reader overcome any language barriers that may impede a full understanding of the subject matter. For example, the concepts included in each volume were selected to complement the subject matter found in existing texts and other books. All but one volume utilize a subject matter chapter arrangement that is most useful for classroom and study purposes.

Entries in all volumes include an up-to-date definition plus a paragraph of *Significance* in which the authors discuss and analyze the term's historical and current relevance. Most entries are also cross-referenced, providing the reader an opportunity to seek additional information related to the subject of inquiry. A comprehensive index, found in both hardcover and paperback editions, allows the reader to locate major entries and other concepts, events, and institutions discussed within these entries.

The political and social sciences suffer more than most disciplines from semantic confusion. This is attributable, *inter alia,* to the popularization of the language, and to the focus on many diverse foreign political and social systems. This dictionary series is dedicated to overcoming some of this confusion through careful writing of thorough, accurate definitions for the central concepts, institutions, and events that comprise the basic knowledge of each of the subject fields. New titles in the series will be issued periodically, including some in related social science disciplines.

—Jack C. Plano
*Series Editor*

# *CONTENTS*

# *A NOTE ON HOW TO USE THIS BOOK*

*The Electoral Politics Dictionary* focuses on terms and concepts common to applied politics as well as federal statutes and court decisions bearing upon this field. Several techniques have been utilized to help the reader locate entries with ease. The entries in the chapters are arranged alphabetically. The reader can explore the implications of a topic by using the cross-references provided at the end of each definition, which point to related materials included in the same chapter or to relevant discussions in other chapters. Entry numbers have been provided for all cross-references.

If the reader is unsure about which chapter to consult for a particular case or concept, he or she may consult the comprehensive index at the end of the book. It includes every term, concept, or case contained in the dictionary, either as a major entry or as a reference within an entry. All indexed terms include entry numbers.

The format of this book is designed to offer the student or general reader a variety of useful approaches to locating information. The book may be used as (1) a *dictionary* and *reference guide* to the language in the field of electoral politics; (2) a *study guide* for students enrolled in courses covering this field; (3) a *handbook* for use by practitioners engaged in applied politics; (4) a *supplement* to textbooks or collections of readings in the field of electoral politics; and (5) a readily usable source of *review materials* for teachers, students, and practitioners in this field.

# *PREFACE*

Precise language is the basic requirement of every intellectual discipline. This is certainly true in the field of electoral politics. We undertook to write *The Electoral Politics Dictionary* in pursuit of clear and precise language for this subject matter.

We have tried to assemble a book that explicates the fundamental elements required for an understanding of electoral politics in the United States. The task involved integration of many ideas, terms, concepts, phrases, and law cases that reflect the multidimensional character of this subject. We hope to reach general readers as well as specific audiences of students and political practitioners. A major objective is to introduce students of applied politics to some of the operational concepts in the field.

The concepts, terms, phrases, and cases selected here represent our best judgment about how to advance the understanding of electoral politics. We did not intend, however, that this dictionary should be an exhaustive reference source. Our selections were guided by such questions as: Does this term, concept, case, or phrase enhance the ability of the reader to communicate in the basic language of the field? Will the entry facilitate the reader's search for knowledge and understanding? Will the dictionary complement and supplement materials commonly used in courses on this subject? By limiting our dictionary to fundamental terms we have been able to provide more thorough descriptions and analyses.

Although all dictionaries are similar, *The Electoral Politics Dictionary* has some distinctive features. First, entries were selected to reflect the major substantive components of electoral politics. The chapters and the entries within each chapter correspond to the leading textbooks dealing with these subjects so that this dictionary can be used more effectively as a teaching and learning tool. Second, each chapter begins with a brief overview that establishes the basic substantive boundaries of the chapter. A third unique feature is the inclusion of a paragraph of *Significance* following each definition. Here we have sought to provide both a historical perspective and an integration of the entry into a larger context. We have also used this section to offer comment and analysis that underscore why we think the entry is important. A fourth feature is the extensive use of cross-references that indicate where additional information contained in the dictionary may be located. Finally, the volume provides a comprehensive index to facilitate location of entries.

The material for this volume was drawn from many sources. It is difficult if not impossible to always identify the original sources of the terms and concepts that have become the foundation of the study of electoral politics. We wish to acknowledge the contributions of the scholars who contributed to this volume by their valuable work in the field of electoral politics. We also wish to acknowledge the stimulation and encouragement given by our department colleagues and students at Western Michigan University. We wish as well to thank the ABC-CLIO staff for their help in the preparation of this volume. We would like to extend special thanks to Professor Jack C. Plano, series editor of the Clio Dictionaries in Political Science and long a valued department colleague. Jack has given our manuscript many hours and given us sound counsel. It is very likely that *The Electoral Politics Dictionary* would never have been written without his involvement and encouragement. Finally, we wish to thank our wives, Bobbi Renstrom and Elise Jorgens, for continued support and many hours spent reviewing chapter drafts. These people made this project possible. We alone, of course, accept full responsibility for errors of commission and omission. We invite communication about any aspect of the book.

—Peter G. Renstrom
—Chester B. Rogers
*Western Michigan University*

# The Electoral Politics Dictionary

# *1. Political Culture and Public Opinion*

Fundamental to the operation of any political system are the basic beliefs, feelings, and opinions that people in the society have about their political system, about how it operates, and about how it should operate. *Political culture* is the term used to describe fundamental, long-term beliefs and values about how politics should and does take place. *Public opinion* is used to refer to shorter-run perceptions people hold about political issues of current importance. The study of political culture and public opinion involves a number of important questions: What is the nature of the political culture and of public opinion? How is political culture passed on to individuals in the society? What factors help to shape public opinion? What is the significance of political culture and public opinion for the operation of the political system? And, finally, how can we determine the values, beliefs, and opinions of the public? In this chapter we will examine these general questions and their specific application in the context of the United States.

At the core of the political culture of the United States is strong support for the fundamental political institutions of the society coupled with considerable skepticism about the officials who are responsible for carrying out the functions of those institutions. Citizens tend to believe strongly in the legitimacy of the Constitution and to think their form of government is the best in the world. There are exceptions, particularly among groups that have consistently faced patterns of discrimination, but, on the whole, people like and want to keep their current form of government. They are not always as positive in their view of the officials running their government. Elections, however, give them a process for removing officials they do not like.

Ideologically, citizens tend toward the middle. Although there is frequent reference to liberal or conservative positions, the majority of people are moderates. Some important principles or ideals people value are democracy, equality of opportunity, free enterprise, freedom, individualism, and limited government. Public opinion in the United States tends to be changeable, inconsistent across issues, and based upon limited information. It is strongly influenced by the media, the principal source of information about what is happening in the society and in the world.

Political socialization is the process by which individuals learn about politics and the political system, the means by which political culture and public opinion are transferred to individuals. A person is not born a liberal or a conservative, a Democrat or a Republican, anti-abortion or pro-choice. These political orientations are learned over time. Although people continue to learn about politics throughout their lives, much of their political orientation is shaped quite early in life. The predominant agents of socialization are family, schools, peers, the media, and events. Early beliefs and values are strongly shaped by the family, even before children reach school age. The schools provide knowledge about the political system as well as instilling commitment to the basic institutions of the society, such as the Constitution, the presidency, and democratic ways of behaving. Peers and the media serve as additional sources of information that can help shape the way people see politics. Events can have a profound impact on how people view the political system, particularly events that were of great significance to many people such as the Great Depression, World War II, the urban riots of the late 1960s and early 1970s, the Vietnam War, and Watergate.

It is important to understand that political beliefs, values, and opinions—the ideas people hold—are crucial in explaining the ways people behave. These ideas constitute a person's political orientation, the perspective that person will have on political matters. In any given situation, this orientation will affect the way an individual behaves. Two people, faced with a similar situation, may behave differently because of differences in political orientation. Imagine two people, one a Democrat and the other a Republican, voting in an election in which they do not know anything about the candidates other than what is listed on the ballot. Because of their different orientations, the Democrat will vote for the Democratic candidate and the Republican will vote for the Republican candidate.

The primary method of measuring political culture and public opinion is survey research. Survey research, or opinion polling as it is sometimes called, involves selecting a sample of the population and asking it questions. If the sample selected is an accurate reflection of the broader population, it is possible to generalize from the sample to the entire population. Sophisticated sampling techniques exist to ensure that representative samples are selected. Survey research is used by scholars, the media, political candidates, and others to estimate a variety of characteristics about the public.

**Affects** **(1)**

Emotions that are directed toward the political system or its component parts. Affects include those parts of a person's political orientation that are based upon feelings or attachments. In studying the way people perceive politics and how that perception shapes their political behavior, political scientists sought to differentiate between emotions (affects) and knowledge or beliefs (cognitions), hypothesizing that each is shaped somewhat differently and in turn has a distinct influence on behavior. Affects refer to the way people feel about the Constitution, democracy, capitalism, Congress, a Supreme Court decision, or any of the other varied components of their political system. In the United States, much of the support for various components of the political system is affective; it is based on positive feelings developed at an early age toward the flag, the Constitution, the nation, governmental institutions, and other symbols. Ceremonial activities such as the Pledge of Allegiance or the singing of the National Anthem strongly reinforce affective support for the political system. *See also* COGNITIONS, 6; POLITICAL ORIENTATIONS, 30; SUPPORTS, 36.

*Significance* Affects are important influences in determining the political stability of a country. If people have positive feelings about the principal actors, institutions, and other elements of their political system, they are prone to support it and its right to take actions even when they dislike those actions. Negative feelings are more likely to generate opposition, even in situations in which governmental actions may be beneficial to those holding the negative feelings. The equivalent at the more personal level commonly occurs—people who are liked and accepted can do virtually anything, whereas those who are disliked find it difficult to gain acceptance regardless of how hard they try. Governments that are liked and accepted have much more flexibility for action and tend to be more stable than those that are disliked. People seldom consider the significance of affects to the way they view politics. It is difficult for individuals to understand that a considerable part of their support for their political system results not from an objective evaluation of or even knowledge about that system but rather from feelings inculcated into them quite early in life. It is all too easy to assume that because we believe that our political system is the best in the world everyone else in the world must believe the same. Doing so ignores the reality that the feelings inculcated into people in other countries encourages support for their political system and that they are as likely to have emotional attachment to their system as we have to ours.

**Agents of Political Socialization** **(2)**
The sources from which people gain their political orientation. Agents of political socialization include the family, the schools, peers, the media, and significant events and are the means by which the political culture of a society is passed on to new generations. Parents are usually the first source of political learning for children. Children observe their parents' behavior, they hear their parents talk, and they develop at an early age many of their parents' orientations. In the United States, the party affiliation of most people is the same as their parents'. The schools are a second major source of political learning. In school, children are taught facts about their political system, but they are also taught positive support for the political system through mechanisms such as saying the Pledge of Allegiance each morning. Peers and the media are additional sources of political socialization. As people interact with their peers, as they absorb information passed along by the media, their process of political learning continues. Finally, major events can influence political learning. Individuals who grew up during Watergate or during other significant periods of the country's political history feel the impact of such events more strongly than others. People who grew up during the Watergate period are more likely to have skeptical or cynical attitudes toward the political system and are more likely to feel alienated from it. *See also* POLITICAL ALIENATION, 25; POLITICAL ORIENTATION, 30; POLITICAL SOCIALIZATION, 31; WATERGATE, 42.

*Significance* Agents of political socialization are the sources of political learning. In a country such as the United States, where there is broad acceptance of the political culture and similarity among the political orientations of most people in the society, the messages passed along from the various agents of political socialization are similar. Children learn that democracy, private enterprise, the Constitution, and so on, are good things—regardless of whether the teacher is a parent, the school system, a peer, the media, or an event. This similarity contributes to the maintenance of a relatively stable political system with high levels of support. In a country with more political subcultures, less agreement about the political culture, and less support for components of the political system, agents of political socialization are likely to communicate much more divergent messages.

**Authority (3)**

The right to take some action. Authority is a type of power legitimated by virtue of compliance with accepted standards or procedures. The political culture and the Constitution determine what is necessary for people to gain authority. Political leaders in the United States have authority by virtue of the office they hold. The person who holds the office of president has the authority (the right) to negotiate treaties with other countries because the Constitution assigns that right to whoever holds the office of president, and people generally consider the Constitution a legitimate source to confer authority. Congress has the authority to pass laws because the Constitution assigns it that responsibility. A police officer has the right to make an arrest if he or she observes someone committing a crime because that authority has been granted by law and is viewed as legitimate by most citizens. *See also* LEGITIMACY, 18; POLITICAL AUTHORITIES, 26; UNITED STATES CONSTITUTION, 37.

*Significance* Authority provides the foundation for governmental action and is particularly important in a democracy such as the United States because ultimately it must come from the people. Political authorities must be able to demonstrate popular support for their right to hold office and for their right to make policy. Elections are the most important way in which top-level government authorities gain the right to hold office and to make policy. The United States Constitution provides for popular election of the president and members of Congress, and state constitutions provide for the election of numerous state and local officials. Other authorities, such as justices of the Supreme Court or cabinet members, gain the right to act by virtue of appointment by elected officials.

**Capitalism (4)**

An economic system or philosophy based on private ownership, the profit motive, and the law of supply and demand. Capitalism is the predominant economic philosophy in the United States. The importance placed on capitalism flows naturally out of beliefs in individualism and the right to private property, which have been important parts of the U.S. political culture since the country came into existence. The economy of the United States has been capitalist throughout most of the country's history, and, although the government has increasingly become involved in the economy during the twentieth century, private ownership and the profit motive remain important parts of the economy. *See also* COGNITIONS, 6; INDIVIDUALISM, 15; POLITICAL CULTURE, 27.

*Significance* Capitalism is an important part of the political culture of the United States. Even as the economy becomes less capitalistic because of government involvement through fiscal and monetary policy and through direct regulation, the belief that the United States has and should have a capitalist economy remains a part of the political orientation of most people. This belief has undoubtedly been reinforced by the conflict between the United States and the Soviet Union, which is viewed by many as a conflict between capitalism and communism.

**Classical Liberalism** **(5)**

A set of political ideas that played a crucial role in the shaping of U.S. political culture, the Constitution, and political institutions. Classical liberalism was a product of seventeenth- and eighteenth-century European thought, brought into the colonies in books by philosophers such as John Locke. It introduced the then revolutionary notion that individuals possessed certain rights simply by virtue of being human, that these rights were not granted by government, but that it was the responsibility of government to protect these rights. Among the values and beliefs articulated by classical liberalism are (1) that government should be limited by the rights of the people, (2) that all persons should be viewed as equal under the law, and (3) that among the rights of the people are the rights to property and to freedom. *See also* CONSERVATISM, 7; IDEOLOGY, 14; LIBERALISM, 19; POLITICAL CULTURE, 27; UNITED STATES CONSTITUTION, 37.

*Significance* Classical liberalism was the dominant influence in the formation of the U.S. government. A version of classical liberalism is articulated in the Declaration of Independence:

> We hold these truths to be self-evident, that all men are created equal, that they are endowed by their Creator with certain unalienable rights, that among these are Life, Liberty and the pursuit of Happiness. That to secure these rights, Governments are instituted among Men, deriving their just powers from the consent of the governed.

The Constitution was designed to set up a government that would be limited and that would ensure the rights of individuals. The impact of these ideas was so great that some have suggested that the reason the United States does not have ideological battles is because the political culture reflects so strongly the tenets of classical liberalism that there is no room for ideological differences. Both present-day liberalism and conservatism can be traced back to classical liberalism.

**Cognitions** **(6)**

Beliefs, opinions, and knowledge about the political system and how it operates. Cognitions refer to what people know or think they know about their country's political system and its component parts. (By contrast, affects refer to how people *feel* about the political system.) Cognitions are one part of a person's political orientation and include perceptions about such things as the Constitution, political institutions, government officials, and political behavior. The belief that "ours is the best country in the world" and the knowledge that in order to vote it is necessary to register are both political cognitions. Cognitions are shaped by political socialization, they are learned, and they do not necessarily correspond to reality. People in the same society may have different, even conflicting, cognitions. In the United States, conservatives tend to believe that the country would be better off with less federal government activity in domestic affairs. Liberals tend to believe that federal government involvement is necessary to solve some of the domestic problems the country faces. *See also* AFFECTS, 1; POLITICAL ORIENTATION, 30; POLITICAL SOCIALIZATION, 31.

*Significance* Cognitions influence the way people behave politically. For example, people who perceive that their actions are important and can have an impact on the operation of the political system are likely to be active participants in the political system. They will vote, join interest groups, work in political campaigns, and possibly even run for office themselves. On the other hand, politically alienated people, who believe they can have no impact on the system, are less likely to participate. People who think their representative in Congress can help them solve a problem they are having with a federal agency are likely to contact that representative, whereas people who are unaware that representatives do such things are unlikely to. Cognitions that encourage political participation are especially important to the maintenance of a democratic political system because democracy is dependent upon popular participation, particularly upon voting.

**Conservatism** **(7)**

An ideological orientation based on opposition to sudden, dramatic change. Conservatives generally believe that existing societal conditions are more agreeable than those that would develop if government intervenes to attempt improvements. Conservatives in the

United States today tend to favor less government activity, particularly less federal government activity that relates to domestic policy or to regulation of the economy. They tend to support a strong national defense and view communism and the Soviet Union as the hard-core enemies of the United States. Conservatives seek to maintain or strengthen traditional institutions such as the family and the church. *See also* CLASSICAL LIBERALISM, 5; IDEOLOGY, 14; LIBERALISM, 19.

*Significance* Conservatism in the United States today is very much in the tradition of classical liberalism in its commitment to limited government, equality of opportunity, and the right to freedom and property. Conservatives share with liberals this classical liberal heritage but interpret it quite differently. Conservatives are likely to oppose government regulation of the economy or the provision of welfare services on the grounds of limited government, while favoring the development of a strong defense and the protection of traditional values by government. The election of Ronald Reagan as president marked a victory for conservatives. Reagan had long advocated conservative principles and had sought the Republican nomination for president with the strong backing of most conservatives in the country. Conservatives are more likely than others to identify with the Republican party in U.S. politics, although not all conservatives are Republicans and not all Republicans are conservatives.

**Demands** **(8)**

Things that people want or expect from their political system. Political scientists attached this particular connotation to the term because of David Easton's extensive work on the relationship of the political system to society. Demands, according to Easton, are one of two ways in which a political system's environment (society) affects the political system. (The second way is supports.) Citizens can make many kinds of demands: Government should lower taxes, improve social security benefits, reduce its role in society, illegalize abortion, protect a woman's right to have an abortion. Demands are the means by which citizens let their government and political officials know what policies they want. Demands can be expressed directly by individuals contacting political officials; or, as is more frequently the case, by interest groups or political parties that aggregate the demands of individuals and communicate them to the political system. Given that demands flow from individuals, and individuals are frequently in conflict, it should not be surprising that considerable conflict exists over demands. In some authoritarian or totalitarian societies, governments tend to discourage or prohibit most people from expressing their demands. In the United States, however, people are encouraged to do so. *See also* INTEREST GROUP, 293; PARTY IN GOVERNMENT, 231; PUBLIC POLICY, 34; SUPPORTS, 36.

*Significance* Demands are to a great extent a reflection of people's orientations. If people believe that the U.S.S.R. is stronger militarily than the United States and that it intends to take over this country, they will probably demand an increase in defense expenditures and a strengthening of overall defense posture. If people believe that the foreign policy behavior of the U.S.S.R. is motivated primarily by fear of invasion and a desire to protect itself, they are likely to demand reduction in tensions between the United States and the U.S.S.R. and the establishment of more-normal relations. Differences in political orientation generate differences in demands. One of the challenges of a democratic political system is for officials to process this variety of demands—many of which are conflicting and not all of which can be met—in such a way that people continue to support the political system even though they do not always get the policies they seek.

**Democracy** **(9)**

A form of government based on the principle of popular sovereignty. In a democracy the ultimate source of authority is the citizenry; political authorities derive their authority from and are responsible to the people. Although it originally evolved in the city-states of ancient Greece, particularly Athens, it was not until the advent of the United States that democracy became a popular and desired form of government. Historically, many people—including most of the participants in the United States Constitutional Convention—feared democracy because they identified it with majority rule or, more explicitly, with "mob rule." Most concepts of democracy today include the notion that individual citizens have certain rights that are protected from government, thus ensuring a degree of protection for individuals from majority rule. Elections are the major device by which popular control is exercised in a democracy. At election time, people can remove from office those people who no longer have popular support. *See also* POLITICAL CULTURE, 27; UNITED STATES CONSTITUTION, 37.

*Significance* Democracy has from the beginning been a fundamental ingredient of U.S. political culture. The Constitution provided for direct election of members of the House of Representatives and indirect election of senators and the president, thereby producing a degree of popular sovereignty. In the early years under the Constitution, there were limits on popular participation because women, blacks, and in some states people not owning property or paying taxes were denied the right to vote. Those limits no longer exist. The franchise has been expanded to include previously excluded groups, and senators are now directly elected by the people, as, for all practical purposes, are presidents. Elections play a key role in maintaining democracy. They provide citizens with the ability to control their government. Since the 1960s, concern about the role of elections in controlling government has increased because of the low level of voter participation and the vastly expanded importance of money and the media in determining who wins elections.

**Equality** **(10)**

The principle that each individual has intrinsic value as a human being and as a consequence deserves a certain similarity of treatment by society and by the political system. Commitment to equality was an important part of the political reaction of the American colonies to England, which still maintained aristocratic notions of position and place in society that limited the opportunities of individuals to the particular class into which they were born. Equality was an essential ingredient of classical liberalism, which so strongly influenced the colonists and continues to be a central element of the U.S. political culture. Equality has a variety of meanings, depending on how "similarity of treatment" is interpreted. In the United States the focus has been on political and legal equality (each person should have the right to vote and to equal treatment before the law) and on equality of opportunity (each person should have equal opportunity for success). *See also* CLASSICAL LIBERALISM, 5; VALUES, 41.

*Significance* Ideas of equality have contributed greatly to the social, economic, and political development of the United States. In theory each individual is entitled to an education, to the right to vote, to equal justice under the law, and to opportunities for upward mobility within society. The practice of equality, however, has not always matched the rhetoric. For much of the history of the country, blacks, women, and other minorities were not provided with equal opportunities. Recent legislation has done much to change this state of affairs, although people at the bottom of the economic order are still least likely to have equal opportunity. Quality education has become essential to equality of opportunity in the complex, postindustrial society of the modern United States. The quality of education provided to the children of the poor is considerably inferior to that provided to most other children, thus greatly decreasing the underprivileged's prospects for competing on any kind of equal basis.

**Freedom** **(11)**

The idea that individuals should be able to pursue their own interests and maintain their own beliefs without interference from government. Freedom, or liberty as it is sometimes referred to, has been an important value in U.S. political culture. People have placed great emphasis on limiting the influence that government should have over their lives. The first ten amendments to the Constitution (the Bill of Rights) were designed, in great part, to protect the freedom of citizens from unwarranted interference by the federal government. These amendments provide for freedom of speech, freedom of religion, and freedom of the press, among many others. *See also* POLITICAL CULTURE, 27; VALUES, 41.

*Significance* Freedom means a variety of things to different people. The desire for freedom from what the American colonists saw as the unfair imposition of taxes and commercial regulations by England was one of the driving forces behind the American Revolution. The desire for freedom from the confinements of civilization drove many early Americans to move to the frontier. The desire for freedom to say what they think, believe, and feel continues to lead many people to immigrate to the United States. What some may see as freedom, however, may appear to others as deprivation of freedom. Slave owners before the Civil War maintained that their freedom included the right to own and use slaves; obviously, the slaves and many others within society shared a different point of view. Business and industry see government regulation as a deprivation of their freedom, but those who support regulation see it as a necessary protection of freedom from discrimination, from exploitation, and so on, depending on the particular regulation.

**Generational Influences** **(12)**

Events or experiences shared by people of a similar age that have a pivotal effect on their political orientation. Generational influences create similarities in political orientation among people of similar age groups by virtue of their shared experiences. People who grew up after World War II are likely to view war, the military, and international relations in a somewhat different manner than those for whom that war was a significant event in their lives. People who grew up in the 1960s experienced the civil rights movement, the war in Vietnam, and urban riots at a time when their political orientation was in its most formative stage. These events remain a vivid part of their experience and their reactions to such events influence their perceptions of other political events. Generational influences are part of the political socialization process and help to shape people's political orientation. *See also* POLITICAL ORIENTATION, 30; POLITICAL SOCIALIZATION, 31.

*Significance* Generational influences always exist, although their particular direction will depend upon the experiences people have lived through. Most of the participants in the United States Constitutional Convention shared two attitudes because of their mutual experiences: (1) hostility toward unresponsive and uncontrollable government because of their colonial experience, and (2) frustration with weak and ineffective government because of their experience with the Articles of Confederation. These generational influences propelled them in the direction of creating a strong central government that was controllable—one that could not exercise arbitrary power. Since the 1960s, the United States has gone through a number of highly charged, critical events—the civil rights movement, urban riots, the Vietnam War, Watergate, and the resignation of a president—that have increased political cynicism and contributed to political alienation. One result has been younger generations that seem less likely to participate in the political system. The most dramatic examples of this development are found in the decreasing number of people, particularly younger people, who are likely to vote or to identify with either of the major political parties.

**Ideologue** **(13)**

A person who tends to interpret the world strictly in ideological terms. The ideologue is a "true believer" so strongly influenced by ideology that her or his beliefs are little influenced by what is happening in the world. Many people are influenced by ideology but are open to some rethinking of beliefs and values based upon encounters with other ideas or observations of world events. For the ideologue, the ideology offers all that is necessary. New and different ideas are to be rejected; facts are generally rearranged to fit preconceptions corresponding to ideological orientation. *See also* IDEOLOGY, 14.

*Significance* Ideologues have at times been powerful actors on the world political scene. Adolf Hitler as an advocate of Nazism provided simple, ideological answers to the complex and difficult problems facing Germany after World War I. He was able to gain substantial popular support, ultimately leading Germany in the conquest of most of Europe. Only Germany's defeat in World War II brought about his demise. Because of the pragmatic nature of politics in the United States, ideologues have not been successful. Although ideologies exist and are relevant to U.S. politics, it is generally the rather pragmatic application of them that seems most appealing to the U.S. public.

**Ideology** **(14)**

A set of values and beliefs about how the society, the economy, and the political system do and ought to function. An ideology provides interconnected answers to questions such as, What is the nature of the good society? How should the economy function? and What should the purpose of the political system be? It also addresses more immediate questions such as, What is the proper role of religion? How should economic benefits be distributed? and How should poverty be dealt with? Major ideologies that are relevant in today's world include liberalism, conservatism, capitalism, communism, and socialism. Individuals who accept a particular ideology tend to have their political orientation shaped by the values and beliefs of that ideology. *See also* POLITICAL CULTURE, 27; POLITICAL ORIENTATION, 30; VALUES, 41.

*Significance* Ideology can influence the political orientation and thus the political behavior of individuals in a society. Societies that have conflicting strong ideologies are likely to be societies in which it is difficult to resolve political conflict because the ideologies provide political actors with preconceived answers for political issues. If each side believes it has the truth, it is not easy to reach agreement when there is a conflict. The political system of the United States has generally been more pragmatic than ideological. Political actors are more likely to look for what works, and thus be able to reach compromises, than they are to engage in ideological battles. An alternative explanation for the lack of ideological battles in the United States is that one ideology, classical liberalism, has played such a crucial role in the development of U.S. political culture and has generated so much agreement about the underlying framework within which politics takes place that there is not much room for ideological debate.

**Individualism** **(15)**

The belief that the individual should be at the center of any conception of society or politics. Individualism provides a sharp contrast to traditional aristocratic thought, which classified people in terms of their caste or position within society, and to modern collectivist thought, which considers individuals as tools for obtaining state or societal goals. Individualism has been an extremely important part of the American experience since colonial days. The "rugged individualist," very much a part of American folklore, represents the idea that people should be able to go their own way, "do their own thing," advance within the society as far as their own talents, ability, and efforts will allow. Society and government exist not to control, dominate, or use people for the purposes of the state but to facilitate individual opportunity. *See also* CLASSICAL LIBERALISM, 5; POLITICAL CULTURE, 27.

*Significance* Individualism has been an important part of American life from the time of the earliest settlers, long before the creation of the current form of government. Many early colonists were seeking to escape the aristocratic class structure that defined their place in society at the time of birth. They sought, and created, a society in which individuals would not be limited by rigid class structure or an overzealous monarch but could pursue their own opportunities. As society became more complex, interdependent government actions placed limits on individuals doing as they pleased, but always within the context of keeping the individual at the center of society. Thus, when the federal government passed laws regulating child labor in the early twentieth century, it was actually placing limits on what factory owners could do. These limits, however, were not imposed in order to advance state control over individuals (the factory owners); rather, they were meant to promote the individual rights of young children who were being exploited.

**Inputs** **(16)**

The means by which conditions in the environment of a political system are transmitted to the political system. Inputs refer to the attitudes people in a society have and the actions they take that influence the operation of their political system. Input can be of two types: demands and supports. Demands are the things people want the government to do. Supports are positive attitudes and actions directed toward the component parts of the political system. The nature of inputs are strongly influenced by the political culture of the society. *See also* DEMANDS, 8; SUPPORTS, 36.

*Significance* The concept of inputs provides a way to better understand the linkages between conditions existing in society and the operation of the political system. When the economy is foundering and there is high unemployment, people react by pressuring the government for job creation policies or unemployment compensation (demands) or by voting against current officeholders (reduction of supports). When economic conditions are good, people are more likely to vote for current officeholders.

**Iran-Contra Affair** **(17)**

A highly secret set of events in 1985 and 1986 that included the sale of arms by the United States to Iran in an attempt to free U.S. hostages and the use of funds from that sale to assist the Contras in their fight to overthrow the government of Nicaragua. The Iran-Contra affair, as these events came to be called, was conducted by a few people operating out of the National Security Council without the knowledge of Congress, key cabinet officials such as the secretary of state and the secretary of defense, and, in the case of the shifting of funds to the Contras, without the knowledge of President Ronald Reagan. Public revelation of these events led to strong criticism of the Reagan administration for allowing such events to take place, extensive investigations, the replacement of a number of people working on the White House staff, and the prosecution of several individuals for violations of the law. *See also* POLITICAL ALIENATION, 25; WATERGATE, 42.

*Significance* The Iran-Contra affair touched off a public spectacle of investigation. The Tower Commission (appointed by President Reagan), two congressional select committees (one for the House and one for the Senate), and a special prosecutor in the Justice Department were involved in efforts to determine what happened and why. There was extensive media coverage of these events and for months the public received information about conflicts between the president and the Congress and about secret activities being conducted out of the National Security Council with little supervision by the president. The Iran-Contra affair weakened the power of President Reagan. His popularity with the public declined, and some people found it difficult to believe that he did not have knowledge of the shifting of funds from the arms sales to the Contras. His decrease in public support also contributed to a decrease in his influence with the Congress. The Iran-Contra affair, like Watergate over twenty years earlier, increased the public's cynicism about the operation of the political system. It is also likely to enlarge the degree of political alienation in the country, thereby contributing to a continuing decrease in political participation.

**Legitimacy** **(18)**

Acceptance by the general population of the right of political institutions or authorities to act. Legitimacy creates or enhances authority because it indicates citizen support for a political body's right to take action, even in cases where popular support might not exist for a particular action. Thus it is possible to accept the right of Congress to create a law while disagreeing strongly with that law. The legitimacy of any political institution or authority is determined by citizen perception, not by the power it may exercise over its citizenry. *See also* AUTHORITY, 3; SUPPORTS, 36; WATERGATE, 42.

*Significance* Legitimacy is particularly important for democratic political systems. Political authorities must maintain citizen support by acting in ways that are viewed as legitimate. Election to office does not provide a blank check to exercise power, only the authority to act within the framework established by the Constitution and the political culture. When political authorities overstep these bounds, they may no longer be viewed as legitimate by many in the population and may, in extreme cases, be removed from office. President Richard Nixon found himself in this position in relation to Watergate. By acting in ways that were improper for the president of the United States, he lost his legitimacy in the view of many citizens as well as many political authorities. Ultimately, he was forced to resign from office.

**Liberalism** **(19)**

An ideological orientation based on the belief that conditions in society can be made better. Liberals favor government involvement in dealing with a variety of problems because they believe such actions will improve the quality of life for individuals within society. Liberals in the United States have supported civil rights activities, government regulation of the economy, and government provision of health, education, and welfare services. They tend to see government, particularly the federal government, as the primary means of coping with the problems faced by those most powerless in society. Liberals have supported civil rights legislation, the Equal Rights Amendment (ERA) to the Constitution, and government programs to aid the poor and other groups they believe to be disadvantaged in society. *See also* CLASSICAL LIBERALISM, 5; CONSERVATISM, 7; IDEOLOGY, 14.

*Significance* Liberals in the United States, like conservatives, are much in the tradition of classical liberalism in their commitment to limited government, equality of opportunity, and the right to freedom and property. Liberals, however, interpret classical liberalism quite differently from conservatives. Liberals support freedom of speech, an uncensored press, and protection of individuals from unfair criminal prosecution on the grounds of limited government, but they also support a great expansion in the role of government insofar as that expansion provides benefits for the people of the society. Liberals gained political power in the United States with the election of Franklin D. Roosevelt in 1932 and have been influential in the years since, particularly under the presidencies of John F. Kennedy and Lyndon B. Johnson. The election of Ronald Reagan in 1980 marked a decline in liberal strength and a rise in conservative strength. Liberals tend to identify with the Democratic party in U.S. politics, although not all liberals are Democrats and not all Democrats are liberals.

**Limited Government** **(20)**

The principle that there are actions or activities that government should be prohibited from taking. Limited government is closely tied to beliefs in citizens' rights—that is, the actions of government are limited by the rights and privileges of its citizens. For example, the right of citizens to freedom of religion stated in the first amendment of the United States Constitution prohibits government from interfering with religious beliefs. Limited government was an important principle in the development of the United States Constitution. The Bill of Rights (the first ten amendments to the Constitution) prohibits Congress from doing a variety of things including establishing a religion, abridging freedom of speech or of the press, preventing people from peaceably assembling or petitioning the government for redress of grievances, forcing people to testify against themselves, establishing an excessive bail, or inflicting cruel and unusual punishment. Other parts of the Constitution include such limits as Article I, which prohibits the suspension of the privilege of the writ of habeas corpus except under unusual conditions as well as the passage of bills of attainder and ex post facto laws. *See also* POLITICAL CULTURE, 27; UNITED STATES CONSTITUTION, 37.

*Significance* Limited government is an important principle that is part of the political culture of the United States. Citizens are socialized early to the idea that the purpose of government is to serve the people, not to act in its own interest. Citizens believe strongly that there are things a government should not do, and government officials who overstep the proper boundaries of behavior may find themselves out of office. Commitment to limited government has remained strong in the United States even as the size and power of government has grown enormously in the years since the Constitution was ratified. The key to understanding why this is the case lies in comprehending changing popular expectations of government. People expect more from government today than they did 200 years ago—or even 75 years ago. Demands for governmental action have greatly expanded but always in terms of provision of services to the public, never in terms of government taking away the rights and privileges of citizens. Government may be larger, but it is still limited.

**Moderate** **(21)**

A nonideological orientation somewhere between conservative and liberal. Moderates tend to maintain that conservatives and liberals are too extreme in the positions they take. Moderates see themselves as pragmatists who support sensible policies, programs, and candidates without concern for ideological content. Approximately 20 to 30 percent of Americans identify themselves as moderates. They tend to be among the least interested in and informed about politics. Their political profile is similar to those people who claim not to have an ideological orientation—neither group tends to be very involved in politics. *See also* CONSERVATISM, 7; LIBERALISM, 19.

*Significance* Moderates are less likely to vote than conservatives or liberals. They are more likely to consider themselves independents rather than identify with either the Democratic or Republican party. Their political behavior is unpredictable both in terms of whom they will vote for and whether or not they will vote. Because they are in the middle, however, they are available to persuasion by candidates of either party, and because they constitute a significant proportion of the population, their vote can make a difference in election results. The candidate or party that can gain substantial moderate support in any given election is likely to do well.

**Neoconservatism** **(22)**

A spin-off from liberalism that occurred in the mid-1960s as a reaction to what were seen as the excesses of liberalism and the new left. Neoconservatism includes a strong anticommunist thrust, acceptance of the welfare state but concern that government has become too large and intrusive, emphasis on freedom as opposed to equality, and support for religion and traditional values. Neoconservatism has been developed and articulated by a small number of intellectuals who have considerable influence because they occupy important positions in academic circles, with the media, and in government. *See also* CONSERVATISM, 7; LIBERALISM, 19; NEOLIBERALISM, 23.

*Significance* Neoconservatism was the first of a number of movements away from liberalism. Neoconservatives share many of the basic values of liberals but believe that the 1960s era of flower children, antiwar activities, permissiveness, and disrespect for authority contributed to a weakening in the fabric of society. Many current neoconservatives once identified with liberalism and the Democratic party but now consider themselves conservative Republicans.

**Neoliberalism** **(23)**
A spin-off from liberalism that occurred in the late 1970s as a reaction to the economic problems of that period and to disenchantment with Jimmy Carter's administration. Neoliberalism maintains a strong commitment to many of the goals of liberalism but adds a new sense of pragmatism, a strong commitment to economic growth and competitiveness, and concern for maintaining a strong defense. Neoliberals generally think that government has to become more realistic and more effective. Government policies should help to stimulate economic growth and increase the effectiveness of U.S. industry in competing with industry in other countries. The government should develop and maintain a strong defense, not by throwing dollars to the Defense Department, but by increasing the effectiveness of the military and by careful strategic decisions about the kinds of weapons systems that are necessary to defense. *See also* CONSERVATISM, 7; INTEREST GROUP, 293; LIBERALISM, 19.

*Significance* Neoliberalism is a reaction to the notion that government can broadly meet the demands of everyone in the society. Neoliberals believe the rise in power of interest groups in the early 1970s has made it difficult to develop public policy that will rationally cope with some of the problems the country is facing. They seek much more targeted government efforts to deal with such issues as the decrease in competitiveness of U.S. industry, the need to combat Soviet aggressiveness, and improvement in the quality of the environment.

**Opinion Poll** **(24)**
A technique used to access people's perceptions about issues or candidates, their political beliefs, their level of political knowledge, or other items of interest to those conducting the poll. Opinion polls make it possible to get an accurate estimate of the views of a large number of people by asking a much smaller number of people. This is done by interviewing a systematically selected sample that is representative of the larger population using a carefully designed questionnaire. Most polls are conducted by telephone, although personal interviews provide an alternative method. *See also* CAMPAIGN POLLING, 165; COGNITIONS, 6; PUBLIC OPINION, 33; SAMPLING TECHNIQUES, 35.

*Significance* Opinion polls provide the most accurate information available about people's political beliefs and opinions. They are used by scholars doing research on political culture, political behavior, and in other areas of political science and sociology. They are used by the media to provide their readers or viewers with information about public opinion or to analyze how people are likely to vote in an upcoming election. They are used by political campaigns to assess voter attitudes and perceptions of candidates as part of the process of developing campaign strategy and tactics. Gallup, Roper, and a number of other national firms conduct polls on a regular basis. Some campaign consultants specialize in polling for campaign purposes. The ability of pollsters to accurately assess voters' preferences has created a major problem in relation to elections. If the pollsters know who is going to win the election before it takes place, and they are publishing their results so that voters also know, why should the voter bother to vote? This has been a particularly pressing problem with presidential elections in which exit polling done in the eastern states has allowed the media to predict who will win the election before the polls have closed in the western states.

**Political Alienation** **(25)**

An individual's feeling of detachment from the political system. Political alienation is the feeling that develops in people that the political system has nothing to offer them, that they can have no meaningful impact on it, that they are as irrelevant to the political system as it is to them. Some people are alienated because of the nature of their early political socialization—they have been taught by parents, schools, peers, and others that politics is irrelevant to them. More common, at least in the United States, alienation occurs because of life experiences. People become alienated because of government policies or actions that they seem unable to cope with or affect. Political alienation is commonly accompanied by low levels of support. *See also* POLITICAL ORIENTATION, 30; SUPPORTS, 36; VOTER TURNOUT, 208; WATERGATE, 42.

*Significance* Political alienation reduces people's willingness or desire to participate in the political system; they see no point to it. In the United States, there is evidence that the decrease in percentage of people voting, participating in political party activity, or even identifying with a political party has been caused by political alienation. People's frustrations with the war in Vietnam, the Watergate disclosures, and other revelations that shook their faith in the way the political system operates have made people more cynical and less willing to invest effort or concern in politics.

**Political Authorities** **(26)**
People who hold office within the political system and who are responsible for making and implementing government policy. Political authorities include, among others, the president, members of Congress, judges, governors, state legislators, mayors, city council members, and government bureaucrats at the national, state, and local levels. In a constitutional system such as that of the United States, the powers, responsibilities, and means of selection of authorities are defined by the Constitution, which also places limits on the types of actions these authorities can properly take. In the United States, the highest level political authorities, such as the president, members of Congress, and governors, are elected directly by the people. Others are appointed by authorities that have been elected (secretary of state, Supreme Court justice, city manager), and others obtain positions by qualifying through some type of merit system (civil servants). *See also* AUTHORITY, 3; DEMANDS, 8; LEGITIMACY, 18; UNITED STATES CONSTITUTION, 37.

*Significance* Political authorities are the people responsible for making and implementing public policy. Their decisions and actions have the force of society behind them. When people make demands on the political system, it is to political authorities that they are appealing for action. Thus, if a group seeks to change military spending policy, it must attempt to influence the president or members of Congress because they are the authorities responsible for those policies. If a group seeks to improve the quality of city garbage collection, it must deal with the city council, the mayor, or other city political authorities. Just as demands are directed toward political authorities, so too are supports. People are most likely to support those authorities who have been responsive to their demands, although it is not always a one-to-one relationship. In many cases, people continue to support authorities who have not met their demands because their support is based on other criteria.

**Political Culture** **(27)**
The fundamental, long-term beliefs and values about how politics should and does take place that are predominant in a society. The political culture of a country provides a framework within which government and politics take place. Political culture is passed on to individuals through the process of political socialization. To maintain legitimacy, governments must operate within this framework; they must not violate basic beliefs and values of the political culture or they will lose the support of people in the society. In most countries

there are political subcultures that may share many of the society's basic beliefs and values but because of ethnic, religious, regional, ideological, or other differences, may perceive politics somewhat differently. When subcultures are significantly different, with few areas of shared values and beliefs, the political system is likely to be unstable. The political culture of the United States includes strong support for basic political institutions such as the Constitution, Congress, the presidency, and the courts, accompanied by considerable skepticism about the political officials who may hold positions within these institutions. It also includes the particular world view that the United States is unique. This sense of uniqueness contains a strong element of traditional nationalism as well as the idea that the country has a singular destiny, whether it is to expand to the Pacific Ocean, as in the nineteenth century, or to be "policeman of the world," as during the mid-twentieth century. Within this sense of destiny is a moral righteousness, a belief that the United States has truth and virtue on its side. U.S. political culture emphasizes such "classical liberal" values as individualism, equality, capitalism, and limited government. Representative democracy is seen as allowing people to control their government while still protecting the rights of minorities within society. *See also* CAPITALISM, 4; CLASSICAL LIBERALISM, 5; COGNITIONS, 6; DEMOCRACY, 9; EQUALITY, 10; FREEDOM, 11; LEGITIMACY, 18; VALUES, 41.

*Significance* Political culture is the glue that holds (or fails to hold) society together. In a country such as Lebanon or a community such as Northern Ireland, where no uniting principles exist upon which all elements of society can agree and where religious and ethnic differences contribute to the maintenance of separate and conflicting subcultures, the nature of the political culture encourages continued fighting. Children are socialized in ways that reinforce conflicts that already exist. In the United States, a substantial body of beliefs and values about politics has been widely accepted by all segments of society, regardless of ethnic, religious, or economic differences. The pattern of political socialization encourages people to think of themselves as Americans who share certain experiences, beliefs, and values and who are in reasonable agreement about the fundamentals of political life. At two points in the history of the United States, basic rifts developed between segments of society that threatened the stability of the system: Differences between the North and South on the issue of slavery led to the Civil War, and the maintenance by whites of racism and discrimination toward nonwhites led to urban riots during the late 1960s and early 1970s. In both cases, after a period of hostility there occurred a movement back toward acceptance of the fundamentals of the political culture and a reduction in group hostilities.

**Political Efficacy** **(28)**
The sense that the things one does will have an impact. Political efficacy refers to the feeling that people's actions can and will make a difference on the operation of the political system. Information about people's sense of political efficacy in the United States is available through survey research that has been systematically done for a number of years by the Center for Political Studies at the University of Michigan. Responses to two items included in the surveys since 1952—"People like me don't have any say about what the government does" and "I don't think public officials care much about what people like me think"—provide measures of political efficacy. According to these data, the country's sense of political efficacy reached its highest point in 1960, when 60 percent of the respondents disagreed with the above two statements. It has declined since 1960, dropping into the 30 to 40 percent range since 1980. *See also* POLITICAL ALIENATION, 25; VOTING, 95.

*Significance* Political efficacy is an important determinant of political participation. People who feel that their actions will make a difference, that they can influence the outcome of elections or policies the government adopts, are most likely to get involved politically. People with a strong sense of political efficacy are much more likely than others to engage in activities such as voting, joining a political party or interest group, or contacting their elected representatives. Events since 1960, beginning with the assassination of President John Kennedy and continuing through other traumatic events of the 1960s and 1970s, have reduced people's sense of efficacy. Because political participation is an important requirement of a democratic political system, great concern has been expressed about the need to increase people's perception of their own political efficacy.

**Political Knowledge** **(29)**
The information that people have about politics, the operation of their political system, and world political events. Political knowledge is the part of cognitions that involves what is known. The average U.S. citizen's political knowledge tends to be very limited. Less than half the population can name their two U.S. senators. People are frequently unaware of the election dates for senators, representatives, governors, and other public officials. Few people can correctly iden-

tify the issue stance of their elected representatives on more than one or two issues. People also tend to have limited knowledge of historical events and the Constitution. Political knowledge tends to come primarily from media coverage that provides short, ahistorical coverage of events with high-excitement value—war, scandals, disasters, and so on. *See also* COGNITIONS, 6; MASS MEDIA, 368; PUBLIC OPINION, 33.

*Significance* Political knowledge is necessary to make reasoned political judgments. Determining whom to vote for, which policies to support, which government programs will be beneficial and which will not requires knowledge about the candidates, policies, and programs. The limited political knowledge possessed by most citizens in the United States creates conditions in which the public is relatively easily manipulated. Candidates are more likely to be elected on the basis of personal characteristics—particularly their ability to make effective use of the media—rather than on issue positions. Citizens do not seem to want much political knowledge, and the way the electoral system is designed discourages candidates from trying to deal with issues.

**Political Orientation** **(30)**

The beliefs, attitudes, values, knowledge, and opinions that individuals hold about how the political system does and ought to operate. Political orientation refers to people's thoughts rather than to their actions. Belief in democracy, support for elections to determine who should hold political office, identification with the Democratic or Republican party, knowledge that U.S. senators are elected for six-year terms, suspicion of the motives of the Soviet Union are all examples of the details that help to make up a person's political orientation. Political orientation is learned through the process of political socialization. Individuals develop their political orientation through interactions with parents, teachers, and peers and, at a more general level, through life experiences. *See also* POLITICAL KNOWLEDGE, 29; POLITICAL SOCIALIZATION, 31; PUBLIC OPINION, 33; VALUES, 41.

*Significance* Political orientation is the primary determinant of how people will behave politically. People's beliefs, values, and knowledge shape their behavior. A person who believes that voting is a critical responsibility in a democracy is likely to vote, whereas someone who thinks that voting is not important is much less likely to do so. People who identify with the Democratic or Republican party are more likely to vote than those who are unaffiliated. People who see themselves as conservative are less likely to support change than people who see themselves as liberal. Thus, in order to explain or predict an individual's political behavior, it is necessary to know his or her political orientation.

**Political Socialization** **(31)**

The process by which people develop their political orientation. Political socialization is the process by which people learn about politics and the political system and develop knowledge, values, beliefs, and feelings about how the political system does and ought to operate. Although political socialization is a life-long process, most political learning takes place at a relatively young age. By the time people are fifteen, they have developed most of their fundamental notions about politics and the political system; additional learning takes place at the fringes, filling in gaps or supplementing knowledge. Political socialization is the means by which political culture and public opinion are passed along to individuals. *See also* AGENTS OF POLITICAL SOCIALIZATION, 2; POLITICAL CULTURE, 27; POLITICAL ORIENTATION, 30.

*Significance* Political socialization contributes to the development of support for the political system in relatively stable systems such as that of the United States. It also helps to shape the pattern of demands people may have in relation to the political system. In the United States, the agents of political socialization (parents, schools, peers, the media, and significant events) tend to provide comparable messages so that children learn to support the political system and have relatively similar demands. As a result, the range of political conflict in the United States is much less than in countries with a less unified political culture and greater disagreement in messages being passed along by agents of socialization. People in the United States may disagree about whether taxes should stay the same, be increased, or be decreased, whether government regulation should increase or decrease, or whether military expenditures are too high or too low; but these are minor disagreements compared to debates over whether the economic system should be capitalist or socialist, whether elections should or should not be held, and some of the other more fundamental debates that take place in societies with less stable political systems.

**Political Trust** **(32)**

The extent to which citizens have confidence in their political leaders and government institutions. Political trust reflects people's perceptions about their government's ability to cope with conditions it faces. The political traumas occurring in the United States since the assassination of President John Kennedy, including the war in Vietnam,

Watergate, and oil shortages, have considerably decreased the political trust that Americans have for their leaders and to some extent for their institutions. There was some evidence that this trust began to increase with the presidency of Ronald Reagan, although the events of the Iran-Contra affair tended to reinforce feelings that all was not well with the government. *See also* IRAN-CONTRA AFFAIR, 17; VOTER TURNOUT, 208; WATERGATE, 42.

*Significance* Political trust affects people's support for the political system. Low levels of trust would make it difficult for the political system to maintain stability and support. Although trust has decreased in recent years in the United States, especially with regard to political leaders, distrust has not reached the point where it substantially decreases support for the political system. A decrease in political trust, along with such factors as a decrease in the sense of political efficacy, seems to have had an impact on political participation, contributing in particular to smaller voter turnouts since 1960.

**Public Opinion** **(33)**

People's perceptions about political issues of current importance. Public opinion refers to people's attitudes, beliefs, feelings, and reactions to events and issues that are of current relevance to the political system. It includes attitudes toward abortion, beliefs about which candidate would make the best president, feelings about how good a job Congress is doing, or reactions to current foreign policy negotiations. Public opinion is similar to political culture, except that it refers to more immediate and more transitory issues. The use of sampling theory and the development of systematic public opinion polling have greatly enhanced knowledge about public opinion in the United States. *See also* COGNITIONS, 6; OPINION POLL, 24; POLITICAL KNOWLEDGE, 29; POLITICAL ORIENTATION, 30; SAMPLING TECHNIQUES, 35.

*Significance* Public opinion is very important in a democratic society such as the United States. If government is to be responsive to popular will, it needs to know what that will is. Studies of public opinion can provide information about what the public wants from government. Several difficulties arise, however, in interpreting the variety of public opinion studies currently available in the United States. First, there is frequently considerable disagreement about the meaning of public opinion studies. Polls asking only slightly different questions may get dramatically different results. In one poll, when asked to agree or disagree to the statement "The decision to have an abortion should be left to the woman and her physician," 73 percent of those interviewed said the decision should be left to the woman. In another poll, when asked whether they would favor or oppose "a ban on all abortions except in the case of rape, incest, or when the mother's life is endangered," 62 percent favored the ban. (The first results are from an NBC News survey of election-day voters in 1984; the second set of results is from a Gallup poll in 1985.) Although the samples for the two studies were somewhat different, the results were dramatically different, reflecting to a great extent the difference in the way the question was phrased. Second, studies suggest that public opinion can be fickle and difficult to understand. People who are interviewed to ascertain their views for public opinion studies have greatly varying levels of political knowledge, with most having very limited political knowledge. Under these circumstances, the answers received will depend greatly on the knowledge available to the respondent. Third, because public opinion has become significant to policymakers, there are occasional efforts to manipulate survey results through the phrasing of questions. Under these circumstances, the studies are more likely to reflect what the pollsters want to hear rather than what public opinion really is.

**Public Policy** **(34)**

The authoritative allocation of values for society. Public policy includes laws passed by legislative bodies, the pattern of implementation of those laws by executive branch officials, and the interpretation of laws and the Constitution by the courts. Public policy is the product of the activities of political authorities; it is an output from the political system. If Congress passes a law regulating pollution emissions, for example, that law becomes part of public policy. If the Environmental Protection Agency were assigned responsibility for implementation of such a law, its actions would also be part of public policy. If a case were brought to court in relation to that law, the decision of the court would also be part of public policy. Public policy in any particular arena is commonly a complex interweaving of the actions of the legislature, the executive (including the bureaucracy), and the courts. *See also* DEMANDS, 8; POLITICAL AUTHORITIES, 26; SUPPORTS, 36; VALUES, 41.

*Significance* Public policy is the means by which the political system affects society. If Congress passes a law to control pollution emissions, the combined effect of the law and its pattern of implementation will have consequences for society in myriad ways. The most direct repercussions would fall to those in violation of whatever standards are created by the law. They would need to change their behavior in order to meet the newly created standards. Doing so, however, might require the purchase of, or perhaps even the development of, new equipment, thereby benefiting whichever business could provide such equipment. People might have to be hired by the company producing the equipment; people might have to be laid off in the company needing the equipment in order to meet the costs of purchasing it; and so on. Whether such a new law will actually decrease the amount of pollution can only be determined over time. People in society who realize the consequences of public policy seek to influence it through their demands. In many cases, they organize interest groups or join already existing interest groups to increase the forcefulness with which they can convey their demands to political authorities.

**Sampling Techniques** **(35)**

Procedures for selecting a small group of people with the expectation that their views will be representative of those of a much larger group. Sampling techniques are varied and complex, but their objective is to ensure that the views of the sample will accurately reflect the views of the larger population from which the sample has been drawn. The most straightforward method is to select a random sample of the population, which is not easy to do because it requires listing by name every person living in the United States before drawing the random sample. Another technique, commonly referred to as stratified sampling, identifies central characteristics of the population such as age, ethnicity, sex, income, education, or region of the country, and ensures that the sample approximates the population on these characteristics. *See also* CAMPAIGN POLLING, 165; OPINION POLL, 24.

*Significance* Sampling techniques that ensure a representative sample are the heart of polling. Sampling theory and the techniques that are derived from it make possible quality investigation into what people think, feel, and believe about politics, politicians, and their government. Before the development of accurate sampling techniques, various unsystematic ways of describing public views existed, but they were generally biased because they were based on unrepresentative samples. The classic example occurred when the *Literary Digest* predicted victory for Alfred Landon over Franklin Roosevelt in the 1936 presidential election based on a poll that included over 2 million of their readers. Although its sample was very large, it was also very biased. Because the sample came from a list of the *Digest*'s readers, it was skewed toward the middle and upper-middle classes. Using currently available sampling techniques, it is possible to predict national election results with a sample of less than 3,000 people.

**Supports** **(36)**

Positive actions and attitudes directed toward component parts of the political system. Supports, along with demands, are the two ways in which society affects the political system. Supports include identifying with country or with nationhood, singing the national anthem or saying the pledge of allegiance, voting, and paying taxes. Supports can be directed at different components of the political system: the political community, the political regime, political authorities, or public policies such as laws, court decisions, and presidential actions. Withdrawal of support by a substantial portion of the population or by important actors can occur in relation to any of the components. If it is focused on the political community or the political regime, withdrawal of support may lead to resistance to the government, or even to attempts to overthrow it. If it occurs in relation to political authorities or policies, efforts to replace those authorities or change those public policies will appear. *See also* DEMANDS, 8; INPUTS, 16; POLITICAL AUTHORITIES, 26; PUBLIC POLICY, 34.

*Significance* Supports are crucial for the continued effectiveness of any government. People support the component parts of the political system for two principal reasons: (1) they are encouraged to do so through the political socialization process, and (2) they are satisfied with what the system is doing—they like its public policies. In the United States, there has commonly been strong support for the political community and political regime and varying levels of support for authorities and policy. Vigorous support for the first two has produced a stable political system, and elections have provided a legitimate way to remove those authorities who are unable to maintain support and to encourage the changing of policies that lack support.

**United States Constitution** **(37)**

The fundamental rules under which government in the United States must operate. The United States Constitution, a brief document, is the oldest operating constitution in the modern world. The Constitution assigns authority to Congress, the presidency, and the federal courts, and to the national political institutions it created; it describes the criteria and the process of selection for the people who will hold office in those institutions. It contains a number of principles—federalism, separation of powers, checks and balances, and limited government—designed to decentralize governmental authority and reduce the prospects of any one political force dominating society. These principles have received as much popular support as the institutions of government throughout the history of the country. *See also* LIMITED GOVERNMENT, 20; UNITED STATES CONSTITUTION: CHECKS AND BALANCES, 38; UNITED STATES CONSTITUTION: FEDERALISM, 39; UNITED STATES CONSTITUTION: SEPARATION OF POWERS, 40.

*Significance* The United States Constitution has had broad popular support throughout the country's history. Because it is brief and provides for institutional arrangements and processes rather than detailing specific policies, the Constitution, with few formal amendments, has remained of central relevance to the operation of the political system. It has proven sufficiently flexible to allow dramatic changes in the operation of the political system without requiring major revision. The words of the Constitution are much the same today as they were 200 years ago, but the government has changed from a small operation of little relevance to most of the people of the country to a large operation upon which everyone in society is in some way dependent.

**United States Constitution: Checks and Balances (38)**
Provisions built into the Constitution that allow each branch of federal government to limit or influence the activities of the other two. Checks and balances were designed by the drafters of the Constitution to ensure that no branch of government becomes too powerful. Checks exist because the separation of powers is not complete; where power is shared among the branches, each has the ability to affect the others. A presidential check on Congress, for example, is his or her right to veto bills it passes. The president can check the federal courts through his or her constitutional power to appoint federal justices. Congress can check the president by removing him or her from office through the impeachment process or by exercising its control over federal spending. Congress can check the federal courts through its control over spending, over the structure and jurisdiction of the courts, and ultimately through the impeachment process. The Supreme Court can check the other two branches through its power of judicial review (the power to declare the acts of the other two branches of government unconstitutional). *See also* UNITED STATES CONSTITUTION, 37.

*Significance* Checks and balances were built into the Constitution as part of the effort to ensure the decentralization of power. The drafters of the Constitution sought to develop stronger political institutions than had existed under the Articles of Confederation but at the same time attempted to ensure that no one institution would become too powerful. They were successful in achieving their goal. Throughout most of the history of the United States, Congress has been the more dominant of the institutions, but checks from the other branches prevented it from becoming all-powerful. With the development of the institutionalized presidency under Franklin Roosevelt, the president has assumed a more dominant role but has at various historical points been strongly checked by Congress or the courts. Some students of and participants in the national political process have come to believe that checks and balances have operated too stringently and made it difficult to develop overall government policy.

**United States Constitution: Federalism** **(39)**
A principle of government built into the Constitution that divides political authority between the federal government and the state governments. Federalism was one of the techniques used by the drafters of the Constitution to decentralize political authority and has been central to the development of the U.S. political system. The Constitution assigns some powers exclusively to the federal government, including the power to declare war, to coin money, and to enter into treaties with other governments. Powers it reserves for the states include police power and power to establish and regulate education and local government. Finally, some powers—such as the power to tax or to regulate commerce—are available to both the state and federal governments. In cases in which there is conflict between state and federal law, the supremacy clause of the Constitution provides that federal laws will be supreme. *See also* UNITED STATES CONSTITUTION, 37.

*Significance* Federalism is one of the important principles built into the United States Constitution that continue to ensure a type of decentralized government in the country. The way in which federalism operates has changed over the years. Initially, state governments and the federal government operated separately and independently, and considerable conflict occurred at times in interpreting the constitutional assignment of powers. Today considerable cooperation exists between the federal and state governments.

**United States Constitution: Separation of Powers** **(40)**
The principle that legislative, executive, and judicial powers should be assigned to separate branches of government. Separation of powers was built into the United States Constitution by establishing Congress, the presidency, and the federal courts as separate branches of government. Although the Constitution creates three separate branches, it assigns them overlapping responsibilities that make them interdependent and encourage the operation of a checks and balances system. Congress is assigned the responsibility of passing laws, but it

cannot implement these decisions itself. Rather, Congress depends on the president and the executive branch for implementation. Further, it falls to the judicial branch to interpret what these laws mean. The president, in turn, is head of the executive branch of government, but the laws he is responsible for implementing and the money necessary for doing so come from Congress, and the Supreme Court has the power to declare his actions unconstitutional. Similarly, the Supreme Court can decide on the constitutionality of the actions of the other two branches, but its members are appointed by the president with the approval of the Senate. *See also* UNITED STATES CONSTITUTION, 37; UNITED STATES CONSTITUTION: CHECKS AND BALANCES, 38.

*Significance* Separation of powers is one of several principles built into the United States Constitution to ensure decentralization of government power. The principle has worked quite effectively to ensure that each branch has a key role to play in the political system and that none has assumed dominance. For most of U.S. history, Congress has been the more powerful institution, although in recent years the presidency has assumed that role. Whichever branch has been more powerful at any moment of history, however, it has been clearly limited by the power of the other two branches.

**Values (41)**

Things that are considered good or desirable, and are preferred over other things. Values can include ideals such as equality, democracy, or freedom; desired conditions such as employment, happiness, or security; desired experiences such as education or travel; or material goods such as wealth, good housing, or other important possessions. In making public policy (outputs), the political system allocates values; it determines who will be entitled to certain valued things. For example, the social security program in the United States provides, among other benefits, that people over the age of 62 are entitled to certain economic benefits (values). Universal public education in the United States ensures that every child will receive the value of an educational opportunity. Other programs provide other values to people in society. A key component of any political culture is what might be called regime values, or values that are central to the operation of the political system and have the support of most of the people in society. Regime values in the United States include freedom, equality, individualism, and free enterprise. *See also* POLITICAL CULTURE, 27.

*Significance* Values vary from one society to another. In some societies, great value is placed on wealth and material possessions, in others on religious status, and so on. There are many things that can be considered desirable by people and the relative ranking of these things will vary from society to society and even within societies. Value priorities are learned through the political socialization process. Once learned, they influence the way people see the operation of the political system and shape people's political behavior. For example, strong commitment to the idea of political equality and equality of opportunity has made it easier for people facing discrimination in the United States to seek redress. The argument on the part of blacks during the civil rights movement that everyone is entitled to equal opportunity, to the right to participate politically, and to vote was made persuasive because of the predominance of the value of equality as a regime characteristic. In a society that does not place value on equality (such as South Africa), such an argument is worthless. One of the best ways to discover who has power within a society is to determine which values that society considers most important and then to see who has them.

**Watergate** **(42)**

A series of events that ultimately led to the resignation of President Richard Nixon on 9 August 1974. An early event in the series was the burglary of the Democratic National Committee offices in the Watergate Hotel complex in Washington, D.C., from which the Watergate scandal takes its name. The break-in was initially considered unimportant, carried out by irresponsible people at the lower level of the Nixon campaign, and thus had no impact on the 1972 election, which Nixon won by a landslide. Subsequent revelations, however, disclosed that the burglary was related to many other improper or illegal activities and that responsibility for these could be traced to high officials within the Nixon White House. As more disclosures developed during 1973 and 1974 as a result of court hearings, congressional investigations, and journalistic explorations, Nixon continued to deny that he had anything to do with either the illegal activities or their cover-up. The dramatic revelation that Nixon had taped most of his White House conversations led to legal efforts to force the president to make these tapes available. When the tapes revealed that Nixon himself had participated in discussions of how best to cover up the various illegal operations, or at least how to cover up their connection to the White House, his doom was sealed. He resigned from office in the midst of proceedings that would have led to his impeachment by the House and probably to his conviction by the Senate. *See also* POLITICAL ALIENATION, 25.

*Significance* Watergate contributed dramatically to the decline of public confidence in government and to an increase in political alienation within the United States. It occurred at a time when the public was already reeling from the assassinations of John and Robert Kennedy and Martin Luther King, the violence of urban riots, and the intense conflict over participation in the Vietnam War. Watergate seemed to strike even deeper, however, because it revealed a government willing to use its power to illegally advance its own goals in ways that violated the rights of its citizens. Watergate represented a threat to U.S. notions of constitutional or limited government. Although President Nixon and his top officials frequently talked about the need for law and order in U.S. society, they seemed to see nothing wrong with violating the law themselves.

# 2. *Political Participation*

*Political participation* refers to activities by individuals within a society that influence or are intended to influence the operation of the political system. Obvious examples come to mind: voting, discussing politics, working in a political campaign. Political participation is at the heart of the operation of a democratic society. Citizens participate in the selection of those who will govern. They are also expected to make known their policy preferences to those who will enact them. Political participation can reflect support for or opposition to the political system and its component parts. Pledging allegiance to the flag or singing the National Anthem reveal and reinforce commitment to the political system; refusing to do so signifies negative feelings toward the system. The most prevalent type of political participation involves efforts to influence the operation of the political system—to have an impact on who will hold office or on what the policies of the country will be. The amount and type of political participation encouraged or allowed may vary from society to society. In countries with democratic political systems, most citizens have sufficient avenues of participation that they feel they can influence government and its policies, although there is considerable variation in participation even from one democratic country to another. In countries in which the political system is not democratic, citizens are likely to be discouraged from any type of political participation other than that desired by government officials. In the United States, political participation occurs in many different ways. Among the most frequent ways that citizens participate are expressing an opinion, talking about politics with friends or neighbors, and voting. Less common activities are signing petitions, serving on community boards or commissions, contacting government officials, and attempting to persuade others how to vote or what to do politically. Some activities involve concerted efforts with others such as participation in an interest group or a political party or working in a political campaign. Probably the least common, and most difficult, type of participation is running for elective office. For most of the activities above, U.S. citizens are more likely to be active than citizens of other democratic countries; the one very important exception is voting.

Several explanations have been developed to explain why some people are more politically active than others. One important concept in explaining activity is efficacy, the feeling that what you do is important and will have an impact. People who are likely to participate in the political arena almost all share this sense of efficacy. They believe that their activities can make a difference. People who are not very active usually do not have this sense of personal efficacy. Education and socioeconomic status also influence an individual's level of participation. The higher their education level and socioeconomic status, the more likely people are to be politically active. Actually, there is considerable overlap among these factors because education and high socioeconomic status seem to contribute to a person's sense of efficacy.

In some situations, low levels of participation occur because of barriers the society has created to discourage participation. For most of the history of the United States, political participation by women and blacks was discouraged. Women were not given the right to vote until the Nineteenth Amendment was adopted in 1920. Blacks were discouraged from voting, particularly in the South, by a variety of techniques such as the poll tax and literacy tests, which were removed in the 1960s. There can also be structural barriers to participation that may not be intentionally directed at any particular group but that may have the effect of discouraging participation. By requiring registration in advance and by holding elections on a working day (Tuesday), the United States makes it more difficult for people to vote than some other democratic countries where registration is automatic and elections are held on Sundays. Such structural barriers are frequently used to explain low levels of voting in the United States.

One significant distinction in political participation is between conventional and unconventional participation. Conventional participation involves activities that are considered "normal," that is, established behaviors or accepted ways of doing things. Contacting your congressman, voting, and joining an interest group would be examples of conventional political behavior in the United States. Unconventional participation involves activities that are extraordinary, that is, considered improper or not viewed as conforming to the rules of the game. Burning your draft card, taking over a building, or kidnapping the mayor would be considered unconventional political behavior in the United States. The definition of conventional and unconventional participation will vary from society to society. Criticizing government activity is a perfectly conventional way of participating politically in the United States, whereas in many countries it would be considered unconventional. The line between conventional and unconventional political participation is fuzzy. Is a protest march or a peaceful demonstration conventional or unconventional behavior? Citizens' views in the United States vary considerably on such a question, although the Constitution clearly protects these types of behavior.

The more difficult it is for people to influence the political system through conventional types of participation, the more likely they are to resort to unconventional types of participation. The United States has a long history of unconventional political participation by groups that have been denied traditional avenues or by people who had access to traditional avenues but who were unable to achieve their objectives by conventional means. American colonists dumped tea in Boston Harbor (the Boston Tea Party) because they could not get England to change her policies. The thirteen colonies revolted against England for much the same reason. In a very real sense, the United States was created through the exercise of unconventional political participation. Later examples include such activities as the attempted secession from the United States by the southern states, the activities of the suffragettes seeking the right to vote for women, many of the activities related to the civil rights movement, urban riots, and protests against participation in the Vietnam War. People have resorted to such methods as revolution, marches, sit-ins, tractorcades, prayer, and protests in their efforts to influence government behavior.

### *Adderley v. Florida*, 385 U.S. 39 (1966) (43)

Held that demonstrators may be barred from assembly on the grounds of a county jail. Adderley and a number of others were convicted of trespassing after they gathered at a county jail to protest the arrest of several students the day before as well as local policies of racial segregation at the jail itself. In upholding the conviction of the demonstrators, the Supreme Court focused on the question of whether the trespass convictions deprived the demonstrators of their freedom of speech. The Court concluded that "nothing in the Constitution . . . prevented Florida from even-handed enforcement of its general trespass statute against those refusing to obey the sheriff's order to remove themselves from what amounted to the curtilage of the jailhouse." That the jail was a public building did not automatically entitle the protesters to demonstrate there. The state, no less than a private owner of property, has power to preserve the property under its control for the use to which it is lawfully dedicated. The security purpose for which the jail was dedicated outweighed the free expression interests of the protesters. The justices felt that to find for Adderley would be to endorse "the assumption that people who want to propagandize protests or views have a constitutional right to do so whenever and wherever they please." The Supreme Court categorically rejected that premise and concluded its opinion by saying that the Constitution does not forbid a state to control the use of its property for its lawful, nondiscriminatory purposes. *See also* COX V. LOUISIANA (379 U.S. 536: 1965), 56; *EDWARDS V. SOUTH CAROLINA* (372 U.S. 229: 1963), 61; *HUDGENS V. NATIONAL LABOR RELATIONS BOARD (NLRB)* (424 U.S. 507: 1976), 68; *PRUNEYARD SHOPPING CENTER V. ROBINS* (447 U.S. 74: 1980), 82; TIME, PLACE, AND MANNER RESTRICTIONS, 89.

*Significance* *Adderley v. Florida* (385 U.S. 39: 1966) involves "speech plus," that is, expression in which conduct beyond the speech itself is involved. In these situations, that action or conduct component may be subject to regulation even if the restriction ultimately impairs the speech. Such regulations—known as time, place, and manner restrictions—must be content neutral and tightly focused. Accordingly, certain areas or buildings may be foreclosed to expressions taking the form of demonstrations or marches because these modes of expression may conflict with other legitimate and substantial public interests. In *Adderley*, the Court ruled the jailhouse grounds to be such a restricted area. Though public, the jailhouse grounds were not seen as an appropriate location for expression because of the essential security interest. Furthermore, a jailhouse is not really a "seat of government," a place where public policymakers conduct public business. Thus a jailhouse and a state capitol building, for example, are not equivalent in that the former may be legally restricted, whereas the latter may not.

**Aggregation** **(44)**

The pulling together of people who share similar political views to make possible concerted political action. Aggregation in the political arena refers to uniting people with coinciding or related interests in order to allow them to more effectively communicate their demands to the political system. To consider one example, thousands of individuals, particularly those whose loved ones have been maimed or killed by drunk drivers, have been bitterly frustrated for years at the lenient treatment given those drivers. As individuals, however, they were powerless to bring about changes. It was not until these people came together in an organization—MADD (Mothers Against Drunk Driving)—and began to provide concerted pressure for new policies to deal with drunk driving that political authorities became more responsive to their demands. *See also* DEMANDS, 8; INTEREST GROUP, 293; POLITICAL PARTY, 235.

*Significance* Aggregation of demands increases the prospects that the political system will respond to those demands. In a society the size of the United States, the demands of any one individual are not likely to be heard. It is only when people with shared interests finds ways to join together that they can increase their effectiveness. Political participation in the United States frequently involves participation in an organized group because such a group is more likely than an individual to have its demands met. Interest groups and political parties are two types of organizations that are consistently involved in demand aggregation.

**Apartheid** **(45)**

Political arrangements in South Africa that require racial segregation and guarantee social, economic, and political superiority to the white minority. Apartheid is the most blatant form of racism because status and opportunity are determined by race. Whites make up 18 percent of South Africa's population and dominate the society. Blacks make up 68 percent of the population and are relegated to positions at the bottom. The remaining population—Asians and coloreds (people of mixed race)—occupy an uncomfortable status somewhere in between but closer to that of blacks. Whites in South Africa maintain their position by denying political rights to blacks and by using intimidation, imprisonment, and violence against those who oppose them, including some fellow whites. *See also* BOYCOTT, 47.

*Significance* Apartheid in South Africa illustrates the importance of political participation in determining public policy. A white minority, by maintaining a monopoly on political decision making, dominates the remainder of the population. Apartheid has generated strong opposition from people and governments throughout the world. In the United States, numerous groups have formed for the purpose of overturning the apartheid system. They have used a variety of techniques including boycotting South African goods, pressuring U.S. companies not to do business in or with South Africa, and urging people and organizations not to purchase stock in companies that continue to operate in South Africa. Congress has passed legislation applying limited economic sanctions to South Africa in the effort to discourage continuation of apartheid. Many of the people and organizations that fought to rid the United States of racism now identify with the cause of black South Africans and are active in organizing opposition to apartheid.

**Boston Tea Party** **(46)**
A protest by American colonists to British taxes on tea and to the granting by the British government of a monopoly in the tea trade to the British East India Company. The Boston Tea Party involved the dumping of large quantities of tea into Boston Harbor in 1773 by Boston radicals dressed as Indians. The Boston Tea Party was the most dramatic of the actions taken by the colonists to resist what they deemed unfair or improper interference with the colonies on the part of the British government. *See also* DIRECT ACTION, 58.

*Significance* The Boston Tea Party was an early and sensational use of unconventional political participation by people who are now considered among the founding fathers of the United States. Most people view the founding fathers with great respect, even awe, and forget that they resisted what they saw as British oppression with illegal and highly controversial actions, including, ultimately, violent revolution. The Boston Tea Party provoked the British Parliament into passing the Coercive (Intolerable) Acts (1774), which led the colonists to convene the First Continental Congress and to begin organizing for armed resistance to the British.

**Boycott** **(47)**
A form of political participation that involves not purchasing or using the products or services of an organization or agency seen as responsible for or contributing to the problems generating the protest. Boycotts use economic power to gain a group's objectives. The American colonists boycotted imported tea as a protest to an act of Parliament. The Montgomery bus boycott, led by Martin Luther King, Jr., provided one of the early, pivotal victories of the civil rights movement. In response to the arrest in 1955 of Rosa Parks, a black woman who refused to sit in the rear of the bus as required by ordinance in Montgomery, Alabama, blacks organized to boycott the use of buses, ultimately bringing about a change in the discriminatory policies of that city. In 1973 many consumers participated in a nationwide meat boycott to protest the increased cost of meat. *See also* CIVIL RIGHTS MOVEMENT, 53.

*Significance* Boycotts provide people with the opportunity to apply economic pressure as a means of altering undesirable conditions. They are most often used by people who feel powerless to bring about the changes they seek by more traditional means. At the time of the Montgomery bus boycott, discriminatory laws and practices disfranchised most blacks in the South; thus, traditional political action to induce the Montgomery City Council to change the ordinance that required black people to ride in the back of the bus was impossible. Refusing to ride the buses, however, was something that any black person could do. Boycotts also afford an opportunity for organizing people for concerted action that may go beyond the boycott itself. As a consequence of the Montgomery bus boycott, many people throughout the United States, particularly in the North, sympathized with the participants and the ranks of the civil rights movement swelled.

**Campaign** **(48)**

A planned, coordinated approach to achieving specifically defined objectives. Campaigns can be designed to reach a variety of goals including election to office, raising money for charity, or winning a military battle. The elements that distinguish a campaign from other efforts to obtain objectives are planning, coordination, and management. Campaigns involve organized efforts that link a variety of components together in ways designed to achieve a common goal. A typical election campaign, for example, would include a fund-raising component to raise the money needed to carry out campaign activities, a volunteer recruitment program to obtain workers, a voter contact program to influence voters, and a management component to develop the initial plans and to ensure that each component effectively implements these plans in a coordinated fashion. *See also* GUBERNATORIAL CAMPAIGN, 184; LOCAL ELECTION CAMPAIGN, 188; NONPARTISAN CAMPAIGN, 191; PRESIDENTIAL CAMPAIGN, 197; PRIMARY CAMPAIGN, 198; SENATE CAMPAIGN, 202.

*Significance* Campaigns encourage political participation. An election campaign, for example, needs volunteers to perform most of the campaign tasks, so an important component of the campaign is to recruit volunteers by encouraging people to become politically active. The campaign needs votes for its candidate, so part of its organizational effort includes a voter contact program to persuade people to vote. All campaigns start with a nucleus of people who in order to obtain some objective need to recruit others to assist them, thus increasing the level of political participation in the country.

***Carroll v. President and Commissioners of Princess Anne*, 393 U.S. 175 (1968)** **(49)**
Struck down an ex parte injunction (an order issued in the absence of one party) prohibiting a rally of militant white supremacists. *Carroll* illustrates the use of court restraining orders to enjoin persons from demonstrating in some way. Such injunctions are frequently, *but not always,* used in situations where permits or licenses to march have been denied. Carroll, a member of a white supremacist organization known as the National States Rights Party, participated in a rally at which aggressively and militantly racist and anti-Semitic speeches were made. At the conclusion of the speeches, it was announced that the rally would be resumed the next night. Local government officials obtained a restraining order in the meantime in an ex parte proceeding. The injunction restrained Carroll and others from holding public meetings for 10 days. The Supreme Court struck down the order primarily because of the way it was secured—the order was issued "without notice to petitioners and without any effort, however informal, to invite or permit their participation in the proceedings." The Court recognized that ex parte orders may be appropriate in some situations, "but there is no place within the area of basic freedoms guaranteed by the First Amendment for such orders." There is "insufficient assurance of the balanced analysis and careful conclusions which are essential in the area of First Amendment adjudication." Furthermore, an absence of information made it difficult for the Supreme Court to construct an order in the narrowest and least stifling terms. *See also* *ADDERLEY V. FLORIDA* (385 U.S. 39: 1966), 43; TIME, PLACE, AND MANNER RESTRICTIONS, 89; *WALKER V. BIRMINGHAM* (388 U.S. 307: 1967), 97.

*Significance* *Carroll v. President and Commissioners of Princess Anne* (393 U.S. 175: 1968) established guidelines through which court orders might be obtained against demonstrators and those having rallies. The permit injunction approach has often been used in such situations. Permits are satisfactory so long as they are confined to reasonable time, place, and manner limitations. Permit or license requirements that are not content neutral or that allow too much discretion to permit-granting officials are typically unacceptable. Civil rights demonstrators often ran afoul of permit injunction regulations. In *Walker v. Birmingham* (388 U.S. 307: 1967), for example, the Supreme Court upheld an injunction issue following the denial of a parade permit. Walker, Martin Luther King, Jr., and others involved in a proposed parade disobeyed the injunction without seeking appellate review of either the injunction or the permit denial that precipitated the court order. The Court found the potentially persuasive objections to the Birmingham permit system to be subordinate to the failure of the demonstrators to obey the court order. A more recent injunction episode involved attempts by the Village of Skokie, Illinois, to prevent an assembly of the National Socialist Party of America, a self-proclaimed Nazi organization. Prior to the assembly, an injunction was secured from a state court enjoining the party from a uniformed march, display of swastikas, and distribution of materials that might "promote hatred against persons of the Jewish faith or ancestry." The Court stayed implementation of the injunction, saying that it deprived the party of its right to demonstrate, at least for the period until full appellate review could occur.

**_Chicago Police Department v. Mosley,_ 408 U.S. 92 (1972)** **(50)**

Ruling that a local ordinance that distinguished labor picketing from other kinds of peaceful picketing was impermissible. The ordinance under challenge in *Chicago Police Department v. Mosley* defined picketing near schools as "disorderly conduct," but excepted peaceful picketing of any school involved in a labor dispute. The question in the case was whether this "selective exclusion from a public place" is constitutional. Because the ordinance treated some picketing differently from others, the Supreme Court's analysis of the First Amendment issue was "closely intertwined" with considerations of equal protection. The "central problem" with the regulation, in the Court's view, was that it "describes permissible picketing in terms of its subject matter"; the "operative distinction" is the "message on the picket sign." The Court said that such content regulation was not permitted. "Above all else, the First Amendment means that government has no power to restrict expression because of its message, its ideas, its subject matter, or its content." Any restriction on "expressive activity" on the basis of content would "completely undercut the profound national commitment to the principle that debate on public issues should be uninhibited, robust, and wide-open." The Court was careful to say that although all picketing at any time must be allowed, "reasonable time, place and manner restrictions may be necessary to further significant governmental interests." Such regulations, however—especially those that control only some expressive activity—must be "tailored to serve a substantial governmental interest" and will be "carefully scrutinized" by the courts. *See also* *ADDERLEY V. FLORIDA* (385 U.S. 39: 1966), 43; TIME, PLACE, AND MANNER RESTRICTIONS, 89; *UNITED STATES V. GRACE* (461 U.S. 171: 1983), 92.

*Significance* *Chicago Police Department v. Mosley* (408 U.S. 92: 1972) examines the regulation of picketing. Picketing, like other activities such as marching or demonstrating, is expression, but it is also more. There is an additional action component that is an integral part of the communication. Picketing is intended to have impact by generating public visibility for a message or position. Independent of the message, the success of picketing or demonstrating is measured by the extent of its exposure. As people engaging in this activity wish to maximize their public presence, they may impinge upon public order. Although public areas are generally regarded as accessible "public forums," certain time, place, and manner restrictions may be imposed by government. Government has an interest in keeping public thoroughfares free of obstruction, for example, and therefore it may restrict access of demonstrators or picketers in such areas so long as the regulation is narrowly focused and nondiscriminatory. The ordinance in *Mosley* was defective because it was not content neutral—it excepted a certain kind of picketing while prohibiting all others.

**Civil Disobedience** **(51)**

Open violation of a law considered by the violators to be immoral or wrong in order to call attention to its alleged immorality. Civil disobedience as a technique for challenging laws was an idea developed in the United States by Henry David Thoreau in an essay of that title written in 1848. Later Mahatma Gandhi drew on the work of Thoreau in establishing the nonviolent resistance to British rule in India that was so instrumental in gaining independence for India. Martin Luther King, Jr., drawing on the tenets established by Gandhi, applied the principles of nonviolent civil disobedience to the civil rights movement beginning with the Montgomery bus boycott and continuing throughout his life. *See also* CIVIL RIGHTS MOVEMENT, 53; DIRECT ACTION, 58; *WALKER V. BIRMINGHAM* (388 U.S. 307: 1967), 97.

*Significance* Civil disobedience provided a way for blacks to confront the long-established racism of the United States. Lacking the political muscle to revise or remove laws maintaining or allowing segregation, blacks made extremely slow progress toward equality until the late 1950s. The formulation and advancement of the principle of civil disobedience by Martin Luther King, Jr., initially during the Montgomery bus boycott and later as the means for advancing the civil rights of blacks throughout the country, provided the civil rights movement with an effective way of demonstrating the brutalities that blacks had to endure. Peaceful, nonviolent resistance to discriminatory laws through such direct action techniques as boycotts, demonstrations, marches, and sit-ins eventually forced the political system to change. Thousands of blacks, along with a number of white allies, spent time in jails throughout the South as a consequence of having publicly violated segregation laws, but the pressure they generated ultimately brought about the removal of the laws they were protesting. Civil disobedience was later used by groups protesting the continuation of the Vietnam War.

**Civil Rights Acts** **(52)**

Laws passed by Congress designed to eliminate discrimination based on race, gender, creed, or national origin. The first civil rights act was passed in 1866, with subsequent ones passed in 1870, 1871, 1875, 1957, 1960, 1964, and 1968. Acts passed in the nineteenth century were designed to protect the rights of blacks in the post–Civil War era, but most provisions were either declared unconstitutional by the Supreme Court or were repealed by Congress. Thus, by the beginning of the twentieth century, little remained to protect the rights of black people. Not until 1957 was another, very moderate, act passed to protect the civil rights of blacks. It established a Civil Rights Division in the Justice Department, created a Civil Rights Commission, and provided the Justice Department with some minimal powers to assist blacks in gaining the right to vote in the South. The Civil Rights Act of 1960 again sought to secure the right to vote for blacks in the South and authorized punishment for people interfering with federal court orders designed to eliminate segregation. The Civil Rights Act of 1964 marked a major change in the approach to civil rights. It was designed to attack discrimination in virtually every area of U.S. life by banning discriminatory practices based on race, color, religion, national origin, and, in the employment arena, sex. The act made illegal arbitrary discrimination in voter registration and prohibited discrimination in public accommodations such as restaurants and hotels. It expanded the power of the Civil Rights Commission, instituted a Community Relations Service to provide assistance in dealing with civil rights problems, and established the principle of equal opportunity in hiring. It gave the federal government teeth to ensure enforcement of civil rights provisions by providing for the withholding of federal funds to state and local programs that practiced discrimination. The Civil Rights Act of 1968 dealt predominantly with housing; it prohibited discrimination in the rental or sale of housing and in advertising or financing that related to housing. *See also* FIFTEENTH AMENDMENT, 63; POLITICAL PARTICIPATION, 79; VOTING RIGHTS ACTS, 96.

*Significance* The various civil rights acts of the last 120 years endeavored to resolve questions of how values such as the right to vote and to participate in politics, the opportunity to compete equally for an education, a house, or a job, and the freedom to act without being discriminated against will be allocated among the various components of society. Most of these values were initally limited to white males who owned property, but they were gradually extended to others in society. The greatest resistance to extending these values came in relation to blacks, most of whom remained slaves until the Civil War and the adoption of the Thirteenth Amendment. The success of civil rights legislation in relation to blacks demonstrates the importance of political participation in maintaining access to societal values. After the Civil War, the right of blacks to participate politically was protected in the South, where most blacks lived, by the federal government and the Union Army. After federal troops were withdrawn in 1876, whites regained political power in the South and the federal government lost concern with the condition of blacks. Southern whites, through the use of violence, intimidation, and state law, made it virtually impossible for most blacks to vote or to participate in other political activities. Lacking the ability to influence the political system, blacks suffered years of segregation and discrimination. Not until blacks resorted to unconventional means of political participation—such as the civil disobedience of the civil rights movement and urban riots—did the political system begin again to respond to their demands. The civil rights acts of the twentieth century *followed* such unconventional political participation; they did not precede it. The successful resort to unconventional political participation made it possible for blacks to regain the right to vote, and since regaining it, they have been more successful in having their demands met through conventional types of political participation.

**Civil Rights Movement** **(53)**

A movement to rid the United States of racial discrimination and segregation. The civil rights movement had its roots in the long struggle of black people for equality of opportunity. This struggle was primarily undertaken by the National Association for the Advancement of Colored People (NAACP), which since the early twentieth century has fought, mostly through the courts, the battle to end racial discrimination. A significant legal victory occurred in 1954 when the Supreme Court ruled in *Brown v. the Board of Education of Topeka, Kansas* (347 U.S. 483: 1954) that the principle of "separate but equal," which provided the legal justification for segregation, was a violation of the Constitution. The civil rights movement involved direct efforts to gain an end to segregation and discrimination not merely in legal decisions but in the practical, day-to-day experiences of blacks. Its first dramatic success occurred with the Montgomery bus boycott in 1955, coordinated by Martin Luther King, Jr., who was then a pastor in a Montgomery church. Reacting to the segregated buses required by state law and city ordinance, blacks organized a boycott of the bus system. In spite of arrests, prohibitions on black carpooling, and other efforts on the part of whites to force blacks to use the bus system, the boycott continued into 1956 when the Supreme Court finally declared the laws requiring segregated buses to be in violation of the Fourteenth Amendment. The movement continued with lunch counter sit-ins, marches, freedom rides, voter registration drives, and other direct action techniques to gain rights for blacks. The predominant organizations of the movement were the Southern Christian Leadership Conference (SCLC), organized out of the efforts in Montgomery; the Congress on Racial Equality (CORE), organized in 1942 but revitalized in the late 1950s; and Student Nonviolent Coordinating Committee (SNCC), organized in 1960. *See also* CIVIL RIGHTS ACTS, 52; DEMONSTRATION, 57; DIRECT ACTION, 58; MARCH, 72; SIT-IN, 83; VOTING RIGHTS ACTS, 96.

*Significance* The civil rights movement differed from earlier efforts to gain rights for blacks in two important ways. First, it entailed a dramatically different way of seeking change. The civil rights movement involved direct confrontation of established patterns of segregation and discrimination. Civil disobedience provided the rationale, and thousands of individuals furnished their bodies to challenge by their actions laws they considered immoral and unjust. "We Shall Overcome," an old Negro spiritual, became the movement's song as people faced police intimidation, mob violence, jail, and, in some cases, even death. Second, the civil rights movement was led by blacks; the principal organizations of the movement were controlled by blacks. Earlier efforts to gain rights for blacks had included significant, and at times dominant, white leadership. Because whites did not face the conditions that blacks did, they were more likely to seek change cautiously and more eager to pursue avenues less threatening to the established social order. The new black leaders of the civil rights movement were much more committed to making change happen immediately; they sought results and were less concerned about maintaining a social order that included racism. To comprehend the impact of the civil rights movement, it is helpful to understand the extent of discrimination that existed as late as the mid-1950s. In the South, the laws in many cases required segregation. Blacks could not go to white schools, sit in the front of buses or movie theaters, eat at white eating establishments, or do virtually anything with whites. In many parts of the South, they were prohibited from voting. In the North, the laws seldom required segregation, but they did not prohibit it. Realtors could decline to show blacks houses in white neighborhoods, businesses could refuse to hire blacks for any but menial jobs, city governments could and did provide much lower levels of service for residents of black neighborhoods, and school systems could and did provide a much better education for white children than for black. The civil rights movement was the single greatest influence in changing these conditions. Its challenge to the established patterns of discrimination was particularly influential in pushing Congress to pass civil and voting rights legislation that has changed the legal status of segregation and discrimination in the United States. Although elements of racial discrimination and segregation do remain, the law now actively seeks to eradicate them rather than to promote or protect them.

**_Coates v. Cincinnati_, 402 U.S. 611 (1971)** **(54)**

Decision that invalidated a municipal ordinance that made it a crime for three or more people to "assemble on a sidewalk and there conduct themselves in a manner annoying to persons passing by." The Supreme Court found the regulation reviewed in *Coates v. Cincinnati* defective for two reasons. First, the Court found the ordinance unacceptably vague because it "subjects the exercise of the right of assembly to an unascertainable standard, and unconstitutionally broad because it authorizes the punishment of constitutionally protected conduct." Conduct that "annoys some people does not annoy others." The ordinance was seen as defectively vague not in the sense that it "requires a person to conform his conduct to an imprecise but comprehensible normative standard, but rather in the sense that no standard of conduct is specified at all." Second, the ordinance was found to violate the constitutional "right of free assembly and association." A state may not make criminal the exercise of the right of assembly "simply because its exercise may be 'annoying' to some people." If such regulation were allowed, the right of people to gather in public places for "social or political purposes would be continually subject to summary suspension through the good-faith enforcement of such a prohibition against annoying conduct." *See also* *CHICAGO POLICE DEPARTMENT V. MOSLEY* (408 U.S. 92: 1972), 50; *COX V. LOUISIANA* (379 U.S. 359: 1965), 56; *SCHAUMBURG, VILLAGE OF V. CITIZENS FOR A BETTER ENVIRONMENT* (444 U.S. 620: 1980), 324; TIME, PLACE, AND MANNER RESTRICTIONS, 89.

*Significance* A governmental restriction may not proscribe conduct that is constitutionally protected. A law that fails to adequately differentiate between activities that may be regulated and those that may not is referred to as overbroad, a defect that is usually fatal to the regulation. The ordinance involved in *Coates v. Cincinnati* (402 U.S. 611: 1971) is a good example of a restriction that suffers from overbreadth. Another illustration can be seen in *Village of Schaumburg v. Citizens for a Better Environment* (444 U.S. 620: 1980), in which the Supreme Court struck down a local ordinance that required organizations soliciting contributions door to door to use at least 75 percent of their receipts for charitable purposes. The purpose of the ordinance was to prevent fraudulent solicitations. The Court objected to the approach because it imposed a direct and substantial limitation on organizations such as environmental education groups whose principal activities are research, advocacy, and public education. Although such organizations obviously do not meet the ordinance definition of charitable, their activities are constitutionally permissible. The Village of Schaumburg's ordinance was simply too inclusive. The Court ruled that, in addition to overbreadth, an enactment may not suffer from either imprecision or vagueness. Regulations must convey standards of conduct that persons of reasonable intelligence can understand. Restrictions that are either overbroad or vague may have a "chilling effect" on expression or some other protected activity.

***Cohen v. California*, 403 U.S. 15 (1971)** **(55)**

Held that expression, even that which may be offensive, is entitled to First Amendment protection. Cohen was arrested in the Los Angeles County Courthouse for wearing a jacket emblazoned with the words, "Fuck the Draft." At his trial, Cohen testified the jacket was his means of stating his intensely held feelings about the draft and U.S. involvement in Vietnam. Cohen was convicted of violating a statute prohibiting "malicious and willful disturbing of the peace" by conduct that is "offensive." The Supreme Court invalidated the statute, ruling that the words rather than the conduct were the issue, and therefore "speech" was being prohibited by the law. In addition, Cohen's words were not directed at anyone. A state cannot excise epithets as offensive by functioning as a guardian of public morality because the First Amendment is "designed and intended to remove governmental restraints from the arena of public discussion." Further, the Court was troubled by the "inherently boundless" nature of what the state was attempting through the statute. "Surely the State has no right to cleanse public debate to the point where it is grammatically palatable to the most squeamish among us." Finally, it was pointed out that language serves a dual communicative function. It conveys not only ideas capable of relatively precise and detailed explication but also otherwise inexpressible emotions. Words are often chosen as much for their emotive as for their cognitive force. The Court concluded,

"We cannot sanction the view that the Constitution, while solicitous of the cognitive content of individual speech, has little or no regard for that emotive function which, practically speaking, may often be the more important element of the overall message sought to be communicated." *See also* *TERMINELLO V. CHICAGO* (337 U.S. 1: 1949), 88; TIME, PLACE, AND MANNER RESTRICTIONS, 89; *TINKER V. DES MOINES SCHOOL DISTRICT* (393 U.S. 503: 1969), 90.

*Significance* *Cohen v. California* (403 U.S. 15: 1971) involved an attempt to punish "offensive" speech. Despite its offensive character, Cohen's message was "pure" speech, in that it does not have an action component but is just the expression itself. Typically, pure speech does not impinge on others as speech plus action might. As a result, regulation of pure speech is generally not permitted. There are exceptions, however, most of which take the form of breach of peace prosecutions. In *Chaplinsky v. New Hampshire* (315 U.S. 568: 1942), for example, the Supreme Court held that provocative "fighting words" are unprotected by the First Amendment. The fighting words exception, however, has been applied narrowly by the courts. Cases such as *Cohen* make it clear that the Court will virtually never permit the content of expression to become the target of regulation, even if that content is provocative, unpopular, or offensive to the public at large.

***Cox v. Louisiana*, 379 U.S. 536 (1965)** **(56)**

Set aside conviction for picketing a state courthouse. *Cox v. Louisiana* arose out of an assembly responding to the arrest of persons picketing segregated lunch counters. The demonstrators marched from a point of assembly to a location across the street from the courthouse where the arrested picketers were housed. Cox urged the group to continue the sit-in, an appeal deemed inflammatory by local authorities. The assembly was ordered to disperse. Cox was subsequently arrested and convicted for three offenses: disturbing the peace, obstructing public passages, and picketing the courthouse. The first two convictions were set aside in a separate decision (*Cox v. Louisiana*, 379 U.S. 536), which drew heavily from the rationale used in *Edwards v. South Carolina* (372 U.S. 229: 1963). The courthouse picketing conviction was more difficult and was handled by itself. The Supreme Court found the law prohibiting courthouse picketing valid on its face because "there can be no question that a state has a legitimate interest in protecting its judicial system from the pressures which picketing near a courthouse might create." But the Court went on to examine application of this ordinance to Cox's circumstances. Failure to define how "near" a courthouse picketers must be requires "on-the-spot administrative interpretation" by officials charged with enforcing the law. The record in this case showed that officials had not suggested the demonstration take place farther from the courthouse. In effect, said the Court, Cox was "advised" that a demonstration at the place it was held would not be too "near the courthouse" under the terms of the statute. As a result, Cox's conviction required reversal. *See also* ADDERLEY V. FLORIDA (385 U.S. 39: 1966), 43; EDWARDS V. SOUTH CAROLINA (372 U.S. 229: 1963), 61; TIME, PLACE, AND MANNER RESTRICTIONS, 89; UNITED STATES V. GRACE (461 U.S. 171: 1983), 92.

*Significance* The right to peacefully demonstrate is protected by the free speech and free assembly guarantees of the First Amendment. Marches, parades, and other demonstrations, because they go beyond mere utterances, may be subjected to reasonable time, place, and manner restrictions to prevent conflicts with the public interest. As was said in *Cox v. Louisiana* (379 U.S. 536: 1965), no group can conduct a demonstration "in the middle of Times Square at rush hour as a form of freedom of speech or assembly." Such regulations must be both narrowly focused and applied in an even-handed, content-neutral manner. If a regulation is neither tightly worded nor content-neutral, it is invalid "on its face." If a regulation is facially valid, its operational characteristics require review. In *Cox*, the Supreme Court found "substantial governmental interest" in safeguarding court buildings from the possible influence and disruption of picketing, thus the precisely drawn restrictions aimed at that objective passed the first hurdle. Situational factors such as the de facto "permission" Cox received to conduct his demonstration across the street from the courthouse mitigated enforcement of the restrictions.

**Demonstration** **(57)**

Unconventional technique for displaying dissatisfaction with government officials or public policy. Demonstrations include such activities as marches, picketing, and sit-ins designed to highlight the cause for which the demonstrators have come together and to create or reinforce a sense of unity among the demonstrators. Although demonstrations involve unconventional political participation, the importance of protecting such participation was recognized early in the history of the United States. Included within the First Amendment to the Constitution are protections of "freedom of speech" and "the right of the people peaceably to assemble, and to petition the government for a redress of grievances." *See also* ADDERLEY V. FLORIDA (385 U.S. 39: 1966), 43; COX V. LOUISIANA (379 U.S. 536: 1965), 56; EDWARDS V. SOUTH CAROLINA (372 U.S. 229: 1963), 61.

*Significance* Demonstrations enable people who lack traditional modes of political power to call attention to their cause and at times influence the behavior of government officials. Demonstrations have been politically important throughout the history of the United States, beginning in colonial times with public resistance to British policies and continuing through the present with marches and rallies urging the government to do more to combat the AIDS (acquired immune deficiency syndrome) epidemic. Demonstrations were a crucial part of the civil rights movement and of the efforts to end the war in Vietnam. They have become an acceptable if extraordinary way of calling people's attention to the concerns of the demonstrators. Their success is dependent on the extent to which the demands of the demonstrators seem legitimate in the eyes of government officials and of the general public. The civil rights movement sought to end discrimination against blacks, to provide them with equal opportunity and the right to vote —goals that at the time seemed legitimate to most people and government officials outside the South. The Ku Klux Klan seeks a return to white protestant supremacy—a goal that most Americans do not currently support (there existed much greater support for this position during the nineteenth and early twentieth centuries). Demonstrations by civil rights workers were successful; demonstrations by the Klan have not gained much support for their position.

**Direct Action** **(58)**

Efforts to bring about change by confronting established patterns rather than operating within them. The Boston Tea Party is a good example of direct action. Rather than trying to persuade the British government to change its policy in regard to granting a tea monopoly, citizens acted directly by dumping tea into Boston Harbor. Direct action can involve civil disobedience but also includes actions such as strikes that, although not illegal, challenge established practices. *See also* BOSTON TEA PARTY, 46; CIVIL DISOBEDIENCE, 51; STRIKE, 86.

*Significance* Direct action has long been an American way of political participation. Throughout U.S. history, people who did not approve of the way the political system was operating or who were strongly opposed to a particular law have acted out their opposition. The Boston Tea Party helped precipitate the American Revolution; Shays' Rebellion contributed to the end of government under the Articles of Confederation and to the drafting of the current Constitution. Direct action has most commonly been resorted to by people who lack traditional means of gaining political power. It was particularly effective for black organizations that were part of the civil rights movement because through the actions of their supporters they could directly challenge and expose the racism so prevalent at the time.

**Disfranchise** **(59)**

To deprive of or take away from a person or group the privilege of voting. Some people in the United States are disfranchised because they have been convicted of crimes, others because they have recently moved and cannot meet the residency requirements for registering to vote until they have lived at the new location for a period of time. The most serious disfranchisements to occur in the United States were of women and blacks. Women were not assured the right to vote until passage of the Nineteenth Amendment in 1920, although previous to that time some states had made provision for women to vote. Blacks were granted the right to vote with ratification of the Fifteenth Amendment in 1870, but a number of techniques were used, particularly in the South, to either discourage them from voting or deprive them of their right to vote. Not until after passage of the Voting Rights Act of 1965 did disfranchisement of blacks come to an end. *See also* FIFTEENTH AMENDMENT, 63; GRANDFATHER CLAUSE, 65; LITERACY TEST, 71; NINETEENTH AMENDMENT, 74; POLL TAX, 81; REGISTRATION, 199; *SMITH V. ALLWRIGHT* (321 U.S. 649: 1944), 84; VOTING RIGHTS ACTS, 96; WHITE PRIMARY, 98.

*Significance* Many Americans are concerned about disfranchisement because the rate of voter turnout in the United States is considerably lower than that in other democratic countries. Is voter turnout low because of disfranchisement or for other reasons? Certainly the use of the poll tax, the grandfather clause, literacy tests, and white primaries involved intentional efforts to deprive blacks of the opportunity to vote, but these restrictions have all been removed. Residency requirements still temporarily disfranchise large numbers of people each election; registration requirements result in even more people being disfranchised because they fail to register.

**Draft Card Burning** **(60)**

A symbolic way of protesting U.S. involvement in the Vietnam War. Draft card burning became a prominent form of civil disobedience for young males beginning in the late 1960s and continuing until the end of the Vietnam War. The United States has used a conscription system for drafting young men into the military services since the Civil War. At the time of the Vietnam War, a selective service system was already in existence that required males to register for the draft when they reached age eighteen. They were issued draft cards that indicated their draft status and were required by law to carry these cards with them at all times. Men would be drafted to serve in the armed forces from the list of those who had registered for the draft. Burning draft cards, particularly at large public protests against the war, was a way for young men to indicate their resistance to the war and to express opposition to the political system that allowed the war to continue. *See also* CIVIL DISOBEDIENCE, 51; *UNITED STATES V. O'BRIEN* (391 U.S. 367: 1968), 93.

*Significance* Draft card burning was symbolic because it in no way changed a person's status within the selective service system. Burning his draft card did not remove a young man from the draft registration list from which selections for military service were made, and in most cases, the selective service system would not even be aware that the card had been destroyed. Other related resistance techniques that had more direct consequences included refusal to register for the draft and refusal to serve in the armed services once drafted. All three acts were violations of the law, so a number of people were prosecuted and served time in jail. Others, facing prosecution, fled to Canada, Sweden, and other countries. In 1974, after the war had ended, President Gerald Ford offered a conditional amnesty to draft resisters.

**_Edwards v. South Carolina_, 372 U.S. 229 (1963) (61)**
Reversed the breach of peace convictions of a group of persons gathered on the South Carolina statehouse grounds to protest against racial discrimination. In this case, the Supreme Court undertook its own "independent examination of the whole record" and found no evidence of violence either on the part of the demonstrators or the crowd watching them. The Constitution does not permit a state to "make criminal the peaceful expression of unpopular views." Here, South Carolina permitted the conviction of demonstrators for speech that was so generalized as to be "not susceptible to exact definition." Furthermore, the demonstrators were convicted because their expression "brought about a condition of unrest." A conviction, said the Court, "may not stand" on such grounds. Any law that, either "on its face" or as "authoritatively construed," is "so vague and indefinite as to permit punishment" for the "fair use" of the "opportunity for free political discussion" is "repugnant to the guaranty of liberty contained in the Fourteenth Amendment." *See also* *ADDERLEY V. FLORIDA* (385 U.S. 39: 1966), 43; *COX V. LOUISIANA* (379 U.S. 559: 1965), 56; TIME, PLACE, AND MANNER RESTRICTIONS, 89.

*Significance* The demonstration in *Edwards v. South Carolina* (372 U.S. 229: 1963) was permitted because there was no violence and because the state capitol grounds, as a seat of government, was viewed as a location dedicated to assembly and discussion of public matters. This demonstration was seen by the Supreme Court as an exercise of fundamental constitutional rights in its most "pristine and classic form." The Court took a further step in *Edwards* that affects situations in which breach of peace ordinances are used to quell anticipated violence or disruption. The Court's "independent examination" of the record led it to conclude that there had not been sufficiently imminent danger of disruption to justify the attempt to disperse the demonstrators in the first place.

**Equal Rights Amendment (ERA) (62)**

An amendment to the Constitution proposed by Congress in March 1972 but not yet ratified by the states. The Equal Rights Amendment (ERA) states that "equality of rights under the law shall not be denied or abridged by the United States or any state on account of sex." It was the centerpiece of efforts by various women's groups, most prominently the National Organization for Women (NOW), to make women's rights equal to those of men. After the seven-year time period for ratification passed, Congress in March 1979 extended the deadline to June 1982, but the amendment never received approval by the 38 state legislatures required for ratification. *See also* WOMEN'S MOVEMENT, 99.

*Significance* Debate over the Equal Rights Amendment (ERA) was intense, particularly as the number of state legislatures approving it moved close to the required number of 38. There is no question that men and women are treated differently by the law in the United States, particularly in the employment arena. Some of the differences involve intentional exclusion of opportunity for women, although these have decreased as women have gained political power through exercising their right to vote. Other differences occur as a consequence of what is seen as protections for women. In the debate over passage, conservatives and women's organizations that favored a traditional role for women opposed the amendment, arguing that although the law treats men and women differently, it does not discriminate in a negative way toward women. Liberals and women's movement organizations that supported the amendment argued that there should be equality of opportunity for all people regardless of their sex.

**Fifteenth Amendment** **(63)**

An amendment to the Constitution designed to prohibit either the state governments or the federal government from denying blacks the right to vote. The Fifteenth Amendment states, "The right of citizens of the United States to vote shall not be denied or abridged by the United States or by any state on account of race, color, or previous condition of servitude." It was adopted in 1870 and was part of the effort, along with the Thirteenth and Fourteenth amendments, to eliminate slavery and to allow ex-slaves and other black people to participate as full citizens within society. *See also* LITERACY TEST, 71; POLL TAX, 81; *SOUTH CAROLINA V. KATZENBACH* (383 U.S. 301: 1966), 85; VOTING RIGHTS ACTS, 96.

*Significance* For a brief period after passage of the Fifteenth Amendment, blacks did exercise their right to vote. This had the greatest impact in the South, where at that time the majority of blacks lived. A number of black officials were elected to Congress, to state and local office, and to the state constitutional conventions, which were drafting new constitutions for states that had seceded from the Union. This era of black political participation drew to a close in 1876 with the disputed election of Rutherford B. Hayes as president. Hayes, in order to gain support from the South, agreed to withdraw federal troops and allow white southerners to regain political control. Southern whites, making use of violence and of questionable legal devices such as the poll tax and literacy test, gradually succeeded in preventing most blacks from voting in most southern states. As blacks moved north, intimidation by whites, although less overt and violent, still tended to discourage them from voting. It was not until the 1960s, many years later, that the civil rights movement was successful in breaking down some of the barriers to black voting. Prohibitions have now been removed, and black voter participation is approaching levels similar to that of others in society.

**Gay Rights Movement** **(64)**

A movement to eliminate discrimination against homosexuals. The gay rights movement developed in the 1960s has sought to create a legitimate place in society for homosexuals. Although approximately 10 percent of the U.S. population is gay, many state laws still declare homosexual behavior to be illegal and subject to arrest and prosecution. Even in states where it is not illegal, homosexuals are harassed and discriminated against in regard to housing, insurance, employment, child custody, health care, and other areas of life. The gay rights movement seeks to change these conditions. It encourages homosexuals to come out of hiding and proclaim their sexual preference as a way of strengthening political efforts to eliminate discrimination. The National Gay and Lesbian Task Force has been active in the political arena, seeking at the state and national levels laws to protect the rights of homosexuals. Its political action committee, the Human Rights Campaign Fund, supports political candidates who are opposed to discrimination based on sexual preference. *See also* MOVEMENT, 73.

*Significance* The gay rights movement, since 1960, has been successful in eliminating antigay laws in almost half the states. It has also contributed to reduction in discrimination against homosexuals. In some areas of the country, particularly in San Francisco and a few other large cities, homosexuals have developed substantial political power because of their numbers. In the early 1980s, two members of Congress who revealed that they were gay were able to win reelection, something that probably could not have occurred before the 1960s.

**Grandfather Clause** **(65)**

A technique used by southern states after the Civil War to prevent blacks from voting. The grandfather clause was used in conjunction with the literacy test or the poll tax. Some states required that people pass a literacy test in order to vote; others required that they pay a poll tax. People who could demonstrate that their grandfathers had voted were not required to pass the literacy test or pay the poll tax. The grandfather clause enabled whites to avoid the literacy test or poll tax requirement, whereas blacks, whose grandfathers had been slaves, could not do so and were thus ineligible to vote unless they could pass the literacy test or pay the poll tax. Many whites would have had difficulty proving that their grandfathers had voted, but the provision was strictly applied only to blacks. Grandfather clauses were ruled unconstitutional by the Supreme Court in 1915 (*Guinn v. United States* 238 U.S. 347: 1915). *See also* DISFRANCHISE, 59; LITERACY TEST, 71; POLL TAX, 81.

*Significance* The grandfather clause was one of the weapons used by southern whites to discourage any political participation on the part of blacks. It provided a supposedly nonracial criterion for determining who could vote that was in reality blatantly racist. By the time the clause was ruled unconstitutional in 1915, the pattern had been firmly established in many parts of the South that blacks could not vote, and ruling it unconstitutional did nothing to change that pattern. Most southern blacks were effectively disfranchised until the civil rights movement was successful in getting some blacks registered during the 1960s. Only after the Voting Rights Act of 1965 had been implemented for several years did overall black turnout begin to match that of white turnout.

**_Harper v. Virginia State Board of Elections_, 383 U.S. 663 (1966)** **(66)**

Declared unconstitutional the use of a poll tax as a voting qualification for state elections. The Supreme Court said in *Harper v. Virginia State Board of Elections* that once the franchise is given, lines may not be drawn that are "inconsistent" with the equal protection clause. The right of suffrage is subject to state standards that are not discriminatory. A state violates that mandate when it "makes the affluence of the voter or the payment of any fee an electoral standard." Voter qualifications have "no relation to wealth nor to paying or not paying this or any other tax." The basic principle that does not permit a state to "dilute a citizen's vote on account of his economic status or other such factors by analogy bars a system which excludes those unable to pay a fee to vote or who fail to pay." To introduce wealth or payment of a fee as a "measure of a voter's qualifications" is to introduce a "capricious or irrelevant factor." *See also* OREGON V. MITCHELL (400 U.S. 112: 1970), 73; POLL TAX, 81.

*Significance* *Harper v. Virginia State Board of Elections* (383 U.S. 663: 1966) was the final nail in the coffin of the poll tax. The poll or head tax was a tax levied against people. It was easily administered and a common method of generating revenue at the state level in the early history of the United States. Other methods of taxation had generally replaced the poll tax by the time of the Civil War, but it was revived in a number of states at the turn of the century to restrict access of blacks to elections. The tax was challenged in *Breedlove v. Suttles* (302 U.S. 277: 1937), but the Supreme Court said the tax was not unconstitutional per se. Numerous legislative attempts to ban the poll tax were unsuccessful in Congress until 1962 when language for the Twenty-fourth Amendment was approved. The amendment, ratified two years later, provided that the right to vote in any primary or general election for federal offices could not be denied "by reason of failure to pay any poll tax or other tax." The amendment did not absolutely foreclose use of poll taxes. Although no such tax or any "milder alternative" could be used in federal elections, several states sought to retain the poll tax as a condition of participation in state and local elections. Using the equal protection clause as the basis of its ruling, the Court held this practice unconstitutional in *Harper*.

**Hatch Act** **(67)**

Law passed in 1939 designed to protect federal civil service workers from being coerced into partisan political activity by their politically appointed superiors. The Hatch Act required civil service employees to abstain from partisan political activity such as contributing to or working in election campaigns and to limit their partisan activity to voting. The intent was to prevent political executives from manipulating their subordinates into assisting the candidates of the party currently in power. The act also includes provisions to prevent federal employees from being fired for political reasons, such as refusing to provide assistance or support for candidates or parties. A second Hatch Act of 1940, which was repealed in 1974, imposed similar limitations on state employees working on projects supported with federal funds. *See also* POLITICAL PARTICIPATION, 79.

*Significance* The Hatch Act has dramatically limited political participation on the part of federal employees since its passage in 1939. Before the Hatch Act, it was commonly expected that federal employees, even though working within the civil service system, could be persuaded by the current administration to support candidates of its party either by working in or contributing to their campaigns. In some cases, employees were eager to provide their support; in other cases, they did so because of coercion from higher up. The Hatch Act solution was to simply prohibit partisan political participation. In the 1970s, pressure developed to modify or repeal the Hatch Act on the grounds that it interfered with federal employees exercising their rights of political participation.

***Hudgens v. National Labor Relations Board (NLRB),*** **(68)**
**424 U.S. 507 (1976)**

Held that the First Amendment did not permit striking workers to picket their employer, whose store was located in a privately owned shopping center. The Supreme Court began its opinion by indicating that the constitutional guarantee of free speech only protects persons from abridgment by government. Although statutory or common law may extend some protection, no protection or redress is provided by the Constitution itself. Given that the shopping center was clearly private, the question became the circumstances, if any, under which private property can be treated as public. The Court reviewed the reasoning from previous cases that found that because large shopping centers were "open to the public," they serve the same function as the "business district" of a municipality and are thus "dedicated" to certain kinds of public use. In this case, the Court simply did not agree that a shopping center is the "functional equivalent of a municipality" and therefore the free expression guarantee "has no part to play in a case such as this." *See also* PICKETING, 77; *PRUNEYARD SHOPPING CENTER V. ROBINS* (447 U.S. 74: 1980), 82.

*Significance* Certain areas may be off-limits for picketing or conducting a demonstration. Access to private property has presented some particularly difficult questions about expression rights. Shopping malls have always been an inviting location for demonstrations because they attract large audiences. Most shopping malls are not publicly owned and thus cannot qualify for "public forum" status in quite the same way as, for example, public streets. Indeed, the question of access to private property, including malls and shopping centers, has been troublesome, and the Warren and Burger Courts responded quite differently. Representative of the Warren Court view is *Amalgamated Food Employees Union v. Logan Valley Plaza* (391 U.S. 308: 1969). In *Logan Valley*, the Supreme Court permitted a union to picket a business located in a shopping center. Given no effective alternative means of communication, the Court ruled the picketing was protected activity. The Burger Court position was less supportive, and it modified *Logan Valley* in *Lloyd Corporation v. Tanner* (407 U.S. 551: 1972), a decision that permitted a restriction on handbilling. In this case, the Court saw adequate alternative communicative means available but also recognized the private character of the shopping center. Although a center invites patrons, there exists no "open-ended invitation for the public to use the center for any and all purposes." Complete abandonment of the *Logan Valley* position came in *Hudgens*—the Court said that the First Amendment simply has no part to play in cases such as these.

**Knownothingism** **(69)**

A movement during the middle of the nineteenth century that vigorously opposed immigration and was strongly anti-Catholic. Knownothingism embodied fear of things foreign, and a desire to return to the safety of an imagined past. The term "knownothingism" developed because opposition to foreigners and Catholics led to the formation of a number of secret, nativistic societies intended to promote "American views," whose members when questioned about their activities would respond, "I know nothing." Knownothings supported "native" American candidates for political office and advocated a 25-

year residence requirement for citizenship. They formed the American Political party, which had brief political influence in the mid-1850s. Knownothingism has come to mean uninformed, largely emotional political activity by people seeking to return to their version of the past. *See also* MOVEMENT, 73.

*Significance* Knownothingism was a reaction to the rapid increase in immigration that occurred in the 1840s. People who viewed themselves as "native" Americans, people whose parents or grandparents had emigrated from Europe, saw their way of life threatened by recent immigrants and responded with bigotry and attempted repression. Knownothingism was a precursor to the Ku Klux Klan, which responded in a similar fashion to immigrants and Catholics, although it reserved its greatest vituperation for blacks. A more recent version of knownothingism is the McCarthyism of the late 1940s and early 1950s which saw Communists everywhere and sought to preserve the American way of life by destroying them.

***Kovacs v. Cooper*, 336 U.S. 77 (1949)** **(70)**

Upheld a city ordinance that prohibited use on the streets of sound amplifiers or other instruments that emit "loud and raucous noises." The Supreme Court mentioned the "broad protection" given the dissemination of ideas and cited the invalidation of a prohibition on door-to-door distribution of handbills and pamphlets. Nonetheless, there were limits. The Court "never intimated" that the visitor could "insert a foot in the door and insist on a hearing." The Court did not think it unreasonable for an ordinance to ban "obtaining an audience for the broadcaster's ideas by way of sound trucks with loud and raucous noises on city streets." The "unwilling listener" is not like the person walking down the street who may refuse to take the pamphlet. In his home, he or she is "practically helpless to escape this interference with his [or her] privacy by loudspeakers except through the protection of the municipality." The right of free speech should allow anyone the opportunity to reach willing listeners, but it is an "extravagant extension of due process" to say that a city cannot restrict use of loudspeakers. Opportunity to "gain the public's ears by objectionable, amplified sound . . . is not more assured than is the unlimited opportunity to address gatherings on the streets." To enforce the free speech protection "in disregard of the rights of others would be harsh and arbitrary in itself." *See also* TIME, PLACE, AND MANNER RESTRICTIONS, 89.

*Significance* *Kovacs v. Cooper* (336 U.S. 77: 1949) was not the Supreme Court's first consideration of the sound amplification issue. A year earlier, in *Saia v. New York* (334 U.S. 558: 1948), the Court invalidated an ordinance that required prior permission of the police chief to use amplification equipment on the streets. Unlike the ordinance in *Kovacs,* the regulation in *Saia* gave a public official complete discretion over the right to be heard. The ordinance in *Kovacs* also required the Court to fully explore the difficult and compounding issue of residential privacy. The Court distinguished the character of the intrusion caused by the communication. Door-to-door solicitations, for example, may be a nuisance, but homeowners can protect themselves by refusing to receive the message. For the homeowner, a sign that he or she is unwilling to be disturbed may prevent an intrusion. No such effective defense, however, exists for the person whose privacy is breached by loudspeakers. Thus, in such cases, government may be permitted to protect people in the privacy of their homes from unwanted speech.

**Literacy Test** **(71)**

A technique used to disfranchise black voters in the South. Literacy tests were designed, on the surface, to determine whether a person was sufficiently literate to be entitled to vote. In reality, however, as applied throughout the South after the Civil War, blacks never passed them even though illiterate whites were able to do so. There were cases of black college graduates flunking the tests. Charles Evers, the first black mayor of Fayette, Mississippi, was asked during a 1946 literacy test, "How many bubbles in a bar of soap?" Literacy tests were suspended by the Voting Rights Act of 1965 and finally prohibited by the Voting Rights Act of 1970. *See also* DISFRANCHISE, 59; *OREGON V. MITCHELL* (400 U.S. 112: 1970), 75; VOTING RIGHTS ACTS, 96.

*Significance* Literacy tests, along with other techniques designed to prevent blacks from voting, contributed to the development of low voter turnouts for blacks. Their use provides yet another example of groups in power systematically discouraging political participation on the part of people they see as a threat. Even blacks who moved north, where they had more opportunity to vote, were much less likely to do so than whites because of their experiences with literacy tests, poll taxes, grandfather clauses, and sheer intimidation during the years they lived in the South. For many years, black voter turnout and political participation in the North were quite low, while that of blacks who stayed in the South remained virtually nonexistent. These patterns did not begin to change until the civil rights movement of the 1960s and the passage by Congress of various civil rights and voting rights acts.

**March** **(72)**

An unconventional variety of political participation designed to call attention to a group's political demands. One of the more famous marches—the march on Washington—occurred as part of the civil rights movement. On August 18, 1963, over 250,000 people, about 25 percent of them white, demonstrated in Washington, D.C., in support of black civil rights. It was there that Martin Luther King, Jr., aroused the audience with his memorable "I have a dream speech" and pictured for them what the United States could be.

> I have a dream that one day this nation will rise up and live out the true meaning of its creed: "We hold these truths to be self-evident, that all men are created equal."
>
> I have a dream that one day on the red hills of Georgia the sons of former slaves and the sons of former slaveowners will be able to sit down together at the table of brotherhood. . . .
>
> When we let freedom ring, when we let it ring from every village and hamlet, from every state and every city, we will be able to join hands and sing in the words of that old Negro spiritual: "Free at last! Thank God Almighty, we are free at last."

The march on Washington was based on a proposal made years earlier by A. Philip Randolph to pressure President Roosevelt and Congress into making defense industry jobs available to blacks. At a meeting with Roosevelt in 1941, Randolph suggested that if the president did not do something to reduce discriminatory hiring practices in defense industries, 100,000 blacks would march down Pennsylvania Avenue that summer. The president was extremely reluctant to involve the federal government in racial issues at that point in time, but he was even more reluctant to have 100,000 blacks marching through the streets of the capital. Within seven days of the meeting with Randolph, President Roosevelt issued Executive Order No. 8022, which created a wartime Fair Employment Committee to deal with the problems Randolph had articulated. Randolph thereupon called off the march. *See also* CIVIL RIGHTS ACTS, 52; DEMONSTRATION, 57; *EDWARDS V. SOUTH CAROLINA* (372 U.S. 229: 1963), 61; VOTING RIGHTS ACTS, 96.

*Significance* Marches provide a way for people who lack traditional political resources to call attention to their concerns. They are particularly effective when there are large numbers of people who can be brought together to participate. A march of 250,000 or 100,000 protesters will potentially have much more impact than one of just 1,000. Randolph's idea for a march was enough to pressure President Roosevelt into meeting his demands even before the march took place. And even though the march did not occur, the idea remained for Martin Luther King, Jr., and others in the civil rights movement to use in 1963. The 1963 march increased pressure for the development of federal policy to deal with racism and contributed to the passage of the Civil Rights Act of 1964 and the Voting Rights Act of 1965.

**Movement** **(73)**

A loose coalition of individuals and organizations seeking similar types of political change. Movements develop because large numbers of people share a particular set of interests and decide to act together on behalf of those interests. A movement is much less structured than an organization. Although there may be communication and coordination among the component parts, there is no overall spokesperson and no individual or organization that can determine the direction of the movement. For example, the women's movement has included many different individuals and organizations over the years, each seeking to improve the condition of women in society. Collectively, they are all moving in the same direction, although at times people or organizations may disagree over specific goals or tactics and may pursue independent, possibly even conflicting, avenues of political action. *See also* CIVIL RIGHTS MOVEMENT, 53; GAY RIGHTS MOVEMENT, 64; WOMEN'S MOVEMENT, 99.

*Significance* A movement brings together people who may in many other respects be quite different but who share a particular set of interests and who become politically active to achieve common goals. The women's movement has involved people both rich and poor, white and black, who shared a similar concern over the status of women in society. Similar diversity existed within the civil rights movement. The larger the participation in the movement, the more likely it will gain its objectives. Most movements are of relatively short duration—they come into existence because of particular circumstances and then fade away after achieving their objectives or because it becomes clear that their objectives are unobtainable or no longer relevant. The reform movement of the late nineteenth and early twentieth centuries challenged the power of the political machine; the civil rights movement of the 1960s confronted the racism and discrimination of U.S. society; the antiwar movement of the late 1960s and early 1970s sought an end to the Vietnam War. Each of these in company with many other movements throughout U.S. history brought important changes in public policy and involved many new people in political action. In most cases, even after the movement ended, the people stayed on, remaining active participants in the political process.

**Nineteenth Amendment** **(74)**
Amendment to the Constitution that was adopted in 1920 and prohibited either the federal or the state governments from denying women the right to vote. The Nineteenth Amendment states, "The right of citizens of the United States to vote shall not be denied or abridged by the United States or by any State on account of sex." Women first obtained the right to vote in Wyoming in 1871 while it was still a territory. At the time the Nineteenth Amendment was adopted, 26 states had already granted women the right to vote. *See also* WOMEN'S MOVEMENT, 99.

*Significance* Passage of the Nineteenth Amendment practically doubled the number of people eligible to vote. It was the single largest increase in the electorate in the history of the country. Leaders of the women's movement, who were instrumental in gaining passage of the Nineteenth Amendment, saw it as the precursor of other rights for women, such as the right to serve on juries and to control their own property after marriage. During the early years after passage, women remained less likely to vote and less likely to participate in other political activities than men. The simple act of making it legal for women to vote could not change the political orientation of most women at that time, who had been socialized to believe that voting and politics were part of a man's world. Gradually, as patterns of political socialization changed, women became as likely to vote as men. Today it is estimated that there are about 10 million more women than men potentially eligible to vote.

***Oregon v. Mitchell,* 400 U.S. 112 (1970)** **(75)**
Upheld congressional power to lower the voting age to 18 for federal elections. *Oregon v. Mitchell* was the case through which the Supreme Court reviewed the Voting Rights Act as it was extended in 1970. The 1970 version of the act retained federal supervisory mechanisms aimed at combating racially discriminatory voting practices used in the original 1965 enactment. The 1970 extension, however, contained three new elements. It prohibited literacy tests and severely limited state residency requirements on presidential elections. The act also lowered the minimum age for participating in both federal and state elections to 18. The Supreme Court divided differently on each of the component elements but upheld bans on literacy and residency requirements by 9-0 and 8-1 votes, respectively. The

question of whether or not to give 18-year-olds the right to vote was more complex. The Court held that Congress had the power to lower the voting age through statute but only for federal elections. The provision lowering the voting age for state elections was invalidated. The Court noted that Congress could alter congressional district boundaries, and by similar reasoning, held that Congress has the power to oversee presidential elections. Under the ruling in *Oregon v. Mitchell,* Congress does not have the authority to statutorily lower the voting age for state and local elections. On this matter, the Court held that the Constitution intended to "preserve to the States the power that even the Colonies had to establish and maintain their own separate and independent governments" unless specifically provided otherwise. The Court indicated that "no function is more essential to that end than the power to determine the qualifications of their own voters for state, county and municipal offices and the nature of their own machinery for filling local public offices." *See also* *SOUTH CAROLINA V. KATZENBACH* (383 U.S. 301: 1966), 85; VOTING RIGHTS ACTS, 96.

*Significance* *Oregon v. Mitchell* (400 U.S. 112: 1970) said several things about congressional power to regulate the electoral process. First, it reinforced the Supreme Court's ruling in *South Carolina v. Katzenbach* (383 U.S. 301: 1966) that the Fourteenth and Fifteenth amendments could be used extensively to eliminate discriminatory voting practices. Second, *Mitchell* said that Congress has unconditional power to regulate federal elections based on powers conferred from Article I. Third, the decision vigorously protected state policy preferences in the area of state and local electoral processes except in those instances in which the Constitution expressly authorizes federal intervention. In other words, *Oregon v. Mitchell* struck a balance between federal legislative power and state sovereignty. The practical effect of the decision was to create the prospect of the 1972 election being conducted with separate registration and balloting procedures, at least for 18- to 20-year-olds. The possibility of such an administrative nightmare prompted the Twenty-sixth Amendment, which lowered the voting for all elections.

**Petition** **(76)**

A request that government take some action. To petition government is to seek a particular action from it. In this general sense, a petition is the same as a demand. More specific forms of petitions have developed in the 1970s. Petitions, for example, are used as a means for placing a candidate's name on an election ballot. They can also be used by people seeking to pressure political officials into particular actions. These people gather the signatures of large numbers of citizens on a written petition requesting the action and submit the document to government officials as a way of demonstrating support for their position. Numerous states have constitutional provisions allowing the initiative, the referendum, and/or the recall, each of which involves an election that is triggered by the submission of a petition containing a legally determined number of signatures. *See also* INITIATIVE, 123; RECALL, 142; REFERENDUM, 144.

*Significance* The right to petition government is protected by the First Amendment of the Constitution, which provides "the right of the people . . . to petition the Government for a redress of grievances." Petitioning government in this general sense is done all the time by various individuals and organizations and is a vital part of a democratic political system. Signing a petition is a more specific act of political participation, one that most people in the United States see as a legitimate way of influencing government and one that a majority of people have used.

**Picketing** **(77)**

Walking or standing in front of an establishment as a way of protesting its activities. The most common form of picketing involves labor union members who are on strike at their work locations or at the headquarters of the organization for which they work. Picketing has also been used by nonstrikers as a way of demonstrating. Teachers have used what they call "informational picketing" to make the case that they are underpaid or that they need more resources to do their job effectively. Civil rights groups have used picketing to protest what they see as unfair hiring practices of an organization. *See also* *CHICAGO POLICE DEPARTMENT V. MOSLEY* (408 U.S. 92: 1972), 50; DEMONSTRATION, 57.

*Significance* The Supreme Court has ruled that peaceful picketing is protected by the First Amendment right to freedom of speech (*Thornhill v. Alabama,* 310 U.S. 88: 1940). It has been most consistently and successfully used by labor unions in their battles with management for higher wages and better working conditions. Picketing serves three functions: It calls attention to the activities of the picketers; it provides an opportunity for them to make their case; and it stops people who support them from crossing the picket line and patronizing the organization being picketed.

**Political Mobilization** **(78)**
Stimulating people with shared interests to get involved in the political system in such a way as to further those interests. Political mobilization can be done by individuals or organizations. Political parties seek to mobilize people to vote for their candidates; interest groups try to mobilize people to become members or to lobby on behalf of the interest group's positions; and political candidates endeavor to mobilize people to work in their campaigns or to vote for them. Political mobilization in a very real sense involves encouraging people to participate politically. *See also*: INTEREST GROUP, 293; POLITICAL PARTICIPATION, 79; POLITICAL PARTY, 235.

*Significance* Political mobilization as a term is relatively recent, although political parties and to some extent interest groups have been involved in encouraging limited political participation since the beginning of the country. Indeed, Samuel Adams, Thomas Paine. and many others who were spokespeople for the American Revolution can be thought of as political mobilizers. The women's movement, the civil rights movement, the anti–Vietnam War movement, and other organizational efforts of the 1960s and 1970s have depended heavily on getting people who were previously inactive involved, frequently in unconventional ways, in the political system. These mobilization efforts have been countered by some of the more traditional interest groups mobilizing more people to support their positions. Today politics has a substantial mobilization component—political parties and interest groups are now expected to organize large numbers of people in an effort to influence the operation of the political system.

**Political Participation** **(79)**
Actions intended to influence the operation of the political system. Political participation can take a variety of forms including voting, discussing politics, working in a political campaign, joining an interest group, demonstrating, or participating in a riot. Some kinds of political participation are expected from citizens, and the process of political socialization encourages these actions. In a democracy such as the United States, citizens are encouraged to participate in the process of selecting government officials through voting and to make known their policy preferences to those who govern. At the time the United States Constitution was adopted, most traditional types of political participation were limited to white males. Gradually the political system has been opened, and today virtually everyone is encouraged to participate, at least at the level of voting. *See also* DEMOCRACY, 9; STRUCTURAL BARRIERS TO PARTICIPATION, 87; VOTER TURNOUT, 208; VOTING, 95.

*Significance* Political participation is necessary for the functioning of a democratic government. Citizens must exercise influence over government officials through the electoral process and have the opportunity to communicate their demands to political officials. Not everyone participates in the same way or to the same extent, however. Education and socioeconomic status are very influential in determining participation. The higher the level of education, income, and social status of an individual, the more likely that person is to vote, join organizations seeking to influence the political system, and act in other ways that would be considered political participation. Poor people, people with limited education, and people with low socioeconomic status are less likely to be politically active in traditional ways because they usually believe that there is little they can do to influence the political system. At times they have been mobilized to participate in less conventional types of activities such as demonstrations, strikes, and so on.

## Political Violence (80)

Illegal activity that is politically motivated and is intended to influence the political system. Political violence is one of the more extreme types of unconventional political participation. It includes violence directed toward property (such as the Boston Tea Party, the Civil War draft riots, and the urban riots of the 1960s) as well as violence toward individuals (such as the lynching of blacks in the South after the Civil War and the assassination of presidents and other important political officials). *See also* BOSTON TEA PARTY, 46; URBAN RIOTS, 94.

*Significance* Political violence has been much more common and effective in the United States than most people are aware. During the 1960s, as the battle to remove racism was taking place, H. Rap Brown suggested that violence is "as American as cherry pie." This country would not have been created without political violence: Violence was used in the colonists' fight against England. Violence was used in the South to prevent slaves from escaping, and violence—the Civil War—ultimately determined the fate of slavery. Violence was used to intimidate blacks in the period after the Civil War, and violence was used by management to discourage union organization throughout most of U.S. history.

## Poll Tax (81)

A fee that must be paid in order to register to vote. The poll tax was used in a number of southern states after the Civil War to discourage blacks from voting. Although the fee itself was nominal, it seemed substantial to poor blacks and poor whites, making voting a luxury many felt they could not afford. The fee often had to be paid months in advance of the time to register, which made the whole process more difficult. In some cases, the poll tax was combined with a grandfather clause that exempted people whose grandfathers had voted from paying the fee. This loophole allowed whites, whose grandfathers could have voted, to avoid paying the tax while requiring blacks, whose grandfathers were slaves, to pay it. *See also* GRANDFATHER CLAUSE, 65; *HARPER V. VIRGINIA STATE BOARD OF ELECTIONS* (383 U.S. 663: 1966), 66; *WALKER V. BIRMINGHAM* (388 U.S. 307: 1967), 97.

*Significance* The poll tax was one of a number of devices used to discourage or prevent blacks from voting. It was part of a systematic effort that took place in the South after the Civil War to remove all political power from black people and to reestablish firm white control in all state and local governments. It was prohibited in elections for federal officials by the Twenty-fourth Amendment, adopted in 1964. Shortly thereafter the Supreme Court declared it unconstitutional for any elections (*Harper v. Virginia State Board of Elections,* 383 U.S. 663: 1966).

**_PruneYard Shopping Center v. Robins,_ 447 U.S. 74 (1980)** **(82)**

Decision that held that demonstrators may access privately owned shopping malls to circulate petitions and distribute political pamphlets. *PruneYard Shopping Center v. Robins* involved a group of high school students who sought to express their opposition to a United Nations resolution against Zionism. They set up a table near the central courtyard of the shopping center, began distributing pamphlets, and asked patrons of the shopping center to sign a petition. The students were orderly and no objection to their presence was registered by any shopping center customer. The students were informed by a shopping center security guard that their activity was in violation of a center policy that prohibited such conduct. The group subsequently filed suit seeking access to the center through court order. The crucial issue for the Supreme Court was whether state protected rights of expression infringed upon the property rights of PruneYard's owners. "A handful of additional orderly persons soliciting signatures and distributing handbills do not interfere with normal business operations." They would not "markedly dilute" PruneYard's property rights. In addition, the Court ruled the shopping center to be open to the public rather than limited to the owners' private use.

Even if the owners disagreed with the demonstrators' message, they could easily disclaim any connection with it. *See also* ADDERLEY V. FLORIDA (385 U.S. 39: 1966), 43; *HUDGENS V. NATIONAL LABOR RELATIONS BOARD (NLRB)* (424 U.S. 507: 1976), 68; TIME, PLACE, AND MANNER RESTRICTIONS, 89.

*Significance* *PruneYard Shopping Center v. Robins* (447 U.S. 74: 1980) addressed the troublesome issue of demonstrator access to private property. The Burger Court position in *PruneYard* represents a compromise between several of its own previous decisions and those of the Warren Court. The Warren Court view is best illustrated in *Amalgamated Food Employees Union v. Logan Valley Plaza* (391 U.S. 308: 1968), in which the Supreme Court upheld the picketing of a business located in a privately owned shopping center because it was a First Amendment protected activity. The Burger Court reconsidered *Logan Valley* in *Lloyd Corporation v. Tanner* (407 U.S. 551: 1972) and upheld a restriction on handbilling. Although a shopping center invites patrons, the Burger Court said, it is not an invitation of unlimited scope. The invitation is to do business with the tenants of the center. There is "no open-ended invitation to the public to use the center for any and all purposes, however incompatible with the interests of both the stores and the shoppers whom they serve." The Burger Court abandoned *Logan Valley* altogether in *Hudgens v. National Labor Relations Board* (424 U.S. 507: 1976). In *Hudgens,* union members attempted to picket the retail store of their employer, which was located in a privately owned mall. Citing *Lloyd,* the Court held that the First Amendment had no part to play in such a case. Thus the Burger Court divorced privately owned shopping centers from First Amendment reach. Through the *PruneYard* decision, however, it did allow protection of expression to flow from state constitutional provisions.

**Sit-in** **(83)**

A form of civil disobedience developed during the 1960s to combat the southern practice of white-only public eating establishments. The first sit-in occurred on February 1, 1960, in Greensboro, North Carolina, when four black college students sat at the lunch counter of an F. W. Woolworth store in violation of the long-standing southern tradition of segregated public eating facilities. When they were refused service, they pulled out books and continued sitting at the counter until the store closed. This action marked the beginning of what was to become an effective tactic of protesting segregation. The students chose Woolworth's because it was a chain store operating in the North as well as the South, and they thought pressures could be generated in the North to change the southern practice of segregation. By the time Woolworth's capitulated, sit-ins had spread throughout the South and were being organized by a number of civil rights organizations, particularly those in which college students were involved. *See also* CIVIL DISOBEDIENCE, 51; CIVIL RIGHTS ACTS, 52; DEMONSTRATION, 57.

*Significance* The sit-in provided the civil rights movement with a remarkably effective technique for highlighting the discrimination and segregation that blacks faced in the South. Because blacks had been denied traditional avenues of political participation in the South, they had no way to directly challenge existing patterns of discrimination. Sit-ins attracted attention, publicity, and media coverage; they also led to arrests of the demonstrators and to political violence against them—which in turn attracted even more media attention. Because of the news coverage given to sit-ins and other demonstrations, people throughout the country became aware of what was happening in the South and did not like what they were seeing. Outside the South, support developed for doing something to end southern segregation. This support ultimately helped to make possible passage of the stronger civil rights legislation that made discrimination illegal.

### *Smith v. Allwright*, 321 U.S. 649 (1944) (84)

Declared that racially exclusive white primaries were unconstitutional as a violation of the Fifteenth Amendment. For years prior to this decision, blacks were excluded from selecting nominees for public office in a number of states because political parties, regarded as legally private entities, could establish their own membership qualifications. The *Smith* case brought this practice to an end. First, the Supreme Court linked the primary to the overall selection process. When primaries "become part of the machinery of choosing officials," they become subject to the same regulations relative to discrimination as general elections. The Court then moved to the privacy issue. The right to vote cannot be "nullified" by a state's creation of an "election process which permits a private organization to practice racial discrimination." The privilege of party membership itself, said the Court, may be of "no concern" to the state, but when that privilege is an "essential qualification for voting, the state makes the action of the party the action of the state." *See also* PRIMARY ELECTION, 140; *UNITED STATES V. CLASSIC* (313 U.S. 299: 1941), 255; WHITE PRIMARY, 98.

*Significance* *Smith v. Allwright* (321 U.S. 649: 1944) eliminated the white primary, which had been effective in discouraging black political participation. Nomination by the Democratic party was a virtual guarantee of election to office in the then "solid South." The racially exclusive party membership qualifications thus prevented blacks from playing any part in the only stage of the process that had an impact. So long as primaries were viewed as separate from general elections and political parties were seen as wholly private entities, the provisions of the Fourteenth and Fifteenth amendments could not be brought to bear on this practice. The Supreme Court's decision in *United States v. Classic* (313 U.S. 299: 1941) made primaries subject to federal regulation when they played an "integral" role in the election process. *Smith* followed three years later with the categorical repudiation of the view that party primaries were private in character. Although other techniques of voting discrimination remained, the *Smith* decision essentially ended the use of the white primary as a means of such discrimination.

***South Carolina v. Katzenbach*, 383 U.S. 301 (1966) (85)**
Considered the scope of Fifteenth Amendment protection of the right to vote and the character of the power granted to Congress to enact appropriate legislation to further that objective. The Voting Rights Act of 1965 abolished devices such as the literacy test and accumulated poll taxes, which had been used to disqualify citizens from voting. The act also provided for extensive federal supervision of elections and required that any new conditions of voter eligibility be reviewed by the U.S. attorney general before implementation. Provisions of the act were triggered if less than 50 percent of citizens of voting age were registered to vote or where fewer than 50 percent of the voting age population had participated in the 1964 presidential election. The Supreme Court began its opinion by noting that the purpose of the act was "to banish the blight of racial discrimination in voting, which has infected the electoral process in parts of our country for nearly a century." Following nearly 100 years of systematic resistance to the Fifteenth Amendment, Congress might well decide to shift the advantage of time and inertia from the perpetrators of the evil to its victims. The targeted nature of the act's coverage was a reasonable legislative option. Congress determined that voting discrimination "presently occurs in certain sections of the country. In acceptable legislative fashion, Congress chose to limit its attention to the geographic areas where immediate action seemed necessary." In sum, the Court viewed the act as an array of potent weapons marshalled to combat the evil of voting discrimination. They were weapons that constitute "a valid means for carrying out the commands of the Fifteenth Amendment." *See also* APPORTIONMENT, 102; VOTING RIGHTS ACTS, 96.

*Significance* The historic Voting Rights Act of 1965 was upheld by the Supreme Court in *South Carolina v. Katzenbach* (383 U.S. 301: 1966). After several previous and largely unsuccessful efforts, Congress took more drastic action to address interference with the right to vote. The legislation was both aggressive and "inventive." The Court's ruling in *Katzenbach* established clear and broad federal power stemming from the Fifteenth Amendment over both federal and state voting practices. The act had a five-year limitation but was extended in 1970, 1975, and 1982. The 1970 extension banned the use of literacy tests. The same extension also set the minimum voting age at 18 throughout the country. The Court held in *Oregon v. Mitchell* (400 U.S. 112: 1970), however, that Congress could only establish age qualifications for federal elections. States retained control over state and local elections. Ratification of the Twenty-sixth Amendment in 1971 superseded the Court's decision in *Oregon v. Mitchell.*

**Strike** **(86)**

A work stoppage by employees for the purpose of gaining or protecting some benefit. In the United States, strikes have been used almost exclusively by labor union members as the ultimate weapon in the battle with management to gain increased salaries or better working conditions. In many other countries, strikes have had more direct political overtones, with workers using them to protest government policies. *See also* DIRECT ACTION, 58.

*Significance* A strike is a form of economic and political participation for U.S. workers. It is direct action on behalf of the interests of the people striking, a way of saying current conditions are no longer tolerable. Strikes put great pressure on management to reach some resolution of the issues being debated because they stop, or at least make much more difficult, an organization's operation. Strikes resemble other direct action techniques in that they are conducted by people not in a position to get what they want by traditional methods.

**Structural Barriers to Participation** **(87)**

Hurdles that are built into the political process that make political participation more difficult. Structural barriers to participation include such things as registration requirements for voting, the holding of elections on weekdays when many people have to work, and requiring the payment of a tax or passage of a literacy test before allowing people to vote. They do not preclude participation; they merely discourage it. *See also* REGISTRATION, 199; RESIDENCY, 145; VOTING, 95.

*Significance* Some structural barriers to participation were designed and used intentionally to discourage participation by particular groups of people; others seem less intentional but nevertheless have the same effect. The white primary, the poll tax, and literacy tests were part of the systematic efforts of many southern states and communities to prevent blacks from voting. Each in turn has been prohibited either by constitutional amendment or by federal law. The registration requirement for voting and the holding of elections on weekdays remain because they are not seen as part of systematic efforts to discriminate against any particular group. It seems likely, however, that each in its own way tends to reduce voter turnout. The registration requirement, for example, has a short-run effect on people who have moved because they have to establish residency before they can register. This requirement may have a special effect on the less educated and less politically involved because they are not likely to think about voting until immediately before an election when it is too late to register. Holding elections during the week makes it more difficult for people with nine-to-five jobs to vote because they have to do so before work, during a lunch break, or after work—the most crowded times for voting.

***Terminello v. Chicago*, 337 U.S. 1 (1949)** **(88)**
Struck down a breach of peace ordinance that includes speech that, among other things, invites dispute. At a meeting, Terminello made an inflammatory speech that created a public disturbance. He was convicted of inciting a breach of peace. The trial court charged the jury that breach of peace includes speech that "stirs the public to anger, invites dispute, brings about a condition of unrest or creates a disturbance." The Supreme Court, however, ruled that the ordinance as applied punished protected speech. The function of free speech, said the Court, is to "invite dispute." It may "best serve its high purpose" when it "induces a condition of unrest, creates dissatisfaction with conditions as they are, or even stirs people to anger." Speech is often "provocative and challenging," so regulation of speech can only occur when it is likely to produce a "clear and present danger of a serious substantive evil that rises far above public inconvenience, annoyance, or unrest." There is "no room" under the Constitution for a "more restrictive view." The Court's conclusion was that no person may be convicted under an ordinance that makes it an offense

"merely to invite dispute or bring about a condition of unrest." *See also* TIME, PLACE, AND MANNER RESTRICTIONS, 89.

*Significance* Government is entitled to protect itself from such behavior as disorderly conduct and breach of the peace. To do so requires careful balancing of free speech and public order interests. In cases such as *Terminello v. Chicago* (337 U.S. 1: 1949), the Supreme Court must determine that breach of peace ordinances, as interpreted and applied by the trial courts, properly define conduct that is not protected. In addition, sufficient evidence must exist that a breach of peace actually occurred. In the instance of *Terminello,* the Court found that the trial judge allowed impermissible regulation of protected speech. The tougher judgment that law enforcement officers at the scene must make can be represented by cases like *Feiner v. New York* (340 U.S. 315: 1951). In *Feiner,* a speaker was arrested to avoid precipitating a disturbance. That decision, however, gave law enforcement substantial latitude to interfere with expression. On the other hand, in *Edwards v. South Carolina* (372 U.S. 229: 1963), the Court concluded that the audience response and the possibility of a disturbance ought not control the opportunity to engage in public communication. Although the *Edwards* approach was more protective of speech that may invite dispute, there are limits. Certain "well defined classes" of utterance that have little "social value" and are not an "essential part of the exposition of ideas" are not protected by the First Amendment. In addition to libel and obscenity, insulting or "fighting words" are among these unprotected classes.

**Time, Place, and Manner Restrictions (89)**
Generally permissible regulations that may be imposed by the state on expression. These regulations do not aim at the expression itself, but rather the how, when, and where of such expression. Time, place, and manner restrictions target speech "plus," that is, expression that requires additional action or conduct beyond mere verbalization. Though the First Amendment extends to most expression, the Supreme Court has said that it does not "give absolute protection" to a person to "speak whenever or wherever he pleases, or to use any form of address in any circumstances that he chooses" (*Cohen v. California,* 403 U.S. 15: 1971). Accordingly, the state may, for example, impose restrictions on sound amplification, the location of demonstrations, the timing of parades or marches, and the location of campaign signs. *See also* *ADDERLEY V. FLORIDA* (385 U.S. 39: 1966), 43; *CITY COUNCIL OF LOS ANGELES V. TAXPAYERS FOR VINCENT* (466 U.S. 789: 1984), 172; *UNITED STATES V. GRACE* (461 U.S. 171: 1983), 92.

*Significance* Time, place, and manner restrictions are evaluated by the courts using three principal criteria. First, any such restriction must be content neutral. That is, it cannot regulate expression on the basis of the expression itself but only on the associated how, when, or where elements. Second, the state must be able to demonstrate a substantial interest for imposing the control. Restricting demonstrations from areas adjacent to hospitals or in-session schools would be such an interest. Finally, time, place, or manner restrictions must be sufficiently narrow in scope to allow alternative ways to communicate particular information. Restrictions that are so broad as to forestall all opportunities for expression will likely be invalidated by the courts.

### ***Tinker v. Des Moines School District,*** **393 U.S. 503 (1969)** **(90)**

The *Tinker* case upheld symbolic gestures as protected substitutes for speech. *Tinker* involved three public school students who were suspended from school for wearing black arm bands to protest the government's policy in Vietnam. They brought suit to enjoin the school district from enforcing its regulation against the wearing of arm bands. The Supreme Court said the arm bands could be worn. The Court found the "silent, passive expression of opinion, unaccompanied by any disorder or disturbance," to be closely akin to "pure" speech. Although the wearing of arm bands was a symbolic action rather than speech as such, the conduct was protected expression as well. The state, said the Court, may not prohibit an expression of opinion without evidence the regulation is necessary to avoid interference with school discipline or the rights of others. The Court also found the ban defective in that it selectively singled out the symbol representing opposition to the Vietnam War while ignoring other political symbols; the regulation was therefore based on content of the message and was selective. *See also* *COHEN V. CALIFORNIA* (403 U.S. 15: 1971), 55; TIME, PLACE, AND MANNER RESTRICTIONS, 89; *UNITED STATES V. O'BRIEN* (391 U.S. 367: 1968), 93.

*Significance* *Tinker v. Des Moines School District* (393 U.S. 503: 1969) established the standard that symbolic expression may be protected by the free speech clause of the First Amendment. *Tinker* was decided at a time when the United States was undergoing a painful public dialogue about the rights of a minority of citizens to protest political actions. The nation was reassessing institutional values that had long gone uncontested. The *Tinker* decision had its origins in the 1930s, when the Supreme Court struck down a state law statute outlawing display of a red flag because it symbolized "opposition to organized government." The Court felt that if such symbolic expression could be restricted, more general political debate would be seriously jeopardized (*Stromberg v. California,* 283 U.S. 359: 1931). More recently, in *United States v. O'Brien* (391 U.S. 367: 1968), the Court upheld a conviction for the burning of a draft card in protest of the Vietnam War. The Court said the gesture was communicative, but it also found that government's interest in protecting the recruitment of persons for military service prevailed when the competing interests were balanced. In a rather unsupportive statement, Chief Justice Earl Warren opined that the Court "cannot accept the view that an apparently limitless variety of conduct can be labelled 'speech' whenever the person engaging in the conduct intends thereby to express an idea." More typically, the Court has supported litigants claiming protection for symbolic expression, but the symbol or gesture associated with the communication will control its permissibility. If the symbol is protected, symbolic expression becomes an effective means of communicating ideas.

**Twenty-sixth Amendment** **(91)**

An amendment to the Constitution that was adopted in 1971 to prohibit either the federal government or state governments from denying people 18 years of age and older the right to vote because of their age. The Twenty-sixth Amendment states, "The right of citizens of the United States, who are eighteen years of age or older, to vote shall not be denied or abridged by the United States or by any State on account of age." The Voting Rights Act of 1970 had given 18-year-olds the right to vote in federal elections; the Twenty-sixth Amendment gave them that right for state and local elections as well. *See also* OREGON V. MITCHELL (400 U.S. 112: 1970), 75.

*Significance* Before passage of the Twenty-sixth Amendment, most states required that people be 21 years old in order to vote. This age restriction became very controversial as the Vietnam War escalated. Young men were being drafted and sent off to fight a war, and in some cases die, before they were allowed to vote. The unfairness of this situation led Congress to include in the Voting Rights Act of 1970 provision for 18-year-olds to vote, but the Supreme Court ruled in *Oregon v. Mitchell,* (400 U.S. 112: 1970) that Congress had the constitutional authority only to lower the voting age for federal elections. Consequently, Congress proposed the Twenty-sixth Amendment, which was rapidly ratified. The amendment gave approximately 11 million people between the ages of 18 and 21 the right to vote. Its importance for the political system has not been great because people of that age are among the least likely to vote or to participate in other ways.

***United States v. Grace*, 461 U.S. 171 (1983)** **(92)**
Struck down a federal law that prohibited picketing and leafleting on the grounds of the U.S. Supreme Court. The language challenged in *United States v. Grace* included within the definition of Court grounds the public sidewalks surrounding the building. The Court began by indicating that "as a general rule," peaceful picketing and leafleting are "expressive activities" protected by the First Amendment. Further, such public places as parks, streets, or sidewalks are typically considered to be public forums, or locations subject only to the narrowest kinds of time, place, and manner restrictions. Although the Supreme Court grounds are not "transformed" into public forum property just because the public may enter the building, the sidewalks that form a perimeter around the building are "indistinguishable from other sidewalks in Washington." Accordingly, those sidewalks must be regarded as public forums. Because the statute under challenge imposed a categorical or total ban on "communicative activity" on public sidewalks surrounding the Court, it could not be justified as a reasonable time, place, and manner restriction. *See also* *ADDERLEY V. FLORIDA* (385 U.S. 39: 1966), 43; *COX V. LOUISIANA* (379 U.S. 559: 1965), 56; *EDWARDS V. SOUTH CAROLINA* (372 U.S. 229: 1953), 61; TIME, PLACE, AND MANNER RESTRICTIONS, 89.

*Significance* *United States v. Grace* (461 U.S. 171: 1983) examined the scope of the public forum concept. Public property such as streets, sidewalks, and parks have been fundamental to the exercise of expression and assembly rights. As a result, they have acquired a special status as public forums, and are typically accessible to citizens as they seek audiences for their ideas. Determination of what constitutes a public forum is a central issue when reviewing restrictions on use of public property against First Amendment challenge. Simply because a facility or property is public does not make it a public forum. Facilities that have not been dedicated to speech or assembly purposes may be placed off limits to public expression. For example, the hallways of a public hospital or jailhouse do not have the same forum status as a town hall or a state capitol building. The ban on expression reviewed in *Grace* restricted the Supreme Court grounds. To the extent that it focused on the Court building and adjacent property, the regulation was a reasonable exercise of governmental power. Though the public could enter the Court building, that alone did not create public forum status. The regulation in *Grace* extended beyond the building and its immediately adjacent grounds, however, and to the degree that it reached perimeter sidewalks that are traditionally public forums, the regulation was disallowed.

***United States v. O'Brien*, 391 U.S. 367 (1968)** **(93)**
Upheld convictions for burning a Selective Service registration certificate. O'Brien and several others publicly burned their certificates in an effort to symbolically influence others to adopt their antiwar beliefs. O'Brien was convicted of violating the provisions of the then-existing federal draft law, which made it a crime to knowingly destroy the certificate. He contended that the First Amendment guarantees all modes of "communication of ideas by conduct" and that his symbolic expression was protected. The Supreme Court said, however, that it could not "accept the view" that an "apparently limitless variety of conduct can be labelled speech whenever the person engaging in the conduct intends thereby to express an idea." Even if the communicative element of O'Brien's conduct was sufficient to bring the First Amendment "into play," the Court said, it did not "necessarily follow" that burning the certificate was protected. When speech and non-speech elements are combined, a "sufficiently important governmental interest in regulating the nonspeech element can justify incidental limitations of First Amendment freedoms." The Court saw use of the certificate as advancing the proper functioning of the system to recruit persons for the military, a "legitimate and substantial" governmental interest. When O'Brien deliberately destroyed his registration certificate, he "willfully frustrated this governmental interest." *See also* *COHEN V. CALIFORNIA* (403 U.S. 15: 1971), 55; TIME, PLACE, AND MANNER RESTRICTIONS, 89; *TINKER V. DES MOINES SCHOOL DISTRICT* (393 U.S. 503: 1969), 90.

*Significance* Symbolic expression uses some action or gesture as a surrogate for words. Once that happens, the expression ceases to be "pure" speech and becomes speech "plus," which is evaluated in a different way. As the Supreme Court emphasized in *United States v. O'Brien* (391 U.S. 367: 1968), the nonspeech component will prevail over the "pure" speech element when evaluating the constitutionality of a regulation. Doctrine on symbolic speech had its origin in *Stromberg v. California* (283 U.S. 359: 1931), in which the Court invalidated a state statute outlawing the display of a red flag because it symbolized "opposition to organized government." The Court was concerned that if symbolic expression such as a red flag could be restricted, more general political discussion could also be jeopardized. The Court has typically supported litigants claiming protection for symbolic expression since *Stromberg* notwithstanding *O'Brien,* a case decided in the midst of the extensive political turmoil associated with the Vietnam experience. If the symbolic action is itself legal, symbolic expression can become an effective communicative technique.

**Urban Riots (94)**

Political violence that spread through the cities of the United States during the mid- to late 1960s. Urban riots involved black violence toward property in every large city and in many smaller ones. At the time, de facto segregation and discrimination in the northern cities were intense. Blacks attended predominantly black schools because of segregated residential patterns, and these schools were inferior to comparable white schools. Blacks faced discriminatory hiring practices, discriminatory housing practices, and a criminal justice system that seemed more concerned with maintaining white dominance than with administering the law. In virtually every instance, the riots were precipitated by some action on the part of police who had come to be viewed by most blacks as enemy enforcers of a white political order. Riots occurred in the black sections of cities and involved destruction of property and other symbols of white political order but did not involve direct attacks on white people. One of the most serious riots occurred in Detroit, Michigan, during the summer of 1967: There were 43 deaths, 324 injuries, and property damage approaching $100 million. Thirty-three of the 43 people killed were black; 17 of the 43, including 2 whites, were looters; many of the deaths were accidental. *See also* POLITICAL VIOLENCE, 80.

*Significance* The riots initially startled many people who believed racial problems primarily existed in the South. Some people tried to pass the riots off as irresponsible looting on the part of a criminal element. A report by the National Advisory Commission on Civil Disorders—appointed by President Lyndon Johnson to investigate the unrest to determine what had happened, why it had happened, and what could be done to prevent future occurrences—suggested

> Our nation is moving toward two societies, one black, one white—separate and unequal.
>
> Reaction to last summer's disorders has quickened the movement and deepened the division. Discrimination and segregation have long permeated much of American life; they now threaten the future of every American.
>
> This deepening racial division is not inevitable. The movement apart can be reversed. Choice is still possible. Our principal task is to define that choice and to press for a national resolution.

The riots triggered much deeper exploration of the extent of racism in the United States and led to efforts to reduce it. For a brief time, the federal government concentrated on removing racism and dealing with the conditions of poverty that existed within both the black community and the white population.

**Voting** **(95)**

Participating in an election by casting a ballot indicating a preference among candidates or on issues. Voting is the most common way to select government officials in the United States and is frequently used to determine policy at the state and local levels of government. At the time the Constitution was adopted, only white males were entitled to vote and in some states even they were not eligible unless they met certain property qualifications. Gradually restrictions on voting were removed. Property qualifications disappeared during the early part of the nineteenth century. Four constitutional amendments helped remove restrictions on the right to vote: The Fifteenth, Nineteenth, and Twenty-sixth amendments prohibited the federal or state governments from denying the right to vote to blacks, women, and people who were 18 years old and older; the Twenty-fourth Amendment prohibited poll taxes used to deny blacks the right to vote. The Voting Rights Act of 1965 has been effective in ensuring that citizens are not denied the right to vote, and today virtually every U.S. citizen who complies with such legal requirements as registering to vote is entitled to vote. *See also* FIFTEENTH AMENDMENT, 63; LITERACY TEST, 71; NINETEENTH AMENDMENT, 74; POLL TAX, 81; VOTER TURNOUT, 208; VOTING RIGHTS ACTS, 96.

*Significance* Voting is the most common form of political participation in the United States. People are taught that they have a civic responsibility to vote, and yet the percentage of those eligible who actually vote is surprisingly small. The highest level of voter turnout was reached in the 1960 presidential election, when 62.9 percent of the voting age population actually voted. By the 1984 election, that percentage had declined to 53.2. Voter turnout in off-year congressional elections when there is no presidential race is always lower, usually in the low forties; in 1978 it fell to 39.4 percent. Voter turnout is still lower in many state and local elections when they are held at separate times from the federal elections; sometimes turnout falls below 10 percent in city council and school board elections. Voting studies clearly demonstrate that education is the most important influence on voting behavior—the more highly educated a person is, the more likely that person is to vote. In the past, women and nonwhites were less likely to vote than white males, but that was a carryover from previous patterns of discrimination. Currently women and nonwhites vote as regularly as white males with the same level of education. One of the remarkable factors about voting, particularly given the tendency of Americans not to vote, is that it does carry power. As groups who had been denied the right to vote acquired it, they were able to have greater influence on the political system. This trend is most clearly demonstrated by the election of hundreds of black officials throughout the South since the 1960s.

**Voting Rights Acts** **(96)**

Laws passed by Congress designed to remove restrictions on the right of blacks and other minorities to vote. The first Voting Rights Act was passed in 1965 and subsequently extended and expanded in 1970, 1975, and 1982. The 1965 act applied to all states and counties in which less than 50 percent of the voting-age population was registered in 1964 (primarily seven southern states). It suspended the use of literacy tests, provided for federal examiners to register voters and to supervise the election process, and required state officials to submit any proposed election law changes to the U.S. attorney general, who could veto them if he viewed them as discriminatory. The 1970 act extended the law for five years and provided some additional provisions, including allowing 18-year-olds to vote and limiting state residency requirements to 30 days in the case of presidential elections. The section providing for 18-year-olds to vote was limited to federal elections by a decision of the Supreme Court (*Oregon v. Mitchell,* 400 U.S. 112: 1970). The 1975 act extended the law for seven years, permanently barred literacy tests, and extended coverage to language minorities (Spanish Americans, Asian Americans, American Indians, and Alaskan natives). The 1982 act extended the law for an additional 25 years, but allowed covered states to get off the list by demonstrating a clear record of no discrimination for ten years. *See also* OREGON V. MITCHELL (400 U.S. 112: 1970), 75; SOUTH CAROLINA V. KATZENBACH (383 U.S. 301: 1966), 85; VOTING, 95.

*Significance* Before passage of the Voting Rights Act of 1965, black and Hispanic Americans of voting age were much less likely to vote than whites. At the same time, there were few black or Hispanic elected officials. In jurisdictions throughout the South and Southwest where a majority of the population was black or Hispanic, whites continued to be elected to Congress, to state legislatures, and to local offices because various pressures—some blatant and openly coercive, others more subtle but nevertheless effective—were used to prevent or discourage blacks and Hispanics from voting. The Voting Rights acts reduced and eventually removed these pressures, with the result that blacks and Hispanics began to register and vote. It was the classic case of dramatic increases in political participation because of removal of barriers to participation. Currently black Americans are about as likely to vote as their white counterparts, and Hispanics are more likely to vote than in the past, although somewhat less likely to vote than their black or white counterparts. This increased participation has had great impact on election results and on public policy. Hundreds of black and Hispanic officials have been elected in the states to which the Voting Rights acts applied, and public policies favorable to these groups have been passed.

***Walker v. Birmingham*, 388 U.S. 307 (1967)** **(97)**
Upheld the convictions of civil rights marchers who disobeyed an injunction and paraded without a license. A demonstration protesting racial discrimination was organized by several civil rights leaders including Martin Luther King, Jr. When they sought a permit to march through Birmingham, Alabama, city officials not only denied the application but also obtained an injunction prohibiting the march from being organized. A march took place nonetheless and brought about the arrest of King and Walker among others. Though the Supreme Court sympathized with the position of the civil rights marchers, it deferred to the injunction. An injunction legally obtained from a court of proper jurisdiction must be obeyed by the named parties, "however erroneous the action of the court may be, even if the error be in the assumption of the validity of a seeming but void law going to the merits of the case." The Court acknowledged that the "generality of the language" of the Birmingham parade ordinance as well as the "breadth and vagueness" of the injunction "unquestionably raise substantial constitutional issues." The way to raise such questions was to apply to the Alabama courts to modify or dissolve the ordinance, but the demonstrators did not do this; nor did they seek an "authoritative construction of the ordinance." This omission was key for the Court. The case would "arise in quite a different constitutional posture" had the demonstrators, "before disobeying the injunction," challenged it and been met with "delay or frustration of their constitutional claims." *See also* *CARROLL V. PRESIDENT AND COMMISSIONERS OF PRINCESS ANNE* (393 U.S. 175: 1968), 49; DEMONSTRATION, 57; TIME, PLACE, AND MANNER RESTRICTIONS, 89.

*Significance* The civil rights marchers confronted a permit system in *Walker v. Birmingham* (388 U.S. 307: 1967). The permit approach is generally suspect because it may allow administering officials too much discretion, which in turn enables them to issue permits based on the message of the applicant. Such was probably the case in *Walker.* This situation was compounded, however, by the existence of an injunction against Walker and the others not to march after their application for a permit was denied. Had Walker sought to set aside the injunction and/or directly challenge the discriminatory denial of the permit, he likely would have prevailed had he gone ahead with the march. Indeed, in a case arising out of the same march, *Shuttlesworth v. Birmingham* (394 U.S. 147: 1969), the Supreme Court did find the Birmingham permit system unconstitutional. The use of the judicial process to supplement administrative decisions greatly augments the need to obey because compliance with the court order is evaluated on bases independent of the original issue. The clear message of *Walker* is that when faced with an injunction, demonstrators can either seek appellate review of the restrictive injunction or disobey. The former approach is clearly the preferred choice of the Supreme Court.

**White Primary** **(98)**

A technique used to permit whites to vote while preventing blacks from participating in primary elections. The white primary was particularly effective in the South, where securing the nomination of the Democratic party was tantamount to election to office. Although the Supreme Court invalidated a state law mandating a racially exclusive Democratic primary in *Nixon v. Herndon* (273 U.S. 536: 1927), primaries were considered discrete from general elections. This distinction permitted many southern states to let political parties operate as private organizations with control over their own membership qualifications. *See also* PRIMARY ELECTION, 140; *SMITH V. ALLWRIGHT* (321 U.S. 649: 1944), 84; *UNITED STATES V. CLASSIC* (313 U.S. 299: 1941), 255.

*Significance* The white primary became an effective technique of discrimination in the 1930s. In the case of *Grovey v. Townsend* (295 U.S. 45: 1935), the Supreme Court ruled that political parties could, as private "clubs," restrict membership and not be subject to the proscriptions of the Fourteenth or Fifteenth amendments. This interpretation was short-lived, however. First, the Court effectively connected primaries to the election process as a whole in *United States v. Classic* (313 U.S. 299: 1941). The Court based its judgment that the primary is an integral element of the election process on the realistic observation that this was the only step in the overall selection process that was of any consequence. A direct reversal of *Grovey* occurred in *Smith v. Allwright* (321 U.S. 649: 1944) in which the Court ruled that political parties were not private entities and, in turn, their activities were no longer immune from Fifteenth Amendment restrictions.

**Women's Movement** **(99)**

A movement to make women's position and status within society equal to that of men. As early as 1776, Martha Adams wrote to her husband, John, "In the new code of laws which I suppose it will be necessary for you to make, I desire you would remember the ladies and be more generous and favorable to them than your ancestors. . . . If particular care and attention is not paid to the ladies, we are determined to foment a rebellion, and will not hold ourselves bound by any laws in which we have no voice or representation." In 1848 several people attended a convention in Seneca Falls, New York, to consider the "social, civil and religious condition and rights of woman." This meeting and the document it produced, "The Seneca Falls Declaration of Sentiments and Resolutions," marked the beginning of the women's movement. The Seneca Falls Declaration was a paraphrasing of the Declaration of Independence and listed "injuries and usurpations on the part of man toward woman" and called for a number of changes designed to make women's position in society equal to that of men. The document and its proponents were viewed as extremely radical by a society that was at the time totally male dominated. Gradually the women's movement split into two camps: the National Woman's Suffrage Association, which continued to call for radical revision of society, and the American Woman's Suffrage Association, which became almost exclusively concerned with gaining the right to vote. Almost imperceptibly, the radical nature of the women's movement was reduced as greater focus was placed on suffrage and less on total equality; in 1890 the two camps merged to form the National American Woman's Suffrage Association. Suffrage became the predominant goal of the movement, with the expectation that the power to vote would bring other changes. Ratification of the Nineteenth Amendment in 1920 was viewed as an overwhelming victory, and the people and organizations responsible tended to cease political activity. The reality was, however, that suffrage brought no immediate change to the position of women. Society was still dominated by men—women were discriminated against in education, employment, law, and most other aspects of life. A woman's role was thought to be in the home taking care of a family while her husband functioned in the outside world. The 1960s brought a rebirth to the women's movement, now frequently referred to as the women's liberation movement. Women again organized and brought political pressure to bear in favor of a more equal position within society. The National Organization for

Women (NOW) and other organizations lobbied at the state and national level for changes in the law that would end discrimination against women. The Equal Rights Amendment (ERA) became the vehicle by which many people hoped to finally end discrimination against women and bring about equality of the sexes. Although the ERA was not adopted, NOW and other organizations and individuals continue to seek equality for women. *See also* EQUAL RIGHTS AMENDMENT (ERA), 66; NATIONAL ORGANIZATION FOR WOMEN (NOW), 312; NINETEENTH AMENDMENT, 74.

*Significance* The women's movement has fought a long battle to improve the lot of women within society. The conditions that Martha Adams complained of in 1776 and that prompted the Seneca Falls Declaration 72 years later were bleak from the perspective of most women. Women did not have the right to vote; they had no voice in the drafting of laws that they nevertheless had to obey; if married they were expected to obey their husbands, who had legal control over their property; and they were denied educational and employment opportunities. In effect, they were almost totally subservient to and dependent upon men. Not all changes that have taken place can be attributed to the women's movement, but it has certainly had great impact. The gaining of suffrage, though not providing the equality many sought, was a major victory that gave women political clout that they could later use. Since the 1960s, an increasing number of women have become active participants in politics, with the result that more women have been elected to political office; in 1984 a woman, Geraldine Ferraro, was nominated by the Democratic party as its candidate for vice-president of the United States. Another area in which the women's movement has achieved success is in changing people's perceptions of the role of women. Behavior is influenced by thought. If people, including women, believe that a woman's proper place is in the home and that it is a man's responsibility to earn a living, they will not be upset by a political/legal system that deals differently with men and women. The Seneca Falls Declaration challenged those beliefs, and even though people identifying with the women's movement at the time were a small and radical minority, they offered a dramatically different way of looking at (thinking about) the relative roles of men and women. The women's movement has continued to push for different ways of thinking about the role of women in society. Indeed, much of their recent success involved opening up opportunities for women in business, law, medicine, and other positions that for most of history have been denied to women.

# 3. *Elections*

Elections are used to fill a vast number of public offices in the United States. At the national level, the president and members of Congress are elected; at the state level, the governor, members of the state legislature, various state executive officials, such as the attorney general and secretary of state, and in many cases state supreme court judges are elected; and, at the local level, city, county, school board, and many other officials are elected. More U.S. public officials obtain their position by election than in any other country in the world. With so many officials to elect, it seems like elections are always taking place. At times it can be confusing as to who is being elected when. Every four years, in even numbered years divisible by four, on the first Tuesday after the first Monday of November, national elections are held for the presidency, the House of Representatives, and one-third of the Senate (on-year elections). In even numbered years not divisible by four (off years), the same process takes place except that there is no race for president. In some states, elections for state officials may be held at the same time as the national elections; in many states, they are held on the first Tuesday after the first Monday in odd-numbered years to separate them from national elections. Elections for local government officials occur at a variety of times depending on state law and local decisions; they are seldom held at the same time as national elections. In addition to the above, primary elections are held to determine who will represent each party in each election. Consequently, it is not unusual for voters to face at least one election per year and in some cases two or more elections.

Elections are central to the existence of a democratic political system. Through elections, citizens can be involved in selecting the political leadership of their society. Elections provide the mechanism through which people can exercise control over their government officials—they can either "throw the rascals out" if they do not like what is happening or they can reaffirm their support by reelecting officials they like. The existence of elections does not guarantee democracy, but it is difficult to imagine democracy without elections. Key to elections working as intended are the processes by which elections are conducted, the regulations operating on those processes, and the extent to which the electorate participates.

At the outset of U.S. history, states controlled virtually every aspect of the election process. Prior to the Civil War, Congress began to restrict certain options available to states, but the major changes commenced after the war with the ratification of the Fourteenth and Fifteenth amendments. These amendments generally aimed at ending discrimination, with the Fifteenth directly focusing on interference with the right to vote. Subsequently, at federal initiative, the electorate was expanded to include women, 18-year-olds, and greater numbers of racial and ethnic minorities. Protection of voting rights from interference, especially that interference motivated by racial prejudice, was not easily achieved. Indeed, U.S. history reflects an almost unending series of legal challenges to various discriminatory strategies utilized to deny voting rights. Included among these strategies are the poll tax, literacy tests, grandfather clauses, white primaries, and general fear and intimidation aimed at keeping blacks from voting. The lengthy process toward elimination of voting interference was highlighted by enactment of the Voting Rights Act of 1965, a comprehensive federal initiative that dramatically increased federal supervisory authority over elections.

Elections can be organized in a variety of ways. To say that we are going to elect someone to office says nothing about the actual procedures to be used other than that there will be a vote. Who will get to vote? Will everyone's vote be of equal weight? Does the winner need a majority of the vote or just a plurality? Must candidates be nominated or can anyone run? These are just a few of the questions that can be asked about the way elections are organized. The reality is that differing ways of conducting elections have differing consequences, so it is important to examine the way elections are structured. The manner in which legislators are elected in the United States, from single-member districts on a winner-take-all basis, strongly encourages the maintenance of a two-party system. In European democracies where proportional representation is used to elect more than one legislator per district, proportional to the votes cast for each party, multiparty systems tend to develop. In the United States, the use of nonpartisan and at-large elections by many cities to elect their council officials tends to discourage voting participation and increase the probability of electing middle and upper-middle class white males. The extended process for electing the president, lasting up to two years at times, encourages some candidates while discouraging others. Furthermore, not all elections are equally competitive. Most congressional districts, for example, are "safe" in that the one candidate is virtually certain of winning either because her or his party is dominant in the district or because of the advantages of incumbency. In cases in which one party is dominant, the primary of that party is the determining stage in the election process. The way in which elections are regulated helps to determine their ability to reflect voter sentiments. For most of the history of the United States, there has been uneven concern about the honesty of elections. Federal legislation passed in the 1970s has brought about a number of changes in campaign practices, including more systematic enforcement of campaign laws. Most states have adopted similar regulations for state and local elections.

There is one additional aspect that pertains to legislative elections. Besides the United States Senate and some city councils and local school boards, most legislative bodies are composed of persons representing a defined district. Each district elects one member to the body. As a matter of constitutional requirement, the number of representatives each district has must be proportional to the size of its population. The apportioning or districting standard of "one person, one vote" has changed the character of most legislative bodies and requires regular revision to stay current with movements of population.

**Absentee Ballot** **(100)**

A legal provision that makes it possible for people who are not able to go to the polls on election day to still cast their ballot. Absentee ballot forms can be picked up in advance of the election, filled out, and returned to proper election officials before election day. They are held until the polls are closed on election day, at which point they are counted along with the rest of the votes. *See also* VOTER TURNOUT, 208.

*Significance* Absentee ballots are used primarily by people who are going to be out of town on election day or who are physically incapacitated and would find it difficult to go to the polls. Some campaigns have made effective use of absentee ballot programs, encouraging people who are not likely to vote but who are supportive of their candidate to cast absentee ballots. This can be a particularly effective campaign technique for candidates with a lot of support among senior citizens or handicapped people. The campaign can provide these supporters with forms requesting that they be sent absentee ballot forms. Doing so greatly increases the prospects that these supporters will vote.

**Absolute Majority (101)**

Over 50 percent of the voters in an election. The difference between an absolute majority and a majority (simple majority) is that some people who participate in an election do not vote in all the separate races or on all the issues. They may vote in the races for president and governor but not in the lower level races and not on the ballot proposals. Candidates or ballot proposals that gain the support of an absolute majority get over 50 percent of all people voting, not just of the people voting in their race or on that proposal. *See also* PLURALITY, 134.

*Significance* Few elections require an absolute majority for victory. To win in most elections, a candidate must receive either more votes than any opponent (plurality) or better than 50 percent of those voting in the race (simple majority). The exception occurs in some states where an absolute majority is required to ratify a state constitutional amendment or call for a state constitutional convention. In such instances, not voting on the issue is the same as voting "no" because a majority of those participating in the election is required for passage.

**Apportionment (102)**

The allocation of legislative seats among and within states. The Constitution requires that "Representatives . . . shall be apportioned among the several States . . . according to their respective Numbers" (Article I, section 2) and requires a decennial census to determine those numbers. Originally each state was to be apportioned one representative for each 30,000 population, with changes in the apportionment to be made after each census. As a result, the size of Congress continued to grow as the population of the country grew. The Apportionment Act of 1929 set a fixed limit of 435 on the number of representatives and required that future representative seats would be redistributed on the basis of the census, creating the possibility that some states would lose seats if their proportion of the country's total population decreased. Although it is up to the states to determine what the actual congressional district lines will be, the Supreme Court has ruled that states must apportion congressional seats on the basis of population (*Wesberry v. Sanders,* 376 U.S. 1: 1963). The Supreme Court also ruled that state legislative seats must be apportioned on the basis of population (*Baker v. Carr,* 369 U.S. 186: 1962) and required so for both the upper and lower houses of state legislatures (*Reynolds v. Sims,* 377 U.S. 533: 1964). *See also* *BAKER V. CARR* (369 U.S. 186: 1962), 106; REDISTRICTING, 143; *REYNOLDS V. SIMS* (377 U.S. 533: 1964), 146; *WESBERRY V. SANDERS* (376 U.S. 1: 1963), 151.

*Significance* The Constitution creates a House of Representatives in which representation is based upon population, which requires seats to be apportioned among the states on the basis of population. This was part of a compromise made during the drafting of the Constitution between those who wanted representation based on population, mostly the larger states, and those who wanted equal representation for each state, mostly the smaller states. The battle and the ultimate compromise reflected an awareness that still exists today that the way legislative seats are apportioned determines the effectiveness with which legislators can look out for their constituents. Throughout most of the history of the United States, state legislatures were reluctant to change district lines, and gradually the rural areas of the country became overrepresented and the urban areas underrepresented. Public policy tended to reflect the imbalance, with Congress and state legislatures showing more concern about the rural than the urban areas of the country. It was not until the Supreme Court in *Baker v. Carr* (369 U.S. 186: 1962) took the first step to require more equal representation that urban areas began getting a better break from public policy.

**At-Large Election (103)**

Election in which more than one candidate is elected from the same district, and the voters are allowed to vote for as many candidates as are to be elected. At-large elections are most frequently used to select members of a city council or to fill judicial positions. Many cities use at-large elections to select their city council. In such cities, council members are elected from the entire city rather than from subsectors of the city, such as wards. If 10 are to be elected, voters are entitled to vote for 10 candidates, and the 10 candidates receiving the highest number of votes win the election. *See also* AT-LARGE CAMPAIGN, 153; SINGLE-MEMBER DISTRICT, 149.

*Significance* Proponents of at-large elections hold that they attract candidates with broader, less parochial concerns who are more likely to make decisions in the interests of the entire unit they are responsible for governing. Thus legislative or judicial bodies whose members are selected by at-large elections are more likely to stay focused on the big picture rather than have their members squabbling over the more narrow interests of particular regions or neighborhoods. Opponents of at-large elections argue that they promote the continued election to office of white, middle-class males who are unresponsive to neighborhood needs and to the needs of minorities within the community. There is considerable evidence that it is more difficult for minorities to win in at-large elections than in single-member–district elections. One solution to these differences for which many cities have opted is to elect their mayor, vice-mayor, and some councilmen on an at-large basis and then elect the other councilmen from regions within the city.

**Australian Ballot** **(104)**

A secret ballot. The Australian ballot requires an election conducted by government officials and paid for by public funds that allows individuals to vote without publicly identifying for whom they voted. Modern voting techniques such as the voting machine or punch-card voting maintain the principle of the Australian ballot, that is, the right of citizens to cast their vote in secrecy. *See also* BALLOT BOX STUFFING, 155.

*Significance* The Australian ballot reduces the prospects of voter intimidation and voter fraud. During the early history of the United States, oral voting and voting through the use of colored ballots prepared by the parties allowed great pressure to be brought to bear on voters because everyone would know how they voted. The Australian ballot has been used in all states since 1868 and provides voters with greater opportunity to vote for the candidates of their choice without fear of reprisal.

***Avery v. Midland County*, 390 U.S. 474 (1968)** **(105)**

Extended the "one person, one vote" principle to local governments. *Avery v. Midland County* involved a challenge in Texas of the districting of the Midland County Commissioners Court. Each of the four districts elected one commissioner to this court, but the county's only urban center, the City of Midland, was one district that contained 95 percent of the county's population. The question in this case was whether the Fourteenth Amendment "forbids the election of local government officials from districts of disparate population." The Supreme Court first determined that the commissioners court was the "general governing body" of the county, and as such, it must comply with the equal protection clause as does the state. The Court said there was "little difference" with respect to the application of the equal protection clause between the exercise of state power through its legislatures and its exercise by "elected officials in the cities, towns, and counties." Were the commissioners court a "special-purpose unit of government" affecting smaller constituencies within the county, the Court would have had to consider whether such a unit may be "apportioned in ways which give greater influence to the citizens most affected by the organization's functions." That issue was not contained in *Avery.* Although the commissioners court may have concentrated its attention on the rural areas of the county, the court had authority to make decisions that affected "all citizens" of the county. Accordingly, the Court held that units like the commissioners court with "general governmental powers over an entire geographic area not be apportioned among single-member districts of substantially unequal population." *See also* APPORTIONMENT, 102; *REYNOLDS V. SIMS* (377 U.S. 533: 1964), 146.

*Significance* Once the Supreme Court established the "one person, one vote" apportionment standard for legislative bodies, a key question that remained was whether it should apply to local governments in addition to state legislatures. *Avery v. Midland County* (390 U.S. 474: 1968) answered this question in the affirmative. Extension of the rule, however, is not to be categorical. The determining factor is the nature of the local unit's scope and function. For the equal population requirement to apply, a local unit must possess at least a measure of general legislative authority, which does not always exist. Just prior to *Avery,* for example, the Court refused to extend the one person, one vote principle in *Sailors v. Board of Education of Kent County* (387 U.S. 105: 1967). In *Sailors,* the Court determined that the functions of the countywide board of education were not policymaking or legislative but rather administrative in character. Even though the board's members were elected from single-member districts, the Court saw no constitutional need to require population equality.

### *Baker v. Carr,* 369 U.S. 186 (1962) (106)

Ruled that legislative apportionment was a matter properly before federal courts. *Baker v. Carr* abandoned the previously held position that apportionment was a political question not subject to resolution by the judicial branch. In the case of *Colegrove v. Green* (328 U.S. 549: 1946), the Supreme Court held that enjoining an election because of malapportionment was beyond judicial authority. Apportionment was of a "particularly political nature and therefore not meet for judicial determination"; for the judiciary to involve itself in such cases would "cut very deep into the being of Congress. Courts ought not enter this political thicket." In *Baker,* the Court changed its position and concluded that the apportionment question was really an equal protection problem containing claims of arbitrary and capricious action. *See also* APPORTIONMENT, 102; REDISTRICTING, 143; *REYNOLDS V. SIMS* (377 U.S. 533: 1964), 146.

*Significance* *Baker v. Carr* (369 U.S. 186: 1962) first addressed the major political problem of legislative malapportionment. By the middle of the twentieth century, malapportionment existed for most state legislative districts as well as for Congress. Years of inattention to shifting populations had produced highly inequitable representation. *Baker* allowed judicial intervention on the matter of reapportionment but left in its wake a great deal of activity directed toward relieving malapportionment. The Supreme Court's introduction of a standard that could guide redistricting came in *Gray v. Sanders* (373 U.S. 368: 1963), in which the Court ruled that the Equal Protection Clause required persons to have an equal vote. Specific reference to "one man, one vote" was made in *Gray*. The following year, the Court applied the one man, one vote standard to apportionment of congressional districts in *Wesberry v. Sanders* (376 U.S. 1: 1964); in *Reynolds v. Sims* (377 U.S. 533: 1964), the Court applied this same standard to the apportionment of bicameral state legislatures.

**Blanket Primary** **(107)**

A type of primary election in which voters may vote for candidates of more than one party. A blanket primary is highly unusual, occurring only in Alaska and Washington. The more common practice is for voters to be allowed to vote in the primary of only one party. *See also* PRIMARY ELECTION, 140.

*Significance* The blanket primary is the most extreme example of attempts to reduce the influence of party in determining who will hold elective office. When voters can pick and choose among candidates from all parties in a primary election, "party" loses its value, and party officials and supporters have no more influence than independents in the determination of who the candidate of their party will be.

**Candidate Orientation** **(108)**

The perceptions, feelings, and attitudes that citizens have about people running for election. Candidate orientation is one of three variables that political scientists commonly use to explain how people vote; the other two are party identification and issue orientation. When it is relevant, candidate orientation is the strongest determinant of how people vote. That is, when voters know enough about opposing candidates (or even about one of the candidates) to feel that they have a clear preference for one over the other, they are prone to vote for their preferred candidate. Voters are most likely to be able to make this kind of choice in highly visible elections, such as those for president, governor, or U.S. senator, in which extensive media coverage and paid advertising provide people with considerable information about the candidates. Candidate orientation includes a number of dimensions: integrity, trust, leadership abilities, management skills, vision for the country, and likability, to mention the major ones. These dimensions or any combination of them plus additional factors may influence voter support for the candidates. Voters may support a candidate because they think he or she is honest, or because they like his or her vision of the future, or because they think he or she will be a good leader. They may dislike a candidate for the same reasons. *See also* ISSUE ORIENTATION, 124; PARTY IDENTIFICATION, 133; TICKET SPLITTING, 253.

*Significance* The effect of candidate orientation on voter behavior has increased since the 1970s because of several changes that have occurred in the United States. First, political parties, which have traditionally been the strongest determinant of whom people vote for, have grown weaker in recent years. The percentage of the population that identifies with a party has decreased, and even those who do identify are more likely to split their ticket (vote for one or more candidates of the other party). As a result, party identification no longer is as influential in determining for whom voters cast their ballot. Second, the media, especially television, have assumed a much more prominent role in overall society. Virtually everyone has a television and spends substantial time watching it. Candidates for major public offices such as the presidency, the United States Senate, or governorships receive extensive coverage on television news programs. In addition, their campaigns purchase substantial television advertising time. All this is reinforced by publicity received in newspapers, news magazines, and so on. The result is that voters today have much more information about candidates for higher office; indeed, by the end of a presidential election, it is almost impossible for a voter not to be familiar with the two major party candidates. When voters feel that they are knowledgeable about the opposing candidates, they are more likely to select on the basis of candidate orientation.

**Canvassing Board (109)**

An official body that is responsible for collecting and tabulating election results and certifying the election winners. Canvassing boards are normally bipartisan and exist at the local and state levels. At the close of an election, the results from each precinct are sent to a city or county canvassing board that tabulates totals for its area. These results are then sent along to a state canvassing board that certifies final election results for elections throughout the state.

*Significance* Canvassing boards are among the least visible parts of the election process. Although they are responsible for officially tabulating results and designating winners, the reality is that the media, eager to communicate election results, report the returns as they are available and even before canvassing boards have performed their function. In all but the closest of races, the winners are known the evening of or the day after the election, whereas state canvassing boards with the authority to officially designate winners may not meet until several days after the election.

**Challenge** **(110)**

An assertion by a poll watcher that someone attempting to vote is not qualified. Challenges can occur on the basis of a number of claims about potential voters, including not being registered, giving a false name, no longer living at the address at which they are registered, and so on. In closed primary elections, voters can be challenged on the basis that they are not affiliated with the party in whose primary they are attempting to vote. Voting is supervised at each polling precinct by bipartisan or nonpartisan officials responsible for seeing that the election is conducted fairly. If a voter is challenged, these officials must determine her or his right to vote. *See also* BALLOT BOX STUFFING, 155; POLITICAL MACHINE, 234.

*Significance* Use of poll watchers by each party to challenge people they believe to be unqualified to vote is a way of protecting the honesty of the electoral system. The old political machine campaign that said "vote early and vote often" referred to people who would vote many times in the same election using different names in different precincts. This so-called graveyard vote (because many of the names used were those of people who were dead) corrupted the system. Challenges are a way of preventing such vote fraud. Challenges can and have been used, however, to discourage perfectly legitimate voters from casting their ballots. Challenges directed against black and Hispanic voters, particularly those who were voting for the first time and uncertain of their rights, have been used in some places to discourage voting.

**Closed Primary** **(111)**
The selection of party nominees in an election in which only people who are identified with the party can participate. To vote in a closed primary, a person must declare her or his party affiliation either at the time of registering or at the time of the primary, depending on state law. Closed primaries are much more common than open primaries (in which voters can vote in the primary of either party without making any public declaration of their party affiliation). *See also* OPEN PRIMARY, 131; PRIMARY ELECTION, 140.

*Significance* Closed primaries strengthen political parties because they require primary voters to identify with a party in order to participate in the process of selecting that party's candidates for election. This procedure encourages people who might otherwise remain independent to opt for one party or another; otherwise, they cannot participate in primary elections.

***Colegrove v. Green*, 328 U.S. 549 (1946)** **(112)**
Ruled that the issue of legislative apportionment was not appropriate for judicial review. *Colegrove v. Green* involved the apportionment of Illinois congressional seats. The legislature had not reapportioned since 1901, and urban areas in the state, especially those in and around Chicago, were substantially underrepresented. One Chicago district, for example, had a population in excess of 900,000, whereas a district in the southern part of the state contained only 112,000 people. The Supreme Court was asked to enjoin state authorities from conducting the 1946 election under the old apportionment statute. The Court refused, saying that what was asked of it was beyond its competence to grant. Historically, said the Court, it has refused to intervene in matters such as these because "due regard for the effective working of our Government revealed this issue to be of a particularly political nature and therefore not meet for judicial determination." The Court said the Constitution provided for responding to such "evils" as malapportionment. Congress was granted authority to secure fair representation in the House. If Congress fails in this task, and standards of fairness are offended, the remedy ultimately lies with the people. For the Court to intervene and sustain the injunction against the conduct of the election would cut deep into the being of Congress. Courts "ought not enter this political thicket." The remedy, said the Court, is to secure state legislatures that would apportion properly or to invoke the ample powers of Congress. *See also* APPORTIONMENT, 102; *BAKER V. CARR* (369 U.S. 186: 1962), 106; GERRYMANDERING, 121.

*Significance* In *Colegrove v. Green* (328 U.S. 549: 1946), the courts were asked to stop the 1946 congressional elections in Illinois because of malapportionment. Urban areas were underrepresented because the state legislature refused to redraw district lines to reflect the current distribution of population. The Supreme Court refused to take such a bold or activist step in *Colegrove*. Rather, it opted to engage in judicial self-restraint by invoking the political question doctrine, wherein the Court holds that the substance of an issue is primarily political or involves a matter directed toward either the executive or legislative branch by constitutional language. In this case, the Court felt Article I, section 4, placed the matter of apportionment "wholly within the authority of Congress." For the judiciary to intervene would constitute a breach of the principle of separation of power. The immediate impact of *Colegrove* was to forestall judicial consideration of the otherwise hopelessly stalemated apportionment question. The Warren Court saw this issue as primarily one of equal protection rather than separation of power and eventually ruled in *Baker v. Carr* (369 U.S. 186: 1962) that legislative apportionment was a matter that could be brought before federal courts.

**_Davis v. Bandemer_, 478 U.S. 109 (1986)** **(113)**
Ruled that claims of political gerrymandering are justiciable. *Davis v. Bandemer* focused on a challenge to Indiana's reapportionment plan devised after the 1980 census. The plan called for a mixture of single- and multimember districts to elect the state House of Representatives. Democrats challenged the plan, alleging it intentionally disadvantaged them. Results from the 1982 election did show a dilution of the Democratic vote. Democratic House candidates received 51.9 percent of the vote cast statewide but won only 43 of 100 seats in the House. The Supreme Court did not find a violation in the Indiana case but ruled that gerrymandering claims are justiciable even where the plan under challenge meets the one person, one vote standard. The mere fact that an apportionment plan makes it more difficult for a particular group in a particular district to elect the representatives of its choice does not render that scheme constitutionally infirm, however. Unconstitutional vote dilution, either on an individual district or statewide level, requires demonstration beyond a mere lack of proportional representation. Unconstitutional discrimination occurs "only when the electoral system is arranged in a manner that will consistently degrade a voter's or a group of voters' influence on the political process as a whole." The principal question in reviewing gerrymandering allegations is whether a particular group has been "unconstitutionally denied its chance to effectively influence the

political process." A finding of unconstitutionality must be supported by evidence of "continued frustration of the will of a majority of the voters or effective denial to a minority of voters of a fair chance to influence the political process." *See also* APPORTIONMENT, 102; GERRYMANDERING, 121; REDISTRICTING, 143; *THORNBURG V. GINGLES* (478 U.S. 30: 1986), 150.

*Significance* Although the Supreme Court refused to set aside the Indiana apportionment plan challenged in *Davis v. Bandemer* (478 U.S. 109: 1986), it did rule that gerrymandering as a practice is subject to judicial examination. Gerrymandering is the practice of establishing legislative district boundaries to give advantage to one party or interest. Gerrymandering was commonly used for years and contributed to enormous disparities in legislative district populations. Generally, the urban areas became seriously underrepresented at both the federal and state levels through malapportionment. In 1962 the Supreme Court ruled in *Baker v. Carr* (369 U.S. 186) that legislative apportionment was an issue appropriate for judicial review—it was justiciable. Subsequently, the "one person, one vote" standard was fashioned. Notwithstanding the new apportionment requirements, gerrymandering may still occur. For this reason, the Court's decision in *Davis v. Bandemer* may have substantial impact because it enables federal courts to intervene in such situations, especially where a racial motive for the gerrymandering may be involved.

**_Dunn v. Blumstein_, 405 U.S. 330 (1972)** **(114)**
Case that examined the use of one-year residency requirements for voting in state elections. The residency requirement was challenged in *Dunn v. Blumstein* on two grounds: that it provided impermissible interference with the right to vote and that it excessively impinged on the right to interstate travel. The central issue for the Supreme Court was whether the state's classification scheme of dividing persons into resident and nonresident categories was unconstitutionally discriminatory. After considering the benefit withheld by the classification (the right to vote) and the basis for the categorization (recency of interstate travel), the Court concluded that the state had to demonstrate a "substantial and compelling reason" for the durational residency requirement. In addition, if there are other ways to achieve its objectives that impinge less upon constitutionally protected activity, the state "may not choose the way of greater interference," but rather must select the "less drastic means" of pursuing its goals. Although protecting the integrity of the electoral process was acknowledged as a "legitimate goal," the Court did not see durational residency

requirements as "necessary to achieve that state interest." Besides being ineffective in combating election fraud, the Court found the year-long period to be "too much." Rather, 30 days was suggested as an "ample enough period of time for the State to complete whatever administrative tasks are necessary to prevent fraud." The Court also set aside the objective of promoting a knowledgeable electorate, seeing it as a "fencing out" process. That new arrivals may have a "different outlook" than established residents is a "constitutionally impermissible reason for depriving them of their chance to influence the electoral vote of their new home state." *See also* OREGON V. MITCHELL (400 U.S. 112: 1970), 75; RESIDENCY, 145; VOTING RIGHTS ACTS, 96.

*Significance* The impact of *Dunn v. Blumstein* (405 U.S. 330: 1972) was to limit voter requirements to minimum registration periods and tests to determine bona fide residence. The success of the challenges to longer durational residency requirements was a product of the Supreme Court's expansion of the scope of the equal protection clause. The first challenge to residency requirements came in *Shapiro v. Thompson* (394 U.S. 618: 1969), a case involving a year-long residency period as a condition for receiving public assistance. As in *Dunn,* the Court focused on the fundamental right to interstate travel and concluded that the requirement penalized those who exercised the right. In 1970, the following year, Congress abolished residency requirements for national elections in the Voting Rights Act. As a result of *Dunn,* most governmental units use a 30-day period, although 50 days was found acceptable in *Burns v. Fortson* (410 U.S. 686: 1973).

**Election** **(115)**
Process that allows citizens to record through voting their preferences on who should hold public office or whether ballot proposals should be made into law. The United States holds more elections than any country in the world. Citizens elect the president and members of Congress at the national level of government; the governor and members of state legislatures as well as a number of other executive officials and judges at the state level; and mayors, city council members, school board members, judges, and numerous other officials at the local level. Citizens determine through primary elections which candidates of each political party will run against one another in the general election. In many states, citizens also vote on ballot proposals through the initiative or the referendum. Some states even have a process that allows citizens to vote an elected official out of office before the end of his or her term through a recall election. *See also*

GENERAL ELECTION, 120; INITIATIVE, 123; PRIMARY ELECTION, 140; RECALL, 142; REFERENDUM, 144.

*Significance* Elections are at the heart of democracy. They provide the means by which citizens can exercise control over government officials. The number of elections held in the United States combined with the fact that many of them are held at different times may have decreased their value in contributing to democracy, however. Although the United States has more elections than any other country in the world, a lower percentage of the voting age population actually participates than in most other countries. There is reason to believe that with so many elections people get bored or confused about whom they are voting for or what they are voting on and thus are less likely to exercise their right to vote.

### Even-Numbered Election Years (116)

Years in which national elections take place. On the first Monday after the first Tuesday in November of even-numbered years, elections are held for all House seats, for one-third of the Senate seats, and, in even-numbered years divisible by four, for the presidency of the United States. In some states, state and/or local elections may also be held at the same time, although frequently state and local elections, particularly elections for school board or city council, are held in odd-numbered years to increase their independence from national elections. *See also* OFF-YEAR ELECTIONS, 130; VOTER TURNOUT, 208.

*Significance* Even-numbered election years, because they always include elections for national offices, generally have the greatest voter turnout. Those even-numbered years in which there is a presidential race generally provide for the largest election turnout. Off-year elections (even-numbered election years in which there is not a presidential race) still generate a greater voter turnout than odd-numbered years when no national offices are filled by election.

### Exit Polling (117)

Interviews with people immediately after they have voted, conducted outside the polling location by survey organizations. Exit polling is used almost exclusively by media organizations, especially the television networks, to predict who will win the election before the official votes have been counted and to help explain or make sense of the election results. By interviewing voters from sample precincts that have been selected in advance, it is possible to accurately predict who will win an election. To date, exit polling has been used predominately in connection with national elections, either presidential primaries or the general elections held in the fall of even-numbered years. Cost is the only reason exit polling could not be used for just any election. *See also* ELECTION COVERAGE, 351; OPINION POLL, 24.

*Significance* It has become common on election night to watch the various television newspeople describe what their exit polls tell them. Each network competes to be the first to predict who will win, and since 1976, exit polls have become important tools in that prediction process. Once the winner or winners are known, the next task is to explain why some candidates won and others lost. Again, exit polls are consulted. They can help to explain how the Catholic vote went or who got the black vote or why people were reluctant to vote for a particular candidate, and so on. Exit polling has become such a powerful tool in predicting election results that some people have argued that it damages the election process. If polling done during the day can be used to predict who will win before the election is even over, many of those who have not yet voted may decide that it is not worth the trouble because they already know the result.

**Federal Election Commission (FEC) (118)**

A bipartisan, six-member commission established by the Federal Elections Campaign Act of 1974 to enforce federal election campaign laws. The Federal Election Commission (FEC) members are appointed by the president with approval by the Senate. All campaigns for federal office (president, Senate, and House) must submit regular reports to the FEC that indicate the nature of campaign expenditures and sources of campaign contributions. The FEC uses these reports to monitor compliance with federal campaign laws. It also makes public the reports that are submitted to it. In addition, the FEC is responsible for implementing the partial public financing of presidential candidates. It determines which presidential candidates qualify for campaign matching funds and how much each should receive. *See also* FEDERAL ELECTION CAMPAIGN ACTS, 180; PRESIDENTIAL ELECTIONS, 136; PUBLIC FINANCING OF CAMPAIGNS, 141.

*Significance* The Federal Election Commission (FEC) is the first federal agency with clearly assigned responsibility for making federal campaign laws work. Laws passed before 1974 were to be implemented in various ways, but no single agency had responsibility for seeing that these laws were complied with. As a consequence, they tended to be ignored. The most blatant example in recent years of illegal campaign activities was the 1972 reelection campaign of

President Richard Nixon; to a great extent passage of the Federal Election Campaign Act of 1974, which included the creation of the FEC, was a reaction to the Nixon campaign. Since its creation, the FEC has monitored campaigns and contributed to cleaning up campaign activity. It does this primarily by requiring reports of spending and fund-raising activities from all federal campaigns and by making that information available to the public and the media. Although the FEC lacks the power to bring criminal charges, it can turn cases over to the Justice Department when it believes crimes have been committed.

## Filing (119)

The legal declaration that a person intends to be a candidate for an elective office. The legal requirements vary somewhat from state to state, but in most cases candidates must file for election with the secretary of state or with a county or city clerk, depending on the office they seek. In some cases, formal notification of the appropriate official is sufficient for filing, but the more common practice is to require that the candidate provide the official with petitions signed by a percentage of registered voters from the jurisdiction in which she or he will run or provide a cash deposit that will be returned if the candidate receives enough votes in the election. Filing entitles the candidate to run against others from her or his party who have filed for the same office in a primary election. The winner of that election will represent the party in the general election. *See also* PETITION, 76.

*Significance* The act of filing indicates seriousness on the part of potential candidates. Many people talk about running for elective office, but far fewer actually get to the point of filing. The legal requirement that everyone file increases the difficulty of running for office, and in the case of incumbents can at times create nightmarish situations. There have been cases of campaign staffs forgetting to file by the legal deadline or filing inappropriately so that it does not count. Incumbents in those situations found themselves having to conduct write-in campaigns in order to get the nomination of their party and thus be on the ballot for the general election.

## General Election (120)

The final election that determines who has actually won an office. General elections are the end product of an election process that may include other elections, such as primaries, to determine who the candidates will be for the final election that determines who has won an office. *See also* PRIMARY ELECTION, 140.

*Significance* Although the general election determines the ultimate winner, it is only the final stage of the process. In some cases, the process of selecting party nominees can be more important, particularly in districts that are safe for one of the parties. The general election for president, although extremely important, occurs after a general election campaign of only a few months. Most of the effort to get elected president involves months of campaign activity leading up to and including presidential caucuses and presidential primaries.

**Gerrymandering** **(121)**
The establishment of boundaries for legislative districts so as to create partisan advantage. In the United States, virtually all legislators at all governmental levels are chosen on a winner-take-all basis from districts in which only one representative is elected. As a result, the incentives are high to maximize the possibility of capturing most of the seats. Gerrymandering is used to gain partisan advantage in legislative elections by techniques such as drawing district boundaries so as to distribute support for one's own party by providing a winning margin in as many single-member districts as possible while concentrating one's opponent's strengths in a relatively small number of districts. *See also* APPORTIONMENT, 102; *DAVIS V. BANDEMER* (478 U.S. 109: 1986), 113; REDISTRICTING, 143; SINGLE-MEMBER DISTRICT, 149.

*Significance* As the Supreme Court decided cases involving legislative apportionment, it articulated guidelines for the establishment of district boundaries. Besides substantially equal populations, districts that are oddly shaped with an "excessive" number of sides or that crisscross natural boundaries or boundaries of political subdivisions are to be avoided. Such guidelines are aimed at discouraging gerrymandering. Nonetheless, most redistricting plans reflect some effort by the party in power to protect or even extend that advantage. The Court recently gave notice, however, that the practice of gerrymandering will receive closer judicial scrutiny. In the case of *Davis v. Bandemer* (478 U.S. 109: 1986), the Court said that claims of gerrymandering involve the issue of representation, a matter that is appropriately before the courts. To prevail on a gerrymandering claim may prove difficult because more is required than simply showing a lack of proportional representation following a single election. A violation must be supported by evidence of "continued frustration of the will of a majority of the voters or effective denial of a majority of voters of a fair chance to influence the political process."

**Incumbent (122)**

An individual who is serving as a public official. Incumbents are the people who already hold office. In the most common use of the term, they hold a public office to which they have been elected rather than appointed. *See also* INCUMBENCY ADVANTAGE, 186.

*Significance* Incumbents, because they already hold office, are in a position to provide services to citizens. They are also apt to be covered by the media because their activities are part of what government is doing. When election time comes, incumbents are much more likely to win than their challengers because of the campaign advantages they have as a result of their incumbency.

**Initiative (123)**

An arrangement in some states that allows citizens to propose legislation or amendments to the state constitution. Citizens interested in doing so must submit to the proper state officials initiatory petitions signed by a requisite number of registered voters. Once signatures on the petitions are validated, the proposal will be submitted to voters at the next election. Such a proposal becomes law (or a constitutional amendment) if the required majority of those voting on the proposal favor it. *See also* REFERENDUM, 144.

*Significance* The initiative was one of a number of reform proposals that gained strength toward the end of the nineteenth century designed to reduce the power of elected officials and political parties and increase the direct influence of citizens. It has been adopted in fewer than half the states but has had great influence on the politics of some of the states that allow it. California is particularly well known for the politics of the initiative because for each election California voters face numerous proposals placed on the ballot through initiatory petitions, some of which directly contradict others on the ballot.

**Issue Orientation (124)**

The way voters perceive the policy positions of candidates in relation to their own policy preferences. Many students and participants of politics believe that issue orientation should be the primary determinant of whom people vote for at election time. In order for issue orientation to play that role, it is necessary for voters to be able to identify the issue positions of each of the candidates for each of the offices on which they will vote. For most voters, who on the whole are not very interested in politics, this is seldom possible. Insofar as these voters are able to identify issue positions of the candidates, they are more likely to see the candidates they like or the candidates of the party they identify with as having positions similar to their own regardless of whether this corresponds to reality. *See also* CANDIDATE ORIENTATION, 108; PARTY IDENTIFICATION, 133; POLITICAL KNOWLEDGE, 29; SINGLE-ISSUE INTEREST GROUP, 327.

*Significance* Although each election brings talk of the importance of issues and virtually every candidate pays token homage to them by articulating his or her stand on the issues, the reality is that issue orientation has little influence in determining how most voters behave. Low levels of political knowledge on the part of voters, a campaign environment that penalizes candidates who seriously address issues, and the ease with which media can be used to enhance candidates' images all contribute to reducing the impact of issue orientation. The major exception is the emergence of some groups in society for whom a single issue is so predominant that their members are willing to cast their ballot on the basis of the candidates' positions on that single interest. Some of these groups are sufficiently well-organized to ascertain the positions of the candidates on the issue of importance to their members and to communicate that information to members in time for them to act on it when they vote on election day.

**Long Ballot** **(125)**

A ballot on which voters must make many choices. A long ballot commonly includes many offices for which the voter must select candidates. The addition of referenda can also add to the length of the ballot. Sometimes called bedsheet ballots, long ballots are common in state and local elections, where voters frequently must elect a variety of executive officials, judicial officers, and legislators. *See also* ELECTION, 115; SHORT BALLOT, 148.

*Significance* Long ballots were at one time thought to contribute to democracy because they allowed voters to select many of their government officials, in some cases all the way down to the local dogcatcher. Today they are seen as contributing to the decline in voter participation in state and local elections. Long ballots are so complicated, providing voters with so many choices among unknown or little-known candidates and on issues that are complex and difficult to understand, that voters at times decide to stay home rather than face the confusion. Recent reforms have sought to reduce the number of candidates on state and local ballots.

**_Mahan v. Howell,_ 410 U.S. 315 (1973) (126)**

Ruled that deviations from precise compliance with the "one person, one vote" standard can be justified. *Mahan v. Howell* was the Burger Court's first opportunity to consider the population standard for apportionment established in *Reynolds v. Sims* (377 U.S. 533: 1964). Virginia had reapportioned its legislature with a plan that varied 16.4 percent from the ideal size. The variation was caused by an attempt to maintain the "integrity" of existing city and county boundaries. The Supreme Court said that the plan reasonably advanced the "rational state policy of respecting the boundaries of political subdivisions" to "avoid the fragmentation" of such subdivisions relative to legislative representation. The Court also considered whether the population disparities in the plan exceeded constitutional limits, and it concluded that they did not. Making such decisions is a judgment call, said the Court, as neither courts nor legislatures are "furnished with any specialized calipers which enable them to extract from the general language of the equal protection clause . . . the mathematical formula which establishes what range of percentage deviations are permissible." *See also* APPORTIONMENT, 102; *REYNOLDS V. SIMS* (377 U.S. 533: 1964), 146.

*Significance* *Mahan v. Howell* (410 U.S. 315: 1973) gave early indication that the Burger Court would tolerate minimal population variations in legislative redistricting schemes. One of the questions following *Reynolds v. Sims* (377 U.S. 533: 1964) was whether the Supreme Court would demonstrate any flexibility in enforcing its equal population requirement. Such cases as *Fitzpatrick v. Preisler* (394 U.S. 526: 1969), where variations were smaller than in *Mahan,* were found unacceptable. The Court appeared to be on a course where it would require in every case a "good faith effort to achieve absolute equality." Decisions like *Mahan* introduced the expectation that limited and well-defended deviations could prevail over rigid mathematical population standards.

**Mandate (127)**

Popular support for or approval of a party's or candidate's policies and programs. A substantial election victory is generally seen as providing a mandate for the implementation of programs supported by the winning candidate or party. The election of Franklin Roosevelt in 1932 provided a mandate for carrying out new programs to deal with the Great Depression. The election of Dwight Eisenhower in 1952 provided a mandate for a more conservative direction in national politics. Mandates are provided by victory in presidential elections or, at the congressional level, by winning control of Congress. *See also* ISSUE ORIENTATION, 124.

*Significance* Presidents commonly claim that their election victory provides them with a mandate to carry out their policies. The difficulty with this interpretation in the U.S. political system is that election success is so little related to issues that most voters are not aware of the policy directions of presidential candidates. Who received the mandate, for example, in 1984, when President Reagan was reelected in one of the largest landslides in the history of the country, when Republicans maintained their narrow margin of control in the Senate, and when Democrats maintained a substantial majority in the House of Representatives? In earlier years when people were more likely to base their vote on party affiliation, a strong presidential victory was accompanied by control of Congress by his party, which could be more clearly interpreted as providing a mandate. Today, with substantial ticket splitting and candidate orientation providing such a strong base for deciding whom to vote for, particularly in presidential elections, it is much more common to have a president of one party and a Congress controlled by the other party. Mandates are difficult to interpret when this happens.

**Nonpartisan Election** **(128)**

An election in which the candidates run with no identification of their political party on the ballot. Nonpartisan elections are most commonly used to select judges and officials at the municipal level. Movement to nonpartisan elections was part of progressive reforms early in the twentieth century. The objective was to purge politics from local government. The reformers believed that nonpartisan contests would minimize the influence of extraneous state and national issues on elections. More important, it was believed that nonpartisanship would emphasize candidate qualifications and eliminate the influence of party machines and local political bosses. Ballot access in nonpartisan elections is typically accomplished by petition. If more than two candidates file for an office, a nonpartisan primary is conducted to reduce the field to two. *See also* AT-LARGE ELECTION, 103; POLITICAL MACHINE, 234; POLITICAL PARTY: FUNCTIONS, 237.

*Significance* The nonpartisan approach to elections has not produced a depoliticized electoral process. Rather, several patterns have emerged. First, parties continue to dominate, although disguised by the cloak of nonpartisanship; that is, parties continue to recruit and finance candidates but not in an overt way. Second, groups and coalitions now perform the role of parties. They may either be associated with the national parties or be ad hoc independent community groups. In either case, slates of candidates are recruited and endorsed for each election. Yet another pattern is one in which individual candidates establish their own organizations. Many people still favor nonpartisan elections, particularly when linked to at-large elections, as a way of keeping local government focused on the interests of the community rather than encouraging partisan or regional bickering. Critics of nonpartisan elections argue that they reduce voter turnout in local elections because parties have no incentive to encourage voting. Critics also see them as favoring the election of an upper-middle-class elite because without the encouragement of parties, it is the higher socioeconomic people who are most likely to vote, and they are most likely to vote for people like themselves.

**Office-Block Ballot** **(129)**

Type of ballot used in general elections in about 20 states in which all candidates for the same position are grouped together under the title of the office they seek. The office-block ballot, sometimes called the Massachusetts ballot, is less common than its alternative, the party-column ballot, in which candidates are grouped together by party rather than by office. *See also* PARTY-COLUMN BALLOT, 132; STRAIGHT TICKET, 250; TICKET SPLITTING, 253.

*Significance* The office-block ballot reduces the emphasis on party by organizing candidates on the basis of the office they seek. It makes voting a straight party ticket more difficult and thus encourages voters to split their ticket. Thus party officials and proponents of stronger parties in the United States oppose the office-block ballot.

**Off-Year Elections** **(130)**

Elections held in years when there is no presidential race. The most common reference to off-year elections occurs during even-numbered years when there are congressional elections but no presidential elections. Off-year elections also include those held in odd-numbered years that are for state and local offices only. *See also* EVEN-NUMBERED ELECTION YEARS, 116; VOTER TURNOUT, 208.

*Significance* The term "off-year elections" developed as a way to refer to those election years when voter turnout would be lower because there was no race for the presidency. This phenomenon remains true today. Voter turnout in off-year elections for Congress is consistently less than 50 percent of the voting age population as compared to over 50 percent when there is a presidential race. Turnout falls even lower in those off-year elections in which there are only candidates for state and local offices.

**Open Primary** **(131)**

The selection of party nominees for elections in which voters need not declare their party identification and may vote in the party primary of their choice. In an open primary, the voter decides in the privacy of the voting booth which primary she or he will vote in. Each voter is limited to voting in the primary of only one party in any given election but may switch to another party in a later election. Because voters do not have to declare a party affiliation, independents are able to participate in open primaries. *See also* CLOSED PRIMARY, 111; PRIMARY ELECTION, 140.

*Significance* In states having open primary elections, voters can select which primary they will vote in on the basis of which party has the most interesting races. In some cases, Democrats will vote in Republican primaries or Republicans in Democratic primaries to attempt to secure the nomination of the weakest candidate, thus improving prospects for their candidate to win the general election. Open primaries reduce the ability of party members and identifiers to control who the nominees of their party will be by allowing outsiders to participate in the selection process. Consequently, proponents of stronger parties generally oppose open primaries.

**Party-Column Ballot** **(132)**

Type of ballot used in general elections in about 30 states in which the names of the candidates are listed in a column under their respective party names. The party-column ballot, sometimes called the Indiana ballot, makes it easier for voters to vote a straight party ticket. *See also* OFFICE-BLOCK BALLOT, 129; STRAIGHT TICKET, 250; TICKET SPLITTING, 253.

*Significance* The party-column ballot increases the probability that voters will vote a straight party ticket because they can check a single party vote or pull a party lever. Party officials and advocates of stronger parties prefer the party-column ballot over its alternative, the office-block ballot, because it encourages straight ticket voting.

**Party Identification** **(133)**

A sense of loyalty to or support for a political party. Party identification is learned at a young age through the political socialization process. In the United States, most people think of themselves as either

Democrats or Republicans—not because they have signed up or pay dues (in most cases, they have done neither), but simply because they identify with one of the two major parties. Party identification for any individual tends to remain constant throughout life. People may vote for a candidate of the opposite party—may even do so on a regular basis—but are unlikely to switch their party identification. Since the 1970s, however, people seem to identify less strongly with "party." The percentage of the population that identifies itself as either Democrat or Republican has decreased over the last 25 years, and the percentage that identifies itself as independent has increased. Since the election of Franklin Roosevelt in 1932, a higher percentage of voters has identified with the Democratic party than with the Republican party, although in the 1980s Republican candidates for the presidency have been successful in persuading independents and Democrats to vote for them. After the 1984 presidential election, surveys actually showed that some voters had switched their party identification, and for a while the percentage that identified with the Republican party was very close to the percentage that identified with the Democratic party. Subsequent polling, however, suggests that part of this movement was a temporary phenomenon. *See also* CANDIDATE ORIENTATION, 108; ISSUE ORIENTATION, 124; POLITICAL ORIENTATION, 30.

*Significance* Party identification directly influences the way people vote and indirectly influences their perceptions of candidates. The strength of party affiliation to determine how people vote has decreased since the 1970s as party identification has weakened and as candidate orientation has become stronger, but it is still the best overall predictor of how a person will vote. Candidate orientation can have an impact on a voter's decision only when the voter has knowledge about the candidates. This situation is most likely to occur in high-level, high-publicity races such as those for president, governor, senator, and to some extent member of the House of Representatives. In most other races, the voter does not have enough knowledge about the candidates to select on the basis of candidate orientation. She or he needs some guide to fall back on to determine whom to vote for. Party identification provides this guide. Even when voters make their decision on the basis of candidate orientation, their perception of the candidates is apt to be influenced by party. Democrats tend to view Democratic candidates more favorably than Republican candidates and vice versa. The perception of candidates is filtered through the screen of party identification. Those people who identify with neither political party—who do not even lean toward one or the other—are the people least likely to vote. People who are interested in and pay attention to politics generally maintain identification with one of the parties, even if they occasionally vote for candidates of the other party. Those people who maintain that they are strict independents, favoring neither party, do so in most cases because they are not interested in politics and thus unlikely to participate in the political process.

**Plurality** **(134)**

The most votes among the competition in an election. Some elections only require that the winning candidate receive a plurality, others that she or he receive a majority. In a race with three or more candidates, if only a plurality is required, a candidate might win with less than 50 percent of the vote. If a majority is required, a run-off election will be held between the two candidates who received the most votes. *See also* RUNOFF PRIMARY, 147; SINGLE-MEMBER DISTRICT, 149.

*Significance* Most elections in the United States only require a plurality in order to win; the exception is that some southern states require a run-off election if no candidate receives a majority in the primary. Elections that require only a plurality to win reinforce the continuation of a two-party rather than a multiparty system. Whoever gets the most votes will win the election; everyone else loses. Under these conditions, parties strive to be inclusive by building coalitions that will ensure victory with a majority of the vote. If a majority were required to win, third or fourth parties could support candidates in the hope that their candidate would make it to the run-off election; at this point, the voter would have to pick between their candidate and the candidate of another party.

**Precinct** **(135)**

The smallest district around which the election process is organized. The country is divided into precincts that commonly contain between 150 and 1,200 registered voters. Each precinct has a polling place where voters cast their ballot at election time. Precincts also provide the organizational basis for political parties, which elect precinct delegates, who in turn serve in larger party organizational units such as ward, city, or county committees. *See also* GOTV (GET OUT THE VOTE), 183; TARGETING, 204; VOTER CONTACT, 207.

*Significance* Precincts provide a neighborhood location for people to vote. They also provide the basis for party and candidate organization to win elections. Voting data from previous elections can be used to approximate the number of straight-ticket Democratic, straight-ticket Republican, and split-ticket voters in each precinct. These data can then be used to target voter contact and GOTV efforts.

**Presidential Election** **(136)**
The process by which voters select a president from among the nominees of the political parties. The formal, constitutional requirement to be elected president is that a candidate receive a majority of votes in the electoral college. Although presidents are elected on the basis of electoral votes, not popular vote, this requirement has become a formality because the electoral college merely confirms results determined by voters on election day. Each state has a number of electoral votes equal to the number of its members of Congress. Thus, for example, Michigan with 18 members in the House of Representatives and 2 senators has 20 electoral votes. In addition, the District of Columbia has 3 electoral votes. There are a total of 538 electoral votes, so to gain a majority a candidate needs 270. If no candidate receives 270 or more votes, the election of the president is determined by the House of Representatives. Candidates gain electoral votes in 51 separate races, one in each state and one in the District of Columbia. The candidate who receives the most votes in a state gets all that state's electoral votes. Thus candidates attempt to determine some combination of state victories that will give them a total of 270 electoral votes. *See also* ELECTORAL COLLEGE, 215; PRESIDENTIAL CAMPAIGN, 197; PRESIDENTIAL ELECTION PROCESS, 137.

*Significance* Presidential elections were designed by the drafters of the Constitution to be indirect—voters would elect electors in each state, who would in turn elect a president. Although that provision is still part of the formal process, the reality is that voters cast their ballots for presidential candidates, not electors, and the electoral college confirms what the voters have decided. Nevertheless, because of the indirect provision for electing a president, the determination of victory is in terms of the electoral vote, not the popular vote. Although it has happened only rarely, a candidate could be elected president without winning the popular vote contest. There have been numerous proposals for amending the Constitution to provide for the direct election of the president, thereby eliminating the electoral vote and the electoral college. To date, none of them has been successful.

**Presidential Election Process** **(137)**
Events and procedures that every four years determine who will be the next president of the United States. The highlight of the U.S. presidential election process occurs when voters cast their ballots for

president on the first Tuesday after the first Monday of November in even-numbered years divisible by four. The total process, however, is long and involved. To be elected president, a candidate must first receive the nomination of one of the two major parties; third-party candidates have no chance of winning a presidential election. To be nominated, a candidate must have the support of the majority of his party's delegates to a national convention held during the summer of the election year. She or he gains the support of delegates by winning presidential primaries and caucus elections that begin in February of that year. Once their nominees have been selected by the Democratic and Republican parties, the general election campaign begins. The winning candidate is the one who receives a majority of electoral votes (270) in the general election. The actual formal confirmation of victory occurs with the electoral college days after the election is over and everyone knows who has won. *See also* CAUCUS, 209; ELECTORAL COLLEGE, 215; NATIONAL CONVENTION, 228; PRESIDENTIAL CAMPAIGN, 197; PRESIDENTIAL ELECTION, 136; PRESIDENTIAL NOMINATION, 138.

*Significance* The presidential election process is the longest, most elaborate, and most expensive way of selecting a chief executive in the world. Candidates must begin years before the actual election if they are to have any chance of winning. Because the delegates who determine the nominee of each party are selected in each of the 50 states and in the District of Columbia, candidates actually compete in over 50 different elections before they can get to the "big one." In order to do well in the primaries and the caucuses, their campaign must be well organized and the candidate must meet regularly with voters in small group situations. Once the nominations are determined, the requirements for success change. Large amounts of money are spent primarily on television advertising, so candidates must have excellent media skills to do well. Many people have raised questions about whether an Abraham Lincoln or a Franklin Roosevelt could survive this process and win election under today's conditions. Other critics have suggested that the length, expense, and other difficulties of the process discourage strong candidates from running because they are unwilling to face the hassle. Proponents of the system argue that the presidential election process provides a testing ground that helps to reveal candidate characteristics and thus reduces the possibility of electing a flawed president.

**Presidential Nomination** **(138)**

The selection by each party of their candidate for president of the United States. Presidential nominations are formally made at each party's national convention in the summer of presidential election years. To receive a party's nomination, a candidate must gain the votes of a majority of the delegates attending the national convention. The reality of current presidential politics is that usually by the time the conventions occur, everyone knows who will be nominated by each party because almost all the delegates are legally committed to a candidate at the time of their selection. These delegates are selected at the state level on the basis of caucuses and presidential primaries, the earliest of which occur in February and the latest in June, at which the candidates compete for support. Inevitably, one candidate will emerge in each party with more than the required number of delegates even before the end of the caucus/primary season and certainly before the national convention. The convention then bestows to the nominee what she or he has already earned in the caucuses and primaries. *See also* CAUCUS, 209; NATIONAL CONVENTION, 228; NOMINATION, 229; PRESIDENTIAL CAMPAIGN, 197.

*Significance* Presidential nominations were originally made by congressional caucuses—members of Congress would meet to determine their party's candidate for president. That process began to break down in 1824, and by the early 1840s, the use of a national party convention to make the nomination became a fixture of presidential politics. Since then, changes in the nominating process have occurred as a result of changes in the way delegates to the conventions are selected. The current pattern of selection, characterized by extensive use of presidential primaries and broad-participation caucuses, has emerged since the 1968 presidential election. It developed as a result of an effort, primarily in the Democratic party, to open up the selection process and thereby reduce the influence of powerful party leaders and increase the participation of women and minority groups. A consequence has been that the national conventions now simply confirm results previously determined by this more open delegate selection process.

## Presidential Primary (139)

A process used for selecting delegates to a party's national nominating convention. The presidential primary has become the most widely used method of delegate selection. Each state may determine whether it will have a presidential primary and, if so, how it will be conducted. In most states, presidential primaries elect delegates who are pledged to vote for a particular presidential candidate. In some states, presidential primaries are not binding and are referred to as mere beauty contests. In other states, only one of the major parties may use the primary to select convention delegates. Further, some states currently use caucuses instead of primaries to register preference for presidential aspirants. In many ways, contemporary caucuses closely resemble closed primaries. *See also* CAUCUS, 209; PRIMARY ELECTION, 140; NATIONAL CONVENTION, 228; NOMINATION, 229.

*Significance* The presidential primary first appeared in the early 1900s and quickly became the most frequently used method of convention delegate selection. Though it experienced a decline in popularity, the presidential primary has enjoyed a resurgence in large part due to delegate selection reforms adopted by the Democrats following their 1968 national convention. Those advocating primaries suggest that they are more democratic, representative, and less subject to control by political bosses and they generate interest for voters. A series of primaries also tends to separate candidates with insufficient support from those with broad-based vote-getting capability. Convention delegates selected during presidential primaries are not legally bound to support the candidate winning the primary, at least beyond the first convention ballot. Other delegates may actually be chosen as nonpledged or uncommitted to a particular candidate. This detracts from the asserted strengths of presidential primaries that they are more representative and minimize dominance of the professional politicians. Opponents of presidential primaries suggest that they are often not decisive and fail to resolve the nomination question. Although not legally bound, delegates to conventions do feel morally bound to remain pledged, which, in turn, makes compromise more difficult. Opponents of presidential primaries would prefer conventions of unpledged politicians who would be most likely to choose the most competitive candidate.

**Primary Election (140)**

The election in which voters determine the candidates to be nominated by a political party to contest for public office in the subsequent general election. The direct primary election was introduced as a nominating device around 1900 as part of the effort to counteract the influence of political machines and bosses. It has become the most frequently used process for the selection of party nominees. There are two basic categories of primary: open and closed. The open primary allows voters to participate regardless of their party affiliation. The unaffiliated, such as independents, may participate in an open primary. A closed primary, on the other hand, is restricted to voters formally affiliated with a party. In either case, a voter may participate in the nomination of candidates from only one party. The primary will either confirm the nomination of a single candidate seeking the nomination or, if many people are seeking the nomination, reduce the field by designating the winner as the party's candidate in the general election. Some states require that a person receive an actual majority of votes before becoming the nominee, so it is often necessary to conduct a runoff primary between the top two finishers from the primary. The direct primary is also used in a majority of states to select national nominating convention delegates. *See also* CLOSED PRIMARY, 111; GENERAL ELECTION, 120; OPEN PRIMARY, 131; PRIMARY CAMPAIGN, 198.

*Significance* Political reformers sought to weaken political machines by turning to such techniques as the direct primary. The direct primary allows voters rather than party bosses more influence in candidate selection. Running successful candidates is the paramount function of parties, and control of candidate selection is a key element in pursuing this objective. In addition to weakening the organizational party in candidate selection, use of the direct primary also diminishes the influence of party among those holding public office. Direct primaries allow officeholders to ignore party objectives because voters will assess their performance directly.

**Public Financing of Elections (141)**

The use of tax revenues to pay all or part of the campaign costs of candidates for public office. Public financing of elections is used in presidential and some gubernatorial elections in the United States. There have been numerous proposals and some bills actually introduced in Congress that would provide partial public financing of congressional elections, but none has yet become law. The Federal Election Campaign Act of 1974 provided for partial public financing of presidential election campaigns for candidates who would accept limits on their total campaign expenditures. Major party candidates who meet certain qualifications, including raising at least $5,000 in each of 20 states from contributions of $250 or less, receive a dollar for dollar match from the federal government for all individual contributions up to $250 that they receive during the campaigns for nomination. In the general election, the federal government provides each major party candidate with the same amount of money, and candidates are not allowed to raise additional funds for their campaigns. The federal funds can be supplemented, however, by party expenditures on behalf of the presidential candidates. *See also* CAMPAIGN COSTS, 160; FEDERAL ELECTION CAMPAIGN ACTS, 180.

*Significance* Proponents of public financing of elections maintain that it allows limits to be placed on campaign expenditures; reduces the influence of large contributors, particularly political action committees; encourages broader participation in the funding of elections; and creates more equal campaign resources for competing candidates. They are able to use the example of experience with partial financing of presidential campaigns to support their case. Since its adoption, only one candidate for president has not agreed to accept campaign expenditure limits in exchange for partial financing; the costs of presidential campaigns have gone down since the period before the law was passed. The dependence of presidential candidates on large contributors and on political action committees has decreased and the importance of gaining the support of small contributors has increased. Finally, no presidential race since passage of the law has had the incredible imbalance of campaign resources of the 1972 Richard Nixon–George McGovern race.

**Recall** **(142)**

An election to determine whether an elected official should be removed from office before the end of her or his term. A recall election is scheduled when the required number of valid signatures on a recall petition that asks for the removal from office of a government official is filed with the appropriate election officials. The choice before voters in the recall election is to keep or remove the challenged official from office. If a majority votes in favor of maintaining the official in office, nothing else needs to be done; if a majority votes to remove, the official loses her or his position and a new election must be scheduled to elect a replacement. *See also* INITIATIVE, 123; REFERENDUM, 144.

*Significance* The recall exists in only a few states, and even in these it can be used only for state or local officials, not members of Congress. It, along with the initiative and the referendum, were reforms proposed by the progressive movement to reduce the power of the political machine and provide voters with more direct influence in government. It is the most direct and powerful means for voters to remove officials in whom they have lost confidence. Until the 1970s, the recall was seldom used except in extreme cases of misuse of office by government officials. Since then, it has been used much more frequently, in many cases not because of misuse of office but because voters are unhappy with policies supported by these government officials.

**Redistricting** **(143)**

The redrawing of legislative district lines. Redistricting is required, in the case of congressional districts, because the Constitution mandates reapportionment of seats in the House of Representatives every 10 years based upon a population census. At such time, states gaining or losing representatives must draw new district lines that correspond to such changes. Redistricting has become necessary in state and local legislative districts because of a series of Supreme Court cases that require legislative districts within a state to be roughly equal in population. *See also* APPORTIONMENT, 102; *BAKER V. CARR* (369 U.S. 186: 1962), 106; GERRYMANDERING, 121; *REYNOLDS V. SIMS* (377 U.S. 533: 1964), 146; *WESBERRY V. SANDERS* (376 U.S. 1: 1963), 151.

*Significance* Redistricting is done by state governments and has been extremely controversial because the determination of legislative district lines commonly influences who will win elections. Until *Baker v. Carr* (369 U.S. 186: 1962), rurally controlled state legislatures refused to redistrict on the basis of population because doing so would decrease the power of rural areas and increase the power of urban areas. Since the Supreme Court has ruled that legislative districts must be roughly equal in population, manipulation of district lines for political advantage is still possible through gerrymandering, the drawing of lines in ways to benefit the party in power. Because of the political nature of redistricting, control of the governor's office and the state legislature at the time of redistricting is of vital importance to each party. If the same party controls each, it can design district lines that will improve the prospects of its candidates until the next census is done.

**Referendum** **(144)**

An arrangement in most states that allows citizens to vote on constitutional proposals and some legislative proposals. A referendum can be held on constitutional amendments, proposed new constitutions, laws already passed (if a sufficient number of registered voters request so by petition), and proposals put on the ballot through the initiative. In addition, some state and local governments submit proposals to voters in what are called advisory referendums to get voter reaction before actually taking action. In most cases, referendums must receive a majority vote for passage, although for constitutional changes, states may require more than a simple majority for passage. *See also* INITIATIVE, 123.

*Significance* Many states adopted some form of referendum in the early part of the twentieth century in response to pressures from the progressive movement to increase direct participation by voters in the determination of public policy. Although the referendum has the virtue of allowing the public to react directly to public policy proposals, extensive use of referendums in some states has greatly added to the length of the ballot voters must cast. This situation has led some voters to become frustrated with the whole process, particularly when many of the proposals are conflicting or confusing, and to conclude that the easiest thing to do is not vote or vote no on all proposals.

**Residency** **(145)**
A requirement for voting based on place of residence. Most states require that people establish residency by living within a voting jurisdiction for a fixed period of time before they are entitled to register to vote. The Supreme Court has suggested that 30 days should be sufficient to establish residency (*Dunn v. Blumstein,* 405 U.S. 330: 1972), and the Voting Rights Act of 1970 stipulates that 30-days' residence in a state is sufficient to qualify a person to vote in presidential elections. *See also* *DUNN V. BLUMSTEIN* (405 U.S. 330: 1972), 114; STRUCTURAL BARRIERS TO PARTICIPATION, 87.

*Significance* Residency requirements were established to prevent people from voting more than once on election day. By requiring the establishment of residency, however, people who have recently moved before an election are deprived of their right to vote. It was this concern that led the Supreme Court and Congress to act to place limits on the amount of time needed to establish residency.

***Reynolds v. Sims,* 377 U.S. 533 (1964)** **(146)**
Established requirements for the apportionment of bicameral state legislatures. *Reynolds v. Sims,* accompanied by several companion cases from other states, held that the one man, one vote principle applied to both houses of state legislatures. The central question was whether there were any constitutional principles that would justify departures from the basic standard of equality among voters in the apportionment of seats in state legislatures. The gravity of the issue was reflected in the Supreme Court's observation that the "right of suffrage can be denied by a debasement or dilution of the weight of a citizen's vote just as effectively as by wholly prohibiting the free exercise of the franchise." Chief Justice Earl Warren declared that legislators represent people, not trees or acres, and these people must have an unimpairable capacity to elect representatives; thus the weight of a citizen's vote cannot be made to depend on where he lives. Population is of necessity the starting point for the consideration of, and the

controlling criterion for judgment in, legislative apportionment controversies. The constitutional demands of equal protection require that a legislative vote not be diluted when compared with those of other citizens living elsewhere in the state. Equal protection also demands that both chambers of state legislatures be apportioned on the basis of population. The Court rejected the federal analogy, calling it inappropriate and irrelevant. Thus population-based representation, "as nearly of equal population as is practicable," became the rule, with only small deviations allowable for flexibility or to prevent gerrymandering. *See also* APPORTIONMENT, 102; *BAKER V. CARR* (369 U.S. 186: 1962), 106; *MAHAN V. HOWELL* (410 U.S. 315: 1973), 126.

*Significance* *Reynolds v. Sims* (377 U.S. 533: 1964) established stringent population guidelines for the apportionment of districts in state legislatures and clearly became the most critical reapportionment case insofar as state and local legislative bodies are concerned. The principle of egalitarianism, a value preeminent among a majority of the members of the Warren Court, clearly governed in this case. When self-governance occurs by electing representatives, every citizen has an "inalienable right to full and effective participation in the political processes of his state's legislative bodies." Equality, reasoned the Warren Court, is essential to the operation of majority rule. Popular majorities ought to elect legislative majorities. Although minority interests are protected by constitutional provisions, it would be unreasonable to sanction minority control of state legislative bodies. Such a condition would "appear to deny majority rights in a way that far surpasses any possible denial of minority rights that might otherwise be thought to result." The extent to which the Warren Court would tolerate deviation from the one person, one vote standard was reflected in *Lucas v. Forty-Fourth General Assembly* (377 U.S. 713: 1964), one of the companions to *Reynolds*. In *Lucas,* the Supreme Court rejected a plan with a 3.6 to 1 variance in one house and a 1.7 to 1 variance in the other house on equal protection grounds. The ruling was made despite approval of the plan in a statewide referendum. The Burger Court permitted deviations of slightly more than 16 percent in *Mahan v. Howell* (410 U.S. 315: 1973). The variance was permitted because it was done to "advance the rational state policy of respecting boundaries of political subdivisions" and did not otherwise exceed constitutional limitations.

### Runoff Primary (147)

A postprimary election to determine which candidate will be a party's nominee in situations in which no candidate received a majority in the primary election. Runoff primaries are held in states, almost exclusively in the South, that require primary candidates to gain a majority in order to receive their party's nomination. In states with runoffs, if no candidate gains a majority in the initial primary, a runoff election is held within a short period matching the two top vote-getters from the primary, thus ensuring that the winner will gain a majority of the votes. *See also* PRIMARY ELECTION, 140.

*Significance* Most states do not have runoff primaries; they declare the winner to be the candidate with the most votes, regardless of whether she or he gained a majority. The runoff primary has played a unique role in the South because from the time of the Civil War until the 1960s, most southern states were one-party, Democratic states. The real competition for elected office took place within the primary of the Democratic party. To gain the party nomination, a majority vote was required, forcing the same coalition building within state Democratic parties in the South as occurred in both major parties in the North. To gain nomination, a candidate ultimately had to gain the support of a majority of the voters, which pushed candidates to develop the broadest possible base. Without the runoff, candidates could have been successful with less than majority support.

**Short Ballot** **(148)**

A ballot with only a few offices and issues on which a voter must decide. A short ballot generally includes a race for the top executive office and for a legislative seat. The ballot for national elections is a short ballot. At most, voters must choose among candidates for the presidency, the Senate, and the House of Representatives (in some years, they only have to choose among candidates for the House). When national elections are held at the same time as state and local elections, the ballot grows longer because races for other offices are added. Many state elections, even when held at times separate from national elections, have a long and complex ballot because they elect numerous state executive officials and provide for voters to decide on a variety of referendums. *See also* LONG BALLOT, 125.

*Significance* A short ballot makes the voter's task much simpler and more manageable. When a voter needs only to choose between candidates for a limited number of offices, it is possible to make a more informed choice. As the number of decisions required of voters—who are for the most part not very interested in politics—increases, they are less likely to be able to cast an informed vote. If voters identify with one of the political parties, they have a means of deciding, even when they do not have information about individual candidates; they can vote for the candidates of their party. On the whole, however, the least informed voters are also least likely to identify with either political party. One solution to their problem of figuring out whom to vote for is to decide to stay home on election day—to not vote for anyone. It is likely that long ballots discourage voter participation and short ballots encourage it.

**Single-Member District (149)**
Election district from which only one candidate is elected. Single-member–district elections are the norm in the United States. The president, members of Congress, governors, state legislators, and many local officials are elected from single-member districts. The predominant characteristic of the single-member district is that there can be only one winner in each district—a candidate must get the most votes to prevail in a single-member district. This is in sharp contrast with elections in many European democracies, which use proportional representation to elect a number of candidates from the same district. *See also* AT-LARGE ELECTION, 103; PROPORTIONAL REPRESENTATION, 239.

*Significance* Single-member–district elections are the strongest contributor to the maintenance of a two-party system in the United States. When there can be only one winner in each district, it is difficult for third or fourth parties to elect anyone to office because seldom can they sponsor a candidate with the ability to beat the candidates of the two major parties. The one sure way to get candidates elected in single-member–district elections is to ensure that they get a majority of the votes, so there are extremely strong incentives to each of the two major parties to build coalitions that will increase the prospects of their candidates receiving a majority of the vote. If more than one candidate were elected from each district on the basis of the proportion of the vote obtained by each competing party, it would be much easier for third parties to elect candidates. Use of single-member districts may distort the relationship of seats and the proportion of popular vote received by a party. One of the major parties may win only slightly more (and possibly even less) than half the popular vote nationally but still win a majority of legislative seats. This situation results from the drawing of district lines throughout the country. On the other hand, the use of single-member districts and the winner-take-all approach does produce legislative majorities and, in turn, more viable and stable governments. Although such simple majorities may not democratically reflect the sentiments of the electorate as well as a multiparty approach, the disadvantages of coalition governments characteristic of multiparty systems are avoided.

**Thornburg v. Gingles, 478 U.S. 30 (1986)** **(150)**
Ruled that the election of a minority candidate (or candidates) from a particular district does not preclude the finding of Voting Rights Act violations. The Supreme Court's decision in *Thornburg* thus makes it easier for minorities to challenge electoral practices and voting schemes as impairing their voting rights. Under review in this case was a redistricting plan for a state legislature that included the creation of several multimember districts that had white majorities in areas where sufficient concentrations of black voters could have formed black majorities if smaller, single-member districts had been created. While challenge to the plan was in progress, an election was held and black candidates fared particularly well. The question before the Court in this case became the effect of 1982 amendments to the Voting Rights Act on circumstances such as these. Prior to 1982, it was necessary to demonstrate that a disputed plan operated as a purposeful device to further racial discrimination. The 1982 amendments changed the focus from intent to electoral outcomes in assessing claims of discriminatory impairment. A unanimous Court said in *Thornburg* that a Voting Rights Act claim is not foreclosed simply because some minority candidates have been successful. A plan that "dilutes" minority votes cannot be defended on the ground that it "sporadically and serendipitously benefits minority voters." *See also* APPORTIONMENT, 102; *DAVIS V. BANDEMER* (478 U.S. 109: 1986), 113; GERRYMANDERING, 121; REDISTRICTING, 143; VOTING RIGHTS ACT, 96.

*Significance* The full impact of *Thornburg v. Gingles* (478 U.S. 30: 1986) is not immediately apparent. In the same term, the Supreme Court ruled in *Davis v. Bandemer* (478 U.S. 109: 1986) that the practice of gerrymandering is subject to constitutional challenge. These two cases would seem to greatly broaden the role of federal courts in monitoring electoral practices and districting plans. At the same time, the Supreme Court could not agree on criteria to be used to review cases such as *Thornburg*. A five-justice majority urged a three-element standard that required challengers to show that (1) they are large and "compact" enough to constitute a majority in the district; (2) they vote "cohesively"; and (3) candidates preferred by the minority are usually defeated by white-preferred candidates. The Court will likely have opportunities to review its decision in *Thornburg* in the near future. The short-term effect, however, may be to discourage use of multimember districts simply because they are harder to defend in Voting Rights Act challenges that apply the ruling made in *Thornburg*.

**_Wesberry v. Sanders_, 376 U.S. 1 (1963) (151)**
Established the "one person, one vote" standard for legislative apportionment. Georgia's congressional district boundaries were challenged in *Wesberry v. Sanders* because one of the districts was more than twice as heavily populated as another. The Supreme Court ruled that Georgia's apportionment was defective. Recognizing that Article I, section 4, has conveyed "exclusive authority" to protect congressional elections to Congress, the Court said that there was nothing in that provision that "immunizes state congressional apportionment laws which debase a citizen's right to vote from the power of courts to protect the constitutional rights of citizens from legislative destruction." The right to vote is "too important" to be "stripped of judicial protection" by such an interpretation of Article I. The Georgia law was defective because it "contracts the value of some votes and expands the value of others." The Court went on to say that language in Article I giving "the people" the power to choose representatives means that "as nearly as is practicable one man's vote in a congressional election is to be worth as much as another's." It would "defeat the principle solemnly embodied in the Great Compromise—equal representation in the House for equal numbers of people," said the Court, if lines drawn by state legislatures could give some voters "greater voice" in electing members of Congress. Although it may not be possible to draw districts with "mathematical precision," there is "no excuse" for ignoring the Constitution's "plain objective" of making "equal representation for equal numbers of people the fundamental goal for the House of Representatives." *See also* APPORTIONMENT, 102; *BAKER V. CARR* (369 U.S. 186: 1962), 106.

*Significance* The first reapportionment case to reach the Supreme Court following *Baker v. Carr* (369 U.S. 186: 1962) was *Gray v. Sanders* (373 U.S. 368: 1963). *Gray* gave the Court an opportunity to begin fashioning particular standards regarding apportionment. The voting practice at issue in *Gray* was something called the county unit system, a technique by which statewide officials were nominated in Georgia. Unit votes based on a combination of the candidate's performance in each county and the number of seats each county possessed in the state legislature produced the nominees. Because the counties' representation in the legislature did not correspond to population, the Court invalidated the process. Although it clearly distinguished this process from legislative apportionment, the Court said the equal protection clause required every person to have an equal vote. Specific reference to "one man, one vote" came from *Gray.* Application of this standard to apportionment of congressional districts came in *Wesberry v. Sanders* (376 U.S. 1: 1963). In *Wesberry,* the Court used language from Article I, section 2, which provides that members of the House be chosen "by the People" to require that as "nearly as practicable," one person's vote in a congressional election must be "worth as much as another's." Thus *Wesberry* made the one person, one vote standard directly applicable to the legislative apportionment process with expanded application of the principle following soon thereafter.

# 4. *Political Campaigns*

A campaign is a planned, coordinated program for attaining intended results. There are many kinds of campaigns—military campaigns, United Way campaigns, election campaigns, to list just a few. *Political campaigns* involve coordinated efforts to attain some political objective: win an election, get a law passed, increase funding for a particular program.

The specific nature of the campaign and the way it is set up will vary depending on the campaign objective. A campaign to get someone elected to office will be different from a campaign to get a law passed. The defining characteristic of any campaign is its goal: What results is it seeking to attain, and what has to happen in order to attain these results. To be elected president, a candidate must win an absolute majority in the electoral college—270 of the total 538 electoral votes available. Winning a majority of the popular vote or having a good media image or raising a lot of money may contribute to winning, but winning is defined in terms of the number of electoral votes gained. An effective campaign would be one that provides the best chance of winning the required number of electoral votes. Such a campaign would begin years before the electoral votes were counted with the development of a campaign plan that identified all the major accomplishments that would be necessary along the path. A presidential candidate must first gain the nomination of his or her party, Democratic or Republican. To do this, he or she must get a majority of delegate votes at a national convention called for the purpose of selecting the party's nominee. Getting a majority of delegates requires competing in primary elections and caucus selection processes and meeting with and trying to gain the support of uncommitted delegates. Once he or she gets the party's nomination, a candidate must then defeat his or her opponent in enough states to gain a majority of electoral votes because electoral votes are awarded on a state-by-state basis with the winner in each state receiving all that state's electoral votes. A campaign is a coordinated effort to achieve all the objectives necessary to ultimately gain that majority of electoral votes.

It is important to understand that other political campaigns would have other requirements for success. A campaign to elect someone to Congress seeks to ensure that the candidate obtains a majority of votes in the general election. Success requires getting the largest percentage of the popular vote. A campaign to elect someone in an at-large election in which more than one candidate is elected from the same district and voters can vote for a number of candidates requires only that the candidate finish high enough among competing candidates to be one of those elected. If five people are being elected from the district, finishing anywhere from first through fifth constitutes success. A campaign to pass a law seeks to ensure that a majority of members in the House of Representatives and in the Senate vote favorably for the legislation and that the president not veto it. For this type of campaign, the focus is on the votes of members of Congress, not the general public. It should be clear by now that we can talk about many different kinds of campaigns. What they all have in common is that they acquire and use resources in planned and coordinated ways to enhance the prospects of achieving some relatively specific objective. Resources can include people, money, knowledge, and experience, to name a few.

The most common type of campaign in the United States is the election campaign, which is the focus of this chapter. People elect the president every four years, members of Congress (435 representatives and 33 or 34 senators) every two years, and thousands of state and local officials on varying timetables. The level of complexity and sophistication of these election campaigns varies considerably, and the rules of the game differ. Many local elections are nonpartisan and/or at-large. The most highly publicized elections involve partisan competition in single-member districts: election for president, Congress, governor, state legislature, and so on. In these elections, a candidate must receive the most votes cast by the voters in her or his district.

Understanding the behavior of individual voters is extremely important in designing an effective campaign to get a candidate elected to office. What causes them to vote the way they do? How is it possible to influence their voting? In general, people in the United States are not interested in politics and as a result are not likely to know much about candidates or issues involved in an election. Many people do not bother to vote. In presidential election years, only slightly over 50 percent of eligible voters actually go to the polls, and in nonpresidential years, less than 50 percent vote. For those people who do vote, the two strongest influences on how they vote are their perception of the candidates (candidate orientation) and how they feel about the candidate's political party (party identification). Candidate orientation is the most influential when people have enough knowledge to choose between the two opponents, or when they have enough knowledge about one candidate to conclude that they favor or oppose that candidate. Party orientation influences the way they see the candidates. Strong Democrats are much more likely to view the Democratic candidate more favorably than the Republican candidate, and vice versa. Because large numbers of people have limited knowledge about politics, many of them lack sufficient knowledge about candidates to make a choice on the basis of candidate orientation. In that case, party affiliation plays a significant role in determining how people vote. It provides voters with a simplified answer to the question, How do I vote? It allows the voter to decide based on the candidate's party, without necessarily knowing anything about the candidate. Issues can also influence how people vote, but for issues to be significant, voters must be relatively well informed.

In election districts where people are overwhelmingly Republican or Democratic, campaigns mean little. The candidate of the dominant party will win the election regardless of what happens in the campaign. It is in districts where neither party is overwhelmingly dominant that campaigns can strongly influence who will win the election. Campaigns usually start with a campaign plan, a document that lays out campaign objectives and describes how a candidate can get enough votes to win the election. A campaign attempts to increase its candidate's share of the vote in two significant ways: persuading people to support their candidate (persuasion), and getting the largest possible number of their supporters to vote on election day [registration and get out the vote (GOTV)]. Persuasion focuses on influencing whom voters will support. It is targeted toward those voters who are undecided or who are weak supporters of one or the other of the candidates. Strong supporters of either candidate are not likely to switch, so campaigns usually do not try to persuade them. Campaigns target their persuasion efforts toward voters they have a chance of influencing. Registration increases the number of supporters who will be eligible to vote on election day. Campaign involvement with registration usually takes the form of encouraging their party to get likely supporters registered. Democratic organizations work with campaigns of Democratic candidates to increase the registration of people likely to vote Democratic, and Republican organizations do the same by focusing on people likely to vote Republican. GOTV seeks to ensure that supporters actually vote. It does a candidate no good to have many supporters if they do not bother to vote. The central focus of an election campaign is on the voters—persuasion, registration, and GOTV. A campaign must acquire and use resources to be successful in carrying out these tasks. People and money are the two most significant campaign resources. The most important person in a campaign is the candidate. She or he is usually the person most likely to be successful in carrying out any of the campaign's activities, whether it is persuading voters, recruiting volunteers, or raising money. But only so much can be done by one person, so many activities that might best be done by the candidate are carried on by volunteers or paid staff. Thus, recruitment of effective campaign workers, whether paid or volunteer, is vital to the success of a campaign. Almost all campaign activities cost money. The higher the level of the campaign and the more the campaign attempts to do, the greater its cost.

**Advance Work** **(152)**

Preparation for the appearance of the candidate. Advance work involves campaign workers (volunteers) visiting locations at which the candidate is scheduled to appear in advance of the candidate to make sure that arrangements are satisfactory. Advance workers make contacts with local people, check out speaking arrangements, make sure there will be satisfactory publicity, cope with potential problems, and do other things that will enhance the effectiveness of the candidate's appearance. *See also* PRESIDENTIAL CAMPAIGN, 197; SCHEDULER, 201.

*Significance* Advance work is most necessary in presidential campaigns. A team of campaign workers will precede the visit of the candidate to a town to gather information that will be helpful to the candidate, to work out the candidate's schedule in detail, and to prepare drafts of speeches that include local color. Advance workers in presidential campaigns tend to be professionals, frequently with media experience, who are adept at ensuring that the candidate's visit will generate the greatest possible positive impact for the campaign. One advance person's trick is to make sure that the candidate is always speaking to packed audiences. The obvious way to do this is to generate large crowds; a more subtle way is to schedule the candidate to speak in small halls. Advance work can also be helpful in more local campaigns. For congressional campaigns, good advance work can improve the prospects of a candidate's visiting with the right people, having the best media contacts, and speaking to the largest crowds in each city or town visited.

**At-Large Campaign (153)**

A campaign to elect a candidate in a multimember district. At-large campaigns differ considerably from most other election campaigns because the rules for at-large elections differ in important ways from most others: (1) more than one candidate is elected from the same district, and (2) voters are allowed to vote for as many candidates as are to be elected. In order to be elected, a candidate need not get the most votes, only enough votes to make her or his rank equal to or above that of the other candidates to be elected. Thus, if nine candidates are to be elected from the same district, success (winning) constitutes finishing anywhere among the top nine candidates in the number of votes garnered. When elections are at-large, they are usually also nonpartisan. *See also* AT-LARGE ELECTION, 153; LOCAL ELECTION CAMPAIGN, 188; NONPARTISAN ELECTION, 128.

*Significance* At-large campaigns need to be designed differently from campaigns in which there can be only one winner. Candidates who share a party identification, a policy orientation, or a common interest can work together in mutually beneficial ways that help all to win. Candidates can also team up and run together. At-large campaigns occur most often in elections for city legislative office or for judicial positions. There tends to be little interest in such races, especially if the election is also nonpartisan. Voter turnout is frequently quite low, often dropping below 10 percent of eligible voters. It is difficult under such conditions for candidates to raise sufficient resources to conduct major campaigns. Candidates who are best able to acquire campaign resources and thus able to mount the most extensive campaigns are most likely to win.

**Balanced Ticket (154)**

The combining of party candidates in such a way as to provide regional, ideological, religious, ethnic, or other kinds of balance to enhance voter appeal. The balanced ticket is most frequently thought of in terms of presidential races, in which each party tries to create balance between its presidential and vice-presidential candidate. If the presidential candidate is from the Northeast, then the vice-presidential candidate should be from the South, West, or Midwest. If the presidential candidate is liberal or conservative, then the vice-presidential candidate is likely to be more moderate. The John Kennedy–Lyndon Johnson Democratic team in 1960 was a classic example of the balanced ticket. Kennedy was a Catholic from the Northeast, a young liberal who demonstrated strong voter appeal; Johnson was a Protestant from Texas, an older moderate who demonstrated great leadership as majority leader in the Senate. Over the strong protests of many of his advisers, Kennedy asked Johnson to become his running mate because he felt Johnson could help the ticket in Texas and other parts of the South and West where Kennedy feared he would be weak. Similar ticket balancing can occur in state and local campaigns, with a party trying to create a balance among its candidates for governor, lieutenant governor, and other state offices or among its candidates for city offices. *See also* CAMPAIGN, 48.

*Significance* A balanced ticket is one way that candidates or parties attempt to ensure electoral victory. The Ronald Reagan–George Bush ticket of 1980 and 1984 provided balance between a conservative and a more moderate Republican. The Jimmy Carter–Walter Mondale ticket in 1976 provided regional balance (Carter from Georgia and Mondale from Minnesota) and balance between an outsider who could run against the establishment (Carter) and an insider who was greatly respected by most of the Democratic establishment (Mondale). There is no guarantee that balancing the ticket will lead to victory; it is simply one more way to broaden a candidate's and a party's appeal. One of the dangers of attempts to balance the ticket is that more emphasis is placed on voter appeal than on ability to govern the nation.

**Ballot Box Stuffing** **(155)**

The illegal influencing of election results through various practices of falsifying vote counts. Ballot box stuffing originally referred to "stuffing" the ballot box with extra votes in the days of paper balloting but now refers to any illegal fixing of election results. Ballot box stuffing was most prevalent in the United States during the era of the political machine. In addition to simply marking thousands of ballots and inserting them into the ballot box before counting, a variety of other techniques existed for influencing results. One such technique, use of the "cemetery vote," involved party workers voting many different times by using the names of registered voters who were dead. The phrase "vote early and vote often" developed as a result of this practice. The modern version of ballot box stuffing involves tampering with voting machines. *See also* POLITICAL MACHINE, 234.

*Significance* Ballot box stuffing has influenced election results at many points in the history of the United States. The presidential election of 1876 between Democratic candidate Samuel J. Tilden and Republican candidate Rutherford B. Hayes was thrown into great confusion because three states—Florida, Louisiana, and South Carolina—submitted two sets of election returns, one set with Tilden winning and the other set with Hayes winning. Republicans who controlled the state legislatures in each state charged Democrats with preventing blacks from voting, whereas Democrats charged that many people who were not registered and others who were not even residents were allowed to vote. The dispute was finally resolved by a commission established by Congress that gave the electoral votes from each of the states to Hayes, allowing him to win the presidential election by one electoral vote. William Safire describes what must be the most extreme case of voter fraud—the New York election of 1844—in which 41,000 people were qualified to vote and 55,000 actually voted (*Safire's Political Dictionary* [New York: Ballantine Books, 1978], p. 104). Although election fraud is much less common today, it still occurs. Candidates must be alert to ensure that they do not end up having an election stolen from them.

**Bandwagon Effect** **(156)**

Tendency for some people to go with the crowd or with the anticipated winner in politics. The bandwagon effect leads many people to end up supporting the campaign of or casting their vote for the candidate who seems to be on top at the moment, rather than rationally evaluating the qualifications of the candidates. Voters end up "jumping on the bandwagon." Since 1976, polling and media coverage have increased the importance of the bandwagon effect. Polls allow reasonably accurate determination of which candidates are ahead at any point in a campaign. When the media publish the results of such polls, undecided voters may be encouraged to go with the candidate who seems to be winning. A more complex version of the bandwagon effect occurs when the media determine which candidates they will cover based on which ones are doing well. Their determination to cover a candidate gives that candidate much greater exposure to the public and thus improves the prospect that the public will jump on that candidate's bandwagon. That most voters have relatively limited knowledge about and little interest in politics enhances the bandwagon effect. Voters who are knowledgeable and interested are much less likely to be swayed by the bandwagon effect. *See also* HORSE-RACE JOURNALISM, 361; POLITICAL ORIENTATION, 30; PRESIDENTIAL PRIMARY, 139.

*Significance* The bandwagon effect can be used by campaigns to increase the prospects of their candidate's winning. The process for selecting the presidential nominee of each party has been strongly influenced since the mid-1970s by the bandwagon effect. The two earliest indicators of how candidates competing for the nomination are doing are the Iowa caucuses and the New Hampshire primary. Iowa and New Hampshire are both small states, each providing only a tiny portion of the delegates who will eventually go to the parties' national conventions and participate in the selection of their party's nominee; however, these states have become overwhelmingly important to a candidate's chance to eventually win the nomination. Most people had no idea who Jimmy Carter was until he finished first among the Democratic candidates in 1976 in the Iowa caucuses and the New Hampshire primary. Suddenly he became the hot candidate, the one the media began to cover and the one on whose bandwagon people began jumping. Since then, the competition has been fierce in those two states because candidates know that they have to do well there or face the prospect of being eliminated, for all practical purposes, from the race.

**_Buckley v. Valeo_, 434 U.S. 1 (1976)** **(157)**

Examined the constitutionality of the Federal Election Campaign Act of 1974 against various First Amendment challenges, including the possibility that regulation of the electoral process impinges upon individual and group expression. By differing majorities, the Supreme Court upheld portions of the act that provided for campaign contribution limits, disclosure, public financing, and the Election Commission. The section imposing limits on expenditures was invalidated. The Court said the act's contribution and expenditure ceiling "reduces the quantity of expression because virtually every means of communicating ideas in today's society requires the expenditure of money." The Court distinguished, however, between limits on contributions and limits on things for which the contributions might be spent. Although the latter represent substantial restraint on the quantity and diversity of political speech, limits on contributions involve "little direct restraint." The contributor's freedom to discuss candidates and issues is not infringed in any way. Even though contributions may underwrite some costs of conveying a campaign's views, the contributions must be transformed into political expression by persons other than the contributor. The Court acknowledged a legitimate governmental interest in protecting the "integrity of our system of representative democracy" from quid pro quo arrangements that might arise from financial contributions. By striking the expenditure limits, the Court allowed unlimited use of personal wealth or expenditures made on behalf of campaigns separate from the actual campaign organization of a candidate. On the matter of disclosure, the Court agreed that the requirement might deter some contributions but viewed it as a "least restrictive means of curbing the evils of campaign ignorance and corruption." The Court also upheld the act's public financing provisions by rejecting a claim that a differential funding formula for major and minor parties was unconstitutional. *See also* CAMPAIGN COSTS, 160; FEDERAL ELECTION CAMPAIGN ACTS, 180; FEDERAL ELECTION COMMISSION, 118; *FEDERAL ELECTION COMMISSION (FEC) V. NATIONAL CONSERVATIVE POLITICAL ACTION COMMITTEE (NCPAC)* (470 U.S. 480: 1985), 287; POLITICAL ACTION COMMITTEE (PAC), 319.

*Significance* *Buckley v. Valeo* (434 U.S. 1: 1976) invalidated that part of the Federal Election Campaign Act of 1974 that sought to limit campaign expenditures. The *Buckley* ruling focused on the spending limits and found that the act's provisions restricting expenditures interfered with political expression of both individuals and organizations. This decision has limited legislative power to regulate certain fundamental campaign activities associated with spending money. In addition, the decision left political action committees (PACs) in a position to expend unlimited amounts on campaigns so long as they remained independent of formal campaign organizations. Indeed, a follow-up ruling on this question used *Buckley* as its controlling authority (*FEC v. NCPAC,* 470 U.S. 480: 1985). This, in turn, elevated the importance of PACs in electoral politics, usually at the expense of political parties.

**Campaign Budget** **(158)**
A major planning and management device for effective campaigns. The campaign budget includes three components: expenditures, fund-raising, and a cash-flow model relating the former two for the entire campaign. Expenditure estimates identify the anticipated campaign expenditures. The magnitude and type of expenditures will vary depending upon the level of the campaign (presidential, congressional, and so on), but typical expenditures might include such items as office expenses (rent, equipment, phones, postage, supplies), media (television, radio, print), fund-raising, staff salaries, travel, volunteer expenses, and anything else that has been built into the campaign plan. Fund-raising estimates identify potential sources of campaign contributions (direct mail, individual contributors, political action committees), and estimate how much can be raised from each. The cash-flow model estimates when each of the expenditures will be necessary and when campaign funds will be available. The timing for expenditures tends to drive decisions about fund-raising, although the cash-flow model can help the campaign to identify places where

expenditures need to be delayed as well as places where fund-raising needs to be stepped up. *See also* CAMPAIGN COSTS, 160; CAMPAIGN PLAN, 164; FUND-RAISING, 182.

*Significance* A campaign budget allows the campaign to make the most efficient use of campaign resources. The campaign that spends $50,000 producing elaborate media spots only to find that it lacks the funds to buy time on television to make use of them is wasting money; yet it is startling to discover how often such situations develop. Use of a campaign budget can reduce the probability of such waste occurring. Development of the budget forces the campaign to relate expenditures to revenues and to make tough choices about which campaign programs can be afforded and which must be eliminated because of lack of funds. Because it is difficult at the time of the development of the campaign plan to accurately estimate how successful the fund-raising efforts will be, many campaigns develop two or even three budgets: an ideal budget, a worst-case budget, and one in the middle. The ideal budget assumes the campaign can raise the money it will need and plans expenditures accordingly. The worst-case budget assumes great difficulty in fund-raising. The middle budget makes the most realistic estimates of fund-raising capacity. Because cash-flow models will be available in each budget, by watching the pattern of fund-raising, a campaign manager can estimate which budget she or he should be operating under.

**Campaign Computers** **(159)**

Computers used to help candidates and their staffs conduct campaigns. Computers make possible or facilitate many campaign activities, including analysis of voting and polling data, maintenance of campaign finance records for campaign reporting, recording voter canvass results for future voter contact, scheduling the candidate, addressing direct mail solicitations, generating reports, and producing documents. Campaigns began making use of computers in the 1960s, primarily for the purpose of analyzing data, and have been finding new applications for them ever since. Computers have changed considerably over the years, becoming smaller, less expensive, and much easier to use. The first campaign computers were large mainframe machines that were too expensive for use except at the presidential level. With the advent of the microchip, computers have gotten smaller and cheaper, and now a campaign at almost any level can afford to purchase a personal or microcomputer. *See also* CAMPAIGN POLLING, 165; SCHEDULER, 201; VOTER CANVASS, 206.

*Significance* Computers have been invaluable to large, expensive campaigns—for president, governor, or senator—since the late 1960s. The advent of smaller, cheaper, and more "user friendly" computers in the 1980s has made them equally invaluable for virtually all campaigns. For between $500 and $10,000, depending on need and prosperity, a campaign can purchase a microcomputer that will make many campaign tasks, especially those related to data analysis, office management, and secretarial functions, easier and faster to perform. Some companies have now developed special software packages for microcomputers that are designed to perform campaign functions.

**Campaign Costs** **(160)**

The financial expenditures involved in the pursuit of elective office. Campaign costs have increased much more rapidly than inflation since the mid-1970s for virtually all elections. The increase is attributable to a variety of factors including greater use of political consultants, more frequent use of paid campaign staff, and more extensive use of paid advertising, particularly television. Easier availability of campaign contributions has also been a factor, however. More sophisticated fund-raising techniques, particularly the development of direct mail fund-raising, and the growth of political action committees (PACs) that seem eager to make contributions have made it easier for campaigns to raise money. The average campaign expenditures for major party candidates for the House of Representatives in 1974 was $53,400; by the 1986 election, it had risen to $260,000. The same pattern exists for senate campaigns. Average cost in 1974 was $437,500; by 1986, it had risen to $2.58 million. *See also* DIRECT MAIL, 177; FUND-RAISING, 182; PAID MEDIA, 193; PAID STAFF, 194; POLITICAL ACTION COMMITTEE (PAC), 319; POLITICAL CONSULTANTS, 196.

*Significance* Campaign costs have risen so dramatically since 1976 that people are reluctant to become candidates unless they have sufficient personal wealth to meet such costs or can be assured of campaign contributions. Because of the likelihood of their reelection, incumbents have a much easier time raising campaign funds than do challengers, so the increase in campaign costs has tended to benefit incumbents. Accompanying the increase in campaign costs has been a change in the source of campaign contributions. Political action committees (PACs) have become much greater contributors to candidates, causing some concern that their influence has become too dominant in the election process. This change can be seen clearly in elections for

Congress. In 1974, political action committees provided 17 percent of the total contributions to candidates for the House and 11 percent of the total for the Senate. By 1986, those percentages had become 36 and 22, respectively, virtually doubling, with every indication that political action committees will play an even larger role in the future.

**Campaign Literature** **(161)**
Written material designed to persuade voters to support a candidate. Campaign literature includes such things as campaign brochures, fliers, direct mail enclosures. The most common type of campaign literature is the campaign brochure, a two- to eight-page information piece that conveys the campaign message and can be used for a variety of purposes including "lit drops" to voters' residences and handouts at events such as fairs or parades or at campaign offices for people who drop by and want to know more about the candidate. Campaign literature is also used extensively in conjunction with direct mail efforts. The carefully written piece that urges potential contributors to send money, uncertain voters to support the candidate, or strong supporters to turn out on election day can be mailed to targeted voters by the campaign. *See also* CAMPAIGN MESSAGE, 163; DIRECT MAIL, 177; LIT DROP, 187; VOTER CONTACT, 207.

*Significance* Campaign literature provides one way of conveying the campaign message. Most campaigns will use various pieces of literature, in addition to other voter contact techniques such as radio and television advertising, to convey the campaign message. These different sources of information about the candidate should be reinforcing—that is, they should carry the same message even if in different packages. For campaigns with extensive resources, the greatest advantage of campaign literature is its ability to convey a targeted message. Senior citizens can be mailed information about the candidate's position on issues important to them; voters identified as concerned about the economy can be sent the candidate's economic message. Campaign literature, although important to any campaign, is more so for lower level campaigns that lack the money to make extensive use of more expensive voter contact techniques such as radio and television advertising.

**Campaign Manager** **(162)**
The person responsible for overall management of a campaign. The campaign manager is responsible for making sure that all parts of the campaign come together at appropriate times and in appropriate

ways. Everyone on the campaign staff reports to the campaign manager. The most important responsibilities of the campaign manager are to ensure that the campaign plan is being implemented, to keep the campaign on schedule in terms of the campaign timetable, and to ensure that others are effectively doing their jobs. A campaign manager also frequently serves as the major point of contact between the campaign and other campaigns, the party apparatus, political consultants, and others important to the campaign but not part of its internal operation. *See also* CAMPAIGN PLAN, 164; CAMPAIGN STRUCTURE, 167; CAMPAIGN TIMETABLE/CALENDAR, 168; CANDIDATE, 170.

*Significance* A good campaign manager frees the candidate to do things that can best be done by the candidate, such as voter contact, media interaction, and fund-raising. The campaign manager makes sure the campaign is operating effectively and thus ensures that the candidate will not have to get involved in management and personnel issues. The candidate needs to have considerable confidence in the campaign manager to be willing to entrust management responsibilities to him or her and to press ahead with appropriate candidate type activities.

**Campaign Message (163)**

The key information that the campaign seeks to convey about the candidate. The campaign message talks about the candidate, her or his beliefs, issue positions, experience, leadership qualifications, honesty, or whatever has been decided upon as the most effective message for winning the campaign. The campaign message is designed to give voters a reason to vote for the candidate. Effective campaign messages are focused, appeal to the voter, and are believable. Campaign messages that try to say everything about a candidate frequently fail because voters pick up an unclear image. In developing the campaign message, polling and other techniques are used to determine voter attitudes. The message can then focus on those aspects of the candidate that are most likely to persuade voters. For example, if the candidate is liberal and the district is conservative, an effective campaign message is not likely to focus on issues or ideology. It might rather focus on effectiveness or leadership qualities, something with which voters in the district can identify. To be effective, a campaign message must be believable. The liberal who tries to persuade voters that she or he is a conservative is not likely to be successful. Rather, voters are more likely to believe that such a candidate cannot be trusted. *See also* CAMPAIGN LITERATURE, 161; CANDIDATE, 170; PAID MEDIA, 193; VOTER CONTACT, 207.

*Significance* The campaign message is what the candidate and the campaign are all about. Once the campaign message has been defined, it becomes central to all facets of the voter contact program. The candidate should convey it as she or he talks to people; the literature and advertising should focus on it; even telephone contacts can include it. President Reagan was very successful in 1984 with the message, "It's morning again in America," conveying the idea that somehow there had occurred a reawakening of U.S. greatness under his presidency and therefore he should continue in office for another term. His opponent, Walter Mondale, was less successful with his campaign message, which included the idea that it would be necessary for the next president to support tax increases, a message voters did not want to hear.

**Campaign Plan** **(164)**

A written document that indicates the objectives of a campaign and what must be done to achieve them. A campaign plan includes the overall strategy for obtaining the objectives, the campaign's organizational structure and job descriptions, a timetable or calendar that assigns target dates for key campaign events, and a budget that estimates campaign expenditures and revenues. A campaign plan is based upon a thorough analysis of what the campaign faces: the strengths and weaknesses of its candidate and the opposing candidate, the nature of the district, and what resources will be available to the campaign. It should be completed before the campaign begins and serve as a guide for what happens during the campaign. *See also* CAMPAIGN BUDGET, 158; CAMPAIGN MANAGER, 162; CAMPAIGN STRUCTURE, 167; CAMPAIGN TIMETABLE/CALENDAR, 168.

*Significance* Development of a campaign plan forces early analysis of what a campaign faces and what it must achieve in order to be successful. Once a campaign begins, there is seldom time for planning, and the intense pressures of coping with or responding to activities of the opposing side, the media, internal campaign problems, and so on, can generate chaos. The plan helps to keep the campaign on track, doing what is necessary to win rather than reacting only to day-to-day events. Not all campaigns make use of a written campaign plan, but the more professional and more successful ones typically do.

**Campaign Polling** **(165)**

A tool for assisting campaigns in divining pertinent voter perceptions about candidates and issues during an election. Campaign polling makes it possible to interview a systematically selected sample of voters from any election district and use their responses to estimate the views of the entire population of the district. In a typical campaign, a baseline poll will be taken before the race begins. The information acquired will be used to help develop the campaign plan and the campaign message. Later polls, frequently using many of the same questions, will be used to help evaluate how the campaign is progressing. Questions are asked about how the candidate and her or his opponent(s) are perceived. Do people like them or dislike them? Do people even know them? How are they regarded ideologically, on issues, as people? Usually a "match race" question will be asked that takes the form of, If the election were held today, whom would you vote for? Questions are also asked about the values, issue positions, party and ideological orientations, and social and economic positions of the people being interviewed. The answers to these questions provide the campaign with a picture of the district—its partisan and ideological mix and the issues people think are important and what their positions on these issues are. The frequency with which campaigns poll depends on campaign resources and the type of campaign. For presidential races and some other highly financed campaigns, polling may be done on a daily basis to monitor the impact of various media messages and provide other useful information. Lower level campaigns may poll less frequently. *See also* CAMPAIGN MESSAGE, 163; CAMPAIGN PLAN, 164; OPINION POLL, 24; SAMPLING TECHNIQUES, 35.

*Significance* Campaign polling is a powerful tool that makes it possible for campaigns to discern what the voters are thinking and how they view the candidates and campaign activities. Such information can be used to design the most persuasive campaign message. Overdependence on polls to determine campaign messages, however, raises important political questions about what it is the candidates are trying to do in a campaign. Are they willing to do anything necessary to win or do they stand for something that they want to communicate to the voters? Do they want the election to represent victory for their particular orientation, values, or policies or are they content to win at any cost? One of the criticisms of polling and related campaign tactics is that campaigns can use polling to find out what the public wants and then attempt to reshape the candidate's image and/or position on issues to correspond to public desires. Richard Nixon's campaign in 1968, for example, was strongly criticized for remaking the candidate's image simply to gain votes. Most candidates and campaigns, however, make effective use of polling results to design the campaign message without going to this extreme.

**Campaign Resources** **(166)**
The assets available to a campaign as it seeks to meet its objectives. Campaign resources include the candidate, campaign workers, money, and time. The more effective a campaign is in expanding and making use of its resources, the more successful that campaign is likely to be. A strong candidate is the most valuable campaign resource because she or he is the person best able to influence voters. The candidate is also the person in the best position to increase other campaign resources—to recruit effective workers (paid staff and/or volunteers) and to raise substantial amounts of money. The campaign plan typically includes provisions for continuing to expand these resources through fund-raising, hiring, and volunteer recruitment. It also includes arrangements for effective use of resources. *See also* CAMPAIGN PLAN, 164; CANDIDATE, 170; FUND-RAISING, 182.

*Significance* Campaign resources are absolutely essential to conducting an effective campaign. Since the 1970s as campaigns have become more expensive and professionalized, candidates devote more of their time and energy to raising money and to ensuring that they have the best possible campaign staff. A campaign, however, must walk a delicate balance between increasing resources and contacting voters. Increasing resources does nothing directly to influence voter behavior. Those resources must be put to use in some type of voter contact program before they can contribute to the campaign's success. A constant tension exists between allocating available resources to further increase resources and allocating them to influence voter behavior. Should the candidate spend time raising money or going to events where direct voter contact is possible? If the latter, the campaign may not have sufficient funds to buy television advertising. If the former, the effectiveness of direct and personal voter contact is lost.

**Campaign Structure** **(167)**
The organizational pattern designed to implement the activities of the campaign as spelled out in the campaign plan. The campaign structure describes the personnel positions necessary for conducting the campaign and delineates the relationship among the people holding these positions. It indicates who is responsible for what activities and who will report to or supervise whom. Typical positions within a campaign are campaign manager, treasurer, accountant, fund-raising

coordinator, field operations director, and volunteer coordinator. The complexity of campaign structures varies considerably depending on the level of the campaign and the resources available. Presidential campaigns have the most complex campaign structure, including some elements of the functional organization described above but also encompassing a number of regional positions that report to the campaign manager. At the other extreme, campaigns for city council, school board, or other local positions are commonly conducted with simple campaign structures, in many cases involving only a few part-time people. *See also* CAMPAIGN MANAGER, 162; CAMPAIGN PLAN, 164; CAMPAIGN TREASURER, 169.

*Significance* An efficient campaign structure greatly improves the prospects for conducting a successful campaign. One of the most difficult aspects of a campaign is ensuring implementation of the campaign plan—making certain that the campaign literature gets distributed, that volunteers are recruited, that money is raised. Too often the assumption is made that these things will somehow just happen or that whoever is available at the moment can do them. This complacency can lead to confusion and chaos, greatly reducing the prospects for campaign success, not only because tasks do not get done but also because people in the campaign get frustrated and are less willing to work. By clearly assigning responsibilities so that everyone working in the campaign knows what is expected, a campaign manager can avoid many of these problems.

**Campaign Timetable/Calendar (168)**

A listing by date of the tasks that a campaign must accomplish. The campaign timetable is part of the campaign plan that provides a guide for what must be done—and when—throughout the campaign. The starting point for developing the campaign timetable is to identify every major campaign program or event—items such as the filing deadline for candidacy petitions, the announcement of candidacy, major fund-raising events, the voter canvass, the media program, the get out the vote (GOTV) campaign. For some of these events—the filing deadline, for example—the date is fixed by outside agencies over which the campaign has no control. For others—the voter canvass, for example—the campaign can determine dates. Target dates are assigned for each event and beginning and ending dates for each program. To complete the campaign timetable, it is necessary to identify for each target date everything that must be accomplished in advance to meet that target date. It is a process of working backwards from each target date, listing advance preparations that need to be made and the dates by which they need to be completed. For example, if the campaign plan includes a GOTV program, most of the contact with voters to encourage them to vote will take place the weekend before the election and on election day. However, in order to make these contacts, volunteers to make phone calls need to be recruited, phones need to be located, the people to be called need to be identified, and their phone numbers looked up. Some of these tasks should be done far in advance of the actual time of the calling. For each key activity of the campaign, it is possible to work backwards to identify those things that need to be done in advance (and how far in advance) so that they can be entered into the campaign timetable. The final product will be a calendar that not only identifies everything the campaign needs to do but also indicates the dates by which each task needs to be completed. *See also* CAMPAIGN PLAN, 164; GOTV, 183.

*Significance* A campaign timetable/calendar is an important part of the campaign plan and serves as an effective management tool during the campaign. Its development requires serious thought about how resources, especially the candidate and time, will be used to achieve campaign objectives. Its use during the campaign reduces the prospect of unpleasant surprises because it allows a manager to make sure that necessary tasks are being completed on time. Without such a tool, for example, it is too easy to get to the big day when hundreds of volunteers turn out for a door-to-door lit drop of campaign brochures and discover that the brochures were ordered too late and will not arrive until the following week.

**Campaign Treasurer (169)**

The person responsible for maintaining campaign finance records and paying the campaign bills. In federally regulated elections, the campaign treasurer is legally responsible for the accurate reporting of campaign revenues and expenditures to the Federal Election Commission on a periodic basis. These reports include a detailed listing of expenditures and identification by name, address, and occupation of contributors of over $100. In state-regulated elections, the legal responsibility of the treasurer varies according to state law. *See also* FEDERAL ELECTION CAMPAIGN ACTS, 180; FEDERAL ELECTION COMMISSION (FEC), 118.

*Significance* The campaign treasurer bears legal responsibility for the financial side of the campaign. For federal elections, the Federal Election Campaign Act of 1974 clearly points to the treasurer as the one campaign official responsible for complying with the reporting and record-keeping components of the act. Because of the complexity of the reporting and record-keeping requirements, most treasurers are accountants. Treasurers also frequently assist with fund-raising.

**Candidate** **(170)**

The person seeking election to office. The candidate, in most cases, is the most valuable resource available to the campaign. Only the candidate can perform some campaign activities, such as making personal appearances, participating in debates, holding press conferences. Other activities that might be carried out by others are more effectively done by the candidate. Examples would include persuading voters, particularly when meeting them in person, taping campaign advertising spots, encouraging volunteers and paid staff, and soliciting campaign contributions. In addition, some activities such as the development of campaign strategy and tactics and the management of the campaign require candidate participation and frequently get more than is necessary because of the candidate's interest. In campaigns for higher office, candidates cannot possibly do all these things, and some of the most important campaign decisions involve making the most effective use of the candidate's limited time—determining what must be done by the candidate and what can be taken care of by the campaign staff or volunteers. In some higher level campaigns, spouses, children, and other family members are used as surrogate candidates, meeting with voters and doing other things that the candidate does not have time for. In campaigns for local office, the candidate is sometimes the whole campaign and does just about everything. *See also* CAMPAIGN MANAGER, 162; CAMPAIGN PLAN, 164; CAMPAIGN STRUCTURE, 167.

*Significance* The candidate is at the core of the campaign; indeed, she or he is the reason the campaign exists. The candidate cannot be the whole campaign, however, except in small-scale local elections; even there, she or he is more likely to succeed by recruiting assistance and dividing the labor. Only the candidate can know what she or he stands for and why she or he is running for office. Others may know more about how to get the candidate elected, however, or how to manage the campaign, raise money, and so on. One of the most crucial tasks a campaign plan can do is to clarify candidate responsibilities and the responsibilities of others in the campaign. In most cases, a candidate is most effective contacting voters, contributors, volunteers, and others, while a campaign manager monitors overall implementation of the campaign plan.

**Celebrity Fund-Raising** **(171)**

The use of celebrities to assist a campaign in raising money. Celebrity fund-raising draws upon the name recognition and popularity of public figures to encourage people to contribute to a campaign. It is particularly effective because federal campaign finance laws limit the amount any individual can contribute to a campaign to $1,000 per election in races for Congress or the presidency. A wealthy supporter can contribute only $1,000 per election; a popular public figure, on the other hand, who can encourage thousands of people to contribute can raise thousands or hundreds of thousands of dollars. *See also* FEDERAL ELECTION CAMPAIGN ACTS, 180; FUND-RAISING, 182.

*Significance* Celebrity fund-raising has become a popular way of raising money and has led candidates to look for support among those who have celebrity status. The president of the United States has always been a good resource for such purposes. A fund-raising dinner attended by the president can raise $500 to a $1,000 per person from hundreds of people, sometimes grossing as much as $1 million. In the 1980s, the entertainment world has provided a number of celebrities who are willing to assist candidates in raising money. A rock star willing to do a concert can pack thousands of people at $25 a head into a stadium and raise $100,000 or more in a single evening, and the people attending need not support nor even be aware of the candidate for whom the money is being raised. Thus, for fund-raising purposes, the support of musicians, movie stars, sports figures, and the like, who can translate their popularity into mass contributions that total more than the $1,000 maximum contribution of wealthy individuals, is invaluable.

***City Council of Los Angeles v. Taxpayers for Vincent,* 466 U.S. 789 (1984)** **(172)**

Ruling that upheld a restriction on the posting of political campaign signs. Taxpayers for Vincent, supporters of a city council candidate, challenged a local ordinance that prohibited the posting of signs on public property, claiming that the restriction was a violation of their First Amendment expression rights. The Supreme Court said that, whereas the First Amendment forbids government from regulating in a manner that advances or restrains expression of particular viewpoints, the ordinance in this case was "content neutral." The Court recognized the restrictive effect the ordinance had on political expression but said that municipalities have a "weighty, essentially aesthetic interest in proscribing intrusive and unpleasant formats for expression." In other words, a city has authority to attempt to "improve its appearance." Further, the regulation was confined in scope. It limited expression only so far as was "necessary to accomplish its purpose of eliminating visual clutter." There were also "ample alternative modes of communication" available to Taxpayers for Vincent. Although they could not post campaign signs on public property, for example, the ordinance did not restrict their right to speak or distribute literature in the locations where sign posting was regulated. Finally, the Court considered and rejected the public forum argument. That public property can be used to communicate—such as posting signs on lampposts or utility poles (locations involved in this case)—does not mean the Constitution "requires such use to be permitted." Public property that is "not by tradition or designation a forum for public communication may be reserved by the government for its intended purposes." *See also* *ADDERLEY V. FLORIDA* (385 U.S. 39: 1966), 43; TIME, PLACE, AND MANNER RESTRICTIONS, 89.

*Significance* *City Council of Los Angeles v. Taxpayers for Vincent* (466 U.S. 789: 1984) made clear that political expression that is typically immune from regulation is not absolutely protected. Regulations of narrow scope may restrict the time, place, and manner in which expression may occur, but such regulations must meet certain conditions. They cannot target the expression itself but rather those elements associated with the expression, and the regulation must be content-neutral. The ban on campaign signs on public property could not have restricted, for example, only posters for the Vincent campaign. In addition, government must have a significant interest for imposing the regulation. Aesthetic concerns in *Vincent* were viewed by the Court as a sufficiently substantial interest to permit a restriction. Finally, the regulation must leave available alternative methods for communicating the information—an opportunity that was available to the Vincent campaign.

**Coattails** **(173)**

The ability of a strong candidate at the top of the party's ticket to gain votes for other party candidates. Coattails have most often been attributed to strong and popular presidential or gubernatorial candidates who are able to translate support for themselves into votes for other candidates of the party who are running for lower level offices. Franklin Roosevelt had strong coattails, particularly in 1932 and 1936, when his popularity helped to elect other Democrats across the country. Richard Nixon in 1972 and Jimmy Carter in 1976 had weak coattails. Even though both men were elected president, other candidates from their parties tended to run more strongly than they did.

Ronald Reagan had relatively strong coattails in 1980, but much weaker ones in 1984. *See also* HOUSE CAMPAIGN, 185; SENATE CAMPAIGN, 202; TICKET SPLITTING, 253.

*Significance* The importance of coattails has decreased since the 1960s because of two major developments: the rise of split-ticket voting, and the increased use of independent campaign operations by candidates, particularly those running for Congress. Even though Ronald Reagan won the 1984 presidential election with one of the biggest landslides in the history of the country, Democrats still maintained a substantial majority in the House of Representatives and held their own in Senate races. Reagan's electoral strength was not translatable into support for other Republican candidates. Voters have become quite willing to split their tickets—to vote, for example, for a Republican presidential candidate and for Democratic candidates for the House and Senate. Voters have been encouraged to split their tickets by independent House and Senate candidates, particularly incumbents, who develop extremely strong campaign organizations.

**Competitive District** **(174)**

An electoral district in which there exists a realistic chance for more than one of the candidates to win. A competitive district is one in which the campaign and the characteristics of the candidate can have an impact on who will win the election. A surprising number of elections take place in safe districts, where everyone knows who will win before the ballots are counted. Districts are competitive where party strength is relatively even and where no popular incumbent is running for reelection. Most states are competitive districts in that statewide races provide candidates from each party with a chance of winning. House of Representative districts and other districts within states are frequently less competitive. The percentage of the vote that the incumbent received in her or his last election is considered a practical guide to the competitiveness of the district. An incumbent who has received less than 60 percent in a two-person race in the last election is considered vulnerable, and the district would be viewed as competitive. Open-seat races—those in which no incumbent is running—are more likely to be competitive. *See also* INCUMBENCY ADVANTAGE, 186; OPEN-SEAT RACES, 192; SAFE DISTRICT, 200.

*Significance* The competitiveness of a district strongly affects the extent to which a candidate can get outside support, particularly financial support from political action committees (PACs). This provides incentive for incumbents to ensure that they win elections by large margins to prevent their districts from being viewed as competitive. A challenger seeking to run for office needs to realistically appraise the competitiveness of the district and, in order to be able to raise campaign support and other assistance, to develop a prospectus that demonstrates the feasibility of her or his winning. The reality is that the best possible candidate running with the best possible campaign cannot win certain elections because the district is safe for the incumbent or the opposing party.

**Congressional Campaign Committees** **(175)**

Party committees in the Senate and the House of Representatives that seek to assist candidates of their party in winning election to Congress. There are four congressional campaign committees: the Democratic Congressional Campaign Committee, which primarily helps Democratic candidates running for the House; the Democratic Senatorial Campaign Committee, which does the same for Democratic candidates running for the Senate; the National Republican Congressional Committee, which primarily helps Republican candidates for the House; and the National Republican Senatorial Committee, which does the same for Republican candidates for the Senate. The House Republicans were the first to create their own organization, doing so shortly after the Civil War because of their fear that President Andrew Johnson would use the Republican National Committee to his advantage in his battle with House Republicans. The House Democrats created their committee shortly thereafter. Senate committees appeared for both parties once the Seventeenth Amendment brought about direct election of senators. Currently, each committee is chaired by a representative or senator of the appropriate party and has a hired staff to carry out most of its activities. The committees raise money that is contributed directly to the campaigns of the candidates whom they are helping. The committees also assist campaigns by providing training and consulting support to make the campaigns as effective as possible. *See also* FUND-RAISING, 182; NATIONAL COMMITTEE, 227; POLITICAL CONSULTANTS, 196.

*Significance* The congressional campaign committees were relatively inactive until the late 1970s. Involved primarily in fund-raising, they contributed the limited funds that they raised almost exclusively to incumbents, the people least likely to need their assistance. In the late 1970s, the Republican campaign committees moved strongly in the direction of direct mail fund-raising, which proved to be successful. They used their funds not solely to contribute to incumbents but also to support challengers and to provide consulting assistance. During the 1980 election, the Republican committees contributed almost

$2.5 million directly to their candidates and spent another $6 million on their behalf, compared with the Democratic committees for the same election year, which contributed slightly over $1 million and spent on their candidates' behalf over $600,000. Since then, the party committees have worked hard to raise money and assist their candidates. The Republican committees still maintain a substantial advantage over the Democratic committees; however, all are now playing a significant role in the campaign process. The existence of the congressional campaign committees reflects a structural weakness of U.S. political parties at the national level. The parties' national committees generally confine themselves to presidential politics and seldom get involved with congressional campaigns, thus the congressional campaign committees fill a vacuum. Even with these committees, the principal campaign organizations for Senate and House candidacies are those established by the individual candidates.

**Demagoguery** **(176)**

The playing upon popular prejudices through the use of inflammatory, questionable, or inaccurate statements to gain the support of voters. Demagoguery is a frequent campaign tactic, particularly of less scrupulous candidates whose campaigns are not going well. The development of sophisticated polling techniques has increased the ability of a demagogue to know what voters are thinking and thus tailor her or his message to them. Candidates often accuse their opponents of demagoguery, whether true or not, as a way of attempting to discredit the opponent's message. *See also* CAMPAIGN POLLING, 165.

*Significance* Demagoguery is an easy but irresponsible way to gain voter support. It is easy because it allows a candidate to play upon popular prejudices and appeal to voters in terms of their biases. It is irresponsible because it reinforces already existing biases and makes it more difficult for other candidates to take responsible positions. For example, for most of the twentieth century, candidates in the South would demagogue on the issue of race, playing to the antiblack prejudices of most southern whites. It was virtually impossible for a candidate who was a moderate on the issue of race to get elected. This situation only began to change since the passage of civil rights legislation ensuring the right of southern blacks to vote.

**Direct Mail** **(177)**

A campaign technique that involves systematic use of the mail to contact large numbers of targeted voters. Direct mail can be used for fund-raising purposes, for trying to persuade voters to support the candidate, or for encouraging voters to vote at election time. Common to all of the above is the use of mail in a targeted way in order to achieve campaign objectives. Direct mail is an important means of getting a candidate's message to large numbers of people. It has become a more common campaign practice with the advent of the computer, particularly the small micro- or minicomputers, because large mailings can be handled efficiently and results can be easily tracked. Direct mail is also used by interest groups to recruit and communicate with members and to raise money. *See also* CAMPAIGN COMPUTERS, 159; FUND-RAISING, 182; GOTV (Get Out the Vote), 183; INTEREST GROUP, 293; VOTER CANVASS, 206.

*Significance* Direct mail fund-raising involves sending prospecting letters to lists of potential contributors who have been selected because there is some reason to believe that they are likely to contribute. A candidate or an interest group with a strong record on environmental protection, for example, might seek lists of environmentalists to mail to, whereas a conservative candidate or interest group might use lists of people who support conservative causes. A response rate of 2 to 3 percent of those contacted in a direct mail fund-raising effort is considered good. The expectation is that on a first mailing to such lists, the campaign will do well if it raises enough money to pay the costs of the mailing. The real money typically is raised after a "house list" of those who have contributed is developed and direct mail fund-raising letters asking for more money are again sent to these people. Such efforts are usually quite successful. Direct mail for purposes of persuading voters or encouraging them to vote on election day is usually done in connection with a voter canvass. The canvass, usually by phone, identifies undecided voters and voters likely to vote for the candidate. Undecided voters are sent information designed to persuade them; supporters are sent reminders just before the election that it is important that they vote.

**Door-to-Door** **(178)**

Localized voter contact that involves the candidate or campaign workers. Door-to-door literally involves going from one house to the next in a neighborhood to contact voters. Some candidates, particularly those running in geographically small districts, will go door-to-door, knocking on doors, introducing themselves, and asking for the support and vote of the people with whom they are talking. Another version is for supporters to go door-to-door in their neighborhood, passing out campaign brochures and urging their neighbors to support the candidate. *See also* LIT DROP, 187; VOTER CONTACT, 207.

*Significance* Door-to-door, when done by the candidate, can be a powerful tactic because it involves personal contact between candidate and voter. It is particularly valuable for candidates for local office or for some state legislative races because the district is small enough that a candidate can actually contact most of the voters in that district.

**Event Fund-Raising** **(179)**

The raising of campaign funds by holding events to which people are encouraged to buy a ticket or make a contribution in order to attend. Event fund-raising attempts to give people who make a contribution something in return: attendance at the event. Many different events and activities can be used to encourage contributions. Some of the more common are dinner parties, swim parties, dances, and roasts. One of the more successful fund-raising events is to bring in a well-known celebrity—the president, a movie star, or a famous musician—as an added enticement to people to attend and make contributions. *See also* CELEBRITY FUND-RAISING, 171; FUND-RAISING, 182.

*Significance* Event fund-raising can be a creative way of enhancing the campaign coffers. Volunteers can be encouraged to hold a variety of fund-raising parties at which people can come to have a good time while still providing funds for the campaign. One innovative version of the fund-raising event is to send invitations to a nonevent, indicating that the campaign is saving the person being invited the effort of having to go to the event; all she or he needs to do is send in a contribution. One possible liability, particularly for large and elaborate events, is that they can take considerable time, effort, and money to organize. The campaign must make sure the net profit from these events will be sufficient to justify such an investment.

**Federal Election Campaign Acts** **(180)**

Acts passed by Congress in 1971, 1974, 1976, and 1979 that provide the legal framework within which campaign financing occurs. The Federal Election Campaign Act of 1971 sought to limit campaign expenditures in presidential elections and provided for public disclosure of contributions of over $100. The law was not to be implemented until the 1976 election. The Federal Election Campaign Act of 1974 was to a great extent a response to the irregularities of Richard Nixon's 1972 campaign. It included ceilings on campaign expenditures for federal elections, public disclosure of campaign contributions, and partial public financing for the presidential nominating process; it also created the Federal Election Commission (FEC). In *Buckley v. Valeo* (424 U.S. 1: 1976), campaign spending ceilings and the process for appointing members to the Federal Election Commission were ruled unconstitutional, leading to the Federal Election Campaign Act of 1976, which amended the 1974 act, taking into consideration the consequence of *Buckley v. Valeo*. The Federal Election Campaign Act of 1979 provided additional amendments to simplify reporting requirements and changed the role that state and local parties could play in presidential elections.

The cumulative result of these acts is to regulate campaign financing for federal elections. Some of the key provisions include limits on campaign contributions, public disclosure of campaign contributions and expenditures, matching funds for presidential candidates before the nomination, federal financing of the general election campaign for major party candidates, limits on campaign expenditures for presidential candidates, and the creation of the Federal Election Commission to enforce the laws. Campaign contribution limits provide that individuals, in any single election, may not contribute more than $1,000 to any candidate, $20,000 to a national party committee, and $5,000 to other political committees and may not contribute more than $25,000 to all of the above in any single year. Political action committees (PACs) may not contribute more than $5,000 to any candidate, $15,000 to a national party committee, and $5,000 to other political committees. Disclosure requirements include reporting to the Federal Election Commission information about contributors and expenditures of $200 or more, which must be submitted on a regular basis, including just before election dates. Provision is also made for what are called independent campaign committees, which may raise and spend money in support of or in opposition to candidates so long as these activities are carried out independently and not coordinated with the campaign of any candidate. Such committees are also required to report to the FEC the same kinds of information required of campaigns.

The acts substantially changed the pattern of financing presidential elections by providing partial public financing to candidates who would agree to accept limits on their total campaign expenditures. The limits set for 1976 were $10 million before the nomination and $20 million for the general election, with cost-of-living increases provided for subsequent elections. National party committees were allowed to spend 2 cents per voting-age person on behalf of their candidate, and state and local parties could spend for such things as campaign buttons or brochures but not for advertising or staff. There are also limitations on expenditures in each state during the nomination process. These limitations apply only to candidates who accept partial public financing. Such candidates can qualify for public matching funds during the primary process by raising at least $5,000 in each of 20 states from contributions of $250 or less. Once qualified, candidates receive matching funds on a dollar-for-dollar basis for every contribution of $250 or less. In the general election, each major party's candidate is provided with the same amount of money and is not allowed to raise additional funds. In 1984, each candidate was allowed to spend $47.3 million. Finally, the Federal Election Campaign Act of 1974 created the FEC to give teeth to the law by actively enforcing it. *See also* BUCKLEY *V.* VALEO (424 U.S. 1: 1976), 157; CAMPAIGN COSTS, 160; FEDERAL ELECTION COMMISSION (FEC), 118; POLITICAL ACTION COMMITTEE (PAC), 319.

*Significance* The Federal Election Campaign Acts were intended to reform the process by which federal campaigns were financed. They sought to ensure that the public would be aware of the source and use of campaign funds; it has been very successful. Campaign reports to the FEC are regularly used by the media to report the financial activities of campaigns for Congress and the presidency. The acts also sought to limit campaign expenditures; in this area, they have had mixed success. In presidential elections, in which public financing was provided in exchange for the agreement to limit spending, they have been quite successful. In campaigns for Congress, in which spending limits were imposed without providing public financing, the limits were declared unconstitutional and subsequently campaign expenditures in House and Senate races have rapidly escalated. An unanticipated consequence of the acts has been the rapid growth of political action committees (PACs) and their increasingly influential role in financing campaigns for Congress, particularly those of incumbents. The acts have also influenced the pattern of campaigning for major-party presidential nominations, by placing great importance on meeting the qualifications for receiving matching funds.

**Free Media** **(181)**

Coverage of the candidate as a news event by the media. Free media coverage provides a powerful and inexpensive way of getting information about the candidate to the public. Coverage of the candidate on the evening news or on the front page of the local newspaper, assuming it is not negative, greatly assists the candidate in gaining voter recognition and conveying information to potential voters. Campaigns seek to communicate through news coverage the same campaign message that is part of their voter contact effort. Campaigns work hard to obtain free media, regularly sending news releases to newspapers and to radio and television stations and calling press conferences when the candidate has information the media would be interested in covering. The candidate's schedule is frequently designed to increase prospects of obtaining free media. Speeches or public appearances are scheduled at times when they are most likely to be covered by the news media. Most campaigns have press or media staff whose primary job is to ensure good, free media coverage. *See also*: CAMPAIGN MESSAGE, 163; ELECTION COVERAGE, 351; PRESIDENTIAL CAMPAIGNS, 197; PRESS CONFERENCE, 389.

*Significance* Free media coverage is essential to most campaigns, particularly higher level campaigns such as congressional, gubernatorial, senatorial, or presidential. Campaigns need free media as a way of supplementing the paid advertising and other techniques they use to get the candidate's message across to voters. As a result, the media can assume an influential role in determining election results. When the media decide whom they will or will not cover and what they will say about the candidates they do cover, they have a powerful impact on a candidate's chances for success. In races for the House of Representatives, for example, the media seldom give much coverage to anyone challenging an incumbent. This factor contributes to the overwhelming success of House incumbents seeking reelection. In the races for presidential nominations, the media tend to cover candidates who seem to be doing well in the polls during the early period. After the Iowa caucuses and the New Hampshire primary, they tend to cover candidates who have done well in one or both of those events. As a result, candidates must exert every effort to do well in the early events or they will be out of the race, not because they have lost electoral votes, but because they have lost media coverage.

**Fund-Raising (182)**

The effort to raise money necessary to finance campaign operations. Fund-raising is one of the central concerns of virtually all campaigns because without sufficient money, most of the activities of a campaign cannot be carried out. The Federal Election Campaign Act of 1974 provides the major legal framework within which fund-raising for Congress and the presidency occurs. Campaigns may receive up to $1,000 per election from each contributor and $5,000 per election from each political action committee (PAC). State laws regulate fund-raising for state and local offices. Campaigns use a variety of techniques for persuading individuals and organizations to make contributions, including personal solicitation by the candidate or by campaign officials or supporters, direct mail, and events. The most successful fund-raising efforts involve careful targeting of individuals or organizations that are likely to be supportive of the candidate. *See also* CELEBRITY FUND-RAISING, 171; DIRECT MAIL, 177; EVENT FUND-RAISING, 179; FEDERAL ELECTION CAMPAIGN ACTS, 180; POLITICAL ACTION COMMITTEE (PAC), 319.

*Significance* Fund-raising has always been important to campaigns, but since the mid-1970s it has become crucial because of the escalation of campaign costs. During 1986, the total expenditure of candidates for Congress was about $400 million, approximately four times the amount spent 10 years earlier for the 1976 congressional elections. In the California Senate race, each party's candidate spent over $11 million for a combined total of almost $23 million. Eighteen candidates for the House of Representatives spent over $1 million each, including one who spent $2.6 million. Campaign expenditures have increased in each election year since the Federal Election Commission (FEC) began keeping records in 1974. Increased campaign costs have elevated the importance of fund-raising for campaigns—to win an election, a substantial fund-raising effort is essential. Campaigns are devoting more of their resources to fund-raising, and candidates are spending more of their time raising money. Political action committees (PACs) have grown in prominence in this setting because of their easy availability as sources of campaign contributions.

**GOTV (Get Out the Vote)** **(183)**

The effort to ensure that voters who support the candidate actually vote. GOTV stands for "get out the vote" and includes a variety of techniques for turning out supporters or likely supporters on election day. The most sophisticated GOTV efforts are those tied to a voter canvass that identifies, among other things, voters who support the candidate. Voters in precincts that tend to vote overwhelmingly for the candidate's party can be added to this list. On the weekend before the election, likely supporters are contacted and reminded that the candidate needs their votes on election day. On election day, they are again contacted and reminded to vote. The campaign maintains poll watchers at each of the voting precincts who check off the names of supporters who have voted. At some point during the day, supporters who have not yet voted may be called again and urged to vote. Accompanying these elaborate contact procedures, campaigns frequently provide rides to the voting precinct and babysitting or other services that will make it possible for their supporters to get to the voting booth. Other less elaborate GOTV efforts may simply involve postcards sent to known supporters urging them to vote on election day or door-to-door contact on election day in precincts containing a high percentage of people likely to vote for the candidate. The thread uniting these efforts is the notion of encouraging a candidate's supporters to actually vote on election day. *See also* VOTER CANVASS, 206; VOTER TURNOUT, 208.

*Significance* GOTV (get out the vote) efforts can mean the difference between winning and losing for candidates in close elections. Only slightly more than 50 percent of those eligible to vote do so in presidential elections, less than 50 percent do so in congressional election years when a president is not being elected, and voter participation falls to less than 10 percent in many local elections. Under such conditions, the campaign that ensures that its supporters do indeed vote can win, even though the majority of people in the district support the opponent. Winning does not mean having the highest number of supporters in the district—it means having the highest number of voters in the district. In local elections where turnout is low, it is possible to link a successful voter canvass to a GOTV effort and virtually ensure victory. In some such elections, it may take only 1,000 votes to win; thus if 1,500 supporters can be called during GOTV efforts, success is virtually guaranteed.

**Gubernatorial Campaign** **(184)**

Campaign to be elected governor of one of the 50 states. Gubernatorial campaigns, because they help to determine who will hold the highest level state office, are viewed by candidates, the parties, the media, and voters as important elections. The office of governor is sufficiently meaningful to generate strong candidates and substantial campaign resources. Campaigns vary considerably from state to state because of the huge population differences and other considerable variations among states. In some states, governors are elected in even-numbered years, at the same time as elected federal officials. In many other states, governors are elected in odd-numbered years, years when there are no national elections. In general, campaign strategy and tactics in any state are similar to those of Senate campaigns conducted in the same state. Campaigns in the larger states approach presidential campaigns in terms of size and money and other resources available. Campaigns in the smaller states have fewer resources available but still attract considerable media interest because of the high level of the office. *See also* CANDIDATE ORIENTATION, 108; EVEN-NUMBERED ELECTION YEARS, 116; SENATE CAMPAIGN, 202.

*Significance* Gubernatorial campaigns are among the larger, more complex campaigns. They typically involve two strong opponents, each with the resources to conduct a vigorous campaign, thus ensuring that each candidate will be relatively well known by the day of the election. The vote for governor, therefore, is more likely to be based on candidate orientation than it is for lower level races in which the opposing candidates are less likely to be familiar to the voters.

**House Campaign** **(185)**

Campaign to be elected to the House of Representatives. House campaigns are important enough to include many of the more sophisticated campaign techniques of higher level campaigns, yet are still small enough to be more easily understood than the larger campaigns. The cost of congressional campaigns has risen dramatically since the mid-1970s, with some campaigns now spending over a million dollars and most campaigns in competitive races spending hundreds of thousands of dollars. Full-scale campaigns in competitive races include extensive fund-raising operations, use of political consultants, and media advertising, and they generally necessitate reasonably careful campaign planning. *See also* CAMPAIGN PLAN, 164; FUND-RAISING, 182; INCUMBENCY ADVANTAGE, 186; OPEN-SEAT RACES, 192; POLITICAL CONSULTANTS, 196; SAFE DISTRICT, 200.

*Significance* House campaigns have become more elaborate and expensive in recent years even as they have become less relevant to who wins most House races. At this level, incumbency advantage begins to be relevant. When House incumbents run for reelection, they win over 90 percent of the time. Most House districts are no longer competitive when the incumbent is running. Congressional campaigns become more competitive when there is no incumbent in the race—because the incumbency advantage has disappeared, these campaigns end up being the hardest fought and the most expensive.

**Incumbency Advantage** **(186)**

The advantage that incumbents have during campaigns by virtue of their already holding office. Incumbency advantage means that incumbents start most elections well liked and better known than their opponents. In elections for most offices, incumbents are able to maintain and build on this initial edge and thus are very likely to be reelected. Presidents have immediate access to the public through the media, so, within limits, they can shape the messages the public will receive about the job they are doing. Senators and representatives have innumerable ways of gaining or maintaining the support of their constituents—helping them with problems with the federal government, sending them information, finding money for district projects, and so on. Thus, because of the job they are doing, incumbents generally start an election with an advantage. Also, incumbents seeking reelection, regardless of party affiliation, have easier access to financial support than their challengers, especially in political action committee (PAC) contributions. Incumbents in the House of Representatives have been successful at maintaining this advantage—they have won in over 90 percent of reelection attempts since 1960. Senators, governors, and presidents have been less successful, although even at the higher level, incumbents are more likely to win than to lose. *See also* HOUSE CAMPAIGN, 185; LOCAL ELECTION CAMPAIGN, 188; TICKET SPLITTING, 253.

*Significance* Incumbency advantage is greatest in elections in which challengers are not able to become as well known as the incumbents and thus are unable to offer the voters a real choice. This situation most often occurs in elections for the House of Representatives and in state and local elections. In these lower level elections, challengers are typically not well known and have a difficult time developing the resources necessary to mount a truly effective campaign. Thus voters must choose between a known, experienced, and popular candidate (the incumbent) and an unknown quantity (the challenger). Under these circumstances, voters usually go with the incumbent. For higher level offices such as governor, senator, or president, the challenger is frequently as well known as the incumbent at the beginning of the campaign because these offices attract stronger challengers. In addition, these campaigns receive such high levels of publicity and have available so many resources for contacting the voter that by the time of the election, the voter is more likely to be in a position to choose between two relatively known candidates. Under these circumstances, the incumbent has less of an advantage.

**Lit Drop** **(187)**

The distribution of campaign literature to voters' houses. A lit drop is a relatively cheap way of getting part of the campaign's message to the voter. There are many ways of organizing lit drops, but the basic idea is that volunteers go from house to house (door-to-door), dropping off campaign brochures. In most cases, the literature is inserted inside the screen or storm door or placed in some other convenient location. It is illegal to use mailboxes for this purpose. A knock-on-door lit drop (knock-drop) is one in which the volunteer knocks on the door and advocates on behalf of the candidate with the resident in addition to handing out the literature. *See also* CAMPAIGN LITERATURE, 161;

CAMPAIGN MESSAGE, 163; DOOR-TO-DOOR, 178; LOCAL ELECTION CAMPAIGN, 188; VOTER CONTACT, 207.

*Significance* Lit drops are conducted by most campaigns but are most valuable for local campaigns. They provide an effective and inexpensive way of getting material about the candidate into the hands of voters. This is especially important for campaigns that lack the resources to convey their message through radio and television. One of the problems with the lit drop is that getting the materials to the house of the voter provides no guarantee that it will be read. Many people tend to throw out this type of material without bothering to do more than glance at the front page.

**Local Election Campaign** **(188)**

A campaign for election to a local office such as mayor, city council, school board, or county commissioner. Local election campaigns, with the exception of some large city mayoral elections, are conducted on a much smaller scale, using fewer campaign resources, than state and national campaigns. They are also frequently at-large and nonpartisan campaigns. *See also* AT-LARGE CAMPAIGN, 153; NONPARTISAN CAMPAIGN, 191.

*Significance* Local election campaigns may involve fewer resources, but their purposes are identical to other campaigns—that is, to most effectively secure and use available resources to attain their candidate's election. Campaigns at the local level that develop campaign plans and in other ways systematically seek to achieve campaign objectives are more likely to be successful than campaigns that are casually put together.

**Name-Recognition Devices** **(189)**

Various techniques for getting the candidate's name known. Principal name-recognition devices include billboards, bumper stickers, campaign buttons, and yard signs. Billboards are used to promote the candidate's name and a brief message, perhaps a campaign slogan. Bumper stickers, buttons, and yard signs seldom have space to include more than the candidate's name. Billboards, bumper stickers, and buttons may be used throughout the campaign. Yard signs are more likely to appear two to three weeks before election day. *See also* NONPARTISAN CAMPAIGN, 191; VOTER CONTACT, 207.

*Significance* Name-recognition devices are most effective in nonpartisan races, in which party identification is not available to give voters cues on how to vote. When a voter is not familiar with the candidates and cannot use party affiliation as a criterion for selection, simply recognizing a candidate's name may be enough to decide in favor of that candidate. Bumper stickers, buttons, and yard signs have an additional advantage that is valuable even in partisan races—they not only develop name recognition, they also demonstrate support for a candidate. They allow people to make a statement to their friends, neighbors, and acquaintances that they support the candidate, which can sometimes help to persuade others to also support the candidate. An additional advantage of bumper stickers and yard signs is that they tend to remain in place and continue to serve their purpose. Buttons are more likely to be worn on the day they are obtained and then put in a drawer, never to be seen again.

### Negative Campaigning (190)

Campaigning that focuses on painting a negative picture of the opponent. Negative campaigning became prominent in the later 1970s, particularly as challengers found that their only chance of election was to convince voters that there was something wrong with the incumbent. The initial response of incumbents was to ignore what their challengers were saying about them and to continue to focus on their own activities. It turned out that negative campaigning worked, however, and some incumbents who ignored the negatives that were being said about them found themselves no longer in office. As a result, incumbents began responding in kind. Negative statements about them led to negative statements by them or their campaign about the opponent. By the 1980s, many campaigns had degenerated to mudslinging efforts. *See also* VOTER TURNOUT, 208.

*Significance* Negative campaigning seems to work because it has helped a number of candidates get elected. No one seems to like it, a great many people disapprove of it, but because it works, there is always the temptation to use it. A major concern expressed about negative campaigning is that it turns voters off—voters become so disgusted with what the candidates are saying about one another that they decide they will not bother to vote. This reaction may provide a partial explanation of the decline in voter turnout since the mid-1970s.

### Nonpartisan Campaign (191)

A campaign for office in a nonpartisan election. Nonpartisan campaigns are similar to other campaigns except that party orientation does not play a role in determining how voters will behave. Candidates run against one another without the support of or identification with political parties. Candidate orientation becomes even more important than in partisan elections, and campaigns must strive to get their candidates known and supported by voters. Heavy emphasis is placed on developing name recognition for the candidate. *See also* CANDIDATE ORIENTATION, 108; NAME-RECOGNITION DEVICES, 189; NONPARTISAN ELECTION, 128; PARTY IDENTIFICATION, 133.

*Significance* Nonpartisan campaigns are more heavily focused on the candidate than partisan campaigns because knowledge of the candidate or at least recognition of the candidate's name provides the only cue for voting. Nonpartisan campaigns occur only in local elections or judicial elections in which it is difficult to generate abundant campaign resources. Candidates who are well known to begin with are likely to maintain that status and thus receive the most votes; thus incumbents running for reelection are very successful. Candidates who have access to substantial campaign resources are also likely to do well. The most common sources of such campaign funding are the candidate's personal wealth or contributions from friends.

**Open-Seat Races (192)**

Elections in which no incumbent is running for office. Open-seat races tend to be the most hotly contested races because with no one having an incumbency advantage, more candidates are likely to believe they have a good chance of winning. If the district is safe for one party, the fiercest competition will take place in that party's primary. If the district is competitive, both the primaries and the general election are likely to be hotly contested. *See also* COMPETITIVE DISTRICT, 174; SAFE DISTRICT, 200.

*Significance* Open-seat races, because they are more competitive, generally attract more campaign contributions and require more elaborate campaign efforts for success. The 1986 congressional elections are representative of the general pattern. The average expenditure for House candidates in open-seat races was $437,000 compared with an average of $334,000 for incumbents and $125,000 for challengers. For Senate candidates in open-seat races, the average expenditure was $3.34 million, compared with an average of $3.30 million for incumbents and $1.74 million for challengers. Candidates in open-seat races spent more, on average, than incumbents—although it was close for Senate campaigns—and far more than challengers facing incumbents.

**Paid Media** **(193)**

The purchase of advertising to help influence the behavior of voters. Paid media include a variety of advertising such as television, radio, newspaper, and billboards. Television and radio provide the most effective advertising for candidates, but each has its advantages and disadvantages. Television advertising is most effective in conveying messages to voters to persuade them to support a candidate, but it is very expensive. It is not uncommon for successful congressional campaigns to spend over $100,000 on television advertising. Presidential campaigns spend millions of dollars on television advertising. Radio, although not quite as powerful as television, is considerably cheaper and can be targeted to much narrower audiences than can television. Most other campaign advertising is much less effective except in local election campaigns. *See also* BROADCAST MEDIA, 339; FREE MEDIA, 181; MASS MEDIA, 368; PRINT MEDIA, 392.

*Significance* Paid media usage has increased greatly in importance since the mid-1970s, corresponding to the increase in importance of electronic media. In previous eras, print advertising was used to supplement the personal contact of candidates and the free media coverage they received. Today, at least for the higher level races, paid media is the major device for getting the campaign's message to the voter. As election day approaches in even-numbered years, it is impossible to watch television without seeing numerous 30-second spots touting the merits of various candidates.

**Paid Staff** **(194)**

People working for the campaign who receive a salary. Paid staff constitute the core of a campaign, the people who will be on the job day after day, night after night. The number of staff that a campaign can hire will depend on the campaign's financial resources. The campaign manager is frequently the first person to be hired and, in a small campaign, may be the only person hired. The manager, if hired early, can participate in drawing up the campaign plan and be responsible for hiring other staff. Other possible paid positions include canvass coordinator, scheduler, field operations coordinator, volunteer coordinator, and office manager, depending on the resources available. Presidential campaigns make the most extensive use of paid staff, including the use of a large number of regional field staff who coordinate the activity of volunteers and party regulars on behalf of their presidential candidate. *See also* CAMPAIGN MANAGER, 162; CAMPAIGN STRUCTURE, 167.

*Significance* Paid staff provide a campaign with professionalism and increased certainty of accomplishing tasks. They compose a core around which the campaign can be built. Almost any campaign job can be done by paid staff or by volunteers. The difference is that paid staff can put in more time and are more reliable. The ideal situation is to have lots of volunteers and a sufficient number of paid staff to make effective use of the volunteers. Because of the value of paid staff, campaigns since 1970 have made more extensive use of them, which in part has contributed to the rise in campaign costs.

**Persuasion** **(195)**

The effort to convince voters to support a candidate. Persuasion is the focus of most voter contact programs. Persuasion efforts most often concentrate on undecided voters or on weak supporters of the candidate (to reinforce support) and of the opponent (to change support). The most persuadable voters are identified through polling and targeting and become the focus of radio and television advertising, campaign literature, direct mail, and other techniques designed to convince them to support the candidate. *See also* CAMPAIGN MESSAGE, 163; CAMPAIGN PLAN, 164; PAID MEDIA, 193; TARGETING, 204; VOTER CONTACT, 207.

*Significance* Persuasion is targeted to limited groups. Not everyone can be persuaded to support a candidate, nor need everyone be. Although most people tend to think of campaigns as trying to persuade everyone to support their candidate, the reality is quite different. Part of the campaign plan involves identifying how many votes the candidate will need to win, and how many and which voters, defined by various groupings, need to be persuaded. The reality is that limits exist to what persuasion can achieve. It is seldom possible for a campaign to persuade supporters of the opposing candidate that they should switch candidates, and only campaigns desperate for votes are apt to try.

**Political Consultants** **(196)**

Campaign professionals who are available for a fee to provide advice and/or services to candidates and campaigns. Political consultants can assist with polling, media development, fund-raising, targeting, campaign management, or any of the other activities necessary for a campaign. Some are specialists, dealing only with a relatively limited area of campaigning; others will provide all-purpose, general assistance to campaigns. Most consultants are identified with either the Republican or the Democratic party and tend to do work primarily for candidates of the party with which they are identified. *See also* CAMPAIGN POLLING, 165; FUND-RAISING, 182; PAID MEDIA, 193; TARGETING, 204.

*Significance* Use of political consultants is a relatively new phenomenon, emerging in the 1960s and vastly expanding in the 1970s. Consultants perform many of the tasks that were previously performed by political parties but do so on a more professional basis. They are the experts, the professionals, the "hired guns" of election politics; they do make a difference. A professionally conducted campaign considerably improves a candidate's prospects for winning, and political consultants contribute substantially to the professionalism of a campaign. Presidential campaigns employ large numbers of consultants, many on a full-time basis. Gubernatorial, House, and Senate campaigns make extensive use of consultants, whereas lower level races, referendum campaigns, and others only occasionally draw on their services. The rise of political consultants has significantly contributed to the vastly increased costs of campaigns. Not only are consultants themselves expensive but the techniques they bring to election politics, particularly their emphasis on paid media, cost a lot of money. Some feel consultants have become so prevalent that elections are being turned into the equivalent of chess games between them.

**Presidential Campaign (197)**

A campaign to be elected president of the United States. Presidential campaigns include quite different stages: (1) the campaign to secure the nomination of the candidate's party, or the nomination campaign; and (2) the campaign to defeat the nominee of the opposing party, or the general election campaign. The goal of the nomination campaign is to secure the support of a majority of the delegates attending the party's nominating convention held the summer before the general election. Each state is allocated a number of delegates to that convention based on formulas determined by the national parties. Each state party, within the framework of state law and national party rules, determines its own process and its own date for selecting these delegates. In addition, the national party can provide for the selection of delegates from party leadership positions or elected offices. Campaigns must compete for these delegates in 50 separate states under 50 different sets of rules over about a five-month time period that normally begins sometime in February and runs through early June of the election year. Campaign plans must include a strategy for emerging from this morass of separate state arrangements with the support of a majority of the delegates. States hold either state caucuses or presidential primary elections to select their delegates; campaign plans would indicate in which and how many of the primaries and caucuses the candidate will commit campaign resources. Historically, the first selection of delegates occurs in the Iowa caucuses, followed shortly by the New Hampshire primary. Campaigns normally put extensive resources into these two states because doing well in the early stages tends to draw extensive free media coverage and to attract supporters and contributors from other parts of the country. As the selection process moves from state to state, candidates who have not done well tend to drop out of the race. Especially since 1980, by the time of the last primary, one candidate has emerged from each party with sufficient delegate support to win his party's nomination on the first ballot of the summer convention. If no candidate has emerged, campaigns continue through the convention, seeking to gain support from the delegates and working until at last one candidate receives a majority of the delegate votes.

Once each party selects its presidential nominee, the second stage of the campaign begins. In the general election, the campaign goal is to win a majority of the electoral votes. Each state has a number of electoral votes equal to the number of its members of Congress (House and Senate), and the District of Columbia has three electoral votes. A candidate wins the electoral votes of a state by winning the popular vote in that state. Party nominees usually use the latter part of the summer, after the national conventions, to recover from the hardships of their previous campaigning and to plan for the general election. The general election is relatively brief, beginning in earnest around Labor Day and running through election day on the first Tuesday after the first Monday in November. Many different activities must be carried out in a short period of time. Basic functions that need to be performed include development (and, in some cases, modification) of the campaign message, scheduling, press relations, research and speech writing, advance work, polling, paid advertising, financial arrangements, and maintaining relations with target groups. Since 1980, campaigns have typically included a campaign director, responsible directly to the candidate, who tries to see that everything gets accomplished and who serves as a liaison to the party and other important target groups. Under the campaign director is the campaign manager, who is responsible for the day-to-day running of the campaign, and under him or her is the field coordinator, who is responsible for supervising regional directors and the heads of special operations. *See also* CAMPAIGN PLAN, 164; CAUCUS, 209; NATIONAL CONVENTION, 228; PRESIDENTIAL ELECTION, 136; PRESIDENTIAL NOMINATION, 138; PRESIDENTIAL PRIMARY, 139; PRIMARY CAMPAIGN, 198.

*Significance* Presidential campaigns have become extremely long and drawn-out affairs, primarily because of the length of the nominating process. Candidates start flocking to Iowa (the first caucus state) and New Hampshire (the first primary state) as much as two years before the final election, and each election year, candidate activities seem to begin a little earlier. The process has been criticized because it makes Iowa and New Hampshire much too critical in the selection process. Candidates must do well in the Iowa caucuses and/or the New Hampshire primary to have much of a chance of winning the nomination, but these states are small and not representative of the country as a whole. Even so, since 1976, most presidential nominees have won the New Hampshire primary. Candidates who do less well than expected in Iowa and New Hampshire may find themselves out of the race even before most of the delegates have been selected. Because these states are so small, campaigns end up focusing on personal contact between the candidate and the voters; issues are frequently ignored. Candidates who are able to spend large blocks of time in the early deciding states and who are effective in personalized campaigning are the most likely to do well, even though they may not make the best presidents. The campaign shifts dramatically once the party nominees have been selected and the general election begins. Television has become the most powerful medium for conveying campaign messages to voters, so campaigns tend to concentrate on creating an effective media image for their candidates. Scheduling is designed to ensure that the candidate will get good coverage on the evening news. Most campaign resources go into the development and airing of television commercials, usually 30-second spots designed to persuade the voter. The focus tends to be on the candidate: What he looks like, how he handles himself, how effective he is in front of the television camera—not on what the candidate represents in regard to public policy.

**Primary Campaign** **(198)**

A campaign to win a party's nomination for an upcoming general election. Primary campaigns are directed toward a more limited range of voters because candidates are trying to convince voters who identify with their party to vote for them. A primary campaign resembles a nonpartisan campaign in that party identification provides no cues on whom to vote for. The campaign message must be one that will appeal to the party's supporters. Candidates in Democratic primary elections will need to gain votes from a population that is on the whole more liberal than the overall population. Candidates in Republican primaries face the opposite situation; their primary voters are more likely to be conservative. *See also* NONPARTISAN CAMPAIGN, 191; OPEN-SEAT RACES, 192; PRESIDENTIAL PRIMARY, 139; PRIMARY ELECTION, 140.

*Significance* Primary campaigns are not common because most primary elections are uncontested. Notable exceptions—cases in which primary elections are likely to be contested and campaigns necessary—are presidential primaries and open-seat elections. Primary campaigns create potential problems for the party and for their winners. One danger is crafting a campaign message that appeals to voters of the candidate's party but is too liberal or too conservative for voters in the general election. Another danger is that primary opponents will say such damaging things about one another that regardless of who wins the primary, victory in the general election will be more difficult.

**Registration** **(199)**

The establishment by individuals of their eligibility to vote. Registration involves providing voting officials, usually city or county clerks, with personal information such as name and address, and then being enrolled on an official list of registered voters. Registration must take place within a specified time period in advance of election day for an individual to be entitled to vote. *See also* STRUCTURAL BARRIERS TO PARTICIPATION, 87.

*Significance* Registration is a legal requirement in the United States. That voters must register in advance of election day decreases voter turnout because by the time of greatest interest in an election, it is already too late to register. Approximately 35 percent of the voting-age population are not eligible to vote because they have not registered. If a campaign can identify unregistered voters who would be likely to vote for its candidate, it can conduct a registration drive to get these people registered, thus increasing the number of potential voters for the candidate.

**Safe District** **(200)**

A district in which only one candidate or one party has a realistic chance of winning an election. Safe districts are those in which the incumbent is so strong that no one has a chance of defeating him or her, or in which one of the two parties is so dominant that only a candidate of that party can win. In the former case, the district is safe for the incumbent; in the latter, it is safe for the party. There are a surprising number of safe election districts scattered throughout the United States. *See also* COMPETITIVE DISTRICT, 174.

*Significance* Safe districts provide little opportunity for campaigns to have an impact on election results. In safe districts the results of the election are predictable before it takes place. Safe districts were common for the Democratic party in the South from the time of the Civil War until the late 1970s. The only campaigns of any significance were primary campaigns to determine who would win the Democratic party's nomination. House of Representative districts have become increasingly safe for incumbents since the 1960s because incumbents have made use of the advantages they have in communicating with and providing services for their constituents, thereby making those constituents reluctant to vote against them.

**Scheduler** **(201)**

The person responsible for putting together the candidate's schedule. The scheduler works closely with the campaign manager to ensure that the candidate's time is being used most effectively to meet campaign objectives. During a campaign, candidates are invited to attend a great variety of events, from debates with an opponent to high school football games. In addition, the campaign plan identifies target groups or targeted areas that require the attention of the candidate. In the latter cases, the campaign must initiate contact and make arrangements for a candidate's appearance. Handling these arrangements is the job of the scheduler. She or he initiates contacts where required, responds to invitations when they occur, and, in conjunction with the campaign manager, makes decisions about where the candidate will appear each day. *See also* CAMPAIGN MANAGER, 162; CAMPAIGN PLAN, 164; CANDIDATE, 170; TARGET GROUPS, 203.

*Significance* The scheduler plays an important role in deciding how the most valuable resource of the campaign, the candidate, will be used. Because the candidate's time is so valuable and so limited, a scheduler who is able to save time for the candidate by making the most efficient travel arrangements, by linking appearances in the same area or region, by clearly indicating what will be expected of the candidate in each appearance and in any other way is a tremendous asset to the campaign.

**Senate Campaign** **(202)**

Campaign for election to the office of United States senator. A senate campaign is a statewide campaign for one of the most coveted political offices in the country. Senate campaigns tend to be highly visible campaigns involving strong, well-known opponents. Because of their visibility and the strength of the candidates, Senate campaigns have access to much greater resources than most other campaigns. The average campaign expenditure for Senate campaigns in 1986 was $2.6 million; included as part of that average were campaigns in some very small states. Political consultants play a prominent role in Senate campaigns because the campaigns can afford to hire them. Because the campaign organizations are necessarily larger and more complex, professionals are needed to manage them. *See also* CAMPAIGN MESSAGE, 163; CANDIDATE ORIENTATION, 108; INCUMBENCY ADVANTAGE, 186; PARTY IDENTIFICATION, 133.

*Significance* Senate campaigns play a substantial role in determining who will be elected to the Senate. Incumbent senators are more likely to face serious opposition and are more frequently defeated than their House counterparts. This fact is attributable in part to the attractiveness of the office of senator, which draws stronger candidates, and in part to the greater visibility of the campaigns, which ensures that by the time of the election, voters will be able to choose between two well-known candidates. Because the challengers are strong, they have the capacity to attract campaign resources and to mount serious challenges to the incumbent. Incumbents raise large amounts of money to protect their seats. Thus the campaigns become more expensive as each candidate tries to effectively get her or his campaign message across to voters. In campaigns in which each candidate becomes relatively known to voters, the importance of party identification decreases and candidate orientation becomes more important. Incumbency advantage also tends to decrease.

**Target Groups** **(203)**

Groups that have been identified by a campaign as likely to be supportive or helpful. Target groups may be identified for a variety of purposes such as for fund-raising, for recruiting volunteers, for supporting the candidate, or for persuasive efforts. Democratic and Republican campaigns usually identify different target groups. Democratic candidates tend to focus on labor organizations, liberals, ethnic groups (particularly black and Jewish), and middle- to low-income individuals. Republican candidates tend to focus on business groups, conservatives, suburban areas, and upper-income individuals. *See also* DEMOCRATIC PARTY, 212; REPUBLICAN PARTY, 241; TARGETING, 204.

*Significance* Target groups are selected by campaigns so as to concentrate campaign resources where they will best meet the campaign's objectives. When a campaign is trying to raise money or recruit volunteers, it is easier and more efficient for it to work with groups that have traditionally supported the candidate or the candidate's party than to appeal to the general public. The campaign plan normally identifies target groups and indicates how the campaign needs to work with each.

**Targeting** **(204)**

The selection of specific groups or individuals as a focus for campaign activity. Targeting takes place in many different ways in a campaign—targeting the most likely prospects for campaign contributions, targeting potential volunteers, targeting undecided voters, and so on. The most extensive use of targeting occurs toward voters. When targeting voters, campaigns seek to distinguish three types, each to be treated differently. Voters who are identified as reasonably strong supporters of the opponent are ignored—the campaign wants nothing further to do with them. Voters who are identified as undecided or as weak supporters of either candidate become the target of various voter contact programs designed to persuade them to support the candidate. Voters who are identified as supporters become the target of the get out the vote (GOTV) program.

Targeting voters takes place at three different levels using three separate techniques: polling, precinct analysis, and voter canvass. Polling is done at the district level and identifies targets by social and economic characteristics such as age, income, religion, and occupation and by region. Precinct analysis takes place at the precinct level; it makes use of results from previous elections to estimate for each precinct the number of persuadable voters and the number of voters who are supporters but unlikely to vote unless strongly encouraged by the campaign. A voter canvass focuses on the individual; it identifies by name, address, and phone number voters who are persuadable or who are supporters. *See also* CAMPAIGN POLLING, 165; GOTV (Get Out the Vote), 183; PERSUASION, 195; PRECINCT, 185; TARGET GROUPS, 203; VOTER CANVASS, 206.

*Significance* Targeting allows a campaign to use its resources most effectively by directing them toward the people most likely to be influenced by the campaign. In any election, most people know how they are going to vote before the campaign begins, and there is little that a campaign can do to change their minds. In competitive districts, the people in the middle—the undecided or uncertain—will determine by their votes who will ultimately win the election. The campaign that can recognize them, discover the problems that concern them, and identify how they feel about the issues can develop a campaign message most likely to appeal to them. This campaign can also target ways that the message is delivered by advertising on radio stations these voters are likely to listen to or by placing television advertising on programs they are likely to watch.

**Volunteers** **(205)**

People who contribute their time and energy to work for a candidate and a campaign. Volunteers make up the unpaid army of workers who are so necessary for carrying out most of the work in campaigns. Volunteers can help raise money, contact voters, address envelopes, chauffeur the candidate, distribute campaign literature, or do virtually any other task required by the campaign. Because they are so important to a campaign, volunteer recruitment and the effective organization, use, and treatment of volunteers play an important role in most campaigns. Larger campaigns commonly assign one or more paid staff members the responsibility for recruitment and care of volunteers. *See also* CAMPAIGN RESOURCES, 166.

*Significance* Volunteers are essential to campaigns. Few campaigns can afford to hire staff to perform all, or even most, of the tasks that need to be performed. Volunteers provide most of the labor for campaigns, thus the care and feeding of volunteers is important. The volunteer who is warmly greeted at the campaign office, who is given something to do, and who is made to feel comfortable and a part of the organization will probably come back and do more work and may even recruit friends as additional volunteers. The volunteer who is ignored, who is not given things to do, or who is made to feel uncomfortable is not likely to return and may even tell friends and acquaintances about how ineffective the campaign is.

**Voter Canvass** **(206)**

Campaign program designed to identify how voters stand in relation to the candidate. A voter canvass contacts voters to determine whether they support the candidate or his or her opponent or whether they are undecided. The voter canvass is always part of a broader voter contact program and serves as a powerful means of targeting voters. It can be done by telephone or in person on a door-to-door basis. The most systematic and efficient canvass uses the telephone to contact lists of registered voters. Volunteers call the registered voters, identify themselves as workers for the candidate, and ask if the candidate can count on the voters' support on election day. Frequently, voters are also asked to identify their party and what they think are the most important issues in the campaign. Workers are urged to call as many people as possible by getting the information quickly and moving on to the next call. The information can then be used for voter contact. People who said they support the opponent are ignored; people identified as undecided are contacted again, usually through a personally addressed letter from the candidate that includes a statement about issues they considered important; people who said they support the candidate are placed in the get out the vote (GOTV) file for further contact shortly before election day to remind them to vote. *See also* GOTV (Get Out the Vote), 183; TARGETING, 204; VOTER CONTACT, 207.

*Significance* A voter canvass is the most powerful campaign technique for targeting voters because it identifies the position of each voter. A canvass is useless, however, unless it is linked to a systematic voter contact program that takes advantage of the targeted information provided by the canvass. Therefore, careful campaign planning is essential if a canvass is to be used. The campaign must have the resources, both financial and human, not only to complete the canvass but to make effective use of the results in the overall voter contact and get out the vote (GOTV) programs.

**Voter Contact** **(207)**

A program designed to convey the campaign message to the voter. Voter contact can include personal contact by the candidate, literature distribution, telephone contact, mail, radio and television advertising, billboards, and other activities whose purpose is to influence voter behavior. The most effective voter contact is part of an overall plan that includes targeting, designing an appropriate campaign message or messages, and systematic and repeated contact with the targeted voters. Such programs may include a mix of contact techniques, although larger campaigns for statewide offices and for the presidency place heavy emphasis on television advertising, particularly for purposes of persuading undecided voters. Local campaigns tend to use radio advertising, literature distribution, and phone and mail contact. *See also* CAMPAIGN LITERATURE, 161; CAMPAIGN MESSAGE, 163; CANDIDATE, 170; PAID MEDIA, 193; TARGETING, 204.

*Significance* Voter contact is what a campaign is all about: the attempt to make contact with and influence voters. All other aspects of a campaign are designed to increase the effectiveness of voter contact programs. Fund-raising and the acquisition of other campaign resources make possible expanded voter contact. The development of the campaign message is for the purpose of influencing voters through voter contact programs. Targeting increases the effectiveness of voter contact programs by getting campaign messages to the people they are most likely to influence. The most effective voter contact occurs when the candidate meets personally with voters, but because only a small percentage of voters can be reached in this way, campaigns devise additional methods of contacting and influencing voters.

**Voter Turnout** **(208)**

The percentage of people eligible to vote in an election who actually do. Voter turnout is seldom over 60 percent in elections in the United States, which makes this country one of the lowest in voter turnout among democracies throughout the world. Turnout is highest for presidential elections, currently somewhat over 50 percent; turnout for off-year elections, usually slightly below 50 percent, is next. In some local elections, such as those for school board or city council, turnout frequently drops below 10 percent. Even in presidential elections, there is considerable variation in turnout from state to state and within states from precinct to precinct. *See also* GOTV (Get Out the Vote), 183; POLITICAL ALIENATION, 25; POLITICAL EFFICACY, 28; SUPPORTS, 36.

*Significance* Voter turnout in the United States is affected by a variety of factors; the most important is socioeconomic status (SES). The higher the SES of an individual, the more likely that person is to vote. Support for the political system and a strong sense of political efficacy increase the likelihood a person will vote, whereas political alienation reduces it. Get Out the Vote (GOTV) programs are a crucial part of many campaigns. By targeting supporters who are unlikely to vote (lower SES, less political efficacy, more alienation) and ensuring that they do indeed vote, campaigns can substantially increase the vote for their candidate.

# 5. *Political Parties*

Political parties are something of a paradox in the U.S. political system. They are regarded by some people as essential and by others as detrimental to democratic processes. A political party is an aggregation of people who formally organize themselves to pursue common political objectives. Although these objectives may vary, foremost among them is electing party members to public office. In several ways, parties provide a linkage between the public and governmental structures, but capturing office is the most effective way of translating political beliefs into public policy.

Contemporary political parties did not exist at the time the U.S. Constitution was ratified. Indeed, many of the individuals who were instrumental in the framing of the Constitution were suspicious of parties. James Madison, for example, saw danger in the potentially divisive influence of ongoing factions. At the same time, the constitutional framers created an environment in which political parties were virtually certain to develop. By requiring the election, at least indirectly, of officials governing at the national level, the framers established the need for a means of public participation in such elections. The political party served this need. The origin of this country's first parties is tied to the question of whether or not the United States needed a new constitution. Those who wished to revise (or scrap) the current governmental structure provided under the Articles of Confederation in favor of a strengthened central government were called Federalists. Following ratification of the Constitution, the Federalists, who focused on advancement of the economic views of Alexander Hamilton, emerged as the first political party in the United States. The Democratic-Republicans, led by Thomas Jefferson, developed about the same time as an opposing faction to the Federalists. The dynamics of partisan conflict were thus set in motion almost immediately after the ratification of the Constitution.

Political parties perform several important functions in the U.S. political system. First, parties formally nominate candidates for public office. The party acts as a recruiting mechanism to ensure that there are candidates to contest for public office. When candidates are numerous, the party acts as a screening agent for the general public. Through the mechanisms of the party, primary elections and nominating conventions are conducted. Second, parties focus voter options. Because elections are usually contested only by nominees of the major parties, voters need seriously consider only a relative handful of candidates. Parties thus allow citizens, many of whom have only limited interest in politics, to participate in elections on a fairly rational basis. Third, parties offer voters some basic philosophical and policy options. Even if citizens are generally unfamiliar with specific candidates or campaigns, the party label provides a handy point of reference. In this way, parties allow voters to indicate broad policy preferences by voting for a party's chosen candidates. Finally, parties facilitate the coordination of public policymaking. Parties permit public officials, structurally separated by constitutional provisions, to fashion coherent policy using shared partisan principles as the basic coordinating element. These common principles are typically contained in the parties' platforms (statements of programs and policy preferences formally adopted at party conventions).

The United States has a two-party system. Although there are more than two party organizations, the winner of virtually all elections for public office will be the candidate of either the Democratic or the Republican party. A number of factors may help explain the two-party system, but the most important reason is the U.S. winner-take-all method of election. Americans elect people to office who obtain a majority of votes (sometimes only a plurality) in an election—there is only one winner. The winner-takes-all approach creates compelling incentives for people to vote for the candidate of one of the two major parties because minor party candidates have virtually no chance of winning. The United States also elects members of its legislative bodies from single-member districts rather than by proportional reflection of party performance in an election. Again, minor parties are not competitive, and voters are inevitably drawn toward one of the two major parties. Accordingly, the two major parties each attempt to create as broad a base as possible in order to attract the largest and most diverse support they can. The two major parties, therefore, are not likely to define their position in narrow ideological terms because to do so would hamper their coalition-building need. Although third parties exist, they typically have a narrow ideological focus, position themselves around a single issue, or become the medium for the candidacy of a particular individual. If these parties grow to represent a large enough group of people, their positions are absorbed by either or both the major parties as part of their ongoing process of coalition realignment. Thus third political parties seem to be either short-lived or of limited impact.

An additional characteristic of the U.S. party system is its highly decentralized structure. The U.S. federal system is largely responsible for this decentralization. Under this system, authority to administer elections is lodged with the states. Candidate selection for offices elected at the state and local levels is conducted by the party organization in place at those levels. The influence of the national party organization on these processes is minimal. Even candidates for the United States Senate and United States House are nominated at the state or district level, which seriously erodes prospects for a disciplined legislative party.

Although the state- and local-level parties have been primary historically, both major parties have attempted to increase the organizational impact of the national party since the mid-1970s.

Notwithstanding the central role of political parties throughout U.S. political history, there is evidence to suggest that the influence of parties is in decline. Polls since the 1970s have consistently reflected that voter identification with parties has weakened, as has the strength of party loyalty for those retaining identification. The measured increase in the level of ticket splitting is a clear manifestation of this diminishing party identification. In addition, some of the traditional campaign functions of parties have been displaced by interest groups and the media, which has prompted parties to engage in certain reforms and redefinition of roles. Both major parties seem engaged in serious self-examination and some transformation of role. Although there will be a role for parties in the political future of the United States, its precise characteristics are unclear.

**Caucus** **(209)**

A gathering of party members for the purpose of selecting party candidates. A caucus may also be used by party members in a legislative body to select leadership and fashion a consensus partisan position on pending legislative business. The congressional caucus was the principal means of nomination early in U.S. history. The Democrats, for example, used a caucus of congressional members to designate the party's presidential nominee. The caucus approach was discarded at the time of Andrew Jackson and replaced by the convention. Subsequent political reforms led to the extensive use of the direct primary as the most representative and democratic approach to candidate nomination, but the caucus has remained a key means for making party decisions. *See also* NATIONAL CONVENTION, 228; NOMINATION, 229; PRESIDENTIAL NOMINATION, 138; PRIMARY ELECTION, 140.

*Significance* Many people were critical of the caucus because it could be secretive, closed, and unrepresentative. In addition to its use by the legislative party, the caucus has once again become a frequently used means of delegate selection for national nominating conventions. The rules governing current presidential-candidate selection caucuses eliminate some of the defects of the earlier caucuses. Presidential caucuses resemble primaries in that any party-registered person may participate. On caucus day, people gather at designated locations and indicate their preference for their party's presidential candidate. Delegates to the nominating conventions are then allocated on the basis of proportion of caucus-participant support. Since 1976, the process of candidate selection has begun with the Iowa caucuses. Presidential hopefuls spend inordinate amounts of resources seeking the support of those who will participate in the caucuses. Although not decisive, the results of the Iowa caucuses tend to establish the serious contenders and often define, at least for the short run, the extent to which candidates will receive media coverage and experience success in raising campaign funds.

**Credentials Committee (210)**

A committee that determines which delegates may be officially seated at a political party's convention. The credentials committee of each party prepares a list of the party's delegates with satisfactory credentials to be seated. Since the 1970s, the parties have accepted their committees' recommended list of delegates without controversy. There have been notable disputes, however, at several national conventions. Challenges to particular state delegations have typically occurred when a serious contest for the nomination exists. The issue in these challenges is not so much who the properly selected delegates are but rather which candidate's bid for the nomination will be furthered. Ultimately, recommendations of the credentials committee are voted on by the convention but may also serve as an early test of strength among or between candidates vying for the nomination. *See also* *DEMOCRATIC PARTY V. LAFOLLETTE* (450 U.S. 107: 1981), 213; NATIONAL CONVENTION, 228.

*Significance* The role of the credentials committee tends to be mechanical at most conventions, but there have been instances in which its recommendations have been pivotal in the ultimate convention choice of a party presidential nominee. The nomination of Dwight Eisenhower at the 1952 Republican National Convention was secured, at least in part, by the seating of his delegates from several southern states rather than the competing delegations of Robert Taft. The 1972 Democratic Convention produced several key battles, one of which involved the composition of the California delegation. Ultimately, the supporters of George McGovern were able to prevail and seat only McGovern delegates from that state. At that same convention, the Illinois delegation led by Chicago Mayor Richard Daley was ousted because, in the view of the convention, the delegates had not been selected in accordance with newly adopted party reforms. A Supreme Court decision following the convention ruled that a state law that interferes with decisions of a party's national convention violates the associations rights of the party (*Cousins v. Wigoda,* 419 U.S. 477: 1975). The essence of the ruling was that parties govern their own conventions, including the matter of delegate selection. Several years later, in *Democratic Party v. LaFollette* (450 U.S. 107: 1981), the Court said that states cannot require a state's convention delegation to vote for the winner of the state's primary election. In other words, a state cannot require a party to violate its own operating rules.

**Critical Election** **(211)**

An election during which partisan realignment occurs. The U.S. party system has been dominated almost from the outset by two major political parties. One or the other of these parties has come into control for a period of time only to be eventually displaced by the other major party. During the time one party maintains control, partisan alignments are relatively stable. The majority party has a consolidated coalition of voters who regularly support and elect the party's candidates. At some point, however, the issues that brought the coalition together become less compelling to a new generation of voters, the coalition deteriorates, and new alignments develop. During this critical election period, a party majority is established or reestablished. *See also* REALIGNMENT, 240; TWO-PARTY SYSTEM, 254.

*Significance* A critical election is one in which new partisan voting alignments manifest themselves. A critical election is usually surrounded by a period during which the realigning takes place. The election itself becomes the time at which the effect of realignment can be measured. Historically, the United States has had several periods during which one of the major parties is dominant. Its dominance eventually ends, and control is assumed by the other party. The critical election brings the change of alignment and control. The election of 1932 is an example of a critical election. Prior to the Great Depression, the Republicans were the dominant party. The events associated with the economic distress prompted a realignment that brought about the emergence of the Democrats with the election of Franklin Roosevelt and his New Deal coalition. This coalition remained stable until the 1950s when Democratic dominance began to erode. Even though the Republicans have been successful in contesting for the presidency over the last several decades, a basic realignment of partisan dominance has not occurred.

**Democratic Party** **(212)**

One of the two major political parties in the United States. The origin of the Democratic party was the Democratic-Republican party founded by Thomas Jefferson in the early 1790s to contest Alexander Hamilton and the Federalist party. The name formally became the Democratic party during the late 1820s as Andrew Jackson instituted his democratic reforms. The Civil War and the slavery issue badly divided the Democrats and provided the opportunity for the new Republican party to emerge. The Democrats were essentially the minority party after the Civil War until the Great Depression and the election of Franklin Roosevelt in 1932. Since then, the party has won the presidency more often than the Republicans and maintained control of Congress for all but eight years. The Jeffersonian party was built around a coalition of farmers and small property owners fearful of expanding government authority at the national level. Contemporary Democrats have abandoned the early states' rightist position and generally favor exercise of federal power. This can be seen in its support of many social welfare and civil rights initiatives. In general, the ideological orientation of the Democrats is more liberal than that of the Republicans. The Democratic coalition has traditionally comprised blue-collar workers, racial and ethnic minorities, the economically disadvantaged, and those from the left of center on the political spectrum regardless of socioeconomic status. *See also* JACKSONIAN DEMOCRATIC PARTY, 220; JEFFERSONIAN REPUBLICAN PARTY, 221; REPUBLICAN PARTY, 241.

*Significance* The Democratic party has undergone considerable change over the years but remains the only major party to span the length of U.S. partisan history. From its states' rights and agrarian origins, the Democratic party of the twentieth century has become known for its support of federal initiatives and of the urban political machine as a base of party organization strength. Andrew Jackson was largely responsible for altering the course of the party. He rejected the aristocratic character of the Jeffersonian party and sought to build a party around the common man. Further, Jackson was committed to grassroots control of the apparatus of government. Through Martin Van Buren, Jackson cultivated the developing urban organizations and forged a coalition of northern urban areas and the frontier. Coupled with Democratic organizational strength at the county level, especially in southern and rural areas, the party was able to forge an effective electoral coalition in the 1930s following partisan realignment brought on by the Great Depression. The Democrats have experienced difficulty in winning and holding the presidency since 1968 because their national candidates have been unable to hold the Roosevelt coalition together. Key defectors have been southerners and blue-collar workers. Even with Republican successes in the presidential contests, however, Democrats have retained control of Congress for an overwhelming majority of the past half-century and remain competitive for U.S. House and Senate seats as well as statewide offices.

***Democratic Party v. LaFollette*, 450 U.S. 107 (1981) (213)**
Allowed a political party to refuse to seat delegates to a national convention who had been selected in ways incompatible with party rules and procedures. Wisconsin law established an open presidential preference primary; it further required delegates to the national conventions to vote in accord with the results of the open primary. The latter requirement was in conflict with the Democratic party's rule that only those willing to publicly affiliate with the party be allowed to participate in the nominating process of the national convention. Suit was brought when the Democratic party indicated that the Wisconsin delegation would not be seated at the convention because its selection process violated party rules. The question before the Court was not whether Wisconsin could conduct an open primary but whether this state, having opened the primary to voters who had not publicly declared their party affiliation, could bind the party to honor the primary results even though those results were "reached in a manner contrary to National Party rules." The Supreme Court ruled that Wisconsin could not so bind the party. The party and its adherents enjoy, said the Court, a "constitutionally protected right of political association." That freedom encompasses association for the "common advancement of political beliefs," and it "necessarily presupposes the freedom to identify the people who comprise the association." The state law prevents the party from screening out those whose affiliation is "slight, tenuous or fleeting," and this screening out process is "essential" to an effective party. Although a state has a "substantial

interest" in the manner in which elections are conducted, a national party has a comparable interest in the way national convention delegates are selected. When the interests were balanced in this case, the Court concluded that state intrusion into the associational freedom of the party was not justified. *See also* NATIONAL CONVENTION, 228; *O'BRIEN V. BROWN* (409 U.S. 1: 1972), 230.

*Significance* The federal courts have generally been unwilling to permit interference with the processes of U.S. political parties. Indeed, for a long period, political parties were regarded as private organizations and thus outside constitutional limits on their conduct. The private club concept was abandoned in the 1940s when the Supreme Court ruled in *Smith v. Allwright* (321 U.S. 649: 1944) that racially exclusive primary elections violated the Fifteenth Amendment. Nonetheless, as reflected in *Democratic Party v. LaFollette* (450 U.S. 107: 1981), parties have been permitted substantial autonomy in conducting their electoral activities. This deference to party autonomy was seen a decade before *LaFollette* in *O'Brien v. Brown* (409 U.S. 1: 1972) when the Court ruled that federal courts ought not interject themselves into the deliberative processes of a national convention, in this case the challenge of a convention committee recommendation regarding the seating of particular delegations. The *O'Brien* decision was based on the political question doctrine, which holds that certain questions are inappropriate for judicial response and better resolved elsewhere. Although it ends up at essentially the same place, the foundation of the *LaFollette* case was the First Amendment right of political association and the freedom political party members ought to have in selecting candidates representing the party before the voters.

**Deviating Election** **(214)**

Presidential election won by the minority party but in which basic partisan affiliations remain intact. A deviating election is caused by an event that alters the existing patterns or by the candidacy of a person who prompts voters to ignore party affiliation at least in casting their ballot for president. Deviating elections have become more common since 1968 because party identification has decreased and candidate orientation has increased in importance in determining how people vote. An election that returns to the previous majority-minority party status is called a reinstating election. The events prompting the deviation may be substantial enough, however, to encourage voters to actually change their partisan affiliation, which, in turn, may cause the minority party to become the majority party. An election that reflects such a fundamental shift is called a realigning election rather than a deviating election. *See also* CANDIDATE ORIENTATION, 108; CRITICAL ELECTION, 211; MAINTAINING ELECTION, 224; REALIGNMENT, 240.

*Significance* A deviating election occurs when the minority party wins control of the presidency. Such an election produces a deviation from the expectation that the majority party, or stronger of the two parties at the time of an election, will retain the White House. Examples of deviating elections are the two wins of Dwight Eisenhower (in 1952 and 1956) and Richard Nixon (in 1968 and 1972). In both cases, Democrats were reinstated to the White House in the succeeding elections (Kennedy in 1960, and Carter in 1976). Furthermore, in none of the deviating elections was the minority party able to gain control of either the House of Representatives or the Senate. Rather than disturbing partisan affiliations, the deviating election finds short-term factors that bring about the defeat of the majority party's presidential candidate.

**Electoral College (215)**

Mechanism by which the president and the vice-president are selected. The electoral college was established by Article II of the United States Constitution, which requires states to select electors equal in number to their representation in Congress. With the three electors from the District of Columbia added with the ratification of the Twenty-third Amendment, there is currently a total of 538 electors. When a person votes in a presidential election, she or he is actually voting for a slate of electors committed to a particular candidate. These electors cast votes on a date following the presidential election. The electors never meet as a national body but cast their ballots from their respective states. If no candidate for president receives an absolute majority of electoral votes, the House of Representatives chooses from the top three candidates in total electoral votes. In the House process, each state delegation has a single vote. Failure to select a vice-president would be resolved in the Senate. *See also* PRESIDENTIAL ELECTION, 136.

*Significance* The electoral college was designed to make selection of the president an indirect process. It was a hedge against possible undesirable consequences that could occur through unrestricted participatory democracy. It was envisioned that the electors would be the established political leadership from a state. The initial design of the electoral college was defective in that it did not anticipate the rapid rise of political parties and their role in presidential selection. Although contemporary electors are permitted to vote for whomever they wish, they are really persons pledged to vote for a particular party's candidates. The design of the electoral college was also flawed in a more functional way. Initially, electors were not able to separate presidential and vice-presidential candidates when casting their votes. Each would vote for two persons to become president, the idea being that the runner-up would be the second best candidate and become vice-president. This procedure produced a tie between Thomas Jefferson and Aaron Burr in 1800, a result that was probably completely unintended by the electors. Although the deadlock was ultimately resolved by the House in Jefferson's favor, the defect was readily apparent. The Twelfth Amendment, adopted in 1803, required among other things that electors vote in separate ballots for president and vice-president. The electoral college has come under substantial criticism over the years. Principal complaints are that it can distort popular vote, it does not function as originally intended, and it gives all of a state's electoral votes to the candidate winning a plurality. Various reform proposals have been discussed, but none has been adopted as yet.

**Favorite Son** **(216)**

A state political figure who is nominated for the presidency at a national convention by members of the state's delegation. A favorite son is typically not a serious candidate but rather a person who is honored by means of placing his or her name in nomination. Alteration of convention rules in 1970 made favorite son candidacies more difficult because, in order for a person to be nominated, she or he must have the support of a minimum of 50 delegates, no more than 20 of whom could come from one state. *See also* NATIONAL CONVENTION, 228; STALKING HORSE, 247.

*Significance* Favorite son candidacies generally occur when a state delegation is unwilling to commit to one of the major candidates for nomination. If a sitting president seeks renomination, favorite son candidacies might be interpreted as dissatisfaction with the president. Aside from extending some personal recognition to the favorite son nominee, favorite son candidacies can keep a state's delegation uncommitted with respect to the more serious contenders for the nomination. After the first ballot, the delegation can assess the status of the contenders and direct its support accordingly. In some cases, the favorite son nominee can negotiate with the delegation's votes among the contenders and possibly secure some future consideration from the candidate to whom the delegation's votes ultimately go. Thus, the favorite son candidacy may have substantial political impact in any presidential election year.

**Federalist Party** **(217)**
The first political party to appear in the United States. The Federalist party was established in the mid-1790s under the leadership of Alexander Hamilton and John Adams. Many of the people who became Federalists were frustrated with the weak government under the Articles of Conferation and supported adoption of an entirely new constitution. The principal issue at the time the party formally began was the expansion of federal power at the expense of the states. The Federalists were the party of the aristocracy, and most of its support came from the commercial interests of the Northeast. The Federalists sought economic expansion on a national level and, to that end, advocated forceful executive and judicial action and such Hamiltonian policies as protective tariffs, assumption of state indebtedness by the federal government, creation of a national bank, and restoration of commercial harmony with Britain. The Federalists were opposed by the Anti-Federalists, ot Democratic-Republicans, led by Thomas Jefferson and James Madison. In a number of respects, the Federalists were the ideological forerunners of the contemporary Republican party. *See also* JEFFERSONIAN REPUBLICAN PARTY, 221; REPUBLICAN PARTY, 241.

*Significance* The Federalist party and John Adams won the election of 1796. Although Adams attempted to follow the policy lead of his predecessor, George Washington, a substantial schism developed between Adams and the Hamilton wing of the party. This rift plus Adams' support for the odious Alien and Sedition Acts contributed to the victory of Jefferson and the Democratic-Republicans in the presidential election of 1800. The Federalist party never recovered, although it continued to contest for the presidency. The War of 1812 gave the Federalists an issue upon which it might rebuild an electoral base, but its opposition to the war was so obstructionist that any chance for revitalization was lost. The party continued to decline, disappearing completely in 1928. The Whig party eventually replaced the Federalists as the principal opposition to the Democrats. The policy priorities of the Federalists outlasted the party's electoral appeal. Prior to departing office, John Adams placed many Federalists, including John Marshall, on federal courts. Marshall was extremely effective in writing Federalist positions into constitutional law through judicial interpretation. It has been suggested that Marshall's doctrines of federal legislative and judicial supremacy were critical to the survival of U.S. federalism.

**Ideological Party** **(218)**

A political party, typically one of protest, based on certain principles or doctrines. Ideological parties are not common in the United States because their world view departs markedly from that offered by the two major parties. Some ideological parties extensively criticize the political establishment. The Socialist or Socialist Workers parties are examples of ongoing ideological parties that have existed for decades. Although they run candidates in every election, they seldom attract much voter support. Since 1976, ideological parties located at the conservative end of the political spectrum have appeared. The Libertarian party is the most obvious example. The Libertarian presidential candidate received more votes in 1984 than any other minor party—upwards of .25 million nationally. Similar to ideological parties are parties of economic protest, which are typically less radical, less enduring, and often tend to be regional in scope. They appeal to groups who perceive themselves as economically disadvantaged largely because of government policies. The Populist party of the 1890s is an example. These parties may experience greater electoral success than the more doctrinaire parties, but they are also more likely to have their economic causes absorbed by one of the major parties, which, in turn, removes the reason for their existence. *See also* SINGLE-ISSUE PARTY, 245; THIRD PARTY, 252.

*Significance* Ideological parties seldom have much electoral impact in the U.S. party system. Ideological parties are characteristic of multiparty systems. The proportional representation approach used in such systems virtually guarantees that a party will win some legislative seats regardless of how extreme, doctrinaire, or regional it might be. In the United States, the two major parties embrace a wide range of political views. Although the two major parties differ on certain issues and general policy approaches, neither is absolutely wedded to a political ideology. Ideological parties act as advocates of alternative approaches to government as well as take specific policy positions. These parties offer a political outlet for the voter who is particularly frustrated or disenchanted with the political process. Ideological parties differ from single-issue parties in scope. The single-issue party is highly focused and pursues one policy objective at the expense of all others. Ideological parties embrace a broad range of policy commitments.

**Independents (219)**
Persons who do not identify with a political party. Independents typically claim that they vote on issue positions and the personal qualifications of candidates. Evidence suggests that independents may not scrutinize either issues or candidates. To the contrary, they may expose themselves to far less political information than active partisans. An independent usually has no formal association with a political party, although some independents register with parties in order to be eligible to vote in primary elections. *See also* POLITICAL PARTY: DECLINE, 236; POLITICAL PARTY: IDENTIFICATION, 133; TICKET SPLITTING, 253.

*Significance* Ever-growing numbers of the electorate consider themselves independents. That is, they do not identify, much less affiliate, with a political party. Since 1960, strong partisan identifiers have decreased by almost 15 percent. In some cases, independents are persons who de-align from a party; others may have never identified with a party. The reluctance especially of new or young voters to identify with a party has been clearly documented. This trend creates organizational problems for parties and special challenges for political candidates. Independents are of sufficient numbers to be decisive in virtually any election, thus they must be specially targeted by most campaigns. This increase in the number of independents has been paralleled by a growth in ticket splitting with persons voting for candidates of both major parties for different offices in the same election.

**Jacksonian Democratic Party (220)**
Successor party to the Jeffersonian Republicans. The Jacksonian Democratic party was a product of the bitter presidential election of 1824. Andrew Jackson, a Jeffersonian Democrat, won more popular votes than any other candidate but lost the election when the House of Representatives selected John Quincy Adams, the candidate of the National Republican wing of the Jeffersonian Democrats. Jackson's supporters then sought control of the party by expanding its base. A coalition of frontier interests (as personified by Jackson himself) and urban organizations led by New Yorker Martin Van Buren was formed. This coalition was built upon the interests of the common man and rejected the more aristocratic character of the established party. The fundamental change was to enlarge the electorate and expand its role in governance. Among the changes in party processes was introduction of the convention as a means of obtaining input from all quarters of the party. The Jacksonian Democratic party built an organization designed to maximize popular support, a strategy

that resulted in the election of Jackson in 1828 and again in 1832. *See also* DEMOCRATIC PARTY, 212; JEFFERSONIAN REPUBLICAN PARTY, 221; WHIG PARTY, 257.

*Significance* The success of the Jacksonian Democratic party in 1828 brought with it a new era in U.S. partisan politics. Jackson wished to make political processes more democratic; to that end, he and the party urged expanded suffrage and heightened electoral accountability of government officials. The popular democracy of Jackson produced larger numbers of elective public offices, most of which had short terms. In response to Jackson and the direction of his party, remnants of the National Republicans and the old Federalist party reappeared in the form of the Whig party and contested with the Democrats through the election of 1852. Eventually, the slavery issue fractured both the Democratic and Whig parties. The Democrats were unable to satisfactorily reconcile competing factions on the issue of slavery and westward expansion, and the party suffered at both the national and the local levels. The impact of this issue on the Whigs was even more severe because the party ceased to exist. Filling the void was the new Republican party, whose emergence defined yet another distinct period of U.S. party history. The Democrats were to remain a major force throughout, and eventually the party restored itself to majority status after the Great Depression. The tenets of Jacksonian democracy remain evident in contemporary Democratic politics.

**Jeffersonian Republican Party (221)**

Party founded in the early 1790s by Thomas Jefferson to oppose the Federalists. The Jeffersonian Republican party, a predecessor of the contemporary Democratic party, was also called the Democratic-Republican party, a name chosen to emphasize their support of representative or republican government. The Jeffersonians embraced the view that small republics, governed by democratically elected officials possessing carefully defined power, provided the most effective government. Accordingly, the party favored states' rights and a federal government with limited authority. The strength of the Jeffersonian Republicans was a coalition of farmers, small property owners, and the state and local political leadership of a number of southern and mid-Atlantic states. *See also* DEMOCRATIC PARTY, 212; FEDERALIST PARTY, 217; JACKSONIAN DEMOCRATIC PARTY, 220.

*Significance* The Jeffersonian Republican party, together with the Federalists, formed the first party system in the United States. The country elected George Washington to the presidency without the presence of parties. During Washington's first administration, members of his cabinet divided over the policy positions advanced by Secretary of the Treasury Alexander Hamilton. The Federalist party developed around the Hamiltonian positions. Leading the opposition was Secretary of State Thomas Jefferson, who eventually resigned from the cabinet to develop an anti-Federalist organization. Jefferson sought the presidency in 1796 but lost to John Adams, Washington's vice-president, by vote of the electoral college. The election of 1800 again matched Jefferson and Adams. Prior to this election, both the Federalists and the Democratic-Republicans formally endorsed their respective candidates; thus, the election of 1800 was the first contested on a partisan basis. Jefferson prevailed and the Democratic-Republican party established itself as the majority party, controlling the presidency and Congress for the next quarter-century. A faction of the Democratic-Republican party known as the National Republicans developed and split the party. Its candidate, John Quincy Adams, won the presidency in 1824, thus ending the era of the Jeffersonian Republicans. What emerged from this split was a realigned party system with Andrew Jackson reshaping the Jeffersonian Democratic-Republican party into the Jacksonian Democratic party.

**Legislative Party** **(222)**

Members of a political party who are serving in a legislative body. The legislative party provides a link between the electorate and the party, and it plays a central role in transforming political promises into public policy. Party is particularly important in determining leadership within the legislative body. Consider the legislative party within Congress. Both the Republicans and the Democrats have a party caucus in both the House and the Senate that includes all party members. The caucus considers policy positions that might be taken by legislative members and decides on candidates for leadership positions. Each caucus selects a party leader and a whip. The whip, along with deputy whips, is responsible for getting members to vote the caucus position, or "party line," on various policy questions. The speaker of the House is also elected on a partisan basis. In addition, party caucuses elect members of the policy committees that attempt to fashion the party position on pending legislation for the caucus. Finally, the caucus designates members who will be involved in appointing party members to the standing committees of the legislative bodies. *See also* PARTY IN GOVERNMENT, 231; RESPONSIBLE PARTY SYSTEM, 243.

*Significance* The impact of the party within Congress has varied throughout history. At no time, however, has the United States ever had disciplined legislative parties similar to those of the British system where party members vote together on all policy questions. The greatest party discipline was evident in the late nineteenth century when the speaker of the House had highly concentrated power. Failure to support the party position often produced sanctions such as loss of a committee chair or membership on an important committee. Eventually, reforms were achieved in both the House and Senate that distributed power among larger numbers of House and Senate members. The result was that party leadership was weakened and the limited discipline that existed prior to the reforms was further diminished. This trend toward decentralization has continued since the 1970s. Members of the House and Senate have worked to build power bases for themselves by distributing influence ever more broadly, particularly to chairs of subcommittees. As a consequence, even more autonomy from the influence of party and legislative party leadership has been created for legislators.

**Local Party Organization** **(223)**

Party organization typically established at the county level. The actual structure of political parties at the local level is often governed by state law, which requires that certain organizational units exist. The most basic unit for local party organization is the precinct, a division of a county or municipality that contains up to 1,400 registered voters and a location for them to vote. The party may have a captain in each precinct, although this is unusual; precinct captains or ward leaders are most often found in urban areas. These leaders will represent their precincts on a county committee. Delegates to county conventions are often selected by primary election to represent the precincts in which they live. County chairs are chosen by the county committee. The chairs are typically unpaid and seldom operate with a staff other than people who also serve on a voluntary basis. *See also* PATRONAGE, 232; POLITICAL MACHINE, 234; POLITICAL PARTY: ORGANIZATION, 238; STATE PARTY ORGANIZATION, 248.

*Significance* The local party organization is partisan politics at the grassroots level. The decentralized structure of U.S. political parties means that the local party retains some importance. The local party is generally organized by county because county officials are elected on a partisan basis, which allows the practice of patronage to be used effectively as an incentive to engage in local partisan activity. Indeed, the old-time political machines operated successfully because they controlled such benefits as government jobs. The county became the arena of patronage as reformers moved municipal elections to a nonpartisan basis. Even in rural areas, the "courthouse gang" operated much like the urban machine. Nonetheless, county organizations tend not to have great power—although a small number of partisans conduct party business year round, local party activity is generally minimal except during campaign season.

**Maintaining Election (224)**

An election in which the majority party retains control of the presidency and Congress. Election contests in the United States have been waged between candidates of the two major political parties. The historical pattern has been that one of these parties establishes its control and maintains its majority status for a period until a realignment produces a change in partisan control. This change of control occurs during a critical election, an election in which new alignments emerge. The opposite of a critical election is a maintaining election, an election that continues the prevailing partisan alignment. *See also* CRITICAL ELECTION, 211; PARTY IDENTIFICATION, 133; TWO-PARTY SYSTEM, 254.

*Significance* A maintaining election produces outcomes based on partisan alignments that remain unchanged from the preceding election. Party alignments are not permanent, but they are relatively stable. That is, fundamental realignments occur infrequently. Between these periods of realignment, one of the major parties may exercise control for several decades. Given this pattern, a maintaining election is to be expected. Consider, for example, the period following realignment in the critical election of 1932. The Democrats, through the coalition produced by Franklin Roosevelt's candidacy and the New Deal program, gained control. The next four presidential elections maintained that partisan alignment.

**Multiparty System (225)**

A political system in which elective offices are held by members of many political parties. Multiparty systems are commonly found in Europe and tend to be distinctive from two-party systems in several ways. First, the parties are more likely to be ideologically based and doctrinaire, which means they usually cannot capture majority support. Rather, they attract segments of the population whose personal views closely correspond to the orientation of the party. Parties of multiparty systems tend to spread across the political spectrum and represent a narrow but diverse portion of the electorate. Second, multiparty systems tend to exist in political systems that use proportional representation as the basis for electing legislators. Parties are awarded legislative seats based on the proportion or percentage of popular vote won in the election. Such proportional representation is the opposite of the winner-take-all approach that characterizes two-party systems. Finally, governments formed out of multiparty systems are based on ad hoc coalitions of parties that are necessary to establish a majority. *See also* PROPORTIONAL REPRESENTATION, 239; TWO-PARTY SYSTEM, 254.

*Significance* Multiparty systems tend to have parties that are not broadly based. Rather than serving as umbrella organizations for wide-ranging coalitions of supporters, parties in multiparty systems are narrowly focused and tend to be ideologically pure. Persons can usually find a party that fits personal preferences. In this sense, parties in a multiparty system may be more reflective of individual preferences than parties in a two-party system. This characteristic creates problems, however, when it comes to governing. Seldom can one party secure majority support. Governments in a multiparty system must usually be formed by coalitions of parties. Coalitions of this kind are fragile and may disintegrate in times of stress, so governments in such systems tend to be unstable. Coalitions are required in two-party systems as well, but the coalition building occurs prior to elections, and compromises are within parties rather than across parties after elections.

***Munro v. Socialist Workers Party,* (226)**
**479 U.S. 189 (1986)**

Upheld a state law that limited general election ballot access to candidates who received at least 1 percent of the total primary vote. Washington established a two-step process for minor-party candidates seeking to get on the general election ballot. Any such candidate must first secure the convention nomination of his or her party. As the official nominee, the candidate would appear on the primary election ballot. In order to access the general election ballot, the candidate needed to receive at least 1 percent of all votes cast for that office in the primary election. The nominee of the Socialist Workers party received only .09 percent, and his name was not placed on the general election ballot. Action was brought claiming abridgement of rights secured by the First Amendment. The Supreme Court upheld this restriction on ballot access. The Court agreed that the right of individuals to "associate for political purposes" and the right of qualified voters to "cast their votes effectively" were impinged here. Such rights, however, are not absolute and are "necessarily subject to qualification if elections are to be run fairly and effectively." Indeed, in reviewing restrictions of this type, the Court said it is "clear" that states may "condition access" to the general election ballot by minor-party or independent candidates upon a showing of a "modicum of support" among the potential voters for the office. When states attempt to justify access restrictions, there is no requirement for a "particularized showing" of a specific adverse condition. To require actual proof of these conditions would "invariably lead" to lengthy disputes over the sufficiency of the evidence and "necessitate" that a state's electoral processes "sustain some level of damage" before the legislature could act. Rather, the Court preferred that legislatures be able to "respond to potential deficiencies . . . with foresight rather than reactively" so long as the response is "reasonable" and does not "significantly impinge" on protected rights. States, said the Court, simply do not have a "constitutional imperative" to "reduce voter apathy" or to assist unpopular candidates to "enhance their chances of gaining access to the general election ballot." The state in this case simply required a candidate to demonstrate a "significant modicum" of voter support, a condition it was entitled to impose. *See also* *BUCKLEY V. VALEO* (424 U.S. 1: 1976), 157; PRIMARY ELECTION, 140; *TASHJIAN V. REPUBLICAN PARTY OF CONNECTICUT* (479 U.S. 208: 1986), 251.

*Significance* The ballot access issue examined in *Munro v. Socialist Workers Party* (479 U.S. 189: 1986) is not new. For years, the Supreme Court refrained from engaging in direct supervision of state electoral processes. That policy began to change with the Warren Court's decision to address the issue of legislative apportionment. Regulations that made it difficult for new or minor parties to get on the ballot were scrutinized more carefully. The Court pointed out in *Munro,* however, that there were cases decided during this same period that establish with "unmistakable clarity" that states may, as a manifestation of their interest in "preserving the integrity of the election process," require candidates to make a "preliminary showing of support" in order to qualify for ballot access. Clearly reflected in such cases as *Munro* is that the Court will permit states substantial latitude in restricting ballot access so long as the access conditions are not unreasonable.

**National Committee** **(227)**

The national executive committee of the two major political parties. The national committees were first established in the mid-1800s by the party conventions. Their function is to conduct party business between the national conventions. The real power of the national committee is quite limited—its first priority is to win presidential elections. To that end, the national committee participates in campaign planning and fund-raising. The national committee is also responsible for planning the party's national nominating convention. The committee also confirms the presidential nominee's choice for national chairperson. If the party nominee loses the election, the national committee often elects a new chair. The Democratic and Republican National Committees both consist of male and female members from each state, the District of Columbia, and the territories, plus the chairs of the state parties. Other members may be added at the discretion of the committees. *See also* CONGRESSIONAL CAMPAIGN COMMITTEES, 175; NATIONAL CONVENTION, 228; STATE PARTY ORGANIZATION, 248.

*Significance* The national committees possess less authority than one might conclude from their location on the party organizational charts. This is true in large part because the real power of the major parties is located at the state and local levels rather than at the national level. The national party and its national committee are driven almost exclusively by presidential politics. Indeed, this presidential focus prompted establishment of the congressional campaign committees as separate entities to provide assistance to the parties' candidates for the House and Senate. Once the national committee confirms the choice of the national chairperson, the party's business is handled through the chair.

**National Convention** **(228)**

A gathering or meeting of party delegates to nominate candidates for president and vice-president. The national conventions are held every presidential election year. In addition to selecting party standard-bearers at the national level, national conventions also adopt a statement of principles and policy priorities called a party platform. Conventions are used at various levels to conduct party business. Indeed, delegates to the national conventions are selected through a series of conventions at the county, congressional district, and state levels. Delegates to national conventions are also chosen by election in states that have presidential primaries. Apportionment of state delegates reflects population but also takes into account the extent to which the state supported party nominees in previous elections. *See also* NOMINATION, 229; *O'BRIEN V. BROWN* (409 U.S. 1: 1972), 230; PLATFORM, 233.

*Significance* The national convention is the principal institution of the political party at the national level. The national convention not only nominates a party's national candidates, but rules that are adopted at national conventions govern party activities, including the process for selecting delegates to future conventions. This authority has been upheld even when convention decisions conflict with state law (*O'Brien v. Brown,* 409 U.S. 1: 1972). The national convention performs two functions that influence the party's chances in the general election. First, the national convention allows various factions within the party to strike compromises. This is particularly important in years when there is a serious contest for the nomination and the need for competing coalitions to unite is high. Second, the convention generates excitement and visibility. It fosters enthusiasm among the party faithful who will carry on the campaign activities. The conventions are extensively covered by the media, and they allow the party leaders, especially the presidential nominee, to be showcased to a national audience. In many respects, a presidential nominee's acceptance speech is the kickoff of the general election campaign.

**Nomination (229)**

Action by which political parties designate persons as their official candidates for elective office. A party may arrive at the nomination of a candidate in several ways: party caucus, petition, primary election, and convention. The most complex nominating process is for the office of president. Formal nomination occurs at a national party convention. Official delegates to the convention are chosen through the use of caucuses, primaries, and/or conventions. Candidacies for the nomination may often be announced a year or more before the first caucuses and primaries that commence in February of presidential election years. Each state completes its own process of delegate selection culminating in June. The two major parties then hold their nominating conventions in July or early August. After these conventions, the nominating process ends and the general election campaign begins. Nomination, followed by legislative consideration of the nominee, is also the process by which appointments are made to executive or judicial offices. *See also* CAUCUS, 209; NATIONAL CONVENTION, 228; PRESIDENTIAL NOMINATION, 138; PRIMARY ELECTION, 140.

*Significance* Nomination is the stage that determines who will contest for office in a general election. If the nomination process does not function fairly, the value of elections would be diminished as a central component of the concept of participatory democracy. This fact is especially true if elections are not competitive in a partisan sense. Where one party dominates the general election process, the only step of consequence in selecting public officials is the nomination of the dominant party's candidate. Until the early 1900s, the convention was the typical means of candidate nomination. Concern that conventions were wholly controlled by the urban political machines led to a number of political reforms. Among these was a replacement of conventions with direct primaries as the principal means of nominating candidates. Since 1980, we have seen a return to conventions as parties attempt to temper the sentiments of partisans in caucuses and primaries with the political reality of mounting successful candidacies.

**_O'Brien v. Brown_, 409 U.S. 1 (1972)** **(230)**
Used the political question doctrine to hold that federal courts ought not interfere with proceedings of a national political convention. *O'Brien v. Brown* developed out of the 1972 Democratic National Convention and involved challenges to delegate seating decisions made by the Convention Credentials Committee. The Supreme Court refused to permit federal court intervention despite the "novel and important" questions presented. The case called for consideration of the issues of whether "irreparable injury" would occur in the absence of intervention and whether the "public interest" was substantially affected. The Court pointed out that if the courts interfered, the convention would be denied "its traditional power to pass on . . . credentials." Remaining out, on the other hand, would "not foreclose" the convention from giving the delegates the relief they sought in court. The Court also recognized the "large" public interest in "allowing the political processes to function free from judicial supervision." Coupled with the availability of the convention itself to serve as a forum for consideration of the Credentials Committee recommendations and the lack of precedent support for intervention, the Court decided against intervention. *See also* DEMOCRATIC PARTY V. LAFOLLETTE (450 U.S. 107: 1981), 213; NATIONAL CONVENTION, 228.

*Significance* The Supreme Court invoked the "political question" doctrine in *O'Brien v. Brown* (409 U.S. 1: 1972) to find that federal courts had no authority over national political conventions. The Court used the doctrine to examine the propriety of the lower court's intervention in the "deliberative processes" of the party convention procedure. Such situations were seen as "essentially political" and involving "relationships of great delicacy." Accordingly, judicial involvement must be approached with "great caution and restraint." So long as the convention itself could resolve these disputes, the "large public interest" was best served by allowing the political processes of the convention to "function free of judicial supervision." In a related situation, the Court ruled in *Democratic Party v. LaFollette* (450 U.S.

107: 1981) that a state cannot require its national convention delegates to vote for the state's primary winner. The decision deferred to the convention's own rules governing the nomination process with emphasis given to the associational rights of the delegates as well as the traditionally detached role of courts from such political processes.

**Party in Government** **(231)**

A political party's elected and appointed public officials. One of the principal objectives of a political party is to place its people in public office. Those reaching office are the party in government. At the national level, the party in government is a party's members of Congress and, for one party, the president. The federal judiciary is usually not included when considering the party in government, although political party affiliation of judges in lower courts is often readily apparent. The task of the party in government is to transform the general goals and policy preferences outlined in the platform into law. Congress is organized on a partisan basis, and although the legislative parties are not particularly disciplined, voting on policy questions is influenced by party more than any other single factor. Similarly, the president serves as a partisan leader; he or she thereby influences which proposals will be introduced or supported by the executive, a factor that is often decisive on which proposals will ultimately be enacted into law. *See also* LEGISLATIVE PARTY, 222; RESPONSIBLE PARTY SYSTEM, 243.

*Significance* There has long been discussion about how closely the party in government ought to reflect public sentiment. There are those who advocate that parties ought to be responsible—that is, the two major parties ought to take distinctive policy positions, with the majority party acting cohesively to turn its programs into policy. The U.S. party system is not responsible because the two major parties neither offer clearly contrasting positions nor exhibit substantial discipline or cohesion within the legislature. Nonetheless, the impact of the party in government can be seen. Legislative bodies are organized on a partisan basis, which has an impact on legislative agendas and the likelihood of particular bills emerging from committees or not. There are also measures that show that, although party discipline is not extensive, there is some party cohesion on policy questions. The effect of party can also be seen on the extent to which a president's agenda is supported in Congress. Members of the president's party clearly are more supportive than members of the opposition. To some extent, party creates a linkage between elective branches that helps forestall legislative-executive stalemate and allows for at least a modest degree of policy coordination.

**Patronage** **(232)**

The practice of giving appointive governmental positions to persons on the basis of partisan activity. Besides jobs, patronage extends to the capacity to direct contracts or licenses, confer honors, or provide other forms of preferential treatment as reward for party work. Patronage is an incentive for people to involve themselves in partisan political causes. Patronage is sometimes referred to as the "spoils system," a derivative of the expression "to the victor go the spoils." Use of patronage or the spoils system dates back to the administration of Andrew Jackson. *See also* POLITICAL MACHINE, 234.

*Significance* The ability to distribute patronage resides primarily within the executive branch at all levels of government. Indeed, the use of patronage was often key to the effectiveness of urban political machines. The principal rationale for patronage is that it provides tangible incentives for party service. It also has the effect of allowing government officials to use loyal partisans who share common political views and policy preferences with program implementation. Critics of patronage argue that abuses in such a system are inherent—that corruption is inevitable. They also suggest that a well-trained and competitively chosen bureaucracy is more productive than persons selected on the basis of mere partisanship. For these reasons, Congress passed the Pendleton Act (Civil Service Act) of 1883, which created a federal civil service selected largely by merit on the basis of competitive examinations. Establishment of civil service at the federal and state levels made patronage largely a local practice. Recent Supreme Court decisions have reached even patronage at the local level, further reducing its impact. In *Elrod v. Burns* (427 U.S. 347: 1976) and *Branti v. Finkel* (445 U.S. 507: 1980), the Court essentially ruled that nonpolicymaking personnel could not be dismissed merely because of party affiliation.

**Platform** **(233)**

A statement of the underlying principles embraced by a political party. The platform generally outlines the objectives a party would pursue if successful in its electoral activities. Platforms are written at party conventions by special platform committees. At state and local conventions, specific positions in the form of resolutions are typically adopted instead of comprehensive platforms that are normally associated with a party's national convention. *See also* NATIONAL CONVENTION, 228; RESOLUTIONS COMMITTEE, 242.

*Significance* Although platforms have frequently been characterized as mere partisan rhetoric, the period dating from 1960 would indicate that the platform serves as an action blueprint for the two major parties. In addition, however, the platform is a means by which a party heaps lavish praise upon itself and directs substantial criticism toward the opposition. More than anything else, the platform showcases the positions on which the party has achieved relative consensus. Although these statements exist on paper as the party's position statement, individual candidates may in essence amend the platform by emphasizing some provisions while distancing themselves from others. In the United States, party platforms do not bind any elected official as they might in Britain, for example, where a responsible party system translates party platforms into governmental policy.

**Political Machine (234)**

A partisan political organization that dominates electoral politics at the local level. Political machines exercised control over elections in part through the practice of patronage, whereby government jobs were exchanged for partisan activity and support. In early U.S. political history, machines provided various social service benefits to those who would support party candidates at the polls; this was most easily done in large urban areas. Political machines were also known to resort to illegal practices such as buying votes and rigging elections to maintain electoral control. A prototype political machine was Tammany Hall in New York City. The Cook County Democratic machine of the 1960s could be mentioned as an example of a political machine, especially during the tenure of Chicago Mayor Richard Daley. *See also* PATRONAGE, 232.

*Significance* Although vestiges of political machines remain, they have lost much of their influence. This loss results in part because what they traded for support is no longer under machine control to the extent it once was. Dealing in government jobs became much more difficult with the advent of civil service and merit selection of bureaucrats. Similarly, many of the benefits that machines traded for votes became the province of government through various social welfare programs. In addition, political reforms such as the direct primary diminished the power of machines and local bosses. In other words, machines eventually lost their capacity to deliver the blocks of votes necessary to control elections. Lost with the demise of the political machines, however, was some attentiveness to personal needs of constituents. Machines responded to voters' problems without any of the bureaucratic delay and red tape often associated with contemporary government.

**Political Party** **(235)**

An aggregation of people who formally organize themselves to pursue common political objectives. The foremost objective of political parties is to exercise power through the election of party members to public office; capturing office is the most effective way of translating political beliefs into public policy. Beyond this, parties link the public and its governmental structures. Political parties as they are today did not exist at the time the Constitution was ratified, but the constitutional framers created an environment in which parties were virtually certain to develop. By requiring the election of those governing at the national level, the framers established the need for a means of public participation in such elections. The political party served this need. The United States has a two-party system; candidates of parties other than the Democratic and Republican parties have virtually no chance of being elected to public office. Although a number of factors may help explain the two-party system, the single most important reason is the U.S. winner-take-all method of election. The winner-take-all approach creates compelling incentives for voters to unite behind one of the two major parties because only their candidates have a realistic chance of winning. Election of members of legislative bodies from single-member districts rather than multimember districts based on a proportional reflection of party performance in an election also encourages the continued existence of the two-party system. Minor parties are not competitive and voters are inevitably drawn toward one of the two major parties. Accordingly, the major parties attempt to become as broadly based as possible. This means that the two major parties will not define their positions in narrow ideological terms because to do so would hamper their coalition-building strategies. One other characteristic of the U.S. party system is its highly decentralized organization. The U.S. federal system is largely responsible for this decentralization. Under this system, authority to administer elections is lodged with the states. *See also* INTEREST GROUP, 293; POLITICAL PARTY: FUNCTIONS, 237; POLITICAL PARTY: ORGANIZATION, 238.

*Significance* Political parties perform several important functions in the U.S. political system. First, parties formally nominate candidates for public office. The party acts as a recruiting mechanism to ensure that there are candidates to contest for public office. When candidates are numerous, the party acts as a screening agent for the public at large. It is through the mechanisms of the party that primary elections, caucuses, and nominating conventions are conducted. Second, political parties focus voter options. Because elections are usually contested only by nominees of the major parties, voters need seriously consider a relative handful of candidates. Parties thus allow citizens, many of whom have only a limited interest in politics, to participate in elections on a relatively rational basis. Third, parties offer voters some basic philosophical and policy options. Even if citizens are generally unfamiliar with specific candidates or campaigns, the party label provides a handy point of reference. In this way, parties allow voters to indicate broad policy preferences by voting for a party's chosen candidates. Finally, parties facilitate the coordination of public policymaking. Parties permit public officials, who are structurally separated by constitutional provisions, to fashion coherent policy using shared partisan principles as the basic coordinating element. These common principles are typically contained in the parties' platforms, which are statements of programs and policy preferences formally adopted at party conventions.

**Political Party: Decline** **(236)**

Reference to the decrease of party influence in the U.S. political process. Individuals who argue that U.S. parties have suffered decline focus on organizational as well as electoral evidence. The political reforms of the early twentieth century eroded the control that political machines exercised over elections. These machines were the strength of the party organizations, especially for the Democrats. With the advent of the direct primary, civil service, and greater involvement by government in providing social services, machines lost their role in candidate recruitment and in controlling jobs and other benefits. The organizational changes were accompanied by a decline in party identification. That is, decreasing numbers of voters used party as the basis upon which election choices were made. To the contrary, a higher proportion of the electorate now view themselves as independents, especially the younger voters. *See also* INDEPENDENTS, 219; PATRONAGE, 232; POLITICAL MACHINE, 234; PRIMARY ELECTION, 140.

*Significance* The decline of U.S. political parties manifests itself in several ways in contemporary electoral politics. First, widespread use of the direct primary reduces the role of party leadership in the critical function of candidate selection. Candidates can go directly to voters and win nomination. Second, use of the mass media and other means of direct contact replaced the party apparatus as the principal way to reach voters. Third, interest groups and their political action committees (PACs) have become the largest source of campaign funding, which allows candidates access to resources to compete for partisan nomination. Each of these situations fosters the bypassing of the political party. Fourth, diminished levels of party identification produce ever-growing numbers of voters who split tickets, voting for candidates of each major party. Finally, with candidates less dependent on parties, those who are elected are less inclined to vote a partisan line—in other words, party discipline is diminished. Notwithstanding these developments, parties continue to exist and play a sizable role in U.S. politics. Indeed, both major parties have engaged in recent reforms in an effort to revitalize themselves.

**Political Party: Functions** **(237)**

Description of the role performed by parties in a democratic political system. The principal function of a political party is the winning of elections by its candidates. It is the party's function of formally nominating candidates for public office that distinguishes it from other organizations, such as interest groups. Before a party can nominate a candidate, it must recruit persons who will be attractive candidates. This selection is part of the larger function of maximizing support. The party must create an image that is broadly appealing to the electorate. By designating a nominee, the two major parties simplify the choices of U.S. voters because the viable candidates for office are typically those of the major parties. In addition, the party provides an ongoing organizational framework into which candidate campaign structures can be linked. For national and statewide campaigns, the party organization is a major source of funding and a means of coordinating campaign efforts. Political parties also play a role in fashioning public policy. Parties provide some choices for voters between alternative policy directions. Although the United States does not have a responsible party system, the two major parties generally embrace different policy options, often in vague language. When elections are over, party becomes the basis on which governments are organized, especially in the legislative branch. In the U.S. system of separated authority, party often serves as a coordinating link among officials in different branches or levels of government. *See also* POLITICAL PARTY: DECLINE, 236; POLITICAL PARTY: ORGANIZATION, 238; RESPONSIBLE PARTY SYSTEM, 243.

*Significance* The functions of U.S. political parties are central to the operation of the electoral process. Parties shape election contests by providing candidates between whom U.S. voters can choose, thereby facilitating participation in elections by ordering and simplifying the process. The control political parties exercise over the electoral process has diminished, however. With the advent of reforms such as the direct primary, the role of party leaders in recruiting party nominees has been reduced. In addition, those who wish to seek party nomination may bypass party organizations and compete directly through primaries. Access to financial resources through the many political action committees (PACs) and exposure to voters through the mass media makes this approach possible. Coupled with these developments has been a reduction in the number of people who formally identify or affiliate with parties. As larger numbers of voters view themselves as independents or unaffiliated, it becomes more difficult for parties to develop any meaningful discipline among partisans elected to office. Nonetheless, the functions of parties retain value for the political process, and both major parties continue to search for ways that they may more effectively fulfill these functions.

**Political Party: Organization (238)**

Structural configuration through which political parties perform their various functions. Political parties are organized at the national, state, and local levels. This structuring creates units of organization at each level at which elections are conducted. At the national level, the two major parties have a national committee and a national chair. The national committee does not possess broad power but has responsibility for conducting the national nominating convention. The national chair generally manages the affairs of the national party and acts as the party spokesperson. Both parties also have congressional campaign committees that coordinate the party's efforts to successfully contest for U.S. House and Senate seats. The state party organization also has a general governing body, called the state committee or state central committee, and a state chair. There is also a level of organization at the county level. In some states, the parties have structural units bounded by congressional or state legislative districts. Finally, there are often lower level organizations within municipalities. It is here that units such as wards or precincts may be organized—this is political organization at the grassroots level. *See also* LOCAL PARTY ORGANIZATION, 223; NATIONAL COMMITTEE, 227; STATE PARTY ORGANIZATION, 248.

*Significance* It is possible to represent the organization of the two major political parties in the United States as a pyramid with the national party on top. Such a diagram would reasonably convey the organizational scheme but would wholly misrepresent the real distribution of power. Rather than higher levels exercising control over those below, U.S. political parties are layered. Although their boundaries may overlap and they may share some common members, each organizational layer is relatively autonomous. At the top of the pyramid is the layer with the most limited power in some respects. The national committees have limited responsibilities and are composed of members selected by state party organizations. National chairs are essentially delegates of presidential nominees, although their visibility can be a major asset to the party as well as a source of power for the chair. The national committees and, to a large extent, the national chairs focus rather exclusively on presidential politics. State and local levels of the party operate independently and possess much of the real power of U.S. parties. This structural fragmentation largely keeps U.S. parties from resembling the more disciplined and doctrinaire parties found in Europe.

**Proportional Representation** **(239)**
An election system that allocates seats in a legislative body to political parties based on their percentage of the popular vote. Under proportional representation, voters cast their ballots for the party (or the party list) rather than for individual candidates. If a party receives 15 percent of the popular vote, its wins 15 percent of the legislative seats. The proportional representation approach carries with it these characteristics: First, it almost always produces a multiparty system. Any party that can gain a minimal share of the vote, usually 5 percent, can elect members to the legislative body. This encourages the formation of political parties because each party is able to capture some fraction of the popular vote from voters politically located most closely to it. Second, proportional representation must have multi- or plural-member legislative districts; legislative bodies must have districts represented by a number of legislators rather than a single legislator. There may be no districts with elections conducted at large, or there may be multimember districts. Thus, a party winning 15 percent of the popular vote can expect about 15 percent of the seats in the legislature. This outcome cannot occur with the winner-take-all, single-member–district approach. *See also* MULTIPARTY SYSTEM, 225; SINGLE-MEMBER DISTRICT, 149.

*Significance* Proportional representation is used in most democratic political systems. It is preferred because it serves the objective of accurately measuring and representing the political sentiments of the electorate. Such a system reflects within legislative bodies even those parties that receive minimal support. The drawback of proportional representation is that it makes formation of a viable government quite difficult. Proportional representation almost never produces a clear majority for a single party. As result, two or more parties must enter into a coalition to establish a government. Such coalitions are usually fragile and may fracture at the first signs of stress. Although the proportional representation approach may be more representative, it is at the expense of government stability.

**Realignment** **(240)**
An election in which fundamental partisan affiliations shift to such a degree that the minority party becomes the majority party. A realigning election is infrequent and occurs only after an event of inordinate impact, such as the Civil War. The history of the U.S. two-party system reveals that one or the other of the major parties has prevailed for extended periods of time. The alignment of voter groups supporting the dominant party is relatively stable and enduring. Periodically, however, the issues that brought one party to majority status become less prominent and are replaced by others. These new issues, typically defined by major events, fracture the majority coalition and create new alignments. Following a critical election period, a new majority party may emerge in a realigning election. *See also* CRITICAL ELECTION, 211; TWO-PARTY SYSTEM, 254.

*Significance* Of the different elections, the realigning election is the most complex. A realigning election actually manifests shifts of basic partisan affiliation that persist beyond a single election. The duration and extent of the change in alignment distinguishes the realigning election from one which temporarily deviates from the existing pattern in a single election. Although modest realignment occurs in any election, a true realignment seems to require a major national event or crisis that actually produces a large number of party converts. Two examples of realigning elections are helpful. The slavery issue and the Civil War brought about the disintegration of the Whig party and a weakening of the Democrats and led to the emergence of the Republicans as the dominant party. The Great Depression drew many affiliates away from the Republicans and created a majority for the Democrats in 1932. This Democratic majority has been maintained ever since, although the potential for realignment has existed since Richard Nixon captured the White House in 1968. Although Democratic dominance has declined, a realignment that restores the Republicans to majority status has not occurred. Rather than realigning, there is evidence to suggest that some voters are de-aligning. That is, rather than change affiliation to the other major party or to a new party, many individuals have chosen to make themselves independent of a party and support candidates on other than partisan grounds.

**Republican Party** **(241)**
One of the major political parties in the United States. The Republican party was largely a product of the slavery issue. Unsatisfied with the antislavery positions of either the Democratic or Whig parties, a group of antislavery persons fashioned the Liberty party in 1840. The Free Soil party was established several years later when the question of slavery in the territories surfaced as the paramount political issue. Although neither of these parties survived as such, they created a political environment out of which the new Republican party could begin. The specific catalyst was the Kansas-Nebraska Act of 1854, which allowed the slavery issue to be decided by the residents of each territory. The Republican party was created to protest this policy. As the Democrats splintered and the Whigs faded away altogether over slavery and related questions, the Republicans established themselves as a major party with the election of Abraham Lincoln as president in 1860. The Republicans were to remain the dominant of the two parties until the election of 1932. The Republican party has generally reflected a more conservative orientation than the Democratic. The Republican voter coalition has traditionally included members of the business community, the more affluent, and the better educated. The farm belt of the Midwest has historically been part of this coalition. In recent years, especially with the candidacy of Ronald Reagan, the Republicans have increased their appeal in the South and among blue-collar workers. Generally, the Republican party has embraced policies that expand foreign trade, restrict growth of social welfare programs, deregulate U.S. business, and favor some form of intervention to deter the growth of Third World communism. *See also* DEMOCRATIC PARTY, 212; WHIG PARTY, 257.

*Significance* The Republican party was established on the basis of its opposition to slavery and its commitment to the preservation of the Union. Following the Civil War, the party was able to expand its base. It was, for example, able to gain strength in the commercial Northeast because of its support of protective tariffs. Its sound monetary policies engendered the support of industrialists. Thus, the party developed across sectional lines and was able to fashion a coalition that embraced businesspeople, farmers, and a number of urban residents. This coalition fragmented in the wake of the economic depression of the 1930s. Following World War II, the Republicans began a recovery by building support in suburban areas and in the previously

Democratic "solid South." This new coalition allowed the Republicans to win the White House with the candidacies of Dwight Eisenhower (1952), Richard Nixon (1968), and Ronald Reagan (1980). Although these victories did not quite bring about partisan realignment, the Republicans did achieve greater electoral success in elections contested at the state level as well as for the U.S. House and Senate. The potential for such realignment still exists, but whether the Republicans actually return to full majority status remains to be seen.

**Resolutions Committee** **(242)**
The committee that drafts a party's statement of basic principles and policy goals. The resolutions committee produces the party's platform for adoption at the national conventions. This function may be second in importance to selection of the presidential and vice-presidential candidates. Resolutions committees that function at county, district, and state conventions typically do not produce comprehensive documents; rather, they fashion short statements on resolutions on specific issues of importance at the state or local levels. The practice today is for the two major parties to begin the platform drafting process well in advance of the convention. Indeed, both parties conduct hearings around the country to permit people to offer their views on what should be included in the document. *See also* NATIONAL CONVENTION, 228; PLATFORM, 233.

*Significance* The work of resolutions committees is important to parties in at least three ways. First, the language of the party platform or its resolutions may help reconcile various factions within the party. A carefully crafted statement of common priorities lends itself to achieving unity within a party prior to a general election. This situation is particularly true when there has been a serious and possibly divisive contest for the presidential nomination. It is also important to avoid, if possible, a floor fight on platform in front of a national audience. Second, the platform may affect the breadth of a party's appeal in a particular election. If platform language reflects priorities that appeal to a broad range of voters, the party's election position is enhanced. Third, although platforms contain statements that do not formally bind candidates if elected, platform pledges are acted upon by the party that wins the election to a large degree; thus, they are not merely semantic exercises.

**Responsible Party System** **(243)**
A party system in which elected party members vote together on policy questions such that the parties can be held accountable for

implementing the programs they promise. Those who advocate a responsible party system argue that parties must take distinctive policy positions and that party members must subscribe to the party's positions. A party system is "responsible" because voters have clear choices between parties, party members holding legislative office are sufficiently disciplined to support the party position on key votes, and, when the party controls the government, its programs will invariably become policy. A good example of a responsible party system is that of Britain where parties are structured in such a way that the top leadership controls the legislative party. This dominance, in turn, creates party discipline such that the majority party's campaign platform may become governmental policy. *See also* LEGISLATIVE PARTY, 222; PARTY IN GOVERNMENT, 231.

*Significance* In a responsible party system, voting for a party has direct policy consequences. The responsible party concept rests on the premise that government is accountable to the electorate and that accountability is most likely to exist when voters are able to choose between unified and disciplined parties. The party prevailing in any election could then be judged on the basis of the policy it enacts and implements. A responsible party system could generate political debate on fundamental policy principles and allow the electorate to more effectively influence that policy. Government would itself become responsible by creating accountability through collective party action. U.S. political parties are structurally decentralized and lack the ideological focus necessary to create any possibility of a disciplined legislative party, however. The structure of government that divides power among three branches and several levels is a further impediment to responsible parties. Those who support such a system suggest that reconstituting the two major parties along liberal-conservative lines would foster responsible conduct by U.S. parties. Although truly responsible parties are unlikely in the United States, evidence shows that the two major parties have begun to pursue party platform positions more carefully.

**_Rosario v. Rockefeller_, 410 U.S 752 (1973) (244)**

Upheld a state requirement that voters formally affiliate with a party 30 days before a general election to be eligible to participate in the subsequent party primary. The Supreme Court rejected the contention that the requirement imposed an "onerous burden" on the exercise of the right to vote or the freedom to politically associate. The cut-off date occurred approximately eight months prior to the presidential primary (held in June) and eleven months prior to the nonpresidential primary (held in September). Although that period may be "lengthy," it is not arbitrary and is related to the "important state goal" of inhibiting party "raiding." The early enrollment deadline makes raiding "all but impossible" because few people will switch party affiliation just prior to a general election on the chance that it will work to their advantage in a subsequent primary election. The early enrollment requirement uses an "insulating general election" as the means of preventing the practice of raiding. Preservation of the "integrity" of the electoral process is a "legitimate and valid state goal," and the time between enrollment and the next primary is "tied to a particularized legitimate purpose and is in no sense invidious or arbitrary." *See also* PRIMARY ELECTION, 140; *TASHJIAN V. REPUBLICAN PARTY OF CONNECTICUT* (479 U.S. 208: 1986), 251.

*Significance* The primary election, in one form or another, has become the preferred nominating method in the 50 states. Many states use the closed primary, an election process in which participation is limited to formally registered party members. The closed primary is favored by political parties because it prevents voters affiliated with one party from "crossing over" and voting in another party's primary in hopes of nominating a weaker candidate, a process known as "raiding." At the same time, a closed primary excludes independent voters from participating and limits the opportunity of many voters to pick and choose the primary in which they wish to participate. *Rosario v. Rockefeller* (410 U.S. 752: 1973) upheld New York's closed primary process and the statutory provisions restricting the period in which voters could change party affiliations. The objective in establishing specified periods for formally changing registration was to prevent "raiding" by cross-over voters. The Supreme Court acknowledged the legitimacy of this objective and the ability of the restriction to advance the objective. Protection of electoral integrity is not an end that may be used indiscriminately to justify state regulation. In *Kusper v. Pontikes* (414 U.S. 51: 1973), the Court found a 23-month lead-time requirement for changing parties to be excessive. Similarly, in *Tashjian v. Republican Party of Connecticut* (479 U.S. 208: 1986), the Court struck down a state law that prohibited parties from opening their primaries to independent voters.

**Single-Issue Party** **(245)**

A political party formed to focus on and promote a position on one public policy question. A single-issue party does not advance a general view or philosophy of government. Rather, its sole purpose is to act as an advocate on an isolated policy issue. The Free Soil party of the mid-nineteenth century is an example of a single-issue party—it fought for the abolition of slavery. The Prohibition party is an example of an ongoing single-issue party. It first appeared in the late 1800s and continues to run candidates for president every four years. The candidates who represent parties that focus on abortion and environmental issues qualified for the ballot in several states in 1984. *See also* SINGLE-ISSUE GROUP, 327; THIRD PARTY, 252.

*Significance* Single-issue parties concentrate on only one issue. Unlike other political parties, single-issue parties have no expectation of electing their candidates to office. Instead, they are engaged in policy advocacy. Occasionally, like the Prohibitionists of the early 1900s, they achieve their policy objective. Even then, however, it is not because the single-issue party wins the election. If a single-issue party advocates a policy position that appeals to a large enough number of voters, one or both of the major parties embrace the position to enhance their own appeal. For example, the Republican party incorporated the issue of prohibition into their platform, succeeded at the polls, and instituted it. Since the early 1970s, single-issue groups have been more effective in influencing the electoral process by supporting or opposing candidates of the major parties rather than formally organizing a party that has no chance of electoral success. Although single-issue party activity may be minimal, single-issue interest groups have increased dramatically in number and have had considerable impact on the electoral process.

**Splinter Party** **(246)**

A political party that splits from one of the major parties. A splinter party is a particular kind of third party. Splinter parties are created when a faction of a major party becomes sufficiently dissatisfied with the party that it spins off or bolts and then challenges the former party with nominees of its own. Splinter or bolter parties have formed several times since the Civil War and have captured substantial portions of the vote in presidential elections. Examples of splinter parties include Theodore Roosevelt's Progressive or Bull Moose party, the States' Rights Democratic party, and the American Independent party. The Progressives spun off from the Republicans and won more than 25 percent of the popular vote and 88 electoral votes in the election of 1912. The States' Rights or Dixiecrat party was a southern splinter party of Democrats and won 39 electoral votes with the candidacy of Strom Thurmond in 1948. Twenty years later, George Wallace and his followers bolted from the Democratic party and won 46 electoral votes and 14 percent of the popular vote. *See also* THIRD PARTY, 252.

*Significance* Splinter parties typically are not ideologically based. Although they may have some issue differences with the major party from which they split, the break usually occurs over the choice of presidential candidate. Because splinter parties tend to form around candidates rather than doctrine, they tend to disappear when the person around whom they organize either fades from the political scene or reconciles with the party from which the faction split. Thus, splinter parties seldom last beyond an election or two. Furthermore, with the exception of the Roosevelt candidacy in 1912, splinter parties seldom determine outcomes in elections even though they may win a considerable share of the popular vote.

**Stalking Horse** **(247)**

A candidate for political office who runs on behalf of or as a cover for an unannounced candidate. Stalking horse candidacies are most often used in pursuit of the presidency. A stalking horse candidate attempts to appear as a bona fide candidate in an effort to measure real or potential support. If support is present, the stalking horse relinquishes his or her base to a stronger candidate who wished to remain undeclared until support could be gauged. If the stalking horse fails to generate support, the person on whose behalf the stalking horse candidacy was attempted does not pursue the nomination. Occasionally, stalking horse candidacies take the form of favorite son candidacies. *See also* FAVORITE SON, 216.

*Significance* The stalking horse acts as a decoy for a potential candidate. The stalking horse candidacy allows support to be measured, albeit indirectly, while protecting a political figure from an unsuccessful or ill-advised candidacy. The stalking horse may test the waters for a candidate representing a particular location on the ideological spectrum or a specific position on an especially controversial public policy issue. Use of stalking horse candidacies has decreased since 1970. Prospective candidates can now measure support more accurately through the use of public opinion polling techniques.

**State Party Organization** **(248)**

Organizational level of political parties defined by state boundaries. The state party has its own resources and possesses a substantial degree of independence from the national party. The organizational structure of parties at the state level resembles their national counterpart. The control mechanism is the state committee, sometimes called the state central committee. State committees vary greatly in size; some have several hundred members. Representation on these committees is usually based on county or legislative district units. Members are selected at local caucuses or conventions, although some states elect members at primaries. The most important functions of the state committee are to select the state party chair and to broadly set party objectives. The management of state party activities falls to the chair and the staff that is assembled by the chair. *See also* LOCAL PARTY ORGANIZATION, 223; NATIONAL COMMITTEE, 227.

*Significance* The state party organization is the principal functioning unit of the two major parties in the United States. Because the national party focuses on presidential politics almost exclusively, the vast remainder of party functions is left to the state and local parties. The state party recruits candidates, engages in fund-raising, develops and executes campaign strategies, and, when successful, organizes government at the state level. The party at the state level has become more critical as more state elections have become competitive since the mid-1970s. The success of state party organizations seems to be a function of the performance of the state party chair. Since 1970, chairs have become well-paid political professionals who establish professional headquarters operations. Unlike the national party, the state party does not possess full operating autonomy. In addition to nationally set party bylaws and to party tradition, state party organizations are governed by state law because of the role state parties play in the conduct of elections.

**_Storer v. Brown_, 415 U.S. 724 (1974) (249)**

Upheld a state law that did not permit an independent candidate a place on the ballot if he or she had a "registered affiliation" with a "qualified political party" within a year immediately preceding a primary election. The Supreme Court decided that the requirement was aimed at "maintaining the integrity" of "various routes" to the ballot and did not discriminate against independents. The policy was aimed at keeping people of one party from running in the primary of another party and at preventing those who had recently lost in a primary from running as independents. The law was based on the concept that the primary was not "merely an exercise or warm-up" for the general election but an integral part of an election process designed to "winnow out" candidates, thereby reserving the general election for "major struggles." The California position was that the general election was not a "forum for continuing intraparty feuds." The statutory provisions advance this policy aim. The direct primary process is protected by refusal to recognize independent candidates who do not "make early plans to leave a party and take the alternate course to the ballot." The regulation works against independent candidacies "prompted by short-range political goals, pique or personal quarrel." The rule also is a "substantial barrier" to a party's fielding an "independent" candidate to "capture and bleed off votes in the general election that might well go to another party." Although a state need not use the approach California did in this case, its perception that the practices regulated by the law may cause "significant damage" was seen as reasonable, as were the regulations employed in relation to it. *See also* MUNRO V. SOCIALIST WORKERS PARTY (479 U.S. 189: 1986), 226; WILLIAMS V. RHODES (393 U.S. 23: 1968), 258.

*Significance* *Storer v. Brown* (415 U.S. 724: 1974) examined the issue of ballot access. Among other provisions, the California Election Code regulated ballot access for independents. Only "bona fide" independents were permitted to petition for a ballot position. A "bona fide" independent was defined by the statute as a person with no registered party affiliation for at least a year prior to the primary election for which ballot access was being sought. Although recognizing that the right of candidacy and the right to vote are closely related and generally protected, the Supreme Court decided that the state objective of protecting the electoral process from disgruntled candidates and divisive candidacies was compelling enough to warrant the regulation. It was also true that the California law reviewed in *Storer* did not categorically deny ballot access to independents but rather only imposed a qualifying condition on such candidates. State regulations that have the potential to be exclusionary fare less well. For example, a state cannot impose excessively high petition signature requirements, unusually brief signature collection periods, or exorbitant filing fees because such regulations are too burdensome and may prevent certain candidacies altogether.

**Straight Ticket** **(250)**

The practice of voting only for the candidates of one political party. Straight-ticket voting is the opposite of ticket splitting, or voting for candidates of both major parties in the same election. Straight-ticket voting is facilitated by party-column ballots that allow a vote to be cast for all of a party's candidates by pulling a single voting machine lever or by marking the appropriate space on a ballot. Voters who identify most closely with a political party typically prefer their party's candidates over the candidates of the opposition party. Such identification is likely to lead to straight-ticket voting. *See also* PARTY IDENTIFICATION, 133; TICKET SPLITTING, 253.

*Significance* Straight-ticket voting places a premium on party and issue positions while minimizing the influence of individual candidates. It also tends to encourage cohesive legislative parties. Certainly straight-ticket voting simplifies the election process for a voter who wishes to use the single criterion of party as a voting cue. The practice of straight-ticket voting runs counter to the notion that voters should support the "best candidate" regardless of party. Those who subscribe to this view would engage in ticket splitting rather than straight-ticket voting.

**_Tashjian v. Republican Party of Connecticut_, 479 U.S. 208 (1986)** **(251)**

Ruled that states may not require political parties to hold primary elections open only to registered party members. Connecticut required that voters in a party primary must be registered members of that party. In an effort to broaden its own electoral base, the Republican party of Connecticut changed its rules to allow registered voters who were unaffiliated with any party to participate in primaries for federal and statewide offices. Possessing insufficient strength to amend the state law itself, the Republicans brought suit in federal court, asserting that enforcement of the law substantially burdened its First Amendment right of association. The Supreme Court decided in favor of the party because its First Amendment interest was so clearly "evident." The freedom to "engage in association" is an "inseparable aspect" of liberty embraced by the freedom of speech. The freedom of association includes "partisan political organization," and the right to associate with the party of one's choice is an "integral part" of this "basic constitutional freedom." Accordingly, the party's attempt to broaden its base is conduct "undeniably central to the exercise of the right to association." The statute in this case limits whom the party may "invite to participate in the 'basic function' of selecting the Party's candidates." The law thus limits the party's "associational opportunities at the crucial juncture at which the appeal to common principle may be translated into concerted actions, and hence to political power in the community." Connecticut contended that the state law prevented "raiding," a practice in which voters sympathetic to one party participate in another party's primary in hopes of influencing the result. Although acknowledging a legitimate state interest in preventing "raiding" and thereby protecting the "integrity of the electoral process," the Court felt that the raiding of the Republican primary by independents was a "notion" only "distantly related" to behavior that might appropriately be regulated. Finally, Connecticut contended that its law protected the "integrity of the two-party system and the responsibility of party government." Here the Court refused to consider the wisdom of open versus closed primaries and was unwilling to let the state substitute its own judgment for that of the party, even if the latter's course was "destructive of its own interests." *See also* DEMOCRATIC PARTY V. LAFOLLETTE (450 U.S. 351: 1981), 213; PRIMARY ELECTION, 140.

*Significance* The Supreme Court's ruling in *Tashjian v. Republican Party of Connecticut* (479 U.S. 208: 1986) permitted a state party to determine the rules by which it conducted its own primary. The Court has generally sought to steer clear of intervening in partisan political processes. In *O'Brien v. Brown* (409 U.S. 1: 1972), for example, the Court invoked the "political question" doctrine when it held that federal courts did not possess the authority to "interject" themselves into the "deliberative processes" of a presidential nominating convention. A decade later, the Court ruled in *Democratic Party v. LaFollette* (450 U.S. 351: 1981) that a state could not require national party convention delegates to support the candidacy of the winner of the state's presidential primary. Notwithstanding this generally noninterventionist tendency, the Court has found the states' interest in some restrictions on the electoral process to be compelling. Typically, these restrictions focus on registration requirements and duration of party affiliation, which were explicitly distinguished from the state law in *Tashjian.* The Court said such regulations were designed to protect parties from the "disorganizing effect of independent candidacies launched by unsuccessful putative nominees." This protection was undertaken to "protect the disruption of the political parties from without," and not to prevent parties from taking "internal steps affecting their own process for the selection of candidates." The Court was careful to point out, however, that *Tashjian* should not be read as blanket support for open primaries or that no state regulation of primary voting qualifications could be sustained. In a footnote, the Court said that party rules seeking to open a primary to anyone, for example, would pose a "different set of considerations" from those contained in *Tashjian.*

**Third Party** **(252)**

A new or highly doctrinaire political party that is usually not competitive in the U.S. two-party system. Regardless of their number, minor parties in the U.S. system are commonly called third parties. In the minds of some, a third party can be distinguished from a minor party on the basis of party origin and electoral impact. According to this distinction, third parties are composed of disaffected members of one of the major parties who break off, bolt, or splinter into a parallel party. The split is usually not the product of an issue or ideology but rather tends to be candidate focused. Such parties have a large enough voter following to have at least some short-term effects on election outcomes. Parties that fit this category are: the Progressive or Bull Moose party, which received more than 25 percent of the popular vote in 1912; the States' Rights Democrats (Dixiecrats) of 1948, who won 39 electoral votes in southern states; and the American Independent party, which won 46 electoral votes with the candidacy of George Wallace in 1948. Minor parties, on the other hand, are seen as issue- or doctrine-based. They tend to have minimal impact on election outcomes but tend to be of longer duration than third parties. Examples of minor parties are the Socialists, Socialist Workers, and Libertarians. Also included in the minor party category are single-issue parties such as the Prohibitionists. These parties focus exclusively on one policy question and ignore all others. *See also* IDEOLOGICAL PARTY, 218; SINGLE-ISSUE PARTY, 245; SPLINTER PARTY, 392.

*Significance* Third parties seldom play a decisive role in election campaigns at either the state or national levels. Rather, they provide an outlet for protest and a means by which policy alternatives may be articulated. History shows that third party movements typically fail unless events become critical. For example, because the Republicans in 1856 embraced strong antislavery and pro-Union positions and offered a sufficiently attractive alternative in presidential candidate Abraham Lincoln, they were able to win the election. In doing so, the Republicans replaced the Whigs as one of the two major parties. This turn of events is the exception, however. Minor parties face several formidable obstacles. First, most voters are firmly affiliated with a major party. And, even if a voter is sympathetic to the positions of a minor party, most know that such parties are not competitive and that tc support them amounts to "throwing away" a vote in the U.S. winner-take-all electoral system. Also, minor parties are often damaged by their candidate focus because once the political figure around which they form passes from the political scene, the party has little to justify its existence. Furthermore, attractive policy positions are subject to seizure by the major parties, which can offer the prospect of actually transforming preferences into actual policy. There are also financial and legal barriers. Third parties can seldom mobilize sufficient resources to effectively spread their message. If, however, a third party candidate receives between 5 and 25 percent of the vote in a presidential election, he or she is eligible to receive federal campaign funds in the next election. Finally, third parties also face difficult requirements to qualify for the ballot.

**Ticket Splitting (253)**

The practice of voting for candidates of the two major parties in the same election. Ticket splitting is the opposite of voting straight ticket, or voting for only candidates of one political party. Split-ticket voting occurs only in a general election because in virtually all primary elections, a voter must use a ballot that contains candidates of only one party. Ticket splitting is a practice favored by those who consider themselves independents or by those who only weakly identify with a party. Ticket splitting is encouraged by a ballot format that focuses on offices (office block ballot) rather than party. *See also* STRAIGHT TICKET, 250.

*Significance* Ticket splitting is done by individuals who vote for the "best candidate." Many voters prefer this method of participating in elections. If a voter rejects the simplification that occurs by voting party, he or she must invest greater energy in examining candidate qualifications and issue positions. The risk is that voters may simply respond to personality rather than real qualifications. Rejection of party by a large number of voters further weakens the possibility of cohesive or disciplined action on the part of elected officials. Ticket splitting often results in different parties controlling the legislative and executive branches, which, in turn, creates the possibility of governmental deadlock.

**Two-Party System (254)**

A political system in which candidates seriously competing for elective office come from the two major political parties. The U.S. two-party system grew naturally from the British example but was at least in part a consequence of early polarization around the question of a stronger central government. The first two U.S. parties—the Federalists and the Anti-Federalists (Jeffersonian Republicans)—split on this fundamental federal-state issue. The history of parties since that time reveals alternations of power between two major parties. Today's Democrats have their origin in the original Jeffersonian party, whereas the Republicans emerged just prior to the Civil War. These two parties have maintained their status as major parties ever since. The U.S. two-party system is also a product of the way public officials are elected. First, the winner is the candidate with the most votes. In addition, we tend not to use multimember or at-large districts for legislatures. Rather, we apportion legislators into single-member districts. A close second-place showing is not rewarded by allocating seats on a proportional basis. On the contrary, the U.S. electoral process is based on a winner-take-all principle, which lends itself to a two-party system. *See also* LEGISLATIVE PARTY, 222; MULTIPARTY SYSTEM, 225; SINGLE-MEMBER DISTRICT, 149.

*Significance* The parties in a two-party system tend to be large coalitions of individuals with fairly diverse interests and views. Such parties tend not to be highly ideological because of their need to be broadly based. Because electoral success typically depends on capturing more voters near the large center of the political spectrum, neither major party can afford to be drawn too far from the center. If a third or single-issue party periodically captures some support, the two major parties tend to embrace the issue to draw voters back into the two-party framework. Before a third party can establish itself as competitive, its base is absorbed. A two-party system tends to simplify voter choices. It also guarantees the election of a party majority to legislative bodies, which allows the winning party to effectively pursue its policy priorities. Finally, because elections tend to be contested near the political center, whoever wins is not likely to depart fundamentally from the status quo, thus political stability is fashioned. It is also a more stable system in that no coalitions of minority parties are required to form a government.

***United States v. Classic*, 313 U.S. 299 (1941) (255)**

Ruled that primaries were part of the election process and subject to federal regulation. Federal charges were brought against several state officials for altering results of a congressional primary. The issue in *United States v. Classic* was whether having such primary ballots properly counted is a right "secured by the Constitution" and enforceable under federal law. The Supreme Court ruled in the affirmative. Although acknowledging the "wide discretion" possessed by the states in conducting elections, the Court said that the framers of the Constitution did not wish to allow states to engage in practices that "defeat the right of the people to choose representatives for Congress." The right to vote, said the Court, includes the right to have the ballot counted at the "general election," and where state law has "made the primary an integral part of the procedure of choice," or where the "primary effectively controls the choice," counting the primary ballots is included in this right. The Court said it could not "close [its] eyes" to the fact that the practical influence of the primary may be so great as to "affect profoundly" the choice at the general election. Unless the constitutional protection of the integrity of elections extends to primaries, the Court concluded, Congress is "left powerless" to effect the "constitutional right of choice." *See also* PRIMARY ELECTION, 140; *SMITH V. ALLWRIGHT* (321 U.S. 649: 1944), 84; WHITE PRIMARY, 98.

*Significance* *United States v. Classic* (313 U.S. 299: 1941) seems like an obvious ruling, but it reversed policy established over several decades that placed the primary outside the election process. The pre-*Classic* view of primaries had its most dramatic impact in the South where it permitted exclusion of blacks from primaries. The origin of the policy grew out of an attempt by Congress to regulate campaign financing in the Corrupt Practices Act of 1910. The act included expenditures made in pursuit of the nomination as well as in the general election. In *Newberry v. United States* (256 U.S. 232: 1921), the Supreme Court had occasion to review this statute and concluded that the primary was wholly independent from the general election. This decision was interpreted as meaning that no constitutional protections reached primaries, including guarantees of equal protection. It was in this manner that blacks were excluded from participating in primaries in a number of states through the private action of political parties. The decision in *Classic* linked the primary to the overall election process, thus overruling the *Newberry* precedent. Although *Classic* did not directly address the white primary, the ruling left the practice vulnerable to close scrutiny. Within three years, in *Smith v. Allwright* (321 U.S. 649: 1944), the Court ruled that parties were not acting as private agents in conducting primaries, a decision that made primaries subject to constitutional limitations.

**Unit Rule** **(256)**

Requirement that state delegations at party conventions vote as a bloc for a single candidate. The unit rule was employed by the Democrats to allow the majority of a delegation to bind the minority to vote as a bloc for the majority's choice. Practices such as the unit rule diminish the representativeness of conventions and were banned by the party prior to the 1972 national convention. *See also* NATIONAL CONVENTION, 228.

*Significance* The unit rule was a device that maximized majority control at a party convention. The vote was prohibited by the reforms adopted by the Democratic Party following the turbulent national convention of 1968. Two commissions were appointed by the Democratic national chair in 1969: The McGovern-Fraser Commission focused on party structure and delegate selection; the commission headed by Rep. James O'Hara dealt with convention rules. The more sweeping reforms involved state party rules and delegate selection. Once adopted by the Democratic National Committee, seating of state delegations at the 1972 convention depended on compliance. Foremost among the reforms were (1) adoption of written rules covering delegate selection, (2) broadening of the base of groups represented at the convention, and (3) safeguarding of process integrity. Among the process safeguards were the elimination of proxy voting and the unit rule. These reforms also required that delegations be selected within the calendar year of the election; this requirement was modified prior to the 1984 campaign. The new Democratic rules also provide for selection of a number (14 percent) of the convention delegates, called superdelegates, on the basis of public office or party positions. These superdelegates return some convention influence to the political professionals. Finally, the Democrats have returned, at least to a limited degree, to a form of the unit rule. The new rule holds that a presidential candidate who wins a decisive proportion of the popular vote in a district may claim all the delegates from that district.

**Whig Party** **(257)**

U.S. political party of the mid-nineteenth century. The Whig party was formed in 1830 by a coalition opposed to the Jacksonian Democrats. Most Whigs came from a faction of the Democratic-Republican party known as the National Republicans, who were unwilling to pursue the Jacksonian priority of democratization of the party and the political system. The National Republicans were not without some strength, having won the presidency in 1824 with John Quincy Adams as their candidate. The Whigs also drew from the old Federalist party. The Whigs advocated a nationalistic economic approach (known as the American system) that drew heavily from economic policies advocated by the guiding spirit of the Federalists, Alexander Hamilton. The name Whig was chosen because its English forerunner had not favored a strong monarchy. The Whigs saw executive power grow under Jackson and often made disparaging reference to "King Andrew." *See also* FEDERALIST PARTY, 217; JACKSONIAN DEMOCRATIC PARTY, 220.

*Significance* The principal leaders of the Whig party were Henry Clay and Daniel Webster. During the 1830s, these two were strong advocates of Whig party priorities such as use of protective tariffs and maintenance of the national bank, positions strongly opposed by Jackson. The Whigs were unsuccessful in contesting Jackson in 1832 but were joined by John C. Calhoun and a number of southern Democrats during the decade. This allowed the Whigs to win the presidency in 1840 with William Henry Harrison defeating Jackson's successor, Martin Van Buren. The Whigs lost the presidency in 1844 but regained it in 1848. The next four years, during the Whig administrations of Zachary Taylor and Millard Fillmore, were the beginning of the end. The central issue of the time, of course, was slavery. Though Whigs were instrumental in reaching the Compromise of 1850, the party was divided by the slavery issue and the sectional factions associated with it. Many southern and proslavery Whigs turned to the Democrats while northerners and antislavery Whigs joined the emerging Republican party. The Whigs ran a candidate (Winfield Scott) for president in 1852 but lost to the Democrats. The Whigs met in convention in 1856 but failed to nominate a candidate of their own, choosing instead to endorse Millard Fillmore, a former Whig and candidate of the Knownothings. By the Civil War, the Republican party had replaced the Whigs as one of the major parties.

**_Williams v. Rhodes_, 393 U.S. 23 (1968) (258)**

Ruled that a state election law unfairly favored the two established major parties. Ohio required that a "new" party submit petitions signed by properly registered voters, totaling 15 percent of the votes cast in the most recent gubernatorial election. The Democratic and Republican parties were able to retain their ballot position simply by getting 10 percent of the vote in the last gubernatorial election. Neither major party was required to submit petitions so long as they met the 10 percent voter support level. The Supreme Court decided this policy violated the equal protection clause and impinged both on the right to vote and to politically associate. The laws give the old, established parties a "decided advantage over any new parties struggling for existence." The right to form a party for the "advancement of political goals means little if a party can be kept off the election ballots and thus denied an equal opportunity to win votes." Furthermore, the right to vote is "heavily burdened" if that vote may be cast for one of two parties "at a time when other parties are clamoring for a place on the ballot." The Court rejected Ohio's contention that it could "promote a two-party system in order to encourage compromise and political stability." The Ohio system did not merely favor a two-party system, said the Court; rather, it favored two "particular parties." The Court found no reason why just two parties "should retain a permanent monopoly on the right to have people vote for or against them." Competition in government policies and ideas is "at the core of our electoral processes and of the First Amendment freedoms." New parties must have the "time and opportunity" to organize in order to meet "reasonable requirements for ballot position, just as the old parties have had in the past." *See also* MUNRO V. SOCIALIST WORKERS PARTY (479 U.S. 189: 1986), 226.

*Significance* *Williams v. Rhodes* (393 U.S. 23: 1968) focused on the issue of party access to the ballot. The Supreme Court has historically permitted states to exercise fairly comprehensive supervisory authority over elections. Regulations that govern party access to ballots, however, began to receive greater scrutiny following the Warren Court's intervention in the legislative apportionment question in the 1960s. Regulations that require some demonstration of support, typically petition signatures or a specified proportion of votes from preceding elections or primaries, have generally been sustained so long as the qualifying levels have been reasonable. Laws like that in *Williams v. Rhodes,* however, which treat major and minor or new parties differently have generally been invalidated. Although states possess a compelling interest in "preserving the integrity of the electoral process," they may not do so by imposing unequal conditions on the opportunity to compete in that process.

# 6. *Interest Groups*

An interest group is an organized body of people who share common objectives. The members act through the group to attempt to influence public policy. Many Americans belong to at least one organized interest group because this kind of association provides a variety of benefits, the foremost being that it amplifies a person's capacity to have an impact on public policy. Next to voting, participating in an organized group is the most popular form of political involvement for ordinary citizens. An interest group differs from a political party in that the winning of elective office is not its principal objective. Also, a political party's policy preferences, as reflected in its platform, cover a wide range of issues; whereas an interest group focuses on only policy decisions that are important to it, regardless of which officeholder made them. Although interest groups may endorse a particular candidate or officeholder, that support will remain only so long as that individual helps advance the group's objectives.

Interest groups are both numerous and diverse, large and small. Some are highly organized, meet regularly, and command substantial resources. Other groups are quite informally organized, seldom meet, and may not even collect the most minimal membership dues. The diversity represented along these variables corresponds highly to the effectiveness of the groups within the political process. The United States has quite a number of interest groups because each tends to focus on a particular issue or set of issues. Given the narrow focus of most groups and the heterogeneous character of the U.S. population, numerous groups must exist to accommodate the broad spectrum of interests. Further, it is clear that engaging in various activities through organized groups is effective. Success, even to a limited degree, offers encouragement to others. The great number of interest groups is also explained in part by the federal-state system. Because public policy decisions are made in a variety of locations—Washington, D.C., state capitols, and city halls—groups are organized to promote and protect their interests in all of these places. Formation of many groups is also facilitated because voluntary association is a constitutionally protected activity. Americans join groups as well because their socialization process places value on it and because organizers of groups are skilled at marketing the benefits of membership. Finally, social and economic conditions and governmental policy initiatives often prompt formation of additional interest groups.

Despite the large number of political interest groups, they can be divided into several major categories. The largest category is the economic interest group. Included here are business and trade organizations, labor unions, and farm groups. The primary objective of these groups is the economic well-being of their membership, which often places them in conflict with one another. This circumstance is viewed by many people as productive because the ongoing competition of interests diminishes the likelihood of any particular interest prevailing indefinitely. The second category comprises groups that grow out of particular political movements—for example, civil rights and women's rights organizations or more ideologically oriented groups such as the American Conservative Union (ACU) and Americans for Democratic Action (ADA). Within the third category are professional associations such as the American Medical Association (AMA), American Bar Association (ABA), and National Education Association (NEA). Although these groups stress the professional interests of their members, they are also heavily involved in protecting their members' economic interests. Public agencies also organize themselves in order to protect their interests in the volatile appropriations processes at the federal, state, and local levels. Organizations representing the interests of city or county governments are numerous, for example. Finally, many public interest groups—such as Common Cause and various environmental groups—have formed since the 1960s; they define their function as protecting the "public interest" as they see it.

Several tactics are employed by interest groups and generally, each is effective in its own way. The first tactic is direct lobbying, whereby representatives of an organization attempt to convince government officials to take particular policy stances by persuasion or through providing officials with reliable information on particular policy questions. The second technique is indirect lobbying, whereby an organization engages in grassroots politics by attempting to generate constituent pressure on government officials. Third, interest groups may become directly engaged in political campaigns either by publicly endorsing a candidate or by providing campaign funds through political action committees (PACs). This form of group involvement in campaigns has grown dramatically since the early 1970s. Finally, groups may use legal action as a means of furthering or protecting their members' interests. Lawsuits are effectively and widely used to compel policy changes, and most suits of consequence are initiated by interest groups.

The bottom line is that interest groups continue to play a significant role in the U.S. political process. Groups provide representation for citizens by communicating views and information to those in positions of formal authority. When people perceive that they have the capacity to influence government, positive attitudes toward the political system are fostered. This, in turn, has contributed to the highly stable political structure in the United States. There are, however, some negative consequences as well. Although to a certain extent groups tend to compete and counterbalance one another, there are significant differences in how well different interests are actually represented. Business and professional interests, for example, have greater resources at their disposal and thus have disproportionately greater influence. The importance of this disparity is magnified by the central role money plays in the political area. Despite the undesirable effects that may result from these inequities, interest groups will continue to perform a constructive function in the U.S. political system.

**Access** **(259)**

Refers to the ability of a group to approach or communicate with officials in the policymaking process. Access is often seen as the prerequisite to wielding any influence on governmental policy. Representatives of interest groups emphasize that they seek access rather than influence through their various lobbying techniques. The actual line of distinction between access and influence is blurred, but it is clear that the latter cannot be achieved without the former. Consider the circumstance of the policymaker who receives information or is accessed by a party representing only one side on a policy question. A more likely situation occurs when the extent of contact or volume of information is markedly different. Interests that have the greatest access to policymakers in order to provide information and arguments are likely to be the most influential. *See also* LOBBYING, 300; PLURALIST THEORY, 318.

*Significance* Access provides the opportunity to communicate with those who possess policymaking authority. Although communication may not always be persuasive, it will at least engage the policymaker's attention. Interests represented repeatedly are likely to have that access translated into impact on substantive policy. It is clear that numerous factors actually affect political outcomes, but for some observers, especially those who subscribe to the pluralist theory, government is seen as operating through competing interests. Key to pluralistic democracy are organized groups that represent interests and a governmental structure that is accessible at a sufficient number of points to permit group impact. Once achieved, access may be utilized by one or more lobbying or interest-representing techniques.

**Agricultural Organization** **(260)**

A group organized to represent the array of farm community interests. The agricultural community is not monolithic, and agricultural organizations reflect that diversity. Farm interests vary substantially by size of farm, by commodities grown, and by the political orientation of the farmers. The largest farm organization is the American Farm Bureau Federation (AFBF), or Farm Bureau, with membership exceeding 3 million. The Farm Bureau has typically opposed governmental intervention in the farm economy and has come to represent the more conservative orientation of wealthier farmers. The National Farmers Union (NFU), on the other hand, tends to reflect the interests of the smaller and lower-income farmers and has strongly supported governmental agricultural subsidy programs. The interests of agriculture are also organized around specific commodities or production specialties such as the Association of Wheat Growers and the National Milk Producers Association. These commodity organizations are the agricultural counterpart to trade associations. *See also* AMERICAN FARM BUREAU FEDERATION (AFBF), 264; ECONOMIC-BASED GROUPS, 282; NATIONAL FARMERS UNION (NFU), 310.

*Significance* Agricultural organizations have a long history of political involvement, but the influence of some of the older organizations declined after the 1970s. Since then, prices for farm products have remained low in an otherwise inflationary economy, and substantial numbers of farmers have been forced to leave farming because of increasing indebtedness and foreclosures. These economic pressures have led farmers to become more militant in making demands on the political process. Some new organizations—the American Agriculture Movement (AAM), for example—have formed as a result. The AAM has organized demonstrations in Washington and various state capitals as a way of dramatizing the farm crisis. It has also urged farmers to withhold products from the market in an effort to raise price levels. If the conditions facing the farm community go unrelieved, these newer and more aggressive agricultural groups may cut into the support for older organizations whose tactics have been less confrontational.

**American Bar Association (ABA) (261)**

A voluntary association of U.S. lawyers. The American Bar Association (ABA) was founded in 1878 to generally improve the legal profession. The initial concern of the ABA was the absence of quality controls on legal education and admission to the profession. The ABA took the lead in tightening accreditation standards for U.S. law schools. Demonstration of proficiency by passing a bar examination as a requirement for entry to the profession was also an area in which the ABA was most active. Its activities eventually were extended beyond professional quality and development to include fostering greater public understanding of the legal system. The main governing body of the ABA is the House of Delegates, but the bulk of the preliminary work of the organization is done through an extensive network of highly specialized sections, divisions, task forces, and standing committees. The ABA puts out a number of publications including the *American Bar Association Journal* (monthly) and the *Washington Summary* (weekly newsletter). A variety of affiliated organizations such as the American Bar Foundation also exist through which research and publications helpful to the profession emanate. *See also* INTEREST GROUP, 293; PROFESSIONAL ASSOCIATION, 320.

*Significance* The American Bar Association (ABA) is the largest of the professional associations, with membership numbering in excess of 330,000. The ABA works closely with state bar associations in pursuing objectives related to professional competence and responsibility. As the national representative of the profession, the ABA has been effective in its support of proposals aimed at improving the U.S. justice system. It has sought or supported reforms that would improve the provisions of child welfare services and enhance delivery of legal services, especially to those unable to afford them. In general, the ABA is sensitive to procedural issues associated with government operations or policies. The ABA also plays a critical role in the selection process for federal judges. A standing committee of the ABA formally examines each federal court nominee and offers its evaluation to the Senate prior to its discharge of the advise and consent function. Occasionally, the ABA is consulted about the qualifications of potential nominees prior to the actual selection by the president.

**American Civil Liberties Union (ACLU)** **(262)**
An organization that seeks to maintain and extend constitutionally protected rights. The American Civil Liberties Union (ACLU) was founded in 1920 and currently is composed of a national office, several regional offices, affiliated units at the state level, and several hundred local chapters. The ACLU consists of two corporate entities at the national level that both share the common objective of preserving individual rights but that differ in the techniques they employ. The first entity is the ACLU, which concentrates on the legislative arena and is the direct lobbying mechanism. The ACLU Foundation, on the other hand, is the litigative arm of the organization. The foundation typically involves itself in lawsuits that raise substantial individual rights questions by directly sponsoring these cases, by providing legal assistance, or by filing amicus curiae, or "friend of the court," briefs that argue the broader constitutional implications of a particular case. The ACLU's public education activities are also conducted under the auspices of the foundation. This includes the regular publication of the ACLU newspaper, *Civil Liberties,* as well as other special newsletters, reports, monographs, and brochures. *See also* CIVIL RIGHTS GROUP, 275; PUBLIC INTEREST GROUP, 321.

*Significance* The American Civil Liberties Union (ACLU) is largely dependent on the performance of its state and local affiliates. Although the national ACLU may successfully litigate some issue before the Supreme Court, the local affiliates act to monitor actual compliance and to take whatever action might be necessary to make sure policy victories become practice. The ACLU has focused generally on issues involving the First Amendment, rights of the accused, and equal protection. This concern for individual rights has found the ACLU directly involved with a number of highly controversial cases or issues, including the Scopes "monkey" trial (the original evolution case), the Scottsboro rape trial, the detention of the Japanese-Americans during World War II, opposition to McCarthyism, the public school Bible-reading controversy, opposition to Vietnam involvement, and even the right of the American Nazi party to demonstrate on public streets. Prominent since the 1970s has been the protection of the rights of women, migrants, and children and the expansion of the right of privacy.

**American Conservative Union (ACU)** **(263)**
An organization established to advance public policy based on the conservative ideology. The American Conservative Union (ACU) was founded in 1964 and currently has affiliates in every state. The ACU

is the oldest and, in its words, "most influential conservative lobbying group in Washington." The ACU actively promotes a conservative political agenda and closely monitors the voting behavior of Congress. It is also active in the broader political arena and addresses selected issues through a public education program that includes publication of the monthly newsletter *Battleline* and sponsorship of the annual Conservative Political Action Conference. *See also* IDEOLOGICAL GROUP, 291; PUBLIC INTEREST GROUP, 321.

*Significance* The American Conservative Union (ACU) has provided an ideological anchor for much of the New Right political agenda. Indeed, the priorities of Ronald Reagan's administration are fully embraced by the ACU, and, in turn, Reagan saw the ACU as key to bringing about a political change in direction at the federal level. The ACU publishes an annual rating of Congress that reflects support of individual members as measured by selected roll-call votes. The ACU has generally supported deregulation of business and federal tax reduction while opposing any increases in federal spending on domestic programs. More specifically, the "correct" legislative vote, according to the ACU, would have included support for MX missile funding, the confirmation of Edwin Meese, funding of Contra aid and rebel forces in Angola, the strategic defense initiative (SDI), removal of the ban on interstate gun sales, the Gramm-Rudman Act, and restricting federal courts from considering cases involving school prayer. The ACU opposed economic sanctions against South Africa, import limits on textiles and apparel, reauthorization of the Clean Water Act, and reauthorization of the "superfund" hazardous waste cleanup program.

**American Farm Bureau Federation (AFBF) (264)**

The largest general farm organization in the United States. The American Farm Bureau Federation (AFBF), or Farm Bureau, is an umbrella structure for upwards of 3,000 county bureaus that exist throughout the country. The AFBF was the outgrowth of a view that government ought to take the lead in developing agriculture. Education and research were seen as the two best general approaches, with the land grant colleges and the agricultural extension service becoming the specific means of delivery. Local farm bureaus initially acted as the sponsoring agencies for the extension service. Although formal financial and other ties no longer exist, this initial linkage was crucial to the development of the AFBF. The AFBF was actually founded in 1919 to join together the numerous local and state bureaus in order to expand focus to broader economic concerns and to facilitate political action in Washington. The AFBF remains an active representative of U.S. farm interests in the political arena. In addition to its continuing commitment to agricultural research and educational programs, the AFBF provides a number of key services to its members, usually through cooperatives. For example, it provides market analyses, technical assistance for production and management matters, supply purchasing services, and farm insurance. Finally, the AFBF produces several publications including both weekly and monthly newsletters. *See also* AGRICULTURAL ORGANIZATION, 260; ECONOMIC-BASED GROUP, 282.

*Significance* The American Farm Bureau Federation (AFBF) has become a generally conservative representative of farm interests. Although supporting government initiatives in the area of soil and water conservation, for example, the AFBF has until recently not supported federal agricultural subsidy programs. In an effort to protect family farming, the Farm Bureau has strongly urged estate tax elimination or at least reform. Other AFBF positions on farm-related issues include pressing for agricultural exemptions to Environmental Protection Agency (EPA) chemical regulations, limiting farmer liability in pesticide damage cases, relaxing meat and poultry inspection processes, and supporting restrictions of foreign investment in land suitable for agriculture. The AFBF also takes positions on other than agricultural issues. For example, it supports school prayer and a constitutional amendment requiring a balanced budget and has opposed certain federal programs it feels facilitate union organizing.

**American Federation of Labor–Congress of Industrial Organizations (AFL-CIO)** **(265)**

The largest labor organization in the United States. The American Federation of Labor–Congress of Industrial Organizations (AFL-CIO) was formed in 1955 and is a broad federation within which several hundred operating unions reside. The AFL-CIO is the product of a merger between the AFL, an organization of largely skilled workers such as those in the building trades, and the CIO, an organization of semi- or unskilled labor from mass production industries. Among the larger operating unions affiliated with the AFL-CIO are the United Steelworkers, the American Federation of State, County, and Municipal Employees (AFSCME), the American Federation of Teachers, and in 1987 the International Brotherhood of Teamsters. The AFL-CIO does not engage in collective bargaining but leaves that function to its individual member unions. Rather, it acts as the political action component of organized labor. The AFL-CIO represents labor before governmental bodies, assists in organizing nonunion workers, coordinates public information campaigns, and is heavily involved in electoral politics. Its Committee on Political Education (COPE) financially supports federal candidates who receive AFL-CIO endorsement. The AFL-CIO also monitors congressional voting records and rates members on the degree to which they support the "interests of workers." *See also* ECONOMIC-BASED GROUP, 282; LABOR ORGANIZATION, 296.

*Significance* The American Federation of Labor–Congress of Industrial Organizations (AFL-CIO) is the country's most powerful labor organization. Accordingly, it devotes a great deal of its resources to improving the living standards, working conditions, and job security of the U.S. workforce. The AFL-CIO aggressively supports policies that improve wage standards, workers' compensation and unemployment benefits, job safety (including strengthening of the Occupational Safety and Health Administration), repeal of section 14(b) of the Taft-Hartley Act, which allows states to have right-to-work laws, and measures that would curtail the export of jobs. The AFL-CIO does not, however, confine itself to labor issues. It supports most urban aid and domestic social welfare programs; strengthening environmental and consumer protection agencies; increasing federal funding for such programs as Head Start, Medicare, Medicaid, and revenue sharing; and economic sanctions against South Africa. The AFL-CIO has also opposed the Gramm-Rudman deficit-reduction plan.

**American Medical Association (AMA) (266)**

A national federation of physician associations. The American Medical Association (AMA) was founded in 1847 for the purpose of promoting the science and art of medicine and the betterment of public health. Its membership numbers around 250,000 and accounts for approximately 70 percent of the nation's practicing physicians. The AMA accredits medical schools, acts as a clearinghouse for medical data, and publishes the *Journal of the American Medical Association* in addition to numerous other publications. Much of the AMA's effort to advance medicine comes through the work of its many councils and committees. It also operates the Institute for Biomedical Research, which involves the AMA directly in the sponsorship of medical research. The AMA also maintains files on suspect practices and practitioners in an effort to eliminate fraud and quackery. The AMA's Council on Drugs is involved in developing testing procedures for new drugs and generally monitors the promotion or advertising of drugs. The governing body of the AMA is the House of Delegates, which comprises over 200 members drawn from the broad array of AMA constituencies. *See also* INTEREST GROUP, 293; PROFESSIONAL ASSOCIATION, 320.

*Significance* The American Medical Association (AMA) maintains an extremely active presence in Washington. The AMA lobbying staff is heavily involved in drafting proposals and appearing before both legislative committees and executive agencies to speak on issues relating to the medical profession. The foremost issues relate to the Medicare and Medicaid programs, health planning, and reforms or regulations aimed at controlling health costs. Historically, the AMA has been successful in its pursuit of measures that would more tightly regulate food and drugs, establish boards of health at the state and local levels, and improve efforts at arresting water and air pollution.

**American Petroleum Institute (API)** **(267)**
A trade association that represents the domestic petroleum industry. The American Petroleum Institute (API) was founded in 1919 and has a current membership of some 200 domestic companies, about 30 foreign companies, and several thousand individuals. The API was designed to promote the interests of the petroleum industry, foster technological development within the industry, and serve as the principal linkage between the industry and government. The API operates from policy decisions made through a committee structure that draws together representatives from virtually all sectors of the petroleum industry. An elected institute chair and president are responsible for management of the professional staff and implementation of adopted policies. In addition to providing a wide range of services to the member companies, the API coordinates industry appearances before Congress and regulatory agencies, engages in direct lobbying, and uses the courts to litigate governmental policies that it views as unreasonable. *See also* BUSINESS ORGANIZATION, 272; TRADE ASSOCIATION, 331.

*Significance* The activities of the American Petroleum Institute (API) are representative of those of a trade association. Although trade associations are business organizations in a broad sense, they do focus on the interests of a particular industry. For example, since the 1970s, interests of importance to the API include tax policy affecting the industry, environmental and transportation regulations, and exploration incentives. More specifically, the API has supported opening more federal lands for energy development, private development of synthetic fuels and governmental subsidies toward that end, greater use of nuclear power, and an easing of various environmental regulations. Furthermore, the API was active in its opposition to the tax package proposed to fund the hazardous-waste cleanup "superfund."

**Americans for Democratic Action (ADA) (268)**
An ideological organization that supports liberal or progressive policies and candidates. The Americans for Democratic Action (ADA) was founded in 1947 by leaders of the liberal community to fashion and advance liberal domestic and foreign policy positions based on the realities and changing needs of U.S. democracy. The ADA seeks to foster public understanding and support for its positions by using public education programs. It also seeks to have its positions become government policy through aggressive direct lobbying of Congress and by attempting to influence the major political party platforms. Like other ideological groups, the ADA depends upon regular newsletters and reports to inform and retain its membership. The ADA was the first group to measure legislative ideology by means of a roll-call vote scorecard. High ADA scores have become a reliable measure of liberal orientation. *See also* IDEOLOGICAL GROUP, 291; INTEREST GROUP, 293.

*Significance* The Americans for Democratic Action (ADA) develop policy positions through a network of standing committees. Representative of recent policy preferences is ADA support for liberalization of long-term unemployment benefits; increases in funding levels for such domestic programs as Head Start, guaranteed student loans, summer youth employment, Medicare, and Medicaid; retaining the ban on interstate handgun sales; and general reduction in defense appropriations, including MX missile production. The ADA has opposed such policies as elimination of cost-of-living adjustments in Social Security benefits, aid to Nicaraguan Contras, repeal of the ban on assistance to Angolan rebels, presidential line-item veto power, the Gramm-Rudman Act, and a proposed ban on federal court consideration of school prayer. Like other ideological groups, the ADA has established a political action committee (ADA/PAC) that directly contributes to the campaigns of liberal congressional candidates.

**Amicus Curiae (269)**
An organization (or individual) that submits arguments in the form of a written brief to a court, expressing views on a legal question before the court. An amicus curiae, which literally means "friend of the court," is not an actual party to the lawsuit. Rather, it is an interested

third party that attempts to provide the court with information or arguments that may not have been offered by the actual parties. *See also* LITIGATION, 299.

*Significance* Amicus curiae participation is a common activity for interest groups that use the courts as a means of furthering group objectives. It typically occurs in cases with substantial public-interest ramifications. As the Supreme Court considered whether a woman has a constitutional right to an abortion in *Roe v. Wade* (410 U.S. 113: 1973), amicus briefs were submitted by 36 pro-abortion and 11 anti-abortion organizations. Amicus arguments tend to focus on the broader implications of a particular case. Submission of an amicus brief is not a matter of right, however. With the exception of amicus participation by an agency of the federal government, an amicus brief may be filed only with the consent of both parties in an action, on motion to the court, or by invitation of the court.

**Association, Right of** **(270)**

The legal right of a group of people acting together to advance a mutual interest or achieve a common objective. The right of association is not expressly protected by the First Amendment but is derived from safeguards for expression and assembly contained therein. The utility of association as a means of achieving political and social goals was acknowledged by the Supreme Court in *NAACP v. Button* (357 U.S. 449: 1958). The Court said, "Effective advocacy of both public and private points of view, particularly controversial ones, is undeniably enhanced by group association." Given the fundamental role of associational activity, government bears an obligation to ensure that interference with such activity does not occur. The Court struck down a state membership disclosure requirement in *NAACP v. Alabama* (357 U.S. 449: 1958) because the regulation adversely affected the ability of the National Association for the Advancement of Colored People (NAACP) and its members to "pursue their collective effort to foster beliefs which they admittedly have a right to advocate." *See also* *BRANDENBURG V. OHIO* (395 U.S. 444: 1969), 271; *KEYISHIAN V. BOARD OF REGENTS* (385 U.S. 589: 1967), 295; *NAACP V. ALABAMA* (357 U.S. 449: 1958), 305.

*Significance* The right of association may have positive effects in a democracy, but regulation may still be imposed. The most troublesome association cases have involved statutory attempts to proscribe subversive organizations and prohibit criminal syndicalism. Syndicalism refers to the takeover of the means of industrial production by workers; criminal syndicalism involves the advocacy of, or participation in, unlawful acts to achieve political change. Many states had criminal syndicalism statutes that were upheld initially because association itself was seen as concerted action threatening public security (*Whitney v. California*, 274 U.S. 357: 1927). The Warren Court rejected this approach because such laws were directed at "mere abstract teaching," or advocacy that is not necessarily related to unlawful acts. Decisions such as *Keyishian v. Board of Regents* (385 U.S. 589: 1967) found "mere membership" in subversive organizations to be insufficient grounds for exclusion from public employment. The Court said laws that sanction membership, unaccompanied by specific intent to further the unlawful goals of the organization, violate constitutional limitations. The right of association is most often protected from regulation by means of the overbreadth doctrine, which cautions that restrictive statutes tend to trap association members indiscriminately. Associational protection has also been applied to organizational involvement in the electoral process.

**Brandenburg v. Ohio, 395 U.S. 444 (1969) (271)**

Ruled that political association is a constitutionally protected activity. Brandenburg, a Ku Klux Klan leader, was convicted for violating a state syndicalism statute that made it a crime to advocate change by illegal means. The Supreme Court reversed the conviction because the law was defective on First Amendment grounds. First Amendment guarantees do not, said the Court, permit a state to "forbid or proscribe advocacy of the use of force or of law violation except where such advocacy is directed to inciting or producing imminent lawless action and is likely to incite or produce such action." The mere abstract teaching of the need to resort to force and violence is not equivalent with "preparing a group for violent action and steeling it to such action." A statute that does not make this distinction intrudes on First Amendment freedoms. By this standard, the Ohio law could not be sustained. The act, said the Court, punished persons who engage in abstract advocacy, and nothing in subsequent proceedings "refined the statute's bald definition of crime in terms of mere advocacy not distinguished from incitement to imminent lawless action." *See also* ASSOCIATION, RIGHT OF, 270; *KEYISHIAN V. BOARD OF REGENTS* (385 U.S. 589: 1967), 295; *NAACP V. ALABAMA* (357 U.S. 449: 1958), 305.

*Significance* The pursuit of political and social goals is generally protected by the First Amendment. Nonetheless, the right of association is not absolute; some regulation may still be imposed. The most difficult associational situations are those in which attempts are made to proscribe subversive organizations and prohibit the kind of conduct involved in *Brandenburg v. Ohio* (395 U.S. 444: 1969). A number of states had statutes like Ohio's, and these laws were initially sustained by the Supreme Court because association was seen as concerted action threatening public security. The first important decision was *Whitney v. California* (274 U.S. 357: 1927). About four decades later, the Warren Court rejected this approach, finding that laws like those in *Whitney* were directed at abstract advocacy not necessarily related to unlawful conduct. Indeed, the Court in *Brandenburg* referred to *Whitney* as "thoroughly discredited" and explicitly overruled it. As a result of *Brandenburg,* abstract advocacy is now wholly protected. Also protected is advocacy that calls for illegal action so long as such action is urged for the indefinite future or when there is no basis for expecting that the audience will be moved to actually engage in illegal conduct.

**Business Organization** **(272)**

Organization designed to promote and protect the interests of private enterprise. The basic objective of business is to be profitable, and business organizations are formed to advance the common interests of businesses in that endeavor. Business organizations are comparatively the largest and most influential groups because the relationship of business and government has generated some of the more fundamental divisive issues in U.S. politics. The interests of those within the business community vary substantially and produce different kinds of participation in the political process. At one level, there are organizations—known as peak associations—that try to represent the full breadth of the business community. The Chamber of Commerce of the United States (CCUS) or the National Federation of Independent Businesses (NFIB) are such organizations. Trade associations represent enterprises within the same industry or trade; they have a narrower focus than peak associations. The American Petroleum Institute (API) and the National Association of Broadcasters (NAB) are examples of trade associations. Finally, many businesses participate in the political process as individual entities. Exxon and General Motors as well as numerous other (and smaller) businesses are fully and directly engaged in trying to influence public policy. *See also* ECONOMIC-BASED GROUP, 282; INTEREST GROUP, 293; PEAK ASSOCIATION, 317; TRADE ASSOCIATION, 331.

*Significance* Business organizations are the largest and most diverse category of interest group. Upwards of 4,000 business organizations exist, and they bring to the political process resources that allow them to exercise substantial influence on public policy. This high number of organizations allows business interests to enjoy multiple representation in the political process to a degree unmatched by any other group. Business organizations devote most of their sizable financial resources to direct lobbying activities, extensive educational efforts in support of the free enterprise system, and electioneering. The latter activity involves making campaign contributions to supportive political candidates through an extensive network of political action committees (PACs).

**Chamber of Commerce of the United States (CCUS)** **(273)**

An umbrella organization that represents business interests on matters of broad significance to the business-industrial community. The Chamber of Commerce of the United States (CCUS) is a peak association whose members are state and local chambers and business organizations as well as individuals. Although local chambers existed much earlier, the CCUS was established in 1912 at the initiative of several locals and with the enthusiastic support of the Taft administration. The idea was to create a national organization that could coordinate and promote business interests. The CCUS defines its purpose as advancing "human progress through an economic, political and social system based on individual freedom, incentive, initiative, opportunity and responsibility." The CCUS is governed by a board of directors and uses an elaborate committee and task force system to develop policy recommendations. Although some recommendations may be adopted by the board, others are submitted to a member referendum. The CCUS has a large staff in Washington that performs most of the direct lobbying. An affiliated lobbying organization, Citizens Choice, actively promotes policies that would reduce the size and scope of government, deregulate business, and reduce the role of labor unions. The National Chamber Alliance for Politics (NCAP) is the principal political action committee; it supports chamber-endorsed candidates and coordinates the political activities of affiliated organizations. Research on a variety of public policy issues is conducted by the National Chamber Foundation. The National Chamber Litigation Center acts as the chamber's "public interest" legal arm. Finally, the CCUS produces such publications as *National Business* and *Washington Report* as well as engaging in other public education activities. *See also* BUSINESS ORGANIZATION, 272; PEAK ASSOCIATION, 317.

*Significance* The Chamber of Commerce of the United States (CCUS) generally supports policies that would reduce government's role in the economy. As a result, the CCUS favors reduction of the federal budget, relaxation of various environmental requirements, and repeal of the Davis-Bacon Act, which regulates wages of construction workers on federal projects. In addition, CCUS supports limiting the power of such agencies as the Occupational Safety and Health Administration (OSHA) and the Equal Employment Opportunity Commission (EEOC), ending the regulation of political action committees (PACs), retaining Hatch Act prohibitions on political activity by federal employees, a different (lower) minimum wage for young employees, and development of nuclear power. The CCUS has also advanced positions on social issues. It favors use of a block grant approach for most social programs, would tighten food stamp eligibility standards, and would eliminate the indexing of entitlement program benefits. In general, the policy orientation of the CCUS has closely paralleled that of Ronald Reagan's administration.

### ***Citizens Against Rent Control v. Berkeley,* 454 U.S. 290 (1981)** (274)

Struck down a municipal ordinance that established a limit of $250 for contributions to committees formed to support or oppose ballot propositions. The Supreme Court noted that the practice of people who share common views "banding together to achieve a common end is deeply embedded in the American political process." The value of such activity is that by collective effort individuals can "make their views known, when, individually, their voices would be faint or lost." The right of association is "diluted" if it does not include the right to "pool money" because such funds are "often essential" if advocacy is to be effective. The Berkeley ordinance permits an individual acting alone to spend without limit but imposes restrictions when contributions are made "in concert with one or more others in the exercise of the right of association." The Court concluded that to place a "spartan" limit, or any limit, on individuals who wish to band together to "advance their views" on a ballot measure while placing none on individuals acting alone is "clearly a restraint on the right of association." *See also* *BUCKLEY V. VALEO* (424 U.S. 1: 1976), 157; *FEDERAL ELECTION COMMISSION (FEC) V. NATIONAL CONSERVATIVE POLITICAL ACTION COMMITTEE (NCPAC)* (470 U.S. 480: 1985), 287; *FIRST NATIONAL BANK OF BOSTON V. BELLOTTI* (435 U.S. 765: 1978), 288.

*Significance* *Citizens Against Rent Control v. Berkeley* (454 U.S. 290: 1981) focused on the expenditure of organizational funds on public issues in the form of ballot proposals. The Supreme Court's ruling was important in several ways. First, it made clear that groups must be able to direct their collective resources into the political process. Given that funds are "often essential" if advocacy is to be "truly or optimally effective," the right of association is "diluted if it does not include the right to pool money through contributions" and then permit those resources to be expended on issues of public concern. Second, the Court saw the political expression of individuals and groups as equivalent. The right of association, said the Court, is restrained if regulations placed on individuals acting jointly do not exist for individuals acting alone. It is clear from other decisions that the Court will not sustain such restrictions on individual contributions. Finally, the Court emphasized the "single narrow exception" identified in *Buckley v. Valeo* (424 U.S. 1: 1976) in which limits on political activity might be permitted—regulation of large contributions to candidates for public office. Under these circumstances, regulation may be appropriate to preserve the integrity of the political system because large contributions might be given to "secure a political quid pro quo from current and potential office holders." As pointed out in *Citizens Against Rent Control,* that same rationale cannot apply to contributions to committees formed to favor or oppose ballot measures.

### Civil Rights Groups (275)

Organizations designed to pursue social and political equality for particular racial, ethnic, gender, or age populations. Civil rights groups have the characteristics of both public interest and single-issue groups. Such groups focus their activities around the "single" issue of discrimination, although success in the pursuit of equality generally has societal benefits that go beyond the groups' own memberships. Groups that would fit into this category are the National Association for the Advancement of Colored People (NAACP), the National Urban League, the National Organization for Women (NOW), the Anti-Defamation League of B'nai B'rith, and the National Association of Arab-Americans. Some organizations such as the American Civil Liberties Union (ACLU) pursue civil rights objectives but are also engaged in the broader protection of civil liberties. *See also* NATIONAL ASSOCIATION FOR THE ADVANCEMENT OF COLORED PEOPLE (NAACP), 304; NATIONAL ORGANIZATION FOR WOMEN (NOW), 312; PUBLIC INTEREST GROUP, 321; SINGLE-ISSUE INTEREST GROUP, 327.

*Significance* The interests represented by civil rights groups are relatively focused. At the same time, economic equality falls within their scope, making civil rights groups somewhat difficult to classify. The number of civil rights organizations is relatively small as is the aggregated membership when compared with the size of their potential constituencies. Nonetheless, civil rights organizations have been generally successful in advancing the cause of their memberships. The struggle for racial equality provides some examples. The first major organization was the National Association for the Advancement of Colored People (NAACP), which was formed in 1909. The NAACP focused its activities around court challenges of discriminatory practices. Its Legal Defense and Educational Fund prevailed in a number of key lawsuits and substantially changed the status of American blacks. Other black civil rights groups have aimed at activating broader membership than the NAACP and have preferred direct confrontation as a principal operating style. The Southern Christian Leadership Conference (SCLC), for example, has historically utilized marches, demonstrations, sit-ins, and economic boycotts as means for influencing public policy. Civil rights groups combating sex discrimination have emerged in the 1970s. These groups have utilized both legal challenges and direct confrontation in the pursuit of gender equality.

**Coalition** **(276)**

An alliance of individuals or groups. The assembling of coalitions is a lobbying technique. A coalition may be formed by several groups that work in the same general policy area. Various women's rights or environmental groups may unite to more effectively utilize their collective resources and heighten their influence on a policy question. Lobbying groups, in turn, try to form coalitions of policymakers who might not otherwise come together. *See also* LOBBYING, 300; LOGROLLING, 301.

*Significance* The character of U.S. partisan politics is such that coalition building is both common and effective. Most coalitions tend to be temporary and narrowly drawn. Even within policy issue categories, coalitions tend to be ad hoc. Although a coalition of women's groups is possible on the question of equal pay, for example, this unity would likely not transfer to the abortion question. It is the technique of coalition building that enables the practice of logrolling to occur. Logrolling allows special and local interests to receive favorable legislative treatment because legislators agree to support each other's home district interests.

**Collective Goods** **(277)**

Benefits or rewards that are distributed to all. Collective goods are the opposite of selective goods, which are not distributed to everyone because of some differential condition or standard. A municipality that collects refuse from all residents provides a collective good—

everyone receives comparable service. If the same municipality distributed special refuse containers to a portion of the population—perhaps owner-occupied residences—and only collected refuse from those with containers, the service would be a selective benefit. Whether a good is collective or selective depends on who is the designated recipient group. A $50 grant to college students to partially cover textbook costs would be a collective benefit for the group defined as college students but would be a selective benefit if the recipient group was defined as college-age persons. *See also* FREE RIDER PROBLEM, 289; PUBLIC INTEREST GROUP, 321; PURPOSIVE BENEFITS, 322.

*Significance* Economists describe collective goods as those that are not subject to differential distribution. Collective goods or rewards are a problem for voluntary associations because group action produces benefits for member and nonmember alike. For many groups, especially public interest ones, this phenomenon creates a marketing challenge known as the free rider problem. That is, a person who benefits from a group's activities while not supporting the group through membership is given a "free ride" by those who do underwrite the costs of the organization. If there are too many free riders, a group's existence may be jeopardized. Short of that, a group may make the distribution of rewards at least partially conditional on membership. This technique is especially effective if the selective rewards are of a material or tangible kind.

**Common Cause** **(278)**

A nonpartisan "citizen lobby" organization. Common Cause was founded in 1970 for the purpose of effecting reforms in the political processes at both the national and state levels. Common Cause has a membership of about 275,000 and is financed exclusively from the dues and contributions of individual members. As a nonpartisan body, Common Cause does not endorse candidates but does evaluate congressional voting records and score presidential candidates on their positions on issues of importance to the organization. Among the major goals of Common Cause have been reform of campaign financing and governmental processes. To these ends, Common Cause engages in direct lobbying and generally monitors the performance of government. It publishes a monthly journal, *Common Cause Magazine,* as well as numerous other studies and special reports. *See also* INTEREST GROUP, 293; PUBLIC INTEREST GROUP, 321.

*Significance* Common Cause is driven by its belief in "open, accountable government and the right of all citizens to be involved in helping to shape our nation's public policies." Over the course of its history, Common Cause has been instrumental in obtaining campaign finance reform, in pushing for "sunshine laws" to open meetings of Congress, in obtaining passage of new ethics standards and financial disclosure regulations for public officials, and in breaking down the seniority system in Congress. It continues to push for reform of congressional campaigns by specifically proposing public financing of elections and limitations on the role of political action committees (PACs). Common Cause would also limit the outside income or honoraria that can be earned by members of Congress. Common Cause has not confined itself to governmental process issues, however. It vigorously opposed U.S. involvement in the Vietnam conflict and has generally tried to block weapons systems it regards as unnecessary. It currently supports nuclear arms control initiatives and opposes further investment in such weapons programs as the strategic defense initiative (SDI), or "Star Wars."

**Consumer Federation of America (CFA) (279)**

An advocacy organization for consumer interests. The Consumer Federation of America (CFA) is an umbrella organization for more than 200 consumer, senior citizen, labor, and other groups. The CFA attempts to advocate proconsumer policy directly before Congress, administrative and regulatory agencies, and the courts. The CFA is governed by a board elected by its members, and various consumer issues are monitored by a structure of specialized committees. Policy resolutions are adopted at an annual meeting, and program objectives are implemented by a professional staff. The CFA also has a State and Local Resource Center that maintains communication with hundreds of consumer and community groups throughout the country as well as local CFA members. The organization regularly publishes two newsletters; the *CFA News,* which reviews public policy actions or consumer matters, and *Action Facts,* which summarizes state and local activities. The CFA also sponsors an annual conference, conducts research through the Paul Douglas Consumer Research Center, and provides an information service that includes legislative voting analyses and the status of proposed legislation. *See also* INTEREST GROUP, 293; PUBLIC INTEREST GROUP, 321.

*Significance* The Consumer Federation of America (CFA), an active lobbying organization, is generally regarded as quite effective in advancing its interests. The CFA has generally supported measures that protect the competitiveness of the marketplace. More specifically, the CFA has opposed oil company mergers, federal support of synthetic fuel development, variable mortgage rates, the joint liability proposal that would limit the responsibility of defendants in product liability actions, and some deregulation such as in the broadcast industry. The CFA has supported proposals such as comprehensive national health insurance and urban mass transit programs.

**Countervailing Theory** **(280)**

View that holds that various interest groups in the political process tend to counterbalance or cancel out each other's impact. The countervailing theory is an outgrowth of the pluralist model of democracy which views society as composed of many diverse interests that compete with one another in order to influence public policy. The countervailing theory argues that the competition among these interests is sufficiently balanced so that no single interest or coalition of interests can dominate the political process in the long term. Some observers, however, reject the pluralist theory and the possibility of counteraction because they see the political system as dominated by a power elite, a small minority with pervasive influence. *See also* ELITE THEORY, 284; INTEREST, 292; LOBBYING, 300; PLURALIST THEORY, 318.

*Significance* The countervailing theory of group politics holds that the public interest is served through the competition of diverse interests as represented by organized groups. Although equivalence in the representation of interests does not exist, evidence suggests that the pluralist model of democracy provides a more accurate representation of the U.S. political system than does the elitist alternative view. The sufficiency of the countervailing theory has diminished since the 1970s, however, because of the advent of single-issue interest groups. Previously, groups tended to represent members across a range of issues—for example, economically based groups like labor unions would take positions on major social legislation. Often, the same groups would contest each other, although specific policy questions would vary. Thus, business and labor would meet in the political arena again and again and, in theory, would counterbalance one another. The increase in the number of groups focusing on single issues has been uneven because on many issues there are no organized opposing groups. Such a void precludes any counterbalancing.

**Direct Lobbying** **(281)**

Activity that seeks to influence policy decisions through direct contact with policymakers. Direct lobbying occurs when a lobbyist has personal, ongoing contact with a member of Congress or congressional staff member or with officials of administrative agencies. Lobbyists represent their positions by providing information and analyses on particular issues or situations. Typically, neither under-the-table payoffs nor threats in the event of nonsupport are exchanged. Rather, lobbyists point out that certain actions would have beneficial consequences for the group represented, with inferences to be drawn from the discussion generally left to the lobbied official. Direct lobbying may also involve testifying at congressional hearings. *See also* ELECTIONEERING, 283; GRASSROOTS LOBBYING, 290; LOBBYING, 300.

*Significance* There are differing views on how effective direct lobbying is. The assumption is that lobbying efforts are successful, but evidence suggests that groups tend to cancel or counterbalance one another. The absence of a clear pattern of impact tends to support this proposition. Although results gained from direct lobbying per se may not be easily measured, this activity does retain access for groups, thereby enabling them to keep positions and supporting data in front of policymakers. It may also be helpful to think of direct lobbying as "defensive," or maintaining the status quo, rather than simply as pushing for changes in public policy. If direct lobbying is defensive, as some observers suggest, it would tend to benefit interests that already enjoy an advantaged position.

**Economic-Based Group** **(282)**

An interest group that organizes for the purpose of protecting the economic interests of its members. Economic-based groups are the longest established and generally the most influential of organized groups. The most numerous are business organizations, a category composed of three levels. First, there are the large umbrella organizations called peak associations. These organizations, such as the National Association of Manufacturers (NAM), attempt to represent business interests generally. Second, there are the more focused trade associations that represent specific business segments. Finally, there are individual businesses and corporations that involve themselves directly with the political process. The economic-based category also includes groups defined by occupation. This subcategory covers labor unions, educational associations, agricultural groups, and professional associations such as the American Bar Association (ABA). *See also* AGRICULTURAL ORGANIZATION, 260; BUSINESS ORGANIZATION, 272; INTEREST GROUP, 293; LABOR ORGANIZATION, 296; PROFESSIONAL ASSOCIATION, 320.

*Significance* Economic-based groups constitute the largest overall category of interest groups because an overwhelming majority of matters moving through the political process involve the economic interests of some segment of the population. Economic or occupational groups are typically able to better influence the political process than other groups because of their generally larger memberships and greater financial resources. Within the economic-based category, however, size of membership and extent of financial resources are not distributed evenly. Groups that represent business interests usually operate with far larger budgets than other groups, and business tends to have its interests represented by more overlapping groups than do, for example, labor or agricultural interests.

**Electioneering** **(283)**
Tactic that involves interest groups directly in political campaigns. Electioneering can take place in a variety of ways. Groups possess several resources that are invaluable to political campaigns. First, their members are potential voters who are linked by communications mechanisms (such as a newsletter) that make them a ready audience for analyses of incumbent performances and other information on candidates. Second, groups can make formal endorsements that may have a persuasive impact on the larger electorate. Third, groups are often the source of campaign workers. Finally, with endorsement usually comes financial support, typically through political action committees (PACs). *See also* CAMPAIGN, 48; DIRECT LOBBYING, 281; GRASSROOTS LOBBYING, 290; LOBBYING, 300; POLITICAL ACTION COMMITTEE (PAC), 319.

*Significance* Electioneering may allow groups to elect candidates who will support their policy preferences as well as enhance a group's capacity to lobby effectively. Constituent pressure from a group that has an established record in the electoral process readily gets the attention of policymakers. Electioneering often makes other lobbying efforts, both direct and indirect, more productive. In addition, the campaign finance reforms of the 1970s created, intentionally or not, strong incentives for groups to establish political action committees (PACs) and channel financial support to selected candidates and their campaigns or make independent expenditures on behalf of endorsed candidates.

**Elite Theory** **(284)**
A view that contends that a small minority of interests controls public policymaking. Elite theory rejects the argument that power and influence are distributed across groups by suggesting that they are concentrated in a handful of stable interests or elites. This small minority has inordinate influence because it controls the pivotal financial and corporate institutions of the country. Although other interest groups do exist, elite theorists argue that only a relative handful, known as

the power elite, really matter. Elite theorists argue that the capacity of elites to control governmental decision making is facilitated by the interlocking of directorates of large corporations and top positions in such executive branch agencies as Defense and Treasury. Elite theory is especially attractive to those who subscribe to the view that the political process is dominated by wealth, to those with a conspiratorial view of politics, or to those who reside at the outer edges of the ideological spectrum. *See also* COUNTERVAILING THEORY, 280; INTEREST, 292; PLURALIST THEORY, 318.

*Significance* Elite theory asserts that the United States is an oligarchy—that is, a governmental system run by a ruling elite. Even though citizens participate in elections and a large number of interest groups exist, issues are defined and outcomes are determined by an inordinately powerful few. Thus, the U.S. political system, according to elitist views, is actually undemocratic. Elite theory offers reasonable explanations for particular cases—for example, why Defense Department contracts for weapons systems have recurring and substantial cost overruns. At the same time, elite theory does not readily generalize. Little empirical support exists for the conclusion that an identifiable elite dominates policymaking across a broad range of issues.

**Environmental Group (285)**

Organization dedicated to protection of the environment and conservation of natural resources. Among the issues of specific concern to environmental groups are such items as clean water and air, construction projects, strip mining, protection of wildlife, preservation of wilderness and open space, oil spills, and energy including many issues associated with nuclear energy. Although a proliferation of groups occurred in the late 1960s and early 1970s, some groups in this category date back as far as the 1890s during which time the Sierra Club was founded. As environmental issues found their way onto legislative agendas in the 1960s, established groups like the National Wildlife Federation doubled and even tripled in size. In addition, many new groups were established such as the Environmental Defense Fund, Friends of the Earth, and Environmental Action. Environmental groups use a variety of means, including conventional lobbying, public education, litigation, and research, in their efforts to influence public policy. *See also* NATIONAL WILDLIFE FEDERATION (NWF), 316; PUBLIC INTEREST GROUP, 321; SIERRA CLUB, 326; SINGLE-ISSUE INTEREST GROUP, 327.

*Significance* There are approximately 100 environmental groups presently engaged in public education and lobbying. Although a few environmental groups predate the 1960s, the most dramatic growth came in the period immediately before and after Earth Day (1970). After a time of virtually no growth, environmental groups became more visible in the 1980s as they challenged the laissez-faire policies of Reagan Interior Secretary James Watt. Once again, memberships in environmental groups increased and some new groups were founded. The issues that prompted the most vigorous opposition were those associated with federal land. Watt favored the opening of these lands for coal extraction and oil exploration. He also supported offshore oil drilling and proposed removal of nearly 1 million acres of federal lands from their classification as protected wilderness areas. The controversial Watt gave environmental groups the opportunity to raise public consciousness about other issues such as nuclear power plant construction and maintenance and disposal of both solid and toxic waste. Besides public education and lobbying efforts, a number of environmental groups sought intervention by courts on matters that they felt threatened the environment. Finally, a number of groups moved into the arena of electoral politics, with some establishing their own political action committees (PACs).

### ***Federal Election Commission (FEC) v. Massachusetts* Citizens for Life (MCFL), 479 U.S. 238 (1986)** **(286)**

Held that section 316 of the Federal Election Campaign Act cannot be applied to nonprofit corporations. This section prohibits corporations from using general funds to make expenditures related to any election campaign for any public office. Massachusetts Citizens for Life (MCFL), a nonprofit, nonstock corporation, was formed to promote pro-life causes. It used its general treasury to prepare and distribute a special election edition of its newsletter. This publication characterized candidates for state and federal offices in terms of their support for or opposition to MCFL's views. The Supreme Court ruled that the special edition of the newsletter was within the prohibition of section 315 but that the statute violated First Amendment protections when applied to corporations such as MCFL. In order to sustain a burden on First Amendment rights, a "compelling state interest" must be demonstrated. At least some of the rationale supporting regulation stems from the "special characteristics of the corporate structure." The "integrity of the marketplace of political ideas" must be protected from the "corrosive influence of concentrated corporate wealth." Direct corporate spending "raises the prospect that resources amassed in the economic marketplace may be used to provide an unfair advantage in the political marketplace." The availability of resources may make a corporation a "formidable political presence, even though the power of the corporation may be no reflection of the power of its ideas." The Court said that groups like MCFL simply do not "pose that danger of corruption." MCFL was formed for the express purpose of "promoting political ideas," and its activities cannot be considered as business. This ensures that its "political resources reflect political support." Because the group sells no shares, persons affiliated with the MCFL will have no "economic disincentive for dissociating" if they disagree with its political activity. In addition, the MCFL's own policies prohibit taking contributions from business corporations or labor unions, which, in turn, prevents it from becoming a "conduit for that kind of spending which threatens the political marketplace." To the extent that section 316 interferes with First Amendment rights of organizations like MCFL as distinct from more appropriate corporate targets, it is "too blunt an instrument" to withstand constitutional scrutiny. *See also* *BUCKLEY V. VALEO* (424 U.S. 1: 1976), 157; *CITIZENS AGAINST RENT CONTROL V. BERKELEY* (454 U.S. 290: 1981), 274; FEDERAL ELECTION CAMPAIGN ACTS, 180; *FEDERAL ELECTION COMMISSION (FEC) V. NATIONAL CONSERVATIVE POLITICAL ACTION COMMITTEE (NCPAC)* (470 U.S. 480: 1985), 287.

*Significance* *Federal Election Commission (FEC) v. Massachusetts Citizens for Life (MCFL)* (479 U.S. 238: 1986) examined the provision of the Federal Election Campaign Act that prohibits contribution of corporate general funds to the campaigns of those seeking public office. The Supreme Court concluded that the act could not apply to nonprofit corporations without violating the First Amendment. Government can use a regulatory approach to campaign financing only where a "compelling" reason exists. In the Court's view, protecting the "marketplace of ideas" from the "corrosive influence" of corporate resources amassed outside the political arena will generally constitute sufficient cause to regulate but not when extended to corporate entities like MCFL, an organization formed for the purpose of advancing a political position. MCFL and similar nonprofit organizations are not businesses and therefore cannot be regulated like businesses. Neither are they likely to jeopardize the integrity of the political process. This ruling thus allows nonprofit corporations to freely engage in the promotion of political ideas.

### ***Federal Election Commission (FEC) v. National* Conservative Political Action Committee (NCPAC), 470 U.S. 480 (1985)** (287)

Ruling that invalidated that portion of the Federal Election Campaign Act amendments limiting a political action committee's (PAC) independent expenditure on behalf of publicly funded presidential candidates. The amendments had established a $1,000 limit. The basis of the Supreme Court's decision was that campaign expenditures like those of the National Conservative Political Action Committee (NCPAC) are expressions protected by the First Amendment. Restrictions on expenditures necessarily limit the volume and depth of discussion as well as the size of the audience reached. The Court also said that the expenditure limitation interfered with NCPAC's associational rights. Such entities as NCPAC allow persons of modest means to join together and "amplify their voices." To restrict the use of their pooled resources would subordinate the voices of those of limited means in favor of those of sufficient wealth to buy expensive media with their own resources. *See also* *BUCKLEY V. VALEO* (424 U.S. 1: 1976), 157; FEDERAL ELECTION CAMPAIGN ACTS, 180; FEDERAL ELECTION COMMISSION (FEC), 118; *NATIONAL CONSERVATIVE POLITICAL ACTION COMMITTEE (NCPAC)*, 307.

*Significance* The Federal Election Campaign Act was passed in the wake of the Watergate scandal. The act limited campaign contributions and required disclosure of both contributions and expenditures. It also provided for publicly funded financing for presidential campaigns and established the Federal Election Commission (FEC) to administer the act. Finally, the act imposed limits on several categories of campaign expenditures. In the case of *Buckley v. Valeo* (424 U.S. 1: 1976), the Supreme Court invalidated the expenditure restrictions while upholding the other provisions. In *Federal Election Commission (FEC) v. National Conservative Political Action Committee (NCPAC)* (470 U.S. 480: 1985), the Court's decision was a logical outgrowth of *Valeo*. Remaining intact under the *NCPAC* ruling is the $5,000 limit on direct contributions to candidates for federal office. This ruling does, however, enhance the role and legitimacy of the political action committee (PAC) within the U.S. electoral process.

### *First National Bank of Boston v. Bellotti*, 435 U.S. 767 (1978) (288)

Ruled that a state could not prohibit use of corporate funds to influence referendum questions. Specifically, the law under review in *First National Bank of Boston v. Bellotti* (435 U.S. 767: 1978) restricted efforts to affect votes on matters other than those "materially affecting" a corporation's property or assets. Expressly included in the statute was the provision that no question "solely concerning the taxation of the income, property or transactions of individuals" would be deemed to materially affect a corporation. The Supreme Court said that expression of views on an issue of public importance is "at the heart of the First Amendment's concern." There is no support for the position that speech loses the protection otherwise afforded by the First Amendment "simply because its source is a corporation that cannot prove . . . a material effect on its business." The Court also rejected the state's contention that the regulation was necessary to sustain the active role of the individual in the electoral process. Even if it were permissible, said the Court, to "silence one segment of society" upon a showing of "imminent danger," there had been no demonstration in this case that the "relative voice of corporations has been overwhelming or even significant" or that there has been any "threat to the confidence of the citizen in government." The Court also pointed out that the "risk of corruption" present in candidate elections is not present in a "popular vote on a public issue." *See also* *BUCKLEY V. VALEO* (424 U.S. 1: 1976), 157; *CITIZENS AGAINST RENT CONTROL V. BERKELEY* (454 U.S. 290: 1981), 274; *FEDERAL ELECTION COMMISSION (FEC) V. MASSACHUSETTS CITIZENS FOR LIFE (MCFL)* (479 U.S. 238: 1986), 286.

*Significance* Regulation of the kind examined in *First National Bank of Boston v. Bellotti* (435 U.S. 765: 1978) frequently surfaced in the wake of the Watergate episode. The Supreme Court's response to the many regulatory initiatives aimed at protecting the integrity of the electoral process was lukewarm at best. Consider, for example, the Federal Election Campaign Act of 1972. Although finding the contribution limits and disclosure requirements constitutional, the Court ruled in *Buckley v. Valeo* (424 U.S. 1: 1976) that restrictions on expenditures placed too great a burden on political expression. Absent a showing that corporate participation "threatened imminently to undermine democratic processes," a state simply does not possess an interest sufficient to justify such an interference with political expression. Key in cases like *Bellotti* and the related case of *Citizens Against Rent Control v. Berkeley* (450 U.S. 290: 1981) was the distinction between ballot issues and candidate elections. Direct financial support of a candidate was seen as potentially system-damaging; it created an opportunity to undermine the political process because of quid pro quo arrangements that might follow financial contributions. Expression by a corporation or other kind of organization on ballot issues simply did not make the system vulnerable to the same kind of threat.

**Free Rider Problem** **(289)**

Refers to the difficulty in attracting those sympathetic to a group's objectives to dues-paying membership. The free rider problem is a phenomenon of marketing generally, but with heightened consequences for voluntary associations. The phenomenon comes from the tendency of people to let someone else make the effort to pursue an objective. The problem may be effectively described using the example of public television subscription funding. Public television is maintained largely through contributions or subscriptions. Even though many people have access to these broadcast stations and regularly watch their programming, not all underwrite the costs of the station by subscribing. This makes subscription drives difficult because the noncontributor has the same access as the contributor and is given, in essence, a "free ride." This same phenomenon obviously applies to any group that seeks benefits that are not restricted to the members of that group. *See also* COLLECTIVE GOODS, 277; INTEREST GROUP, 293; MATERIAL BENEFITS, 302; PUBLIC INTEREST GROUP, 321.

*Significance* The free rider problem has been more troublesome for public interest groups than for other categories of interest groups because public interest groups deal with collective and generally nonmaterial benefits. Absent this kind of incentive, people are reluctant to make a contribution or pay membership dues. Nonetheless, many public interest groups are able to attract enough people who believe in the cause to allow maintenance of the organization, although it has become increasingly necessary to augment revenues by seeking foundation or other independent funding. If too many individuals get a free ride, however, a group's existence may be threatened, in which case a group might attempt to attract more support by focusing on material benefits available only to group members.

**Grassroots Lobbying** **(290)**

Activity that attempts to influence policymakers through constituent pressure. Grassroots lobbying is often called indirect lobbying because it does not involve lobbyist contacts. Grassroots lobbying can be used in conjunction with direct lobbying. It may take the form of letter-writing campaigns or protests such as demonstrations or marches. Groups that engage in grassroots lobbying are usually most effective when they can command cohesive voting behavior from their memberships. Such groups maintain current voting records of legislation, keep their members apprised of how particular legislators have voted, and formally endorse candidates who are most supportive of their group's position. *See also*: DIRECT LOBBYING, 281; ELECTIONEERING, 283; LOBBYING, 300.

*Significance* Grassroots or indirect lobbying uses constituents to influence policymakers' behavior. Although such tactics are often used to supplement direct lobbying activities, they may also be effective on their own. Consider, for example, the impact of conservative religious groups in the 1980s. Some chose the indirect, or grassroots, approach instead of establishing a lobbying office in Washington. Through constituent pressure, they sought to advance their views on matters like abortion and school prayer. Constituent pressure became more substantial as some groups became active in the election process and eventually could claim at least a modest role (often more) in determining election outcomes. The main drawback of grassroots activities is that they are difficult to sustain. Unlike a Washington lobbyist who may remain an ongoing presence, a demonstration or letter-writing campaign is likely to be a short-term phenomenon. As time passes, a group's demands may fade from the consciousness of policymakers.

**Ideological Group** **(291)**

An organization that pursues a wide range of goals based on an integrated set of underlying values. Ideological groups differ from economic-based groups in that the goals that are pursued are typically nonmaterial in character. To the extent that ideological groups attempt to represent interests broader than their own membership, they resemble public interest groups. Their focus is relatively broader and more symbolic and abstract than most public interest groups. Members of ideological groups are loosely bound by common values that emphasize the fundamental elements of a political system. The ideological framework of this kind of group provides the foundation for specific issue positions. Expression of the ideological position is often the only personal objective of this group's members. The liberal Americans for Democratic Action (ADA) or the conservative American Conservative Union (ACU) are examples of ideological groups. *See also* AMERICAN CONSERVATIVE UNION (ACU), 263; AMERICANS FOR DEMOCRATIC ACTION (ADA), 268.

*Significance* Ideological groups tend to interact with the political process much as other groups do. Their ideological basis may make such groups quite influential. The success of ideological groups is typically a function of the extent to which those they seek to influence identify with the broad value premises of the group. For this reason, ideological groups located on the extremes of the political spectrum have been uniformly unsuccessful in U.S. politics. In addition to developing policy positions, testifying before congressional committees, and engaging in direct and grassroots lobbying, ideological groups rate officeholders, particularly legislators, and make indices of their voting records a part of the public education program. The

Americans for Democratic Action (ADA), for example, was the first to measure a legislator's voting record for ideological position and assign support scores to every member of Congress. Compilation of such legislative scorecards has now become standard practice for a large number of groups, ideological and otherwise.

**Interest** **(292)**

A term used to indicate a right, claim, or share of something. An interest is anything in which there is advantage or value. Thus people pursue interests either on behalf of themselves as individuals or as members of groups that share a common interest or interests. One might have an individual or shared interest in virtually anything; economic value or advantage, protection of the environment, "good" government, gun control, military preparedness, or deregulation of the trucking industry are a few of limitless examples. Groups organized for the purpose of pursuit of shared interests are called interest groups. Interests that are not collective or shared by all are called selective or special interests. Interest groups that attempt to advance special or vested interests are often referred to as special interest groups, usually with a negative connotation. *See also* COLLECTIVE GOODS, 277; INTEREST GROUP, 293; LOBBYING, 300.

*Significance* A free society permits its citizens to pursue their interests even if they are selfish and exclusive. Often interests are not compatible. For example, domestic manufacturers of steel may want import restrictions on low-priced foreign steel. Obtaining such restrictions would benefit the manufacturers but would also result in consumers having to pay higher prices for items containing steel. In other words, the problem with the pursuit of most interests is that they may not be good for the nation as a whole. James Madison warned of this danger of special interests—or "factions," as he called them—but ultimately concluded that greater harm would occur by regulating or suppressing associational or interest group activity. According to Madison, the better response to self-interest advocacy is to have government act as a mediator among competing interests to protect minorities from injury by any majority interest that might develop. The pluralist response to the same issue is that many diverse interests exist and are represented by groups, but no single group or interest is likely to dominate in an ongoing fashion.

**Interest Group** **(293)**

An organized group of people who share common objectives. The members act through the interest group to attempt to influence public policy. It is largely through interest groups that linkages are established between individual preferences and priorities and the governmental institutions and processes established to act on these preferences and priorities. People who share a common occupation or views on governmental policy options do not themselves constitute an interest group. It is only when these people organize themselves and consciously attempt to influence public policy that an interest group is created. An interest group is different from a political party in that it does not have the winning of elective office as its principal objective. In addition, the policy preferences of a political party—at least those reflected by its platform—cover a wide range of issues. Interests groups, on the other hand, tend to selectively focus on policy decisions most important to them regardless of which officeholder made them. Although interest groups may endorse a particular candidate or officeholder, their support will remain only so long as that person helps advance the group's particular objectives. The tactics employed by interest groups are several in number, and generally each is effective in its own way. The first is direct lobbying, whereby representatives of an organization attempt to convince government officials to take particular policy stances. The second technique is indirect lobbying, whereby an organization engages in grassroots politics by attempting to generate constituent pressure on government officials. Third, groups may become directly involved in political campaigns through public endorsement or by providing campaign funds. Finally, groups may use legal action as a means of furthering or protecting their members' interests. *See also* CIVIL RIGHTS GROUPS, 275; ECONOMIC-BASED GROUP, 282; IDEOLOGICAL GROUP, 291; INTEREST, 292; PUBLIC INTEREST GROUP, 321; SINGLE-ISSUE INTEREST GROUP, 327.

*Significance* Large numbers of Americans are members of at least one organized group. This kind of association provides a variety of benefits but foremost is that it amplifies a person's capacity to have an impact on public policy. Next to voting, participation with an organized interest group is the most likely form of political involvement. Interest groups are both numerous and diverse, large and small. Some are highly organized, meet regularly, and command substantial resources; others are quite informally organized, seldom meet, and may not even collect the most minimal membership dues. The diversity represented along these variables directly corresponds to the effectiveness of the groups in the political process. Interest groups can be divided into several major categories. The largest category is the economic interest group, which includes business and trade organizations, labor unions, and farm groups. These groups have as their primary objective the economic well-being of their membership. The second category encompasses groups that grow out of particular political movements as exemplified by civil rights and women's rights organizations. Professional associations such as the American Medical Association (AMA) or National Education Association (NEA) constitute the third category of economic interest group. Although these groups stress the professional interests of their members, they are also heavily involved in protecting their members' economic interests. Public agencies also organize themselves in order to protect their interests in the volatile appropriations processes at national, state, and local levels. Organizations that represent the interests of city or county governments are numerous, for example. Finally, we have recently seen the formation of many public interest groups such as Common Cause and various environmental groups that define their function as protecting the public interest as they see it.

**Iron Triangle** **(294)**

Reference to a three-sided relationship of congressional committees, executive agencies, and interest groups. The terms "cozy triangle" or "policy subgovernment" are often used to refer to the same mutual support pattern. The three-way alliance is based upon compatible interests. Most congressional policy choices are made in committees (or subcommittees). Each of these committees has oversight responsibilities over an executive agency's program(s). These programs, in turn, operate to the benefit of particular interest or client groups, and lobbyists are retained by them to protect these interests. Over the course of time, committee and agency staff people and lobbyists develop a shared interest in protecting the status quo. The term "iron" is used to characterize the closed, almost impenetrable nature of these subsystems, although it also suggests a permanence that may not exist. An example of such a triangle is the relationship among members of appropriations committees concerned with defense expenditures, procurement officers of the Defense Department, and weapons contractors. These three groups are linked in an arrangement that will inevitably provide power and campaign support, large budgets, and contract income to those parties respectively. *See also* INTEREST GROUP, 293.

*Significance* The iron, or cozy, triangle operates because the members of the alliance have priorities that intersect. The committee members want reelection, the bureaucrats want program expansion, and the interest groups want their policy preferences adopted. Key to the relationship is interest group involvement. An agency with strong support is likely to have favorable legislative oversight, whereas absence of such support may engender minimal congressional support. Some contemporary political analysts see the iron triangle idea as insufficient in describing the current policymaking process for two reasons. First, proliferation of interest groups makes it more difficult for rigid and exclusive triangles to form or maintain themselves. Second, congressional changes in the policy process instituted in the mid-1970s have decentralized power and created substantial overlap of authority, reinforcing the tendency toward greater accessibility by many groups.

***Keyishian v. Board of Regents*, 385 U.S. 589 (1967) (295)**
Required that more than mere membership in organizations be demonstrated before the imposition of restrictions on associational rights. *Keyishian* examined several New York statutes known collectively as the Feinberg Law that authorized the Board of Regents to monitor organizational memberships of state employees. The board was required to generate a list of subversive organizations in which membership was prima facie evidence for disqualification from public employment, including appointments to academic positions. While the person being terminated could have a hearing, the hearing could not address the matter of subversive classification of the organization. Keyishian and several other faculty members in the state university system were dismissed because of their membership in the Communist party. The Supreme Court struck down the Feinberg Law and rejected the premise that "public employment, including academic appointment, may be conditioned upon the surrender of constitutional rights which could not be abridged by direct government action." The Court found "mere membership" to be an insufficient basis for exclusion: "Legislation which sanctions membership unaccompanied by specific intent to further the unlawful goals of the organization or which is not active membership violates constitutional limitations." The Court also said the laws "sweep overbroadly in association which may not be proscribed." The regulations "seek to bar employment for both association which legitimately may be proscribed and for association which may not be sanctioned." The flaw of overbroad sweep was as fatal as the flaw of vagueness. *See also* ASSOCIATION, RIGHT OF, 270.

*Significance* *Keyishian v. Board of Regents* (385 U.S. 589: 1967) overturned *Adler v. Board of Education* (342 U.S. 485: 1952), decided 15 years earlier. *Adler* had found these same laws constitutional, deciding that teachers "have no right to work for the State in the school system on their own terms." The *Adler* position was that the state may inquire into the fitness and suitability of a person for public service, and past conduct may well relate to present fitness. In addition, one's associates, past and present, may properly be considered in determining fitness and loyalty. "From time immemorial, one's reputation has been determined in part by the company he keeps." *Keyishian,* however, rejected such thinking. Shortly after *Keyishian,* in *United States v. Robel* (389 U.S. 258: 1967), the Supreme Court voided a McCarron Act provision that prohibited any member of a Communist-action organization from working in a defense facility. As in *Keyishian,* the Court found that the statute "casts its net across a broad range of associational activities, indiscriminately trapping membership which can be constitutionally punished and membership which cannot be so proscribed."

**Labor Organization** **(296)**

Association of workers whose objective is improvement of the economic well-being of employees. Labor organizations typically seek to accomplish their objectives through collective bargaining. Although the number of labor organizations or unions is comparatively small, they represent more members than any other interest group. Workers who are members of a union number approximately 20 million. The overarching labor organization is the American Federation of Labor–Congress of Industrial Organizations (AFL-CIO), which is a broad federation of most operating unions. About 14.5 million unionized workers belong to unions affiliated with the AFL-CIO. Operating unions join workers of common occupation or the same or closely associated industries. Examples of such operating unions are the United Automobile Workers (UAW), the American Federation of Teachers (AFT), and the International Ladies Garment Workers Union (ILGWU). Some unions are independent and remain outside the AFL-CIO umbrella. *See also* *AMERICAN FEDERATION OF LABOR–CONGRESS OF INDUSTRIAL ORGANIZATIONS (AFL-CIO)*, 265; ECONOMIC-BASED GROUP, 282; INTEREST GROUP, 293; UNITED AUTOMOBILE WORKERS (UAW), 332.

*Significance* Labor organizations are principally interested in improving working conditions and compensation received for work. Labor organizations have also been active in the political arena, generally supporting social welfare programs among other things. Labor organizations engage heavily in direct lobbying but have also been extremely active in the electoral process. The political vehicle for the AFL-CIO—for example, the Committee of Political Education (COPE)—employs a large professional staff that engages in fundraising, voter registration, and candidate-support activities. COPE provides in excess of $1 million to the campaigns of endorsed federal candidates alone. The influence of labor organizations on the political process has declined in recent years, in part because of a decrease in blue-collar jobs and a resulting decrease in the proportion of the workforce belonging to unions. (This proportion now stands slightly below 20 percent.) More important, union leadership can no longer "deliver" the union vote because labor-union members no longer vote as a cohesive bloc. Traditionally, union rank and file supported the Democratic party, but in 1984, almost half of the labor vote went to Ronald Reagan despite leadership endorsement of the Democratic ticket.

**Landrum-Griffin Act** **(297)**
Enactment that tightens Taft-Hartley Act restrictions on labor unions. The Landrum-Griffin Act (the Labor Management Reporting and Disclosure, or Labor Reform, Act) was passed in 1959. The act basically requires unions to submit reports on union operations, especially finances, to the secretary of labor. The act also bans Communists, individuals with criminal records, and individuals with competing business interests from serving as union officers and makes it a crime to misuse union funds. Finally, the act seeks to protect certain rights of union members, such as the use of secret ballot when electing officers, the requirement of formal hearings for any disciplinary matters, and the guarantee of member access to union financial records. *See also* TAFT-HARTLEY ACT, 329.

*Significance* The Landrum-Griffin Act was adopted in response to growing concerns about union corruption. Congress had conducted a series of investigations and uncovered misconduct on the part of some union officials. To some extent, the act was passed to help clean unions protect themselves from corruption. Also part of the agenda, however, was the pursuit of policies that subjected unions to greater governmental control. This represented a substantial policy change from that of the mid-1930s and 1940s, which had been almost nurturing of the labor movement.

**League of Women Voters (LWV)** **(298)**
A nonpartisan political organization that seeks to influence public policy through informed political activism. The League of Women Voters (LWV) was founded in 1920 and succeeded the National American Woman's Suffrage Association upon ratification of the Nineteenth Amendment. The league's first function was to assist women in effectively discharging their newly won political

responsibilities. Its overriding objective has been to pursue open and accountable government through informed citizen participation in the political process. The LWV is actually two complementary entities based in Washington—the league is the political advocacy and membership component, and the League of Women Voters Educational Fund is the research and public education organization. The league also has approximately 1,300 affiliates at the state and local levels. Since 1976, the LWV Educational Fund has been responsible for sponsoring presidential debates. In addition, the league actively advocates its policy positions through direct lobbying and generally acts as a governmental watchdog. In this latter capacity, the league regularly rates Congress on selected votes, organizes letter-writing and telegram campaigns, and has resorted to the courts to litigate legal questions of importance. *See also* COMMON CAUSE, 278; INTEREST GROUP, 293; PUBLIC INTEREST GROUP, 321.

*Significance* From the outset, the League of Women Voters (LWV) opted to remain outside the realm of partisan politics. As a result, the LWV neither supports nor opposes candidates for public office. The league, however, actively presses its position on many public policy issues. It establishes an issue agenda and then determines its positions through a process of research and member agreement. Among the issues identified as priorities for the 1980s are support for a verifiable nuclear freeze, equitable pay for women and minorities, environmental protection and affirmative programs aimed at environmental cleanup, the protections contained in the 1982 amendments to the Voting Rights Act, and protection of reproductive rights. The league has opposed a constitutional amendment prohibiting abortion, opposed trade protectionism, and supported continued U.S. funding of the United Nations.

**Litigation (299)**

The use of lawsuits as a means of pursuing group objectives. Interest group involvement in litigation can take several forms. First, the group itself may be the actual party to a lawsuit. Environmental groups, for example, may sue on behalf of their members (and possibly the public at large) to stop construction of a nuclear power plant or the leasing of protected federal land. A group also might sponsor litigation brought by an individual or group of individuals. This can be done by underwriting some of the expense of the litigation or by providing expert legal assistance to the litigants. Finally, a group may participate in litigation through third party, or amicus curiae, briefs, a process that allows a group to offer arguments supporting the group's position on an issue before a court. *See also* AMICUS CURIAE, 269; LOBBYING, 300.

*Significance* The use of litigation as a technique of forcing policy changes is quite common today, and interest groups have been at the forefront of using legal advocacy. The success of the NAACP Legal Defense Fund is illustrative. Starting in the 1930s, the National Association for the Advancement of Colored People (NAACP) contested a variety of discriminatory policies and practices in the federal courts rather than lobbying legislative bodies that contained segregationist members. It was through NAACP litigation that the policy of segregating public schools was declared unconstitutional in *Brown v. Board of Education* (347 U.S. 483: 1954). These court successes, in turn, led to dramatic civil rights advances on other fronts in the 1960s. As the federal courts have become more conservative during the years of Ronald Reagan's presidency, conservative groups have become more active in using the courts to pursue policy priorities.

**Lobbying** **(300)**

The actions of a group or individuals aimed at influencing the content of public policy. Lobbying can occur in several different ways. A group that engages in lobbying must make tactical decisions with regard to who is being lobbied and which approach will maximize a group's effectiveness. When a group wishes to make direct contact with a policymaker, it typically utilizes a lobbyist. The lobbyist represents the group's position directly to the policymaker, an approach known as direct lobbying. A group may lobby indirectly by involving its membership in the effort to influence public policy. This method, often referred to as grassroots lobbying, is usually a supplement to direct lobbying. Groups may also focus lobbying activities on the public in an effort to gain broad citizen support for their positions. Separate but nonetheless related is a group's use of electioneering, a technique whereby a group actually becomes involved in election campaigns. Finally, a group may lobby through the courts by involving itself in litigation of issues of particular importance to it. *See also* DIRECT LOBBYING, 281; ELECTIONEERING, 283; GRASSROOTS LOBBYING, 290; LITIGATION, 299; LOBBYING, 300.

*Significance* It is a mistake to think of lobbying as solely direct lobbyist contacts with members of Congress. Although all groups may not utilize all lobbying tactics or access other than legislators, there are a variety of techniques that can be directed at different officials. The courts and literally hundreds of executive agencies are frequently the target of lobbying. In addition to the influence that might be sought by direct and grassroots lobbying, groups also attempt to win public support through educational or information campaigns. This method might involve traditional public relations efforts with literature, speakers, or media advertising. It might also involve conducting research in order to produce data that supports a group's position on an issue. A variation of this theme is the publishing of indexes of voting records, which has utility for electioneering efforts as well.

**Logrolling** **(301)**

An agreement between legislators to support each other's proposals. Logrolling allows legislative bargaining to occur so that each legislator is able to advance the particular interests of his or her state or home district. Logrolling takes place when those who represent particular interests are unable on their own to ensure passage of legislation favorable to their interests; they therefore enter into a coalition so that they possess sufficient votes to enact two or more bills. For example, a group of legislators may wish to secure funding for urban mass transportation while another group may wish to expand agricultural subsidies. The two groups may agree to vote in favor of both. As a result, each group of legislators may wind up voting for a low-priority program—maybe even one that they each would oppose in the absence of the agreement—but by doing so, both groups secure enough votes to also pass an item of high priority to their own districts. *See also* COALITION, 276.

*Significance* Logrolling may be regarded as legislative vote trading or back scratching. What it involves is a coalition of highly motivated legislative minorities who use this approach to reach ends not otherwise possible. Logrolling is the technique by which appropriations are voted for local projects or programs. Such appropriations are referred to as "pork barrel" legislation. The most extreme logrolling scenario is the occasional "Christmas tree" proposal that contains an advantage for numerous special interests. None of the component provisions could win in isolation, but when aggregated, they gain sufficient support to be enacted.

**Material Benefits** **(302)**

Goods that have measurable value. A material good or benefit usually has monetary value or is transferable into goods that have monetary value. Material benefits differ from both solidary and purposive benefits. Solidary benefits are derived from the act of association itself, whereas purposive benefits are based upon group objectives. Neither solidary nor purposive benefits have monetary value as such. An overlapped distinction of benefits separates tangible rewards from those that are symbolic. Again, the measure of value is the distinguishing characteristic. *See also* COLLECTIVE GOODS, 277; PURPOSIVE BENEFITS, 322; SOLIDARY BENEFITS, 328.

*Significance* Material benefits are tangible—they have utility or monetary value. Material benefits are also extrinsic rather than intrinsic in that they are derived from the benefits that come from associational activities. Organizations that are principally interested in members' economic well-being are likely to provide or protect material things. Workers may join a labor union because it is able to improve their level of compensation as well as working conditions. These benefits have monetary value and utility. Presence of material benefits, particularly if distributed only to group members, allows an association to easily retain current members as well as attract new ones.

**Moral Majority** **(303)**

An organization of religious conservatives active in the political arena. The Moral Majority was founded in 1979 by the Rev. Jerry Falwell, a Baptist minister and television evangelist. It claims membership in excess of 6 million and describes its purpose as opposing those who would destroy the "traditional family and moral values on which our nation was built." Over the course of its short history, the Moral Majority took positions on issues outside the scope of its name and original charter. As a result, a new umbrella organization known as the Liberty Federation was established in 1986. The Moral Majority continues as a subsidiary and focuses on what it calls "strictly moral" issues. In addition, a new lobbying and educational entity called the Liberty Alliance has been created as a separate subsidiary of the Federation. *See also* IDEOLOGICAL GROUP, 291; INTEREST GROUP, 293.

*Significance* The original charter of the Moral Majority defined the organization as political and pro-life, pro–traditional family, and pro–strong national defense. The Moral Majority initially featured its opposition to abortion, to legal acceptance of homosexuals, to the Equal Rights Amendment (ERA), and to pornography. The Moral Majority claimed responsibility for the registration of several million new voters prior to the 1980 election, in which it supported the election of Ronald Reagan and a number of conservative U.S. Senate candidates. These successful candidacies may have been substantially aided by these new voters and the several million dollars the Moral Majority expended in the campaigns. More broadly, the Liberty Federation supports the Strategic Defense Initiative (SDI), the Balanced Budget Amendment, and aid to the Contras in Nicaragua and opposes an unverifiable nuclear freeze.

**National Association for the Advancement of Colored People (NAACP)** **(304)**

A U.S. civil rights organization. The National Association for the Advancement of Colored People (NAACP) was founded in 1909 as an outgrowth of the Niagara Movement. The NAACP operates through a network of local affiliates in an effort to eliminate racial discrimination. Though it once was viewed as quite radical, the NAACP has from the outset chosen not to use direct confrontation, focusing rather on litigation and legislative lobbying as its principal tactics. Its Legal Defense and Educational Fund has achieved substantial success in the courts. As the civil rights movement grew in militancy in the 1950s, the NAACP retained its more restrained approach and left the mass-action activities to other groups. The 1970s and 1980s have seen the NAACP focus largely on issues involving the economic well-being of blacks. A centerpiece of this emphasis has been its advocacy of effective affirmative action employment policies. *See also* ASSOCIATION, RIGHT OF, 270; CIVIL RIGHTS GROUP, 275; CIVIL RIGHTS MOVEMENT, 53; INTEREST GROUP, 293; *NAACP V. ALABAMA* (357 U.S. 449: 1958), 305.

*Significance* The National Association for the Advancement of Colored People (NAACP) has preferred to use the federal courts to advance the interests of civil rights. The NAACP was responsible for a number of early decisions including those striking down the use of the grandfather clause (*Guinn v. United States,* 238 U.S. 347: 1915) and the white primary (*Smith v. Allwright,* 321 U.S. 649: 1944) as discriminatory devices that illegally interfered with the right to vote. Topping any list of court victories, of course, is *Brown v. Board of Education* (347 U.S. 483: 1954), in which the NAACP was able to obtain a ruling that declared segregation of public schools to be unconstitutional. The NAACP has been instrumental in establishing associational rights. In the 1950s, the NAACP confronted Alabama's attempt to limit the organization's activities in the state, including an effort by Alabama to obtain NAACP records and membership lists. The Supreme Court ruled in *NAACP v. Alabama* (357 U.S. 449: 1958) that the forced disclosure of such material would unlawfully interfere with the right of association. Several years later, in *NAACP v. Button* (371 U.S. 415: 1963), the Court upheld the NAACP's efforts to generate litigation as a form of political expression.

***NAACP v. Alabama*, 357 U.S. 449 (1958)** **(305)**
Examined the nature of constitutional protection for the freedom of association. *NAACP* involved an attempt by the state of Alabama to compel disclosure of the NAACP membership list as a means of inhibiting operation of the organization. The association refused to disclose the list and was cited for contempt and fined, but the Supreme Court reversed the contempt judgment. The Court's opinion provided the foundation of the concept of the constitutional right of association. In its opinion, the Court first had to resolve the matter of standing. Alabama argued that the NAACP as an organization could "assert constitutional rights pertaining to the member," but the Court found the association's "nexus with them is sufficient to permit that it act as their representative." The Court determined in fact that the NAACP is the "appropriate party to assert these rights, because it and its members are in every practical sense identical." The Court then moved on to the infringement of protected freedoms threatened by the compulsory disclosure. It recognized that "effective advocacy of both public and private points of view, particularly controversial ones, is undeniably enhanced by group association." The compelled disclosure was viewed as affecting "adversely the ability of the [NAACP] and its members to pursue their collective effort to foster beliefs which they admittedly have a right to advocate." The Court saw disclosure as having adverse consequences in two ways. First, the association itself would likely suffer diminished financial support and fewer membership applications. Second, disclosure of the identity of members might prompt "economic reprisal, loss of employment, threat of physical coercion, and other manifestations of public hostility." *See also* ASSOCIATION, RIGHT OF, 270.

*Significance* *NAACP v. Alabama* (375 U.S. 449: 1958) marked the beginning of a new era for associational rights. The decision not only recognized the efficacy of group activity but acknowledged that such activity was constitutionally protected. In a similar judgment (*Shelton v. Tucker,* 364 U.S. 479: 1960), the Supreme Court struck down a state statute that required public school teachers to disclose annually every organization supported by their memberships or contributions. The Court determined that even a legitimate inquiry into a teacher's fitness and competence "cannot be pursued by means that broadly stifle fundamental personal liberties when the end can be more narrowly achieved." Although not directly involving the disclosure issue, the NAACP was able to affirm another dimension of associational freedom in *NAACP v. Button* (371 U.S. 415: 1963). *Button* upheld the NAACP's strategy of representing membership interests through litigation. Many states have enacted antisolicitation laws that prohibit the "stirring up" of lawsuits. In the case of the NAACP, the Court recognized such activity as a means for achieving lawful objectives and a form of political expression. Indeed, "for such a group, association for litigation may be the most effective form of political association." Litigation that seeks vindication of constitutional rights is a different matter from avaricious use of the legal process purely for personal gain.

**National Association of Manufacturers (NAM) (306)**
A peak or umbrella organization of U.S. manufacturing. The National Association of Manufacturers (NAM), founded in 1895, has a membership in excess of 12,000 companies. A large proportion of these members are small businesses, although these companies produce almost 75 percent of U.S. manufacturing output. NAM has a number of focused policy committees that act to advise its board of directors and professional staff. With particular expertise in economic policy, labor-management relations, and environmental issues, NAM engages in direct lobbying by providing testimony at congressional hearings. It also has a legal division that files third-party amicus curiae briefs in important law cases. NAM regularly informs its members on the status of legislation and regulatory developments through its newsletters and other publications. NAM assists its members in forming political action committees (PACs) as well as conducting their own lobbying activities. The organization is also engaged in public education efforts that focus on the general goals and objectives of the business community. NAM is affiliated with several state organizations and national trade associations and closely coordinates its activities with other leading peak associations such as the Chamber of Commerce of the United States (CCUS). *See also* BUSINESS ORGANIZATION, 272; CHAMBER OF COMMERCE OF THE UNITED STATES (CCUS), 273; PEAK ASSOCIATION, 317.

*Significance* The National Association of Manufacturers (NAM) generally represents business interests and acts as an advocate for the U.S. free enterprise system. It actively pursues a comprehensive program of policy objectives. These policy preferences can be broken into several categories that include deregulating business and reducing the number of regulatory agencies that exist; increasing productivity (often by anti-union tactics or by advocacy of limitations on labor force restrictions such as rigorous enforcement of Occupational Health and Safety Administration [OSHA] regulations); controlling government spending and reducing the deficit (NAM generally favors cutting federal domestic spending); enhancing U.S. competitiveness in the international economy; and relaxing environmental and energy regulations.

**National Conservative Political Action Committee (NCPAC)** **(307)**

A registered political action committee whose purpose is to influence the outcome of elections. The National Conservative Political Action Committee (NCPAC) is one of the most prominent of the "new right" organizations. In addition to contributions to selected campaigns, NCPAC's principal activity is to make independent political expenditures on behalf of conservative candidates. NCPAC also makes similar expenditures aimed at defeating liberal incumbents. *See also* FEDERAL ELECTION CAMPAIGN ACTS, 180; FEDERAL ELECTION COMMISSION (FEC), 118; *FEDERAL ELECTION COMMISSION (FEC) V. NATIONAL CONSERVATIVE POLITICAL ACTION COMMITTEE (NCPAC)* (470 U.S. 480: 1985), 287.

*Significance* NCPAC has been successful at generating large sums of money by contacting enormous numbers of small donors around the country through direct-mail campaigns. Although much of its revenue goes to support the costs of its own staff and money-raising campaigns, NCPAC was given some credit for the ouster of several liberal U.S. senators in the 1980 election. Acting separately from the formal campaigns of Republican candidates, NCPAC ran negative media advertising aimed at discrediting targeted incumbents. Similar attempts by NCPAC in subsequent congressional elections have been substantially less effective. Nonetheless, the NCPAC's use of independent expenditures has become a common approach for influencing elections and has enhanced the role of political action committees (PACs) in the electoral process. Finally, it was NCPAC's challenge of the expenditure limitations imposed by the Federal Election Campaign Act that permitted the Supreme Court the opportunity to strike down these provisions. In *FEC v. NCPAC* (470 U.S. 480: 1985), the Court held that these expenditures are the political expression of a group of people who spend pooled resources to "amplify their voices" in the political process. Such activity is legitimate, said the Court, and is thus protected by the First Amendment.

**National Education Association (NEA)** **(308)**

A professional association of teachers, administrators, and school counselors. The National Education Association (NEA) has a membership of approximately 2 million and seeks to operate as the national representative of educators. The NEA sits atop a structure that has almost 10,000 affiliates operating at the local school-district level.

The political activity of the NEA is conducted under the auspices of its legislative program. Policy positions developed from the membership by the Legislative Committee are formally adopted at the annual assembly. Legislative input is also solicited on specific issues in the publication *NEA NOW*. The legislative program is responsible for monitoring legislative performance on selected topics and regularly issues the NEA legislative report card. NEA's political action committee, NEA-PAC, evaluates candidates for federal office and provides financial support to those it endorses. *See also* INTEREST GROUP, 293; PROFESSIONAL ASSOCIATION, 320.

*Significance* The legislative program of the National Education Association (NEA) is organized by tiers. The first tier includes legislative issues developed and initiated by NEA that receive the highest priority. The current first-tier priority initiatives are increased federal funding of education and a federal policy that protects collective bargaining rights of educational employees at all levels. The second tier consists of issues initiated by the federal government that require ongoing NEA activity. Illustrative of this second tier of issues is asbestos abatement, full protection of civil and human rights (which includes enforcement of civil rights laws), reproductive freedom, affirmative action, full support of the Department of Education, and opposition to public funding of nonpublic schools through tuition tax credits, vouchers, or "free choice" mechanisms. The third tier contains issues that warrant continuous monitoring but activity only when necessary. These issues typically range outside the educational arena—for example, environmental protection, national health insurance, and fair housing.

**National Farmers Organization (NFO) (309)**

An association of farm and ranch producers that uses collective bargaining as its principal means of representing producer interests. The National Farmers Organization (NFO) originated as a protest movement in response to the economic distress of producers in the 1950s. The NFO sought to influence government to increase price support programs. Dissatisfied with its lack of success, the NFO turned to collective bargaining with food processers as a means of developing sufficient control of the agricultural marketplace to drive product prices to profitable levels. A series of "holding actions" in which selected products were withheld from the market eventuated in production and price contracts. The NFO is unlike other agricultural organizations that are federations of state affiliates. It is a producer group that acts exclusively as a marketing agent for its membership and does not provide other services available from other groups. The NFO encourages its members to retain their associations with other groups in order to obtain the benefits offered through them. The NFO maintains a lobbying staff in Washington, produces a syndicated farm news program for radio, and publishes a monthly newsletter. *See also* AGRICULTURAL ORGANIZATION, 260; ECONOMIC-BASED GROUP, 282.

*Significance* The National Farmers Organization (NFO) is one of the more militant agricultural groups. Its use of collective bargaining distinguishes it from other farm groups and often leads to opposition to its efforts to gain new members. In 1979, the NFO founded its own political action committee, Grass Roots in Politics (GRIP), to directly participate in federal elections. The NFO views domestic farm policy as outdated and inadequate because its forces farmers into overproduction, which, in turn, is the root of oversupply and long-term depressed price levels. The NFO supports a new approach that would include minimum pricing and market orders. Short of a comprehensive change, the NFO supports policies that would benefit small, individual producers as distinct from nonfamily corporate producers. More specifically, the NFO supports crop insurance, deregulation of haulers that transport food products, broadened loan and credit assistance, and increased funding for the food stamp program.

**National Farmers Union (NFU) (310)**

An agricultural organization that seeks to represent family farming interests. The National Farmers Union (NFU) was founded in 1902 and is composed of state farmers unions. The NFU tends to be a relatively militant organization, generally opposing large agribusiness interests while favoring subsidy programs for small farmers. The policy positions of the NFU are developed at a series of conventions culminating in a national convention that formally makes policy decisions. The NFU maintains a lobbying office in Washington, carefully monitors legislation and administrative regulations that affect family agriculture and rural life, and lobbies directly for progressive farm legislation. The NFU also uses a grassroots operation called the Congressional Action Committee as a means of reaching members of Congress regarding pending legislation. *See also* AGRICULTURAL ORGANIZATION, 260; ECONOMIC-BASED GROUP, 282.

*Significance* The National Farmers Union (NFU) is one of several general agricultural organizations. It is a federation that spans particular commodities, although its strength is in the wheat belt of the

Midwest. Its positions have focused on small family-farm interests. Accordingly, the NFU has generally favored price supports, soil conservation programs, and embargo protection. More specifically, it has supported federally underwritten crop insurance, development of synthetic fuels, regulation of strip mining, and more beneficial provisions regarding estate taxes.

## National Federation of Independent Business (NFIB) (311)

An association of small, independent business organizations. The National Federation of Independent Business (NFIB) was founded in 1943 to promote the free enterprise system and give independent and small businesses greater impact in developing public policy at the national as well as the state level. The NFIB is heavily involved in direct lobbying with Congress and various government agencies, particularly the Small Business Administration. Its representatives appear before congressional committees and offer testimony on behalf of small businesses. Similarly, they appear before platform committees of the major political parties in an effort to have small-business interests properly represented within the priorities stated in each party's platform. In addition to the publication of a quarterly assessment of the economy and a legislative update, the NFIB directly solicits member opinions through its *Mandate* newsletter. The *Mandate* survey results actually shape NFIB policy positions, and the results are distributed to members of Congress and selected agencies of the executive branch. *See also* BUSINESS ORGANIZATION, 272; PEAK ASSOCIATION, 317.

*Significance* The National Federation of Independent Business (NFIB) has more than 500,000 members, which makes it the largest individual membership business organization in the United States. It is one of the few national organizations in which the membership directly sets the direction of its political activities. The NFIB generally supports cuts in federal spending, reducing Social Security programs other than retirement, reducing the impact of OSHA regulations, and eliminating estate taxes for small businesses. More specific positions that NFIB has taken in the 1980s include support for federal deficit reduction (including the Gramm-Rudman Act), federal tax reductions, presidential line-item veto power, and the balanced budget amendment. The NFIB has opposed attempts to remove Davis-Bacon small-business exemptions for defense contracts and the proposed "superfund" value-added tax.

**National Organization for Women (NOW)** **(312)**
Organization established to combat discrimination against women. The National Organization for Women (NOW) was founded in 1966 and consists of a national organization, regional and state affiliates, and local chapters. NOW is engaged in a broad array of activities that include direct lobbying, litigation, public education programs, research, and the publication of a monthly newsletter entitled *National NOW News.* A number of task forces are in place to monitor such issues as gender discrimination in education, the workplace, the media, and credit access. NOW has also been involved with the issue of reproductive rights. *See also* CIVIL RIGHTS GROUPS, 275; INTEREST GROUP, 293.

*Significance* The National Organization for Women (NOW) has aggressively pursued adoption of public policy that it believes would reduce inequities based on gender. At the top of its agenda is adoption of a constitutional amendment that deals with women's equality. NOW has also sought to combat pay inequities in the workplace. Beyond equal pay for equal work, NOW seeks to have compensation based on the principle of comparable worth. It also embraces such positions as pro-choice for abortion; the right to individual determination of life style, which includes sexual preference; reform of what it feels is a discriminatory Social Security system; and policies that advance homemakers' rights.

**National Rifle Association (NRA)** **(313)**
A voluntary membership association dedicated to the advancement of the interests of U.S. gun owners. The National Rifle Association (NRA) was founded in New York in 1871 by a small group of National Guard officers who were seeking to improve member marksmanship and establish riflery skill requirements for the guard. The purposes of the NRA have, since the 1960s, been defined in terms of exercising a constitutionally protected right to possess arms. The NRA maintains that so long as U.S. citizens use firearms lawfully, their right to own firearms cannot be violated. The NRA conducts an extensive firearm safety education program, seeks to promote firearm proficiency among law enforcement and military forces, and is dedicated to the betterment of the sports of shooting and hunting as "wholesome" recreational activities. It produces public service spots for the broadcast medium and publishes two widely circulated periodicals, the *American Hunter* and the *American Rifleman,* and numerous other pamphlets and manuals. *See also* INTEREST GROUP, 293; SINGLE-ISSUE INTEREST GROUP, 327.

*Significance* The National Rifle Association (NRA) is extremely active politically. Direct lobbying is conducted by the Institute for Legislative Action (ILA), a Washington-based entity. Since its establishment in 1975, the NRA-ILA has aggressively endeavored to prevent enactment of restrictions on gun ownership and use. The institute is especially active at the state and local levels where comprehensive gun control initiatives are more likely. The NRA has a political action committee known as the Political Victory Fund that supports candidates who are sympathetic to their pro-firearm position. At the federal level alone, the NRA has endorsed and financially supported candidates in more than half of the congressional races in any given election year. It has one of the most sophisticated candidate evaluation processes in Washington. Candidates for federal office are asked to fill out a questionnaire concerning guns and gun control. Scores are determined for each candidate and sent to NRA members in the respective states and legislative districts. The NRA is also extremely effective at indirect lobbying because it is able to mobilize substantial expressions of sentiment when gun regulations are proposed at any level.

**National Right-to-Life Committee (NRL) (314)**
An organization that opposes abortion. The National Right-to-Life Committee (NRL) was founded in 1973 in response to the *Roe v. Wade* (410 U.S. 113: 1973) decision of the Supreme Court, which legalized abortion. NRL claims a membership of 11 million through more than 1,800 affiliates in all states and the District of Columbia. The NRL was initially chartered as a lobbying and "social action" organization. It publishes a biweekly newsletter entitled the *National Right-to-Life News* and has established a political action committee (PAC) and an educational trust fund to allow it to more fully engage in electoral and public information activities. In addition to its direct lobbying activity at the federal level, NRL acts to coordinate anti-abortion activities and serves as an information clearinghouse for its state and local chapters. *See also* INTEREST GROUP, 293; SINGLE-ISSUE INTEREST GROUP, 327.

*Significance* The National Right-to-Life Committee (NRL) is one of the many pro-life or anti-abortion organizations that currently exist in the United States. Prior to *Roe v. Wade* (410 U.S. 113: 1973), the abortion question had been almost exclusively a state issue. The Supreme Court's decision changed that and provided the impetus for the establishment of many national organizations on both sides of the abortion controversy. The ultimate objective of NRL is adoption of a constitutional amendment that would categorically prohibit abortion.

Short of achieving that goal, NRL has been instrumental in promoting a number of legislatively enacted restrictions on abortion over the years, including the right of medical personnel to refuse to participate in the performance of abortions. Possibly the most critical of the restrictions, however, is the limitation on the use of federal Medicaid funds to finance abortions. Federal funds cannot be used to promote abortions, either.

**National Right-to-Work Committee** **(315)**
A single-issue organization that opposes compulsory union membership. The National Right-to-Work Committee views federal law that recognizes a union to represent all workers in a particular bargaining unit as an encroachment of individual freedom. Especially offensive is the union practice of expending compulsory dues for political purposes the committee feels are not supported by the workers paying the dues. The committee seeks to restore freedom of choice for workers by promoting right-to-work laws. Such laws, authorized at the state level under section 14(b) of the Taft-Hartley Act, prohibit union membership as a condition of employment. The committee conducts an extensive public education campaign that highlights the abuses of compulsory union membership and aids in the establishment of state organizations to counter that policy. *See also* BUSINESS ORGANIZATION, 272; SINGLE-ISSUE INTEREST GROUP, 327; TAFT-HARTLEY ACT, 329.

*Significance* The National Right-to-Work Committee was founded in 1955. Its initial focus was protecting section 14(b) of the Taft-Hartley Act from repeal. Spurred by early success, the committee actively sought to have states exempt themselves from the compulsory membership laws through 14(b). To date, 20 states have adopted the right-to-work position. The committee continues to seek similar action in the remaining states and clearly would support a change in federal policy to that end if it were proposed. Short of total success on the question, the committee pursues legislation that would prohibit use of union membership dues for political purposes. In addition to direct lobbying, the committee puts out a variety of publications ranging from a monthly newsletter to numerous pamphlets and monographs.

**National Wildlife Federation (NWF)** **(316)**
Citizen organization dedicated to promoting the "wise use" of natural resources. The National Wildlife Federation (NWF) is the largest organization of its kind and is composed of affiliate organizations at the state level. NWF policy positions are developed through the affiliate

structure and implemented by a professional staff of more than 600. The NWF has an extensive public education component that includes a number of publications aimed at a wide-ranging audience including preschoolers. The NWF also funds conservation and wildlife research and attempts to foster cooperation and coordination among other natural resource organizations. Finally, the NWF attempts to influence natural resource policy through direct involvement within the legislative, administrative, and legal processes. *See also* ENVIRONMENTAL GROUP, 285; INTEREST GROUP, 293; PUBLIC INTEREST GROUP, 321.

*Significance* The National Wildlife Federation (NWF) is the most conservative of environmental groups. The NWF is more willing than other such groups to balance environmental interests with developmental or economic interests. As a result, the NWF will more readily accept multiple-use approaches to natural resources and public lands. It has also been less inclined to urge broad and extensive federal regulation than many other environmental groups. Nonetheless, the NWF lists as major achievements its role in, among other things, establishing the "superfund" to finance the cleanup of chemical wastes, extending the Clean Air and Clean Water Acts, limiting oil and gas leasing in wildlife refuge areas, and forestalling changes in federal strip mining regulations. The NWF will also resort to litigation, as it did in the early 1980s to stop ocean dumping of waste and the leasing of North Dakota land for coal mining.

**Peak Association (317)**

Broad organization that attempts to represent the entirety of the business community. Though peak associations are quite limited in number, they are extremely influential due to the breadth and diversity of their memberships. Among the most visible and prominent peak associations are the Chamber of Commerce of the United States (CCUS), Business Roundtable, National Federation of Independent Business (NFIB), and the National Association of Manufacturers (NAM). Peak associations engage in some of the same lobbying activities that trade associations do. They differ from trade associations, however, in breadth of focus and membership homogeneity. Peak associations mobilize around issues that have an impact on the interests of the business community at large and leave issues more directly affecting a single industry to the trade associations. The membership of peak associations is wide-ranging but usually includes businesses and business organizations such as trade associations. *See also* BUSINESS ORGANIZATION, 272; CHAMBER OF COMMERCE OF THE UNITED STATES (CCUS), 273; ECONOMIC-BASED GROUP, 282; NATIONAL ASSOCIATION

OF MANUFACTURERS (NAM), 306; NATIONAL FEDERATION OF INDEPENDENT BUSINESS (NFIB), 311.

*Significance* A peak association is an organization of smaller groups. Because of its size and general focus, the peak association is an unusually visible organization. Peak associations can also command great resources. Consider, for example, the Chamber of Commerce of the United States (CCUS), a broadly based confederation of state and local units, trade associations, and individual businesses. Its membership exceeds 250,000, its budget is approximately $75 million, and its professional staff numbers more than 400 persons. Policy objectives are implemented primarily through this professional staff. Business Roundtable, on the other hand, is an organization of chief executive officers of the largest and most prestigious companies. Because of the character of its membership, its staff is relatively small and the members interact with the political process directly. The activities of peak associations revolve around issues that have an impact on the business community at large, such as taxation, consumer protection, and worker compensation issues. On such issues, peak associations are relatively effective.

**Pluralist Theory** **(318)**

A view that society is composed of many diverse interests. Pluralist theory suggests that these interests—derived from cultural, social, and economic differences, among others—compete with each other for a share of power and influence in the political process. The pluralist view embraces the notion that through the process of competition no single interest can dominate. Rather, competing interests counterbalance one another, with each group retaining some access and some degree of influence on policy decisions. Pluralists would argue that the ends of democracy are served by the multiplicity of groups. Not only do groups input their views on public policy questions, but, in doing so, groups serve as representatives for individuals. *See also* COUNTERVAILING THEORY, 280; ELITE THEORY, 284; INTEREST, 292.

*Significance* The pluralist view of democracy differs markedly from that of elitist theory. The latter sees a stable and inordinately powerful minority dominating governmental processes and policy. The pluralist, on the other hand, sees specific questions resolved through a competitive process that involves numerous and diverse interests. This competitive process moves across a broad range of matters with different interests prevailing on particular issues rather than a single elite dominating them all. The competition among interests allows a wide spectrum of input to be processed within governmental structures before policy decisions are made. Although governance through group access departs somewhat from traditional concepts of public participation and rule by the majority, citizen access to government is the key element in either case. Given that a readily identifiable and stable elite does not seem to prevail across all policy issues, the pluralist theory seems a plausible explanation of the U.S. political scene.

**Political Action Committee (PAC) (319)**

A formal committee of an interest group designed to raise monies that can be used to support political candidates favorable to the group. Political action committees (PACs) had their origin prior to World War II, typically as political mechanisms of labor unions. For years, however, these committees played only an incidental role in the political process. Passage of the Federal Election Campaign Act of 1971 dramatically enlarged their influence. The federal law permitted PACs to receive and disperse contributions of up to $5,000 to congressional campaigns. The effect, intended or not, was to make PACs a convenient conduit for individuals, groups, and corporations to contribute to political campaigns. *See also* FEDERAL ELECTION CAMPAIGN ACTS, 180; *FEDERAL ELECTION COMMISSION (FEC) V. NATIONAL CONSERVATIVE POLITICAL ACTION COMMITTEE (NCPAC)* (470 U.S. 480: 1985), 287; INTEREST GROUP, 293.

*Significance* At the present time, there are approximately 5,000 registered political action committees (PACs). PACs were responsible for more than a third of the funds made available to congressional campaigns in 1986. PACs are also permitted to make unrestricted independent expenditures on behalf of publicly funded presidential candidates. Most PAC activity in the form of campaign contributions is done by three broad categories of PACs. First, of course, are the PACs that represent economic interests—for example, labor and corporate PACs. Next, there are PACs established by professional and trade associations. Finally, there are the ideologically based PACs—for example, the National Conservative Political Action Committee (NCPAC), an organization dedicated to the election of conservatives to public office. The period since the mid-1970s has seen the proliferation of PACs and a dramatic expansion of their impact on the political process. This heightened impact will likely remain for the foreseeable future, with a commensurate loss of impact for political parties.

**Professional Association** **(320)**

Organization designed to advance and protect the interests of specialized professionals. As reflected in their activities, professional associations share some of the characteristics of trade associations and labor unions. On the one hand, professional associations are interested in advancing their respective professions. They provide technical services and act to disseminate information to their members through the publication of journals and the sponsoring of conferences. At the same time, these associations are attentive to the economic needs of the profession. Professional associations cut across both the public and private sectors and vary substantially in size and focus. Among the larger and more influential professional associations are the American Bar Association (ABA), the American Medical Association (AMA), and the National Education Association (NEA). Occupying the other side of the continuum are associations that serve highly specialized or academic professionals. *See also* AMERICAN BAR ASSOCIATION (ABA), 261; AMERICAN MEDICAL ASSOCIATION (AMA), 266; NATIONAL EDUCATION ASSOCIATION (NEA), 308.

*Significance* The political involvement of professional associations varies widely. Some associations participate infrequently in the political process and then only when a political issue happens to intersect their relatively narrow or focused interests. Other associations are constantly active. The American Medical Association (AMA) is continually involved in trying to influence the fashioning of health policies, especially those like Medicare that directly affect doctors' incomes or those that may affect the degree to which health care is regulated by government. Similarly, the American Bar Association (ABA) exercises influence on issues that involve change in the legal process and court system. In addition, the ABA plays a major role in the evaluation of nominees for the federal judiciary.

**Public Interest Group** **(321)**

An organization that pursues objectives that are not limited to its own membership. Examples of public interest groups that seek to represent widely held interests include consumer and environmental groups. Public interest groups first appeared in the nineteenth century and generally focused on such substantive policy issues as slavery, prohibition, or women's suffrage. The Progressive movement of the early twentieth century focused largely on various reforms within the governmental process. Public interest groups are sometimes referred to as citizens' groups. During the late 1960s and early 1970s, the number of public interest groups increased significantly as larger numbers of people had the means to financially underwrite the costs of such organizations. For many, their affiliation with public interest groups was a conscious reaction to the growing influence of special or vested interests in the political process. *See also* COMMON CAUSE, 278; ENVIRONMENTAL GROUP, 285; LEAGUE OF WOMEN VOTERS (LWV), 298; SINGLE-ISSUE INTEREST GROUP, 327.

*Significance* Public interest groups often claim broad support and assert that they promote the public interest. In reality, they promote their particular perception of the public interest, which may or may not be broadly acceptable to the public. In addition, the public interest label may be adopted by a group because it may enhance the public image of the organization or it may facilitate governmental access. Nonetheless, many public interest groups currently exist, and they must be recognized as serious participants in the political process. Take, for example, Common Cause. Established in 1970, the organization has generally sought to heighten governmental accountability. In particular, Common Cause has successfully advanced campaign finance reforms such as public financing and public disclosure of campaign contributions and expenditures. Similarly, many groups have been established by consumer advocate Ralph Nader. These include Public Citizen, an umbrella organization that supports investigations into practices affecting the consumer; Congress Watch, the direct lobbying arm of the Nader group; Critical Mass, which focuses on safety standards for nuclear power plants; and the Health Research group, which focuses on the delivery, quality, and cost of health care.

## Purposive Benefits (322)

Benefits derived from the goals or objectives of a particular association. Purposive benefits are typically altruistic, although rewards are produced by enjoying the benefits that come from an association's efforts. Forestalling gun control proposals, for example, is a proposive benefit enjoyed by members of the National Rifle Association (NRA). Unlike material benefits, purposive benefits are not likely to have monetary value. They are also likely to be collective in character in that they are not limited to the group members who pursue them. *See also* COLLECTIVE GOODS, 277; PUBLIC INTEREST GROUP, 321.

*Significance* Certain interest groups are sustained largely through the efforts of individuals who receive purposive rewards or benefits from their membership within those groups—for example, public interest or ideological groups provide rewards that tend to be both collective and symbolic rather than selective and material. Individuals who belong to such groups are usually highly committed to the goals of the organization—"true believers," if you will. For these persons, the ideological, "good government," or specific-issue agenda provides sufficient rewards in and of itself to produce formal membership affiliation. Actions are rewarded for the instrumental effect they may have in achieving group objectives but also for the mere expression of certain values. Although not enough of these people exist to sustain all such groups, they do constitute the indispensable core of the long-standing ones.

**Regulation of Lobbying Act** **(323)**

Legislative enactment aimed at controlling interest group lobbying activities. Throughout the history of the United States, there have been concerns that interest groups are too influential and that special interest politics threaten the integrity of the political process. Despite these concerns, interest group politics including lobbying have generally remained free of stringent regulation because to impose limits on such activity interferes with basic First Amendment freedoms. The Regulation of Lobbying Act was actually part of Title III of the Legislative Reorganization Act of 1946. It called for only minimal limitations. Specifically, the act requires the registration of persons or organizations that receive money for the "principal purpose" of influencing Congress. The registration processes include disclosure of lobbyist identity, employer, and the amount and purpose of expenditures. The act also requires lobbyists to submit quarterly activity reports, which are published in the *Congressional Record.* Penalties including fines and/or imprisonment and a ban on future lobbying were established for violators. *See also* FEDERAL ELECTION CAMPAIGN ACTS, 180; LOBBYING, 300.

*Significance* There is much doubt that the Regulation of Lobbying Act has any real impact on lobbying activities. As soon as the act went into effect, its defects as a regulatory device became obvious. The "principal purpose" language was a key problem. Groups that did not make direct contact with Congress or those that were able to claim their principal purpose was not lobbying fell outside the registration requirement. Futhermore, the act covered only congressional lobbying contact and did not extend to executive or regulatory agencies. The act was also vague as to the kinds of contacts that were regulated, leaving it to lobbyists to determine which activities were reached by the law. The act also exempted from registration groups spending their own resources for lobbying in contrast to those who "solicited" funds for lobbying purposes. Lobbyists also had great discretion in determining which expenditures needed to be reported as lobbying costs. Finally, the law contained no effective enforcement provisions. Nonetheless, the Regulation of Lobbying Act remains the only one in existence. Although some new legislation was introduced in the wake of Watergate, nothing directly aimed at lobbying practices emerged. Substantial changes were made in regulations governing campaign financing, however, which do impact on interest group activity.

**_Schaumburg, Village of v. Citizens for a Better_ Environment, 444 U.S. 620 (1980)** **(324)**

Struck down a local ordinance that used the overbreadth doctrine. In the *Village of Schaumburg v. Citizens for a Better Environment,* the Supreme Court examined a local ordinance that prohibited door-to-door solicitations for contributions by organizations not using at least 75 percent of their receipts for charitable purposes. A charitable purpose excluded such items as salaries, overhead, solicitation costs, and other administrative expenses. An environmental group was denied permission to solicit because it could not demonstrate compliance with the 75 percent requirement. The organization sued, claiming First Amendment violations, and the Court struck down the ordinance. The primary objection was the overbreadth of the ordinance. The Court noted that a class of organizations existed to which the 75 percent rule could not constitutionally be applied. These were organizations "whose primary purpose is not to provide money or services to the poor, the needy, or other worthy objects of charity, but to gather and disseminate information about and advocate positions on matters of public concern." The cost of research, advocacy, or public education is typically in excess of 25 percent of funds raised. The Court felt that to lump together all organizations that failed to meet the 75 percent standard imposed a direct and substantial limitation on protected activity. Although the village interest in preventing fraud may generally be legitimate, the means to accomplish that end must use more precise measures to separate one kind from another. *See also* *COATES V. CINCINNATI* (402 U.S. 611: 1971), 54; *SECRETARY OF STATE OF MARYLAND V. J. H. MUNSON COMPANY* (467 U.S. 947: 1984), 325.

*Significance* *Village of Schaumburg v. Citizens for a Better Environment* (444 U.S. 620: 1980) is important because it produced a requirement that statutes carefully distinguish between lawful and unlawful behavior. This ruling is particularly important when it comes to the regulation of groups and parties whose function is to engage in public discussion of public issues. The *Schaumburg* reasoning was later applied to a state limitation on charity fund-raising expenses in *Secretary of State of Maryland v. J. H. Munson Company* (467 U.S. 947: 1984). Maryland had enacted a statute designed to prevent abusive and fraudulent fund-raising by prohibiting a charity from spending more than 25 percent of its gross income for expenses. The Supreme Court invalidated the law, saying that fund-raising for charities was so intertwined with speech that it required First Amendment protection. In *Coates v. Cincinnati* (402 U.S. 611: 1971), the Court struck down a city ordinance that prohibited three or more persons from assembling on public sidewalks and conducting themselves in such a way as to "annoy any police officer or other persons who should happen to pass by." The Court found that the ordinance "makes a crime out of what under the Constitution cannot be a crime." It was also impermissibly vague because it conveyed no standard of conduct and "men of common intelligence must necessarily guess at its meaning."

***Secretary of State of Maryland v. J. H. Munson* Company, 467 U.S. 947 (1984)** **(325)**

Struck down a state law that limited the amount a charity could expend in fund-raising to 25 percent of the amount raised. The regulation in *Secretary of State v. J. H. Munson Company* did have a waiver provision for situations in which the limit would "effectively prevent" a charitable organization from generating revenue. The law was challenged by a professional fund-raiser whose fee was regularly in excess of the limit. Despite the waiver, the Supreme Court found the regulation overbroad and therefore unconstitutionally burdensome on free expression. The waiver was "extremely narrow" and was to "no avail" to an organization whose high fund-raising costs were "attributable to legitimate policy decisions about how to use its funds, rather than to inability to raise funds." Organizations with high costs due to information dissemination, discussion, and advocacy "remain barred" from carrying on "protected First Amendment activities." The law was flawed by overbreadth and possessed "no core of easily identifiable and constitutionally proscribable conduct that the statute prohibits." In all its applications, the law operated on a "fundamentally mistaken premise that high solicitation costs are an accurate measure of fraud." Where means were chosen to pursue an objective that was too "imprecise," applications of the law created an "unnecessary risk of chilling free speech." *See also* ASSOCIATION, RIGHT OF, 270; *SCHAUMBURG, VILLAGE OF V. CITIZENS FOR A BETTER ENVIRONMENT* (444 U.S. 620: 1980), 324.

*Significance* The Supreme Court's ruling in *Secretary of State of Maryland v. J. H. Munson Company* (467 U.S. 947: 1984) was the second recent decision on charitable fund-raising. In *Village of Schaumburg v. Citizens for a Better Environment* (444 U.S. 620: 1980), the Court struck down a local ordinance barring door-to-door solicitations for organizations that did not use 75 percent of their fund-raising proceeds for "charitable purposes." The waiver feature contained in *Munson* was a technique used by many states to limit the effect of the *Schaumburg* ruling on their efforts to regulate solicitations by charitable organizations. The Court, however, was unpersuaded that the waiver resolved the defect found in *Schaumburg.* There remain, said the Court, charitable organizations that will continue to be affected by the law despite the waiver because their activities, protected as they might be, have a cost that exceeds the limit. *Munson* not only speaks to the need for organizations to have sufficient room to operate and raise money, but also reiterates the need for regulations to be both narrow and precise such that they do not apply overbroadly and consequently interfere with protected activity.

**Sierra Club (326)**

One of the nation's leading environmental groups. The Sierra Club was founded in 1892 for the purpose of protecting natural resources and environmental quality. It is governed by an elected board, with basic policy and organizational issues coming before a larger council. Beneath the national organization, it operates through a structure of regional, state, and local chapters. Through the Sierra Club Foundation, research is sponsored and educational materials produced. The Sierra Club Legal Defense Fund utilizes legal remedies to protect environmental interests. The Sierra Club also engages in direct and constituent lobbying, with emphasis on providing Congress and its committees with technical assistance and expert testimony on ecosystem issues. *See also* ENVIRONMENTAL GROUP, 285; INTEREST GROUP, 293; PUBLIC INTEREST GROUP, 321.

*Significance* Despite its being one of the older environmental organizations, the Sierra Club has experienced dramatic membership growth since 1980. Similarly, the level of litigation and political activity heightened, especially during James Watt's tenure as secretary of the interior. The Sierra Club has even gone so far as to establish the Sierra Club Committee on Political Education (SCCOPE), its own political-action arm. The Sierra Club has supported such policies as reauthorization of the Clean Air and Clean Water Acts, protection of Alaskan lands, suspension of water projects and nuclear plant construction, mass transportation, and retention of federal ownership of wilderness areas. It has also effectively used the courts to advance its positions. In 1983, for example, it was one of six environmental groups that jointly blocked removal of almost 1 million acres of land from protected status.

**Single-issue Interest Group** **(327)**

A group that pursues objectives with exclusive focus on one policy issue or area. Single-issue interest groups have a public interest character in that positions they advance often affect more than their own memberships. Groups organized around the abortion question are good examples. They seek either a ban on abortion or preservation of abortion as a personal choice guaranteed by law. Whichever policy position prevails will apply to everyone, members as well as nonmembers. At the same time, single-issue groups can be distinguished from public interest groups by their unyielding, uncompromising, and sometimes militant pursuit of their singular policy objective. Although single-issue groups have long occupied a place on the political scene, such groups have increased substantially since the late 1960s, which, in turn, has elevated their visibility as organized groups. Single-issue interest groups engage extensively in both direct and indirect methods of lobbying. *See also* NATIONAL RIFLE ASSOCIATION (NRA), 313; NATIONAL RIGHT-TO-LIFE COMMITTEE, 314; PUBLIC INTEREST GROUP, 321.

*Significance* Single-issue interest groups are composed of individuals who focus their energies on one issue. Although members of other groups may strongly support the issue positions of their own organizations, that commitment typically cannot match the intensity of commitment possessed by those who join single-issue groups. Accordingly, single-issue groups are usually more aggressive, confrontational, and uncompromising. They have also cultivated media visibility to the extent that some are able to exercise disproportionately more influence in the political process than other kinds of groups. The National Rifle Association (NRA) and its success in preventing adoption of gun control measures is illustrative. The NRA has been able to mobilize a large membership and engage in extremely effective grassroots lobbying at the federal as well as state and local levels of government. Single-issue groups are also active in the election process. Groups that support or oppose abortion have attempted to frame election contests around that single issue. Although claims of playing a decisive role in such elections may be overstated, these groups often succeed in drawing heavy media coverage to their cause.

**Solidary Benefits** **(328)**

Benefits derived from the act of associating. Solidary rewards include such benefits as the sense of affiliation or belonging, any special status that might come from group membership, and enjoyment of the social aspects of membership. Solidary rewards are independent of the goals of the association. *See also* MATERIAL BENEFITS, 302; PURPOSIVE BENEFITS, 322.

*Significance* Solidary benefits are intrinsic—that is, they are benefits that come from nothing more than association itself. Nonetheless, solidary benefits may provide sufficient incentive to attract or retain members to a group. Solidary and purposive rewards are especially important for ideological or public interest groups because such groups typically deal in collective goods that are not material in nature.

**Taft-Hartley Act** **(329)**

Enactment that imposed certain regulations on labor unions. The Taft-Hartley Act (the Labor-Management Relations Act of 1947) was actually a modification of the National Labor Relations (Wagner) Act. Taft-Hartley did retain some portions of the Wagner Act and continued, for example, formal regulation of unfair labor practices by employers. Taft-Hartley targeted such tactics as secondary boycotts but also banned the closed shop and union political spending. The act also provided a number of "cooling off" mechanisms, including court orders that may be used in serious strike situations. In addition, Taft-Hartley established reporting requirements for unions that allowed government to monitor the internal operations of unions. *See also* LABOR ORGANIZATION, 296; LANDRUM-GRIFFIN ACT, 297; NATIONAL RIGHT-TO-WORK COMMITTEE, 315; WAGNER ACT, 333.

*Significance* The Taft-Hartley Act was an outgrowth of the view that unions had gained too much power. Coupled with evidence of union corruption and the suspicion that some union leaders were political subversives, the Republican-controlled Congress passed Taft-Hartley over the veto of President Harry Truman. It did represent a departure from the union-protective position manifest in the Wagner Act and thrust the government more fully into the labor-management arena. Taft-Hartley had an additional provision, section 14(b), that attempted to limit union shops by permitting states to exempt themselves from federal law otherwise requiring union shops. This right-to-work exception under 14(b) has been adopted by 20 states.

**Teamsters** **(330)**

The largest labor union in the United States. The Teamsters are formally the International Brotherhood of Teamsters, Chauffeurs, Warehousemen, and Helpers of America and have a membership in excess of 2 million from the transportation, trucking, and warehousing industries. The Teamsters union was founded in 1899 as a loose confederation of locals. A stronger organization featuring five regional conferences eventually emerged, with the conferences taking the lead in Teamster political activities. Under the presidency of Jimmy Hoffa, the structure was centralized further, with the national union even taking over contract negotiations. Despite some successes at the bargaining table, Hoffa, like his predecessor Dave Beck, became the target of federal investigations of union misconduct. It was at this time that the Teamsters were expelled from the American Federation of Labor–Congress of Industrial Organizations (AFL-CIO). Following Hoffa's conviction for jury tampering, some of the power concentrated at the national level returned to the locals and councils of locals. The Teamsters continued to be plagued by legal problems as an unaffiliated or independent union in the 1970s and 1980s. In 1987, following a leadership change, the Teamsters reaffiliated with the AFL-CIO. *See also* ECONOMIC-BASED GROUP, 282; LABOR ORGANIZATION, 296.

*Significance* The Teamsters union is politically quite active and, because of its size, the union possesses the potential to be a significant factor in the electoral process. The political arm of the Teamsters is an entity known as Democratic Republican Independent Voter Education (DRIVE). The national leadership of the Teamsters has been more willing than their organized labor counterparts to support Republican presidential candidates. As a result, the two campaigns of Ronald Reagan showcased the Teamsters' endorsement in their attempts to appeal to labor rank and file. The Teamsters also score congressional voting records. Among the key issues for Teamsters have been opposition to deregulation of the trucking industry, support for strengthening OSHA, and opposition to a national trucker's license, especially one with more stringent drunk-driving standards than for other motorists.

**Trade Association** **(331)**

An organization of businesses or enterprises in the same trade or industry. A trade association is an integrative organization that unites businesses that are typically competitors but that have common political interests. Trade associations have the most offices in Washington;

therefore, they are the principal source of political activity on behalf of the business community. Upwards of 2,000 trade associations have representatives permanently located in Washington. Trade associations vary greatly in size and political influence. The National Home Builders Association, for example, has over 130,000 members and an annual budget exceeding $12 million. Others have extremely modest memberships and financial resources. *See also* AMERICAN PETROLEUM INSTITUTE (API), 267; BUSINESS ORGANIZATION, 272; ECONOMIC-BASED GROUP, 282; PEAK ASSOCIATION, 317.

*Significance* Trade associations are organizations whose members are businesses. Trade associations engage in a broad variety of activities; foremost among these is influencing governmental policy on matters that affect the entire industry. Such questions usually involve taxation and regulations directed at the industry. For example, the American Petroleum Institute (API), the trade association for the petroleum and natural gas industry, has been active in advocating, among other things, repeal of the windfall profits tax, decontrol of natural gas, and the opening of onshore as well as offshore governmental lands for energy exploration. In addition to political activities, trade associations typically provide technical assistance that allows members to more effectively address industry problems. These activities may include counsel on matters of industry health, industry practices, marketing, industry data processing, environmental protection, public relations, and public education.

**United Automobile Workers (UAW) (332)**

Labor union that represents virtually all employees involved in the production of motor vehicles and aircraft. The United Automobile, Aerospace and Agricultural Implement Workers of America (UAW) was formed in 1935 and gained its first significant recognition following its strike of General Motors in 1937. Though initially chartered by the American Federation of Labor (AFL), it joined the Congress of Industrial Organizations (CIO) in 1936 where it remained until the merger of the AFL and CIO in 1955. Near the end of Walter Reuther's presidency, the UAW became an independent union, a status it maintained until it rejoined the AFL-CIO in 1981. The UAW has a nonpartisan political component known as the Community Action Program (CAP). Through a network of approximately 160 regional CAP councils, the UAW is able to participate in the political process in a variety of ways. CAP actively works to register union members to vote and conducts turn-out-the-vote efforts on election days. CAP is also involved in public information campaigns that feature legislative voting records. Finally, CAP endorses candidates and contributes to the campaigns of endorsed candidates from funds generated in voluntary fund-raising drives for UAW V-CAP, the UAW's registered political action committee (PAC). *See also* ECONOMIC-BASED GROUP, 282; LABOR ORGANIZATION, 296.

*Significance* The United Automobile Workers (UAW) has a long history of political involvement. The UAW was a participant in the creation of the Congress of Industrial Organizations' (CIO) political action committee (PAC) in 1943, an entity that was merged into the American Federation of Labor's (AFL) Committee on Political Education (COPE) in 1955. The policy positions advanced by the UAW are adopted at national conventions that are held regularly. Highest priority is assigned to issues that are most closely associated with the economic interests of the UAW. Protection of the U.S. automobile industry through import restrictions and extension of unemployment compensation benefits, for example, have been especially important. In addition, the UAW has supported efforts to eliminate employment discrimination, pass the Equal Rights Amendment (ERA), fund public transportation and public employment programs, and provide cost-of-living adjustments for most public assistance programs.

**Wagner Act** **(333)**

Federal enactment that protected the right of employees to organize themselves and engage in collective bargaining with their employers. The Wagner Act is the popular name of the National Labor Relations Act of 1935. The act defined certain interferences with the right to organize and bargain as unfair labor practices and established the National Labor Relations Board (NLRB) to enforce provisions of the act. The NLRB is empowered to adjudicate claims of proscribed practices and issue cease-and-desist orders to employers found in violation. *See also* LABOR ORGANIZATION, 296; TAFT-HARTLEY ACT, 329.

*Significance* The Wagner Act is regarded as the Magna Carta of the labor movement. The act legitimized union activity and legally protected it. During the decade following enactment, union membership increased dramatically. With the growth in membership came greater political influence for unions. When partisan control in Congress changed from Democratic to Republican following World War II, the labor-protective tone of the Wagner Act was diminished by enactment of the Taft-Hartley Act, although basic protection of collective bargaining remained national policy. The Wagner Act was based on congressional authority over interstate commerce. The Article I authority drawn on for the Wagner Act was more extensive than had been recognized by the courts prior to 1935, thus some question existed as to constitutionality of the initiative. The Supreme Court, in the wake of the "Court-packing" threat, did uphold the act in the case of *National Labor Relations Board v. Jones and Laughlin Steel Corporation* (301 U.S. 1: 1937).

# 7. *The Mass Media*

The *mass media* are the means of communicating with large and widely dispersed audiences. There are two types of mass media: one communicates through the printed page; the other communicates by broadcasting the spoken word over airwaves or wire. Newspapers and magazines are components of the printed media. Radio, television, and even the telephone belong to the broadcast media. Although the mass media have a variety of functions, several bear directly on the political system. The ways in which the mass media gather and report the news have a particular impact on the political process. They determine which items are worthy of dissemination and emphasis; they offer comment on and interpretation of the news; they provide political background and context; and they shape public attitudes about events and persons, especially government officials who are actors in news stories.

The historical development of the mass media is tied to their ability to gather and disseminate information. Technological improvements are significant in this regard. Also significant is the public, which consumes what the media disseminate, and continues to demand more from them. The development of the print and broadcast media into means of mass communications took different paths. The first newspapers were highly focused and were often organs of political parties or groups. Production was both costly and slow, thus most early newspapers were not widely circulated. As printing techniques improved, the penny paper, which attracted broader readership, was introduced. The telegraph permitted news to be communicated more quickly and widely, which led directly to the first wire services, a significant contribution to the timely reporting of events. News gathering was also enhanced by the use of reporters, a technique first developed seriously during the Civil War. Finally, newspapers began to engage in sensationalizing the news as well as seeking to expose corrupt practices. This latter activity was the precursor of investigative journalism. Each of these activities contributed to the transformation of newspapers into widely circulated publications. Magazines developed more slowly, but, with the introduction of the weekly newsmagazine soon after World War I, a medium of national scope was established for the first time.

The medium of radio first began broadcasting in 1920. The number of stations that broadcast—to say nothing of the number of radios that received—grew quickly. Several years later, the first network was created, linking individual stations and permitting the establishment of a truly national medium. Broadcasts added a dimension impossible to capture in print. The appeal of radio was not lost on political figures. Many have followed the lead of Franklin Roosevelt, who used radio quite effectively to communicate to the American people. Television added the dimension of video, which generated even greater appeal. Television has grown to such an extent that virtually every household in the country is equipped to receive television broadcasts. Television certainly enhanced the capability to communicate immediately to vast audiences.

The media in the United States are privately owned. Indeed, this private ownership is concentrated in the hands of a relative few, but not without consequence. On the one hand, it politically insulates the media from unwarranted government influence or interference. At the same time, the private media are driven by revenues linked to audience shares. This condition may influence decisions on newsworthiness of events because audience appeal becomes part of the editorial matrix. Thus it becomes possible, if not likely, that the media's money-making function of entertainment overlaps their journalistic efforts. The suggestion has been made that private ownership distinguishes U.S. mass media from its counterparts in other political systems. Although greater political freedom for the media is the result, the media—especially the broadcast media—are subject to regulations, notwithstanding the First Amendment. These regulations target several problems. The federal government requires licensure of all broadcasters in order to protect the finite, public airwaves from actions detrimental to the public interest. Thus, for example, broadcast frequencies are assigned so that broadcasters cannot interfere with each other's broadcasts. Most regulation in this area is administered by the Federal Communications Commission (FCC). Some regulations target the substance of broadcasts. Licenses may be jeopardized by broadcasting "indecent" material. Broadcasters are also obligated to operate according to certain access rules (for example, the equal time and fairness doctrines) so that licensees do not prevent certain viewpoints from being heard in a community. Like the print media, the broadcast media must live within the legal limits that govern issues such as access to information, source confidentiality, and libel.

The media clearly have a substantial impact on politics that manifests itself in several important ways. First, the media practically shapes the political agenda of the country. By featuring particular items, issues, or people, priorities are established that guarantee that these items, issues, or people will be in the spotlight and discussed. Second, the media have great impact on the electoral process, beginning with candidate selection. Traditional partisan routes to nominations are now being displaced by candidacies that are taken directly to the electorate via the media. In addition, candidates need different strengths than previously. An appealing television presence often becomes more valuable than political experience. The media also influence elections by producing debates, offering support of one candidate over another by issuing endorsements, by disclosing projected election outcomes even before the balloting is complete, and by simply being available to those who can afford to purchase time and promote a carefully packaged candidate in 30- or 60-second ad spots. Finally, there is good reason to believe that the media can have an impact on public policy, both domestic and foreign, by the way they handle it. We need look no further than our painful experience in Vietnam to see the impact of the media on national policies. On balance, it is abundantly clear that the aggregate effect of the media on U.S. politics is considerable.

## Agenda Setting (334)

Making a list of items to be considered or addressed. Agenda setting in the political context refers to establishing the list of issues or items that need governmental attention. One of the ways the media affects the political process is in the setting of agendas. In selecting which news items to feature and which to ignore, the media assign priority to some issues over others. The issues assigned priority will be those in the forefront of the public's consciousness, the issues upon which public officials will act. The capacity of the media to set agendas is limited, however. Some issues or events featured by the media simply do not capture the public's attention. In such instances, the media are unable to establish an issue as a priority; this happens most often with substantive policy matters. It is also true that public officials use the media to influence political agendas—the media cover what public officials and candidates for office choose to emphasize. *See also* BIAS, 337; NEWSWORTHINESS, 380.

*Significance* The media have an impact on agenda setting, but media influence on political agendas is not evenly distributed. Rather, disproportionate influence is exercised by the major news organizations, such as the three leading television networks, the two news wire services, and the print media with national markets. The latter comprise the principal news weeklies *Time, Newsweek,* and *U.S. News and World Report* and several daily newspapers, including the *New York Times, Wall Street Journal, Washington Post,* and *USA Today.* Aside from influencing the behavior of public officials by establishing priorities, these major media influence what the remainder of the media will cover. As political figures respond to issues assigned priority by the major media, their responses will be reported by these secondary media, thereby reinforcing the view that these issues are important and deserve attention.

**Backgrounder** **(335)**

Conversations between public officials and the press to provide background information. Backgrounders may take the form of press conferences or briefings, but generally information disclosed "on background" cannot be attributed. Information received by the media in a backgrounder is often described as coming, for example, from "government sources" or "highly placed officials." Other information obtained "off-the-record" but in a more surreptitious manner than the backgrounder is referred to as a "leak." Information received on background differs from that obtained off-the-record in that information obtained by means of the latter cannot be disclosed even if the source is withheld. Journalists who violate either of these boundaries will quickly have no background or off-the-record sources. *See also* LEAKS, 364; PRESS CONFERENCE, 389.

*Significance* The backgrounder serves several purposes for the source. As background, the information may allow the media to cover the official more favorably. The backgrounder also permits officials to float "trial balloons" or to try out ideas or proposals on other officials or the public without being directly linked until a reaction has been measured. Officials can also "send messages" in an attempt to influence the behavior of others. Consequences of an action (or inaction) may be anonymously suggested such that the target perceives them in a less threatening way. Journalists have mixed feelings about backgrounders: They dislike the restrictions but understand that they must often pay this price for access and information not available otherwise.

**Beat System** **(336)**

Newsgathering technique that assigns reporters to particular persons, places, or subject matter. The beat system developed because certain sources of information are ongoing. Placing reporters around those sources maximizes the volume of information that can be obtained from such sources. News organizations typically have a number of beats in Washington. Some reporters are assigned to cover the president, Congress, the Supreme Court, executive departments such as state, or international institutions. Other reporters may be assigned substantive issues like business or energy that may require them to monitor several agencies or locations. Reporters assigned to particular beats are responsible for gathering newsworthy information, but the search is often facilitated by regular contacts with press secretaries or other staffers responsible for press liaison. *See also* WIRE SERVICE, 403.

*Significance* The beat system provides a framework for newsgathering. Because the bulk of news comes from identifiable and regular sources, there is utility in simply assigning reporters to cover these sources exclusively. The beat approach best enables news organizations to achieve fullest coverage of the source. It also heightens the quality of coverage in that the reporter gains greater expertise about his beat through familiarity. By covering only the Supreme Court, for example, a reporter becomes more knowledgeable about the Court and thus better able to report on its activities. The various beats combined supply news organizations with an extraordinary proportion of the information reported by the media. The beat system also has an impact on the uniformity of reported news. Because news sources are patterned, most news organizations assign reporters to the same beats. This means that reporters covering a State Department news briefing, for example, will have essentially the same information to report.

**Bias** **(337)**

Partiality or prejudice with respect to a person or viewpoint. Critics of the media argue that their reporting of news is biased because it is influenced by the political orientations of the journalists and the owners of the news organizations. Typically, the contention is made that the news correspondents are biased in a liberal direction, whereas the media owners are conservative. Evidence suggests that these broad characterizations may be true. Nonetheless, most of those who study the media conclude that ideology or partisanship does not work its way into news reporting in a substantial or consistent fashion. The media that may have appeared to be more favorable toward Walter Mondale in his challenge of Ronald Reagan in 1984 was the same media that seemed to treat Jimmy Carter somewhat negatively in his contest against Reagan just four years earlier. If a pattern of bias does exist, it may be against officeholders, a phenomenon that may simply be a product of journalistic skepticism. *See also* EDITORIAL, 349; ELECTION COVERAGE, 351; NEWSWORTHINESS, 380.

*Significance* The early press in the United States communicated a great deal of political bias. Indeed, the early press were organs of political parties and dutifully conveyed the party line. As the media became independent of parties, they also sought to be more objective and professional in their treatment of news. As a result, it is almost impossible to find overt bias in newsgathering by the contemporary media. Nonetheless, potentially biasing factors do exist. First, a number of judgments are involved in covering the news—newsworthiness must be determined. Essentially, this process involves deciding which stories will be covered and how much emphasis each will receive. Such determinations cannot be made mechanically. Second, a commercial factor enters with respect to newsworthiness. The media need to attract audiences, which becomes a major criterion in selecting news items.

**_Branzburg v. Hayes_, 408 U.S. 665 (1972)** **(338)**

Held that newspersons must disclose sources of information to a grand jury and rejected the argument that newspersons possess a privileged relationship with their sources. After having published reports about drug use and manufacture, Hayes was subpoenaed to appear before a state grand jury and identify the individuals whom he had seen using and making illegal narcotics. Hayes refused to testify and was cited for contempt. The Supreme Court said that the First Amendment "does not invalidate every incidental burdening of the press that may result from the enforcement of civil or criminal statutes of general applicability." In balancing the interests of protecting the criminal process and the newsgathering function of the press, the former must prevail. The consequential but uncertain burden on the press is not sufficient to treat newspersons differently from any other citizen. They must respond to relevant questions put to them in the course of a valid grand jury investigation or criminal trial. The burden in *Branzburg* was not a prior restraint, a tax, a penalty on content, or a compulsion to publish. The Court suggested, however, that the impact of its holding would be limited. "Only where news sources themselves are implicated in crimes or possess information relevant to the grand jury's task need they or the reporter be concerned about grand jury subpoenas. Nothing before us indicates that a large number or percentage of all confidential news sources fall into either category." Finally, the Court argued that abuse or harassment of the press would be subject to ongoing judicial monitoring. *See also* *HOUCHINS V. KQED, INC.* (438 U.S. 1: 1978), 362; *RICHMOND NEWSPAPERS V. VIRGINIA* (448 U.S. 555: 1980), 400.

*Significance* *Branzburg v. Hayes* (408 U.S. 665: 1972) said that even an unconditional freedom to publish would be of limited value if information gathering was unprotected. Nonetheless, the Supreme Court refused to interpret the First Amendment in such a way as to create the privilege sought by Branzburg. To protect that function, several states have adopted shield laws to protect the confidentiality of sources. No such legislation exists at the federal level, although *Branzburg* did prompt introduction of such proposals. The Burger Court also rejected other claims of the press regarding its rights in gathering information. In *Saxbe v. Washington Post* (417 U.S. 843: 1974), the Court upheld federal prison regulations that prohibited press interviews with designated or particular inmates. The Court said the Constitution does not impose on government the "affirmative duty to make available to journalists sources of information not available to members of the public generally." Four years later, in *Houchins v. KQED, Inc.* (438 U.S. 1: 1978), the Court upheld a refusal to allow media access to a county jail that had been the site of a prisoner's suicide and allegations of violent incidents and inhumane conditions. The Court saw the case as one involving a "special privilege of access" such as that denied in *Saxbe*—it was a "right which is not essential to guarantee the freedom to communicate or publish."

**Broadcast Media (339)**

Electronic means by which the spoken word is transmitted. Although several devices may carry spoken words, radio and television are typically regarded as the primary components of the broadcast or electronic media. Radios were introduced into the United States in 1920, heralding a new political era. Broadcast enabled politicians to make direct contact with audiences and allowed them to reach many who were not reached through newspapers. Within 30 years, the number of radio stations had grown to more than 3,000, and nearly 90 percent of U.S. households owned at least one radio. Many of the local stations throughout the country were eventually linked by several radio networks that turned radio into a medium of national scope. Television was operating on an experimental basis in the late 1930s, but dramatic development of the technology occurred after World War II. Growth of television paralleled that of radio. A large number of local television stations, most of which were affiliated with the three major networks, quickly developed. Like radios, Americans bought television receivers, so by 1980, less than 2 percent of U.S. households did not own at least one television set. Television had one major advantage over radio, however, in that it provided the visual dimension. Through television, news and political events could be seen from one's living room. The broadcast media enjoy First Amendment protection but have historically been subjected to greater regulation than the print media. *See also* COMMUNICATIONS ACT OF 1934, 344; MASS MEDIA, 368; NETWORK, 378; PRINT MEDIA, 392.

*Significance* The broadcast media have altered the U.S. political landscape. Broadcasting is a medium that can reach virtually every house nationwide. Franklin Roosevelt was the first president to effectively utilize broadcasting for political advantage. His fireside chats allowed him to communicate directly with the electorate and cultivate support for his political agenda. Broadcast coverage of candidates has also had a dramatic impact on the electoral process. Events such as broadcast debates and political advertising are principal examples. The impact of the broadcast media is not confined to election campaigns, however. On a daily basis, the broadcast media serve as the primary source of news and other information for most Americans. The function of reporting and interpreting the news enables the broadcast media to influence public opinion, which, in turn, has direct consequences on governmental policies and the processes of policymaking.

**Cable Television (340)**

Transmission of television signals through a cable rather than through air. Cable television is the term used to refer to community antenna television (CATV). Cable television first appeared around 1950, although its impact was limited for a number of years in part because of Federal Communications Commission (FCC) regulations that sought to protect the established broadcast networks from competition from cable. This approach changed over the years as government officials recognized the value of cable for reaching people who could not be serviced by conventional broadcast stations. In addition, cable technology did not require use of public airwaves for transmission of programs. Cable offered the possibility for a great many new channels, thus relieving the access pressure resulting from the limits of the broadcast spectrum. *See also* DEREGULATION, 348; NETWORK, 378.

*Significance* New communications technologies such as cable television offer the possibility of many channels of programming and substantially greater public access. Great content diversity can be provided through the increased number of channels supported by these technologies. In addition, cable systems provide special public access opportunities, typically nonprofit programming time made available by local companies as a condition of operating a local cable franchise. Cable television in a broad sense, and public access cable more specifically, prompted the FCC to consider removal of various access regulations that have existed for the broadcast media. Although cable television itself has been deregulated by the FCC, other political obstacles remain. Cable companies are often regulated at the local level, and cable companies are generally required to obtain franchises from local authorities, a process that is often highly politicized.

***Chandler v. Florida*, 449 U.S. 560 (1981) (341)**

Examined implementation of media coverage provisions in a trial in which the defendant objected to such coverage as a violation of the Sixth Amendment's requirement of a fair and impartial trial. The Florida Code of Judicial Conduct permitted electronic media and still photographic coverage of trial and appellate proceedings within the discretion of the presiding judge. The Supreme Court decided in *Chandler v. Florida* that, absent a specific showing of prejudice, permitting the coverage was constitutional. An absolute ban on broadcast coverage could not be justified, said the Court, simply because of possible or potential risk. The Court preferred the Florida approach because it provided safeguards for certain problem cases. The Florida guidelines "place on trial judges positive obligations to be on guard to protect the fundamental right of the accused to a fair trial." The mere presence of the broadcast media does not inherently adversely affect the process. The burden is on the defendant to show that his or her case was influenced by the coverage. The Florida process allows review on appeal of allegations of compromised proceedings because of media coverage. Chandler could demonstrate no specific adverse impacts on the trial participants that were sufficient to constitute a denial of due process. *See also* *NEBRASKA PRESS ASSOCIATION V. STUART* (427 U.S. 539: 1976), 377.

*Significance* *Chandler v. Florida* (449 U.S. 560: 1981) reflects the Supreme Court's deference to the discretion of trial judges in managing problems that relate to media coverage of criminal trials. Just as in *Gannett Company v. DePasquale* (443 U.S. 368: 1979) and *Richmond Newspapers, Inc. v. Virginia* (448 U.S. 555: 1980), the Court left critical assessment of possible adverse effects to the presiding judge. This approach squares with the Burger Court's preference for letting the totality of circumstances provide the basis for resolving questions of law. *Chandler* also represents a swing away from *Gannett,* a swing begun in *Richmond Newspapers.* Courtroom coverage by electronic media has the potential to be most problematic in terms of fair trial standards, yet in *Chandler,* the Court refused to find such coverage inherently violative of due process. *Chandler* placed the burden of proof with the defendant by requiring the accused to demonstrate prejudice; *Gannett* had allowed an accused simply to request closure. Absent a showing of adverse effect, a defendant cannot simply terminate coverage or achieve closure by request alone. In such circumstances, the free press and public trial interests outweigh the interests of the criminal defendant.

### *Columbia Broadcasting System, Inc. (CBS) v.* Federal Communications Commission (FCC), 453 U.S. 367 (1981) (342)

Upheld FCC application of a reasonable access rule to broadcast stations for candidates for federal office. The Federal Election Campaign Act of 1971 allowed revocation of a station license for failure to allow "reasonable access" to broadcast by "legally qualified" candidates for federal office. A complaint was filed with the FCC by President Jimmy Carter's campaign organization after it had unsuccessfully sought to buy time for political advertising. The major networks refused to make time available, arguing, among other things, that they were not prepared to sell time nearly a year before the election. The FCC ruled their refusal to be a violation of the law and order compliance. The Supreme Court supported both the order and the statutory basis for it. The Court agreed with the networks that the law created a "right of access" that broadened political broadcasting obligations, but the Court did not see this as "unduly circumscribing their editorial discretion." When a broadcaster accepts a franchise for the "exclusive use" of part of the public domain, that franchise comes "burdened by enforceable public obligations." Although the broadcaster is entitled to the "widest journalistic freedom consistent with" those public obligations, it is the "right of the viewers and listeners, not the right of the broadcasters, which is paramount." The First Amendment, said the Court, has its "fullest and most urgent application" when campaigns for public office are involved, and the law here contributes to free expression by enhancing the ability of candidates to present views and information. The law creates a limited right of access in that legally qualified candidates can buy advertising time. The law does not, in the estimation of the Court, "impair the discretion of broadcasters to present their views on any issue or to carry any particular type programming." *See also* FAIRNESS DOCTRINE, 353; FEDERAL COMMUNICATIONS COMMISSION (FCC), 354; REBUTTAL, RIGHT TO, 398.

*Significance* The Supreme Court upheld in *CBS, Inc. v. FCC* (453 U.S. 367: 1981) that Congress can require broadcasters to allow candidates for federal office access to the broadcast medium. The rule recognized in this case is similar to others that apply to the broadcast medium. It attempts to balance the interests of the broadcasters and the need to regulate in the public interest those using a channel monopoly. Maintenance of reasonable access by candidates is likely to remain regulated. Despite the language of this case, the Court's position on access has not been altogether clear. For example, in *CBS v. Democratic National Committee* (412 U.S. 94: 1973), the Court determined that a broadcaster policy of refusing to sell editorial advertisements was an acceptable practice and not incompatible with the fairness doctrine or the reasonable access rule. In that case, the Court said Congress intended to defer to broadcasters the widest journalistic freedom consistent with its public responsibilities and did not mandate a categorical right to broadcast access.

**Commercial Speech** **(343)**

Speech that advertises a product or a service or that has a business purpose. Commercial speech is a category of expression that has historically not been viewed as protected speech and therefore has been subject to substantial regulation. The commercial speech doctrine, for example, permitted the regulation of gender-referenced help-wanted advertisements in *Pittsburgh Press Company v. Human Relations Commission* (413 U.S. 376: 1973). The advertising involved in that case was not only commercial in character, but it engaged in illegal employment discrimination. Any First Amendment interest that may extend to commercial speech is "altogether absent," said the Court, when the commercial activity is itself illegal. *See also* *NEW YORK TIMES V. SULLIVAN* (376 U.S. 254: 1964), 381; *PITTSBURGH PRESS COMPANY V. HUMAN RELATIONS COMMISSION* (413 U.S. 376: 1973), 385.

*Significance* The commercial speech doctrine allows censorship of particular content, expression that is generally related to business activities. Despite the Supreme Court's holding in *Pittsburgh Press*

*Company v. Human Relations Commission* (413 U.S. 376: 1973), the doctrine has been substantially eroded. The narrowing of the doctrine began in *New York Times v. Sullivan* (376 U.S. 254: 1964), where the Court ruled a political advertisement that allegedly libeled a public official was not commercial speech. The definition was narrowed further by the Burger Court in *Bigelow v. Virginia* (421 U.S. 809: 1975) and *Virginia State Board of Pharmacy v. Virginia Citizens Consumer Council, Inc.* (425 U.S. 748: 1976). In the former, the Court protected the publication of an advertisement by an organization offering services related to legal abortions in another state. The Court held that the advertisement "conveyed information of potential interest and value to a diverse audience," not merely a commercial promotion of services. In the latter case, the Court struck down a statute that made advertising of prescription drugs a form of conduct that could lead to suspension of a license. The Court argued that even if the advertiser's interest is a purely economic one, such speech is not necessarily disqualified from protection. Consumers and society have a "strong interest in the free flow of commercial information." The effect of these decisions is to virtually eliminate the previously unprotected category of commercial speech.

**Communications Act of 1934** **(344)**

Federal enactment aimed at regulating the broadcast media. The centerpiece of the Communications Act was the Federal Communications Commission (FCC). The FCC was empowered to regulate broadcasting in the "public interest." The act replaced the Federal Radio Act of 1927, which had established licensure requirements for broadcasters through a Federal Radio Commission. The Communications Act replaced the Federal Radio Commission with the FCC and mandated it to regulate broadcasting in several ways: The FCC has authority to regulate ownership concentration, to evaluate broadcaster performance as part of the licensure procedure, to require that some broadcast time be devoted to local or public interest content, and to establish fair treatment rules for those who wish to access the public airwaves. Another section of the act made it a federal crime to engage in wiretapping. *See also* CABLE TELEVISION, 340; DEREGULATION, 348; FEDERAL COMMUNICATIONS COMMISSION (FCC), 354.

*Significance* The Communications Act of 1934 does not precisely define the mission of the Federal Communications Commission (FCC). As a result, the FCC has had to address fundamental questions such as the direction of broadcast industry development and whether regulation or lack of regulation best serves the public interest. Over the course of its history, the FCC has not earned the reputation of an aggressive industry regulator. Nonetheless, it has established regulations that reach the organizational interrelationships within the broadcast industry. Under the act, the FCC limits, for example, the number of AM radio, FM radio, and television stations that can be owned by a single company. The FCC also affects broadcast content in that various access rules such as equal time require stations to make facilities available to various interests. The broadcast industry has long argued that it is overregulated and that some FCC regulations inhibit the exercise of their broadcasters' free expression rights. The present FCC seems to concur, at least in part, and has moved in the direction of broadcast deregulation.

**Concentrated Ownership** **(345)**

Refers to control of U.S. newspapers and broadcast stations by a relatively small number of owners. The mass media in the United States are largely privately owned and that ownership is increasingly concentrated. One of the direct consequences of private ownership is concentration. As private entities, the media seek to be financially profitable. Successful newspapers and broadcast stations make money because they have large enough audiences to sell advertising space or time. The audience or market reached by a particular newspaper or broadcast station cannot be enlarged easily, so ownership of media in several markets becomes the best way to grow. In this way, ownership becomes concentrated. Estimates are that there are approximately 9,000 commercial radio stations, 1,200 television stations, and 1,700 daily newspapers. Most of these are not independent but rather are linked in some fashion including ownership. An overwhelming majority of television stations are affiliated with the large broadcast networks; many of the daily newspapers are owned by national or regional chains. The Gannett Company, for example, owns over 80 daily papers across the country plus a number of radio and television stations. The trend since the late 1970s is to expand the size of these chains. Patterns of ownership take several forms. One form is simple multiple ownership whereby individuals or corporations own media of the same kind. A chain of 20 newspapers is an example of multiple ownership. Another pattern involves cross-media ownership whereby several media are combined. Finally, some media are owned by large conglomerates that also own nonmedia businesses. Although the print media remain largely unregulated with respect to ownership concentration, the electronic media are subject to structural limits established by the Federal Communications Commission (FCC). Fearful of concentration, the FCC initially allowed a single owner only one AM radio, one FM radio, and one television station in a community. The current ownership rule permits a single person or corporation as many as 12 each of AM, FM, and television stations. These structural restrictions have been the subject of much debate and full deregulation is likely in the near future. *See also* MEDIA MARKET, 371; NETWORK, 378; NEWSWORTHINESS, 380; WIRE SERVICE, 403.

*Significance* Concentrated ownership of the media tends also to concentrate media influence. Concentration of owners enables small numbers of people or corporations to control newsgathering and communication. A worst-case scenario would be a group of powerful owners manipulating news flow to serve their own private or political interests. Even if that does not occur, concentrated control offers consumers only a limited number of news source choices. Further, the choices that do exist are probably not meaningful with respect to content diversity because the national and large regional organizations use a virtually standardized approach to newsgathering and reporting. Ownership concentration is a natural product of private media ownership. Owning a number of stations or newspapers is intended to heighten the chances for commercial success. Commercial success, in turn, depends on maximizing audience appeal, which is typically done by aiming at the "middle range" of prospective media consumers—an approach that makes coverage similar if not uniform.

**Crisis Coverage** **(346)**

Treatment given by the media to events that pose a danger or threat to the public. Crisis coverage includes reports on natural disasters, major accidents such as airplane crashes, outbreaks of violence, or assassinations of public officials. When such incidents occur, the public expects government to take appropriate action and expects the media to keep people apprised of the latest developments. In times of crisis, the media and government tend to function in concert. The media become an easily utilized means for officials to communicate with the public. In addition, the media as an institution are uniquely capable of gathering and disseminating the volume of information that is produced from a crisis situation. Beyond basic information, the public also depends on the media for interpretation of crises as a prerequisite to fully understanding what happened. A natural disaster such as an earthquake may require little interpretative discussion. The attempted assassination of a president, on the other hand, may be sufficiently complex as to need substantive interpretation in order to build understanding and perspective. *See also* NEWSWORTHINESS, 380.

*Significance* Crisis coverage generates extremely large audiences. Public need for news is great, and the media are clearly capable of delivering crisis-related information. Media coverage of crises has both desirable and undesirable consequences. First and foremost, crisis coverage reduces uncertainties by providing information. Any hard information, even bad news, can diminish anxieties. Such coverage also fosters a support dynamic as people become aware that they are not going through a crisis alone. Crisis coverage may also reassure the public that government authorities are adequately responding to the situation. On the other hand, crisis coverage may prompt panic or other irrational behavior on the part of some people. It may even incite illegal conduct, as was the case with coverage of the urban riots in the 1960s. Crisis coverage may also draw people to the scene of a crime or disaster, which may, in turn, impair those trying to respond to the crisis appropriately. In order to avoid such consequences, most media have developed crisis coverage strategies. These strategies consider a wide range of issues associated with coverage and set forth policy decisions that will govern media conduct during crises.

**C-SPAN (Cable Satellite Public Affairs Network) (347)**
A cable news facility that covers activities of the federal government on a 24-hour basis. C-SPAN stands for Cable Satellite Public Affairs Network, and it includes full coverage of proceedings in the House of Representatives in its programming. Prior to 1979, broadcast coverage of congressional proceedings was limited to extraordinary events such as the Watergate investigation and the House Judiciary Committee deliberations on the impeachment of President Richard M. Nixon. No coverage of sessions in the House or Senate chambers was permitted. In 1979, the House abandoned this policy; the Senate followed in 1986. Through the facilities of C-SPAN, which is carried by more than 1,500 cable systems, the broadcasts of House and Senate activities are regularly watched by large numbers of people. *See also* CABLE TELEVISION, 340.

*Significance* It is estimated that upwards of 500,000 people watch House proceedings on C-SPAN. The potential audience is substantially greater given that approximately 35 million people subscribe to cable systems through which C-SPAN can be accessed. Placing Congress in front of the television camera was not universally welcomed. Proponents asserted that full coverage would enhance congressional visibility vis-à-vis the president as well as positively affect the quality of floor debate. It was argued by opponents of the plan that television would actually modify behavior—that there would be more and longer speeches, more "grandstanding" by House members, and a possible power shift to those who could make the best media appearance. Insufficient data exists upon which to fully judge the effects of televising congressional proceedings, but it appears that the House now spends more time in sessions and the speeches are more numerous and feature more visual materials. C-SPAN does allow those outside Congress to more readily monitor its activities. C-SPAN also becomes a convenient source from which the media may capture taped segments of floor speeches for use in news broadcasts. That the Senate has decided to allow television within its chambers reveals its perception that full coverage has political impact.

**Deregulation (348)**

The elimination of governmental controls over particular industries or activities. Substantial support for deregulation of the broadcast industry after more than 50 years of rather extensive regulation has recently developed. The Communications Act of 1934 provides the authority for current regulation of the broadcast media. That act and the Federal Radio Act, which preceded it in 1927, were regulatory initiatives aimed at protecting the scarce public resources associated with broadcast transmission, especially broadcast frequencies. This objective was pursued by granting licenses to a limited number of broadcasters who, in turn, were expected to utilize their franchises in the best interests of the public. Regulations were established, with license renewal made conditional on compliance with these regulations. The regulations currently in effect for the broadcast media primarily target broadcast content and concentration of ownership. The basic regulatory scheme begun in the mid-1930s remains, although many believe a compelling reason no longer exists for regulation. *See also* EQUAL TIME PROVISION, 352; FAIRNESS DOCTRINE, 353; FEDERAL COMMUNICATIONS COMMISSION (FCC), 354; LICENSURE, 366; REBUTTAL, RIGHT TO, 398.

*Significance* The arguments for deregulation of the broadcast media focus on three main points. First, the underlying scarcity condition no longer exists. Competition within the broadcasting industry has heightened dramatically. The advent of cable technology and the ever-increasing number of broadcast stations may offer sufficient access without regulation. Second, specific content regulations such as the right to rebuttal, equal time, and fair treatment rules too severely impinge broadcasters' First Amendment rights. If the greater number of outlets can minimize the access problem, government may no longer have a sufficiently compelling interest to interfere with broadcasters' free press rights. Third, there is growing sentiment that some of the regulations are actually counterproductive. Take, for example, the equal time or rebuttal rules. Those rules were designed to protect public access rights but may in reality diminish access. Broadcasters, in the face of having to give candidates for an office or people subjected to personal attacks reply time, may not make time available to any candidate nor run any broadcasts that touch on controversial issues. In aggregate, there is a strong case for deregulation of broadcasting, and the likelihood of such a policy direction is currently rather high.

**Editorial** **(349)**

An argument or expression of opinion issued by the media. An editorial typically takes a position on a public issue and urges some kind of action. Opinions presented through editorials are to be kept wholly separate from reporting news, and they are accordingly designated as opinion by both the print and electronic media. Editorial positions taken by the media may be a natural outgrowth of the ideological orientation of the editors. Some media can be identified as more conservative or liberal in their editorial stances. Editorials may also be the product of investigative journalism, which uncovers or examines some undesirable practice. In such cases, the media then urge corrective actions of some kind. Freedom to offer editorial views is protected by the First Amendment, although it is subject to some regulation, especially within the electronic media. Under Federal Communications Commission (FCC) regulation, broadcasters must allow time for responsible replies to editorial comments. *See also* AGENDA SETTING, 334; EDITORIAL PRIVILEGE, 350; INVESTIGATIVE JOURNALISM, 363.

*Significance* Editorial prerogative encompasses more than the media offering their position on some matter. It involves comprehensive control over content. The selection of which news items to cover, how to report or interpret them, and how much time or space to devote to them are editorial judgments. Typically, however, these judgments are based on professional rather than partisan or ideological criteria. Coverage of news does not contain an advocacy character. The media may choose to engage in advocacy, but they do so in clearly marked editorial columns, usually on separate pages devoted exclusively to opinion and comment. Editorials tend to point out problems and call for particular action, typically governmental action. In this way, the media may get issues on the public agenda and foster public support for a particular solution. A form of editorial that has a direct impact on the political process is the candidate endorsement. This is a media recommendation to voters to support a candidate for public office. Such endorsements may be especially influential in close contests or in campaigns that otherwise lack publicity.

**Editorial Privilege** **(350)**

The extent to which publishers may be insulated from the need to disclose information about editorial judgments. Editorial privilege is a singular benefit claimed by the press. Such a benefit would allow the press to enjoy a special position or advantage over others. Generally speaking, the Supreme Court has been reluctant to elevate the press to this privileged level. If the editorial processes are covered by such a privilege, for example, a plaintiff in a libel action would not be able to inquire of a publisher about the source of information used by the publisher. Neither could the plaintiff inquire about the information-gathering process itself or the basis upon which journalistic judgments were made, including the publisher's state of mind. The Court rejected the claim of such privilege saying that the First Amendment does not distinguish the media from any other sources from which parties in a libel action may obtain evidence. *See also* *HERBERT V. LANDO* (441 U.S. 153: 1979), 360; *HOUCHINS V. KQED, INC.* (478 U.S. 1: 1978), 362; NEWSPERSON'S PRIVILEGE, 379.

*Significance* Editorial privilege involves the scope of control the media have over their own activities. The greater the special status or privilege accorded the press, the greater its control. Among other things, editorial privilege would better protect publishers from libel actions because it would not allow plaintiffs in such suits to inquire about editorial processes and judgments. The Supreme Court rejected the existence of this kind of editorial privilege in *Herbert v. Lando* (441 U.S. 153: 1979). Indeed, the Court has typically been reluctant to say that beyond its basic protections the First Amendment conveys special privileges to the press. For example, the Court has rejected the view that the First Amendment gives newspersons the right to protect the confidentiality of sources or to access any government sources of news or information.

**Election Coverage** **(351)**

Attention given by the media to political campaigns as a part of its news-reporting function. The public receives most of its information about political candidates through the media. Political contact is initiated by individual campaigns when candidates purchase advertising time or space. Political information is also communicated by the media in their coverage of the election process as a series of news events. Although many people will not be directly influenced by media election coverage, the way the media report on candidates and campaign activities can affect undecided voters, a small but potentially decisive segment of the population. Media election coverage tends to be almost uniform because news organizations usually report the same things. Generally, election coverage emphasizes discussion of the personal attributes of candidates, sometimes at the expense of substantive issues. This situation occurs because in addition to having a professional responsibility to report important social and political events, the media need to maximize their audience appeal. Thus, personalities may be assigned higher priority than issue positions. Nevertheless, the media constitute the only institution that has the resources to gather and distribute the information that most voters use to make electoral judgments. *See also* AGENDA SETTING, 334; BIAS, 377; FREE MEDIA, 181; HORSE-RACE JOURNALISM, 361; PAID MEDIA, 193.

*Significance* Media election coverage affects the political process in several ways. For example, the candidate most likely to be elected, especially to a federal or state office, is the one who is able to perform well on television because most large campaigns depend on broadcast advertising and press interviews for public exposure. The mass media also allow candidates without political experience to compete because name recognition can be established more quickly than in the past. Consequently, self-starters and newcomers have been more willing to run for office, and the role of political parties in candidate recruitment has declined. Candidacies may now be taken directly to the electorate rather than having to depend on party organizations to give them their blessing. Media coverage of the electoral process has its greatest impact on presidential selection. Because the media need to appeal to the broadest audience, they tend to engage in horse-race journalism—that is, they portray campaigns in terms of who is winning and losing at a given moment. Expectations are established by candidate positions in the horse race, which has consequences on how the public perceives a candidacy. This, in turn, influences subsequent poll performances, fund-raising, and other key campaign components.

**Equal Time Provision (352)**

Rule that requires broadcasters to give candidates for the same office an equal opportunity to utilize their stations. The equal time provision is one of the access rights contained in section 315 of the Communications Act of 1934. The rule requires that a broadcaster selling time to a candidate for Congress, for example, would have to allow any other candidate for that particular seat an opportunity to the same amount of time at the same rates. The rule covers all candidates for a specific office independent of their electoral prospects, thus even minor party candidates can compel broadcasters to permit them access. If a broadcaster prefers to sell no time to political candidates, the rule does not apply. Neither does the rule apply to news coverage situations in which a station or network journalist reports candidates' activities. *See also* COMMUNICATIONS ACT OF 1934, 344; DEREGULATION, 348; FAIRNESS DOCTRINE, 353; FEDERAL COMMUNICATIONS COMMISSION (FCC), 354; REBUTTAL, RIGHT TO, 398.

*Significance* The equal time provision was designed to ensure equal access opportunities for political candidates. The rationale for such access regulations as the equal time provision is grounded in the notion that broadcasters are licensed by government to operate as near monopolies, thus they should not be able to air only the content that they prefer. Although the intent of access regulations is reasonable, their effect often does not well serve the access objective. Evidence suggests that many broadcasters prefer not to make time available to certain candidates, particularly at the state and local levels, rather than open themselves to equal time requests. For this reason, among others, the Federal Communications Commission (FCC) and Congress are being urged to abandon or modify many of these regulations.

**Fairness Doctrine** **(353)**

A policy established by the Federal Communications Commission (FCC) that requires the holder of a broadcast license to afford a reasonable amount of air time to issues of public significance and to replies by persons of differing viewpoints from those expressed by the station. The fairness doctrine embraces the concept of equal time, which requires that if a station gives or sells a party or candidate time during a political campaign, it is obligated to make equal time on the same basis to any opposing party or candidate. The fairness doctrine was enacted by Congress in the Communications Act of 1934 and is enforced by the FCC through its licensure authority. *See also* EQUAL TIME PROVISION, 352; FEDERAL COMMUNICATIONS COMMISSION (FCC), 354; *RED LION BROADCASTING COMPANY V. FEDERAL COMMUNICATIONS COMMISSION (FCC)* (395 U.S. 367: 1969), 399.

*Significance* The fairness doctrine reflects the position of Congress that the public is entitled to hear competing views on issues. Because the broadcast media use scarce public airwaves and because licensing provides a type of monopoly, the media have been subject to the regulation despite enjoying substantial First Amendment protection. The fairness doctrine as a particular regulation on the broadcast industry has been upheld by the Supreme Court in *Red Lion Broadcasting Company v. Federal Communications Commission (FCC)* (395 U.S. 367: 1969). Over the years, the doctrine has been the subject of much discussion and criticism. Many people have come to believe that the traditional scarcity argument no longer applies and that maintenance of the doctrine too greatly restricts the freedom of broadcasters. In an action taken in mid-1987, the Federal Communications Commission (FCC) finally abolished the doctrine. That decision, however, may have short-lived effect as Congress clearly has the authority to reestablish the standard by statute. Indeed, in anticipation of FCC reversal of the doctrine, Congress cleared a piece of legislation to write it into law, but the bill was vetoed by President Ronald Reagan. This contest will certainly continue.

**Federal Communications Commission (FCC) (354)**
An independent regulatory commission created by Congress in the Communications Act of 1934. The Federal Communications Commission (FCC) enforces provisions of the Communications Act, such as the regulation of interstate and foreign communication by radio (including two-way), television, wire, cable, and satellite. The FCC consists of seven members appointed by the president for staggered seven-year terms. As with other independent commissions, FCC members are buffered from control by the president or Congress; removal from office can only occur for cause. *See also* EQUAL TIME PROVISION, 352; FAIRNESS DOCTRINE, 353; *RED LION BROADCASTING COMPANY V. FEDERAL COMMUNICATIONS COMMISSION (FCC)* (395 U.S. 367: 1969), 399.

*Significance* The principal power of the Federal Communications Commission (FCC) is that of licensure. Through its power to grant licenses to broadcasters, the FCC can enforce the various regulations, such as the fairness and equal time doctrines, under which the broadcast media must operate. Traditionally, the broadcast media have been subject to more stringent regulation than the print media because the public airwaves are seen as scarce resources that require regulation in the public interest. The differential regulatory treatment has been upheld by the Supreme Court in such cases as *Red Lion*

*Broadcasting Company v. Federal Communications Commission (FCC)* (395 U.S. 367: 1969). In the early 1980s, the FCC engaged in the deregulation of telephone service. Evidence suggests that the FCC now favors at least partial deregulation of the broadcast industry, in which case the role of the commission would be substantially narrowed.

***Federal Communications Commission v. League of Women Voters*, 468 U.S. 364 (1984)** **(355)**

Ruling that disallowed a ban on editorializing by federally funded broadcast stations. The prohibition was contained in the Public Broadcast Act of 1967 and challenged by several noncommercial stations as well as the league. The Supreme Court began its examination of the ban by recognizing that the broadcast medium "operates under restrictions not imposed on other media." Nonetheless, this regulation was seen as "specifically directed at a form of speech—namely, the expression of editorial opinion—that lies at the heart of the First Amendment." In addition, the ban was "defined solely on the basis of the content of the suppressed speech." A regulation motivated by a "desire to curtail expression of a particular point of view" is the "purest form" of an abridgment of free speech. Finally, the Court said that the ban on editorializing by every station receiving federal support "far exceeds" what might be necessary to prevent governmental interference or to prevent the public from assuming that the editorials represent the "official view of government." As a result, the regulation "impermissibly sweeps within its prohibition" a wide range of protected expression. *See also* FEDERAL COMMUNICATIONS COMMISSION (FCC), 354; PUBLIC BROADCASTING ACT OF 1967, 394.

*Significance* *Federal Communications Commission v. League of Women Voters* (468 U.S. 364: 1984) touched on two important media regulation issues. First, it once again pointed out that the broadcast media are more subject to government regulation than the print media, but not absolutely. A ban on editorializing is aimed at "precisely that form of speech which the framers of the Bill of Rights were most anxious to protect." The Supreme Court made it clear that, were a similar ban on editorializing imposed on the print media, the Court would "not hesitate to strike it down." Second, the case required the Court to rule on the justifications for the ban as advanced by government. Principally, the ban was intended to safeguard the independence of public broadcasters. The Court found this justification insufficient given the totality of the ban. It believed that alternatives might be found that less drastically restrict expression. Such a judgment by the Court represents a second-guessing of Congress, a position four members of the Court were unwilling to take in *FCC v. League.* Thus it is possible that in the future, the Court may reverse itself by deferring to congressional judgment on what constitutes a threat to public broadcaster independence and thereby permit Congress to impose the editorial ban as a condition of public funding.

**_Federal Communications Commission v. Pacifica Foundation_, 438 U.S. 726 (1978)** **(356)**

Acknowledged the power of the Federal Communications Commission (FCC) to regulate the broadcast of "indecent" material. A radio station broadcast a monologue that contained several words of questionable propriety for daytime airing. A complaint was received by the FCC from a parent whose child had heard at least a portion of the broadcast. The FCC did not formally sanction the station but placed the complaint in the station's license file for later review. The Supreme Court supported this action. The key issues in the case were whether the FCC's action constituted forbidden "censorship" and whether speech "concededly not obscene" may be restricted as "indecent." In answer to the first question, the Court concluded that the ban on censorship precludes the FCC from editing broadcasts in advance but does not extend to the review of content of completed broadcasts. The power to regulate "indecency," the Court said, stemmed from the "uniquely pervasive presence" of the broadcast media. Indecent or offensive material presented over the air confronts the citizen not only in public but in "the privacy of the home, where the individual's right to be let alone plainly outweighs the First Amendment rights of an intruder." Because an audience is constantly "tuning in and out," prior warnings are inadequate to completely protect the listener or viewer from "unexpected" content. To simply say that the broadcast can be turned off when the objectionable material is first heard is "like saying that the remedy for an assault is to run away after the first blow." *See also* FEDERAL COMMUNICATIONS COMMISSION (FCC), 354; PRIOR RESTRAINT, 393.

*Significance* The regulation of obscenity is possible because, as a category, obscenity is unprotected expression. *FCC v. Pacifica Foundation* (438 U.S. 726: 1978) went even further in the case of broadcaster regulation by recognizing the authority of the Federal Communications Commission (FCC) to reach speech that is not quite obscene but rather only "indecent" or "offensive." Another important consequence of *Pacifica* deals with the matter of censorship. Although the FCC is not allowed to engage in censorship per se, the Supreme Court did not view consideration of the complaint against Pacifica in the licensure context to be improper conduct. Finally, *Pacifica* represents an extremely strong reiteration of the rationale that allows substantially greater regulation of the broadcast media as distinct from the print media. Unlike other cases that emphasized the need to regulate airspace as a scarce and public resource, *Pacifica* featured the "obtrusiveness" of the broadcast media and easy access to it by children, a potentially more far-reaching rationale for supporting regulation.

**Freedom of Information Act of 1966 (FOIA) (357)**
Federal statute that requires agencies to allow access to certain information. The Freedom of Information Act (FOIA) was signed into law in 1966 and amended in 1974. The act gives the press and the public a legal basis from which to obtain release of government documents. Several categories of information are exempt from these disclosure requirements. Although executive agencies have generally issued their own implementing regulations, the first step typically involves formal application for particular information. Those who are denied access to requested information may resort to the courts. In such situations, the courts review the reasons for withholding materials. The burden falls with the withholding agency to demonstrate damage that would result from disclosure. *See also* INVESTIGATIVE JOURNALISM, 363; MEDIA ACCESS, 369.

*Significance* The Freedom of Information Act (FOIA) was enacted in the belief that greater public access would enhance the accountability of public officials. Indeed, the early experience with requests submitted under the act was that too many materials had been inaccessible previously. The act is not easily used in that the request process is cumbersome and time delays are not uncommon. Further, agencies are continuously attempting to reduce the scope of the act. In addition, many documents remain out of the act's reach. Nonetheless, information obtained through use of the act has produced various, substantial revelations concerning such issues as covert Central Intelligence Agency (CIA) activities and threats to public health from unsafe pharmaceutical products or nuclear power plants.

**Free Press Clause (358)**
A clause of the First Amendment that prohibits Congress from enacting any law that abridges freedom of the press. The free press clause restrains both federal and state governments from, among

other things, imposing prior restraint on the print media. A prior or previous restraint is a restriction on publication before it takes place or before published material can be circulated. Such restraint typically occurs through licensure or censorship procedures. The First Amendment prohibits prior restraint because restriction of expression before it can occur constitutes a threat to both free speech and to a free press. Exceptions to the prohibition may be justified if publication threatens national security, incites overthrow of the government, is obscene, or interferes with the private rights of other persons. The basic dimensions of prior restraint were established in *Near v. Minnesota* (283 U.S. 697: 1931). The free press protection also extends to regulations that may come subsequent to publication. Generally, such restrictions must be narrowly drawn and reviewed against demanding standards so that government does not gain censoring influence over content. In other words, the media must retain almost total editorial control. Neither may the press be ordered or commanded to publish. Finally, the media cannot be singled out for special regulation or taxation. *See also* *NEAR V. MINNESOTA* (283 U.S. 697: 1931), 378; *NEW YORK TIMES V. SULLIVAN* (376 U.S. 254: 1964), 381; *NEW YORK TIMES V. UNITED STATES* (403 U.S. 713: 1971), 382; PRIOR RESTRAINT, 393.

*Significance* The free press clause protects the information-gathering function of the press, although an absolute right of access and confidentiality of sources does not exist. Freedom of the press occasionally collides with the fair trial interests of criminal defendants. Some limitations may therefore be imposed on the press to minimize prejudicial pretrial publicity. The press cannot be barred from criminal trials, however, and it cannot be restrained from reporting what is observed there except in extraordinary circumstances. The broadcast media are permitted to cover criminal proceedings provided that they do so with no adverse consequences to the accused. Several forms of published expression remain unprotected by the free press clause. Obscenity, for example, has consistently been held to be subject to government regulation. Another area outside free press clause protection is libel, which is printed material that defames a person. Despite its unprotected character, libel has been narrowly defined by the Supreme Court, especially where public officials are concerned. Debate on controversial public issues cannot be inhibited by threats of libel actions. The broadcast media are affected by a First Amendment interest but are also subject to government licensure regulation because of the difficulty of access to the airwaves.

**Gag Order** **(359)**
An order by a court that is directed at media representatives to prohibit the reporting of a court proceeding. A gag order is an injunction intended to minimize publicity that might prejudice a criminal trial. An injunction is a judicial order that either prohibits a party from acting in a particular way or requires a specific action by a party. Except in extreme circumstances, the Supreme Court has limited the use of such an order because it can violate freedom of the press. A gag order is also a court order that prevents a disruptive litigant from further interference with a court proceeding. The order might go so far as to bind and literally gag an unruly litigant, as in *Illinois v. Allen* (397 U.S. 337: 1970). A gag order may be issued against the lawyers and litigants in a case, prohibiting them from discussing certain aspects of the case. Sometimes a gag order results in sealing portions of a file or the transcript of certain testimony in a trial in order to protect infants, mentally ill persons, or a patent or trade secret. *See also* *NEBRASKA PRESS ASSOCIATION V. STUART* (427 U.S. 539: 1976), 377; PRIOR RESTRAINT, 393.

*Significance* A gag order is used to prevent prejudicial pretrial publicity. It is an extreme measure and constitutes a substantive encroachment on freedom of the press. It may only be considered as an extraordinary or last resort where extreme and highly prejudicial publicity exists. Before it can be used, a trial judge must carefully weigh three factors set forth in *Nebraska Press Association v. Stuart* (427 U.S. 539: 1976): the nature and extent of coverage, the likely impact of alternative measures on mitigating the publicity, and the anticipated effectiveness of the gag order on foreclosing damaging publicity. Other alternatives such as change of venue or delay in the commencement of a criminal prosecution are more accepted means of protecting the fair trial rights of an accused person.

***Herbert v. Lando*, 441 U.S. 153 (1979)** **(360)**
Declared that a plaintiff in a libel action is entitled to inquire into the editorial processes of the defendant. Herbert was a retired army officer with extended service in Vietnam. He received widespread media attention when he accused his superior officers of covering up reports of atrocities and other war crimes. Herbert conceded that his public figure status required him to demonstrate that the defendants had published a damaging falsehood with actual malice. About three years after Herbert's disclosures, CBS broadcast a report on Herbert and the charges against him on the program "60 Minutes." Lando

produced and edited the program and also published an article on Herbert in the *Atlantic Monthly*. Herbert's suit alleged that the "program and article falsely and maliciously portrayed him as a liar and a person who had made war crime charges to explain his relief from command." In attempting to develop proofs for his case, Herbert tried to obtain the testimony of Lando before trial, but Lando refused, claiming that the First Amendment protected him against "inquiry into the state of mind of those who edit, produce, or publish, and into the editorial process." The Supreme Court ruled against Lando. The Court held that the First Amendment does not restrict the sources from which a plaintiff can obtain evidence. Indeed, "it is essential to proving liability that plaintiffs focus on the conduct and state of mind of the defendants." If demonstration of liability is potentially possible, "the thoughts and editorial processes of the alleged defamer would be open to examination." Such examination includes being able to inquire directly from the defendants whether they knew or had reason to suspect that their damaging publication was in error. The editorial privilege sought by Lando would constitute substantial interference with the ability of a defamation plaintiff to establish the ingredients of malice. Further, the outer boundaries sought by Lando are difficult to perceive. In response to the concern that opening the editorial process was an intolerable, chilling condition, the Court suggested that if claimed inhibition flows from the fear of liability for publishing knowing or reckless falsehoods, that condition is precisely what *New York Times v. Sullivan* (376 U.S. 254: 1964) and other cases have held to be consistent with the First Amendment. Spreading false information in and of itself carries no First Amendment credentials. If a plaintiff is able to demonstrate liability from direct evidence "which in turn discourages the publication of erroneous information known to be false or probably false, this is no more than what our cases contemplate." *See also* LIBEL, 365; *NEW YORK TIMES V. SULLIVAN* (376 U.S. 254: 1964), 381.

*Significance* *Herbert v. Lando* (441 U.S. 153: 1979) established that the editorial practices of a defendant publication could be accessed by a plaintiff in an attempt to show malice. *New York Times v. Sullivan* (376 U.S. 254: 1964) had set in motion the requirement that malice be demonstrated in libel actions brought by public officials. *Lando* carried the implications of such a demonstration to the point of imposing on freedom of the press by rejecting the notion of editorial privilege. Another issue raised in *Sullivan* relates to the matter of public figures. *Sullivan* protected publications from libel suits where critical comment had been made about government officials. Soon thereafter the category of government official was expanded to include public figures, private citizens who are in the midst of public events, or persons who attract wide public attention.

**Horse-Race Journalism** **(361)**

Media coverage of politics that emphasizes winning and losing over substance. Horse-race journalism describes a typical media approach to election campaigns. Such coverage features aspects of campaigns that are most associated with "winners" and "losers"—for example, poll results, crowd sizes at rallies, or extent of financial support. The horse-race approach leads to designations of candidates in horse-race terms such as frontrunners, dark horses, and long shots. The "who is leading, gaining, trailing, or fading" emphasis of horse-race journalism is easily recognized in presidential election years as the caucuses and primaries run their course. Although less likely, horse-race journalism can occur outside the campaign context as well. Consider, for example, the Senate deliberations over the Supreme Court nomination of Robert Bork. The media engaged in horse-race journalism to the extent that they assigned priority to the head count of senators who announced their intention to support or oppose the nomination. *See also* BIAS, 357; ELECTION COVERAGE, 351; PRESIDENTIAL CAMPAIGN, 197.

*Significance* Horse-race journalism is the product of the media's need to appeal to the largest possible audience. The contest or horse-race aspect of politics tends to be more interesting to most readers or viewers than matters of substance. The horse-race emphasis, in turn, affects public opinion. The presidential nominating process provides a good example. Designation of a candidate as the frontrunner or favorite in a particular caucus or primary creates performance expectations. If the candidate exceeds expectations, the campaign gains strength. Failure to perform to expectations may lead to eroding momentum, diminished chances in the next primary or caucus, greater difficulty in raising money, and so on. Such a candidate often turns to staged media events in an effort to recover, a strategy that subordinates even further the meaningful discussion of issues.

***Houchins v. KQED, Inc.*, 438 U.S. 1 (1978)** **(362)**

Rejected press claim of right to access a county jail. KQED, a local broadcast company, was not permitted to inspect and photograph the portion of a jail where a prisoner suicide had occurred and that reportedly had been the location of abusive incidents. KQED asserted that the right to gather news gave them an "implied special right of access to government controlled sources of information." The Supreme Court disagreed. The Court recognized that prison and jail conditions are "clearly matters of great public importance" and that the media serve an important function by acting as the "eyes and ears" of the public. Nonetheless, "like all other components of our society media representatives are subject to limits." The media are neither a "substitute for" or an "adjunct of" government and are "ill-equipped to deal with problems of prison administration." The role of the media must not be "confused" with that of government; each has "special" functions both "complementing" and "sometimes conflicting with each other." Neither the public importance of the conditions of penal facilities nor the media's role for disseminating information affords a basis for "reading into the Constitution a right of the people or the media to enter these institutions." The First Amendment protects the media's freedom to "communicate information once it is obtained." Nothing in the amendment or in case law on the subject has "intimated that the Constitution compels the government to provide the media with information or access to it on demand." The Court concluded by saying that the issue here was a claim to the special privilege of access, something that is "not essential to guarantee the freedom to communicate or publish." *See also* BRANZBURG V. HAYES (408 U.S. 665: 1972), 338.

*Significance* As reflected in *Houchins v. KQED, Inc.* (438 U.S. 1: 1978), the Supreme Court has been reluctant to recognize a special position for the press. Freedom of the press has been viewed as a guarantee to communicate or publish. Accordingly, government cannot, for example, impose a prior restraint, direct that certain content be published, or levy a targeted tax on the press. Beyond that, the press is entitled to no further rights or privileges than the general public. This position was evident in *Branzburg v. Hayes* (408 U.S. 665: 1972) wherein the Court rejected the press assertion of newsperson's privilege, or right to protect the confidentiality of news sources. The Court said the press had the same obligations as any citizen to provide relevant information to the criminal investigation process. The reasoning in *Branzburg* applies to the information-gathering issue in *Houchins* and *Saxbe v. Washington Post* (417 U.S. 843: 1974). As the Court said in *Saxbe,* a case that involved access to federal prisoners, the Constitution does not impose on government an "affirmative duty to make available to journalists sources of information not available to members of the public generally."

**Investigative Journalism** **(363)**

Especially extensive media examination of a subject. Investigative journalism is an outgrowth of the old practice of muckraking. Investigative reporting usually targets suspect practices in either the public or private sector, or examines the effectiveness of selected public policies. Investigative journalism typically requires a substantially greater investment of media resources on a subject than regular news coverage treatment. Since the early 1970s, the media have created special investigative units to engage in the extensive information gathering that is required of investigative journalism. The results of investigative inquiries are either reported in serial fashion in the print media or revealed as special segments of news broadcasts. Because the electronic media operate under severe time limitations, they are often unable to develop the same background depth as the print media. Occasionally, separate programming is built around investigative documentaries. The success of such programs as "60 Minutes" reflects the audience appeal of investigative reporting. *See also* MEDIA ACCESS, 369; MUCKRAKING, 374; WATERGATE, 42; YELLOW JOURNALISM, 404.

*Significance* Investigative journalism is a kind of media manipulation of the political process—it is intended to have an effect. Investigative reporting typically focuses on suspect or corrupt practices. The exposure of misconduct may motivate the misbehaving official to change his or her ways. More likely, the exposure will prompt a public demand for punishment of the wrongdoer or changes in public policy. The resignation of President Richard Nixon was at least in part a result of the *Washington Post*'s investigation of the Watergate affair. Social responsibility is not the only motive for investigative journalism, however. Investigative reporting is both valued within the profession and has audience appeal, as reflected in broadcast ratings. Because investigative journalism makes the media direct participants in the political process, several basic ethical issues have been raised by the endeavor, not the least of which are the media's potential bias and loss of credibility as reporters of political events.

**Leaks** **(364)**

Informal and sometimes surreptitious release of information. A guarantee of source anonymity is imperative if a reporter is to obtain leaked information. Leaks occur for a variety of reasons. In some cases, the official who leaks information may be acting without authority—for example, in the release of suppressed or sensitive materials. In other instances, the leak may be a form of "whistle blowing" and contain information pertaining to misconduct. Other leaks may be aimed at gauging the response of other officials or the public to a particular proposal. Finally, leaks may be used to disrupt or interfere with the plans or proposals of political opponents. *See also* INVESTIGATIVE JOURNALISM, 363; PACK JOURNALISM, 383.

*Significance* News leaks have mixed consequences. They permit disclosure of information that might not otherwise be released, which allows issues to reach public attention. They may also provide information that uncovers corruption or misconduct. The reporters who played a pivotal role in developing the Watergate scandal depended on leaks from several persons inside Richard Nixon's administration. Leaks may also have negative consequences. They may be used for political gain or they may cause damage if disclosed materials are especially sensitive. This latter is most likely to occur in the context of foreign relations where extremely delicate negotiations on a wide range of matters are frequently in progress.

**Libel** **(365)**

The use of false and malicious material that injures a person's status or reputation. Libel has consistently been held to be a category of unprotected speech. Relief from libel may be pursued through either civil or criminal proceedings. Libel laws may not inhibit debate on public issues, however, even if the debate includes vigorous and unpleasant attacks on government and/or public officials. In such situations, statements must be made in print with reckless disregard of their falsehood and with actual malice before libel occurs. Plaintiffs in libel proceedings may inquire into the editorial processes of defendant publications as a means of establishing state of mind as an ingredient of malice. Oral defamation is called slander. *See also* FREE PRESS CLAUSE, 358; *HERBERT V. LANDO* (441 U.S. 153: 1979), 360; *NEW YORK TIMES V. SULLIVAN* (376 U.S. 254: 1964), 381.

*Significance* Libel actions afford some protection from defamatory statements made through the media. The use of civil suits to obtain money damages has become the principal approach to seeking redress. As is clear from decisions like *New York Times v. Sullivan* (376 U.S. 254: 1964), however, libel laws cannot be used to create a "pall of fear and timidity" within the media, especially related to discussion of public matters. For this reason, libel laws distinguish between public and private figures and afford the latter greater opportunity to recover from adverse comments by the media. If a person within the "public figure" classification is to prevail in a libel action, "reckless disregard" of the truth and "actual malice" must be demonstrated, standards that are difficult to meet. A public figure is likely to be a government official, elected or otherwise, but may also be a private citizen "in the midst of doing a public thing" or someone who attains wide public attention.

**Licensure** **(366)**

The granting of permission to engage in a particular activity. Licensure has been the principal method by which government has regulated the electronic media since the passage of the Federal Radio Act in 1927. Licensing is administered by the Federal Communications Commission (FCC) under authority of the Communications Act of 1934. Included in the licensure process is the assignment of individual frequencies to each broadcaster so that signals do not interfere with one another. Indeed, broadcasters who wished to avoid the scrambling of transmissions invited this aspect of regulation. The need to license the electronic media is based on the premise that the airwaves they utilize are both public and finite. Such scarce resources require regulation in order to protect the public interest from irresponsible conduct of the few who enjoy the privilege of holding a license. The FCC enforces regulations that reach electronic media ownership and broadcast content through the licensure process. No parallel licensing exists for the print media. *See also* DEREGULATION, 348; FEDERAL COMMUNICATIONS COMMISSION (FCC), 354.

*Significance* Licenses granted by the Federal Communications Commission (FCC) to broadcasters are not permanent. This licensure feature allows the FCC to generally secure compliance with regulations that exist for the electronic media. Several factors govern an FCC decision on whether to grant or renew a license. Prior to renewal, licensees must show that they have been good stewards of the public airwaves. Broadcasters must demonstrate that they are both attentive and responsive to the needs of their broadcast areas, which includes performing local public service functions. In addition, broadcasters must not have accumulated a record of failing to fulfill access obligations. Withholding the license does not occur often, but the possibility of such an action is typically sufficient to produce satisfactory performance of broadcasters.

**Managed News** **(367)**

Information that is generated and distributed by government. News is managed by government officials in an effort to affect favorably what is published or broadcast by the media. Such manipulation can occur in several ways. First and possibly most important, officials can control the flow of information. The media typically receive information through press releases, briefings, or news conferences. The scope and substance of these news sources are largely within the control of the official using them. Second, officials may create circumstances that enhance favorable coverage—for example, the carefully designed media event. Finally, officials attempt to cultivate the favor of the media through actions that capitalize on the media's ongoing need for information. *See also* MEDIA ACCESS, 369; PRESS RELEASE, 390.

*Significance* The ability to manage news may have substantial benefit for public officials. Managed news is not necessarily information that is untrue or even misleading, but its release is controlled in such a way as to place an official in the most favorable position. The press conference offers the possibility of news management. An opening statement guides the course of the news conference toward issues the official who is holding the conference wants covered and away from those that are controversial. News releases may be controlled not only in content but in timing to enhance impact. Withholding news may heighten attention devoted to other stories by reducing competition for media coverage. Conversely, release of several items at the same time may help bury an unfavorable one. The news blackout may be utilized prior to major announcements in an effort to increase their media visibility and impact. News management also involves coordination of flow so that negative or inconsistent releases are minimized if not eliminated. Often executive department staffers are required to obtain clearance prior to releasing information, not so much to censor its release but to ensure that discussion of the same topic by two or more administration officials is compatible. The press is aware of such management devices and generally dislikes these efforts to manipulate it; but, because it depends on these sources for news, it has little choice but to accommodate to the situation.

**Mass Media** **(368)**

Means used to communicate with large numbers of people. The mass media refers to either the published or electronically transmitted word when it is used for broad communication. Use of the published word is called the print media and typically includes daily or weekly newspapers and magazines. The most common examples of the broadcast or electronic media are radio and television. A medium allows a printed or spoken word to connect the sender of the message to the receiver. Media that support or allow communication to large, diverse, and widely distributed audiences are the mass media. The mass media serve several key functions for the political system, including reporting information, shaping citizen attitudes and behavior, and influencing political agendas and governmental policies. The mass media have evolved to a level of such importance within the political process that they are often called the fourth branch of government or the Fourth Estate. In addition to certain direct consequences on the political process, the mass media are significant because of the extent to which they intersect with the lives of so many Americans. It is estimated, for example, that nearly three people in four read newspapers, and nearly 90 and 100 percent of households own radios and televisions, respectively. It is further claimed that the U.S. adult population spends upwards of half its leisure time exposed to one or another form of mass media. Such a volume of exposure cannot fail to have political consequences. *See also* BROADCAST MEDIA, 339; PRINT MEDIA, 392.

*Significance* The impact of the mass media on the political process is variable and thus difficult to measure with precision. Nonetheless, some broad effects may be readily identified. First, the mass media are the source of virtually all political news. What the news media choose to report and how they do so has an effect on what we know. Second, media determination of what is newsworthy often defines the political agenda for political actions by assigning high priority to issues that are reported as distinct from those that are not. Third, the mass media also influence the electoral process in that they place a premium on candidates who, for example, are able to use television effectively. Use of the broadcast media for political advertising, especially the short or spot advertising, has changed the approach to election campaigns. Finally, mass media coverage of particular issues may have consequences on public policy itself. Continued focus by the mass media on matters such as the foreign trade deficit may generate public demand for change in those policies.

**Media Access (369)**

Refers to the media's capacity to reach necessary sources of information. If the media are to inform the public, they must be able to access information. The media function of acting as a watchdog on behalf of the public requires access to meetings, documents, government officials, and other sources of information. Media access is an indicator of a free press. The greater the extent of access, the more freely the media can fulfill their fundamental function. The primary point of tension involves access to government-controlled sources. Clearly, access cannot be absolute, so the question focuses on how much access is sufficient to balance the competing needs and interests involved. *See also* FREEDOM OF INFORMATION ACT, 357; *HOUCHINS V. KQED, INC.* (438 U.S. 1: 1978), 362; INVESTIGATIVE JOURNALISM, 363.

*Significance* Media access is denied when meetings are closed to the press, when documents and records are classified in ways that place them out of reach, and when officials make themselves unavailable to the media. Inhibiting access prevents the press from reporting the actions of government officials to the public. Access, then, is clearly critical to effective newsgathering. An important issue becomes the extent to which the First Amendment might protect media access. Several views exist. The least protective view holds that the First Amendment prohibits only arbitrary governmental interference with access. A more protective position is that access is a constitutional right and, as such, government would need to demonstrate far greater justification for denial of access than merely defending against claims of arbitrariness. The most protective view is that access is not only a press right but, in addition, the press is entitled to gain access to sources unavailable to the general public. Current press law in the United States rests in the middle position. Press claims of privilege or special access have consistently been rejected by the Supreme Court in such cases as *Saxbe v. Washington Post* (417 U.S. 843: 1974) and *Houchins v. KQED, Inc.* (438 U.S. 1: 1978). In doing so, the Court has said that the First Amendment imposes no affirmative duty to make information specially available to the press and that special as distinct from protected access is not essential to the right to communicate or publish.

**Media Event** **(370)**

A situation designed to produce or lend itself to media coverage. Success or failure in contemporary politics is often a function of media coverage, so political actors deliberately attempt to create events that are likely to receive media attention. An example of a media event is the press conference, an event to which the press is called by a public figure but at which no actual news is given. Rather, it is an opportunity for the public figure to dramatize positions and make statements that can be utilized on news broadcasts. Often media events do not feature speeches but convey positive visual images of a public figure. Media events tend to feature politicians "in action," such as at a construction site for a new plant, in order to emphasize a position on an issue like employment or economic development. *See also* ELECTION COVERAGE, 351; FREE MEDIA, 181; PRESS CONFERENCE, 389.

*Significance* Media attention is a critical factor in electoral success, so politicians will create situations, or media events, that will draw coverage. Campaigns in particular are designed to maximize media exposure. Tailoring media opportunities and providing a context that enhances the image of candidates is of highest priority. Officials seeking reelection are better able than their challengers to obtain media coverage; they are also better able to use their incumbent status to portray themselves as "looking official" or "in action." The end that is sought through a media event is a short phrase that will serve as an attractive segment for news broadcasts. Beyond the words, the media event is used to provide visual background that, it is hoped, will enhance a candidate's image.

***Media Market*** **(371)**

Area in which a broadcast station or the print media have an audience. The size of a media market is defined by the distance across which a broadcast signal can be received or printed materials can be distributed in a timely fashion. The span of a media market may also be thought of in consumer terms—that is, the audience within a media market is one that is able to respond to advertisers' messages carried through the media. Clearly, media that serve the major metropolitan areas have substantially larger markets than those outside such areas. It is estimated that there are nearly 400 print and 300 broadcast markets in the United States. Most of the newspapers and broadcast stations in the United States are part of multimedia and cross-media organizations, thus media ownership in this country is quite heavily concentrated. *See also* CONCENTRATED OWNERSHIP, 345; FEDERAL COMMUNICATIONS COMMISSION (FCC), 354; PAID MEDIA, 193.

*Significance* The extent to which media markets may be concentrated is determined by the Federal Communications Commission (FCC). Except for limits imposed by antitrust regulations, the print media may compete in as many markets as they wish (which explains the growth of regional and national newspaper chains). Broadcast media, on the other hand, are limited. Under FCC regulations, a single entity may own combinations of television and AM and FM stations but cannot own more than 12 stations in any of the three categories. Market and market size per se are not principal factors in this regulatory scheme. They do, however, have important consequences for the development of political campaigns. Media advertising is a fundamental ingredient in a successful campaign, so campaign resources must be spent to ensure that larger markets are covered effectively. Running a campaign over an area with several markets requires expenditures in each and is considerably more costly than campaigning over an area with but one densely populated market.

### *Miami Herald Publishing Company v. Tornillo*, 418 U.S. 241 (1974) (372)

Struck down a state right-to-reply law for newspapers. The law said that if the character or the record of a candidate for public office is "assailed" by a newspaper, the candidate may demand a free-of-cost opportunity to reply. Failure to comply was deemed a misdemeanor. The Supreme Court found this law offensive to the First Amendment. Any law, said the Court, that creates a "compulsion to publish" anything that would not otherwise have been published is unconstitutional. Having a responsible press is a "desirable goal," but press responsibility can neither be "mandated by the Constitution" nor can it "be legislated." The statute here "operates as a command" in the same way as a regulation that forbids the publication of specified material. Furthermore, the statute "exacts a penalty" on the basis of newspaper content. It costs money and time and takes up space in the newspaper. The law may also lead editors to conclude that the "safe course" is to avoid the controversy associated with political coverage. In this way, a government-enforced right of access policy "inescapably damages the vigor and limits the variety of public debate." Beyond this, the law "fails to clear" the First Amendment barriers because of its "intrusion into the function of editors." A newspaper, said the Court, is more than a "passive conduit" for news and comment. The choice of material that goes in, decisions about length and treatment, and so on constitute the "exercise of editorial control and judgment." It has "yet to be demonstrated" how government regulation of this "crucial process" can be done compatibly with the First Amendment. *See also* *COLUMBIA BROADCASTING SYSTEM (CBS), INC. V. FEDERAL COMMUNICATIONS COMMISSION (FCC)* (453 U.S. 367: 1981), 342; FAIRNESS DOCTRINE, 353; *RED LION BROADCASTING COMPANY V. FEDERAL COMMUNICATIONS COMMISSION (FCC)* (395 U.S. 367: 1969), 399; REBUTTAL, RIGHT TO, 398.

*Significance* The Supreme Court's ruling in *Miami Herald Publishing Company v. Tornillo* (418 U.S. 241: 1974) reflects the striking differences in the extent to which the print and broadcast media are subject to regulation. The unique nature of the broadcast media renders them more subject to regulation. The frequencies and airspace utilized by the broadcast media are scarce public resources, unlike the readily available ones upon which the print media depend. Because the broadcaster is using public resources, the rights of the audience as against the interests of the broadcaster are more likely to prevail.

Furthermore, broadcasting has an "intrusive" character that requires greater regulation than does the printed page. Thus, although a reply requirement could be upheld by the Court in *Red Lion Broadcasting Company v. Federal Communications Commission (FCC)* (395 U.S. 367: 1969), an identical requirement imposed on the print media is an impermissible prior restraint. Even though a state may indirectly control access to the print media such as through the regulation of publishing monopolies, access may not be secured by tampering with published content. The right-to-reply rule at issue in *Tornillo* was not content-neutral and thus constituted an impermissible prior control.

### ***Minneapolis Star and Tribune v. Minnesota Commissioner of Revenue*, 460 U.S. 565 (1983)** (373)

Held that a state use tax assessed against the cost of ink and paper used in the production of publications violated the free press protections of the First Amendment. The Supreme Court reiterated that press protection was not absolute and that either the states or the federal government may subject newspapers to "generally applicable economic regulations without creating constitutional problems." In examining the Minnesota tax, the Court found no legislative history nor "any indication" beyond the structure of the tax itself of any "impermissible or censorial motive on the part of the legislature." The legislature, however, chose not to apply its general sales and use tax to newspapers. Rather, it created a "special tax" that applies only to "certain publications protected by the First Amendment." The Court found Minnesota's use tax "facially discriminatory" by "singling out" publications for treatment "unique" to Minnesota tax law. The Court then needed to determine whether the First Amendment "permits such special taxation." A tax that "burdens rights protected by the First Amendment" cannot stand unless the "burden is necessary to achieve an overriding governmental interest." The Court said that there was "substantial evidence" that differential taxation of the press "would have troubled the Framers of the First Amendment." The power to tax differentially "gives a government a powerful weapon against the taxpayer selected." When a state imposes a "generally applicable tax, there is little cause for concern." But when the state singles out the press, the "political constraints" that prevent a legislature from passing "crippling taxes of general applicability are weakened," and the threat of "burdensome taxes becomes acute." That threat can "operate as effectively as a censor to check critical comment by the press." *See also* NEAR V. MINNESOTA (283 U.S. 697: 1931), 376.

*Significance* The Supreme Court found First Amendment defects in a state tax against certain publications in *Minneapolis Star and Tribune v. Minnesota Commissioner of Revenue* (460 U.S. 565: 1983). The free press protection of the First Amendment was first extended to the states in the famous prior restraint decision of *Near v. Minnesota* (283 U.S. 697: 1931). Soon thereafter, the Court examined the matter of taxation of the press in *Grosjean v. American Press Company* (297 U.S. 233: 1936). The Court struck down a state tax because it found the levy to be punitive in character. The *Minneapolis Star* had based its challenge of the Minnesota use tax on the *Grosjean* decision, but the Court found the impermissible censorial motive lacking. Nonetheless, the Court held that differential taxation of the press was suspect and could be justified only by demonstrating a compelling state need. The First Amendment, however, has not been used to preclude states from subjecting publishers to general regulations including taxation.

**Muckraking** **(374)**
Journalistic practice of investigating and exposing corruption and misconduct. Muckraking is a technique originally designed to heighten readership of a paper. The exposés produced by "raking muck" tended to be sensational, with factual accuracy taking a backseat to the entertainment value. Nonetheless, muckraking was an early manifestation of investigative journalism and often had more laudable motives than mere market sales. The disclosures produced through muckraking were seen as valuable in that they were likely to prompt some corrective action, a result that generally served the public good. *See also* INVESTIGATIVE JOURNALISM, 363; YELLOW JOURNALISM, 404.

*Significance* Muckraking in one form or another has existed for a long time. Exposure of misconduct by people with authority and influence is an element of responsible journalism. It differs from other journalistic functions, however, in that it is intended to prompt a response from the political process. Many analysts include the investigative element as a journalistic technique for manipulating the political process. This, of course, raises a number of ethical and other questions about how to engage in investigative journalism. Responses to these questions are typically framed around the objectives of present-day muckraking, which include stimulating public demand for reform, directly motivating public officials to consider remedial action, or developing sufficient publicity to enable government officials to actually effect reforms. The investigative reporting of the Watergate episode pursued these objectives and was instrumental in invigorating the media's commitment to social responsibility.

**National Media** **(375)**
Media that can reach an audience distributed across the country. The national media are limited in number but possess disproportionate influence. Components of the national media include the broadcast networks, the wire services, and newsmagazines such as *Time, Newsweek,* and *U.S. News and World Report.* Newspapers typically do not engage national audiences, although *USA Today* (published by the Gannett Company), and, to a limited extent, the *New York Times* and *Washington Post* are distributed nationally. The national media have the resources to devote to national and international newsgathering. The body of reporters who make up the Washington press corps include representatives of the national media. *See also* CONCENTRATED OWNERSHIP, 345; NETWORK, 378; WIRE SERVICE, 403.

*Significance* The national media have a great deal to do with how Americans perceive government and the policies it adopts. The news, at least that which has a national or international focus, is reported to most Americans by the national media. Usually, Americans receive the news from one of the three major television networks. The next most frequent source of news is newspapers. With few exceptions, newspapers depend on one or both of the two national wire services for national and international news. Thus, the sources of national and international news are concentrated in the hands of a small number of national media; this source concentration tends to produce content similarity. Each of the national media assigns reporters to news beats (places where newsworthy events are most likely). The White House press corps, for example, is a group of reporters assigned to cover the president. These reporters generally represent the national media. They attend the same briefings and press conferences, and they receive the same news releases. As a result, they basically report similar if not identical things. If it were not for the national media, however, it is unlikely that independent and local media could provide national news. Even so, efforts have been made to counter some of this centralized national control and make the media more responsive to local needs. Included in these efforts are print media with state or local focus and an underground press that contains specialized information for relatively small audiences.

***Near v. Minnesota,* 283 U.S. 697 (1931)** **(376)**
*Near* was the Supreme Court's first significant censorship decision. The decision established the doctrine of previous or prior restraint, and it emphasized that the core of free press protection is freedom from governmental censorship of published material. The doctrine of

prior restraint is built on the proposition that restraint of expression *before* it occurs constitutes a grave threat to free speech. Near published a weekly newspaper that engaged in vicious attacks on various public officials in Minneapolis. He was subsequently enjoined from publication under provisions of a Minnesota statute that authorized the abatement of any "malicious, scandalous and defamatory newspaper, magazine or periodical" as a "public nuisance." The Court found the statute unconstitutional. In doing so, the Court first determined that the "liberty of the press and of speech is within the liberty safeguarded by the due process clause of the Fourteenth Amendment from invasion by state action." The Court found the statute defective in that it was "not aimed at the redress of individual or private wrongs." Rather, it was aimed at distribution of material "for the protection of the public welfare." Although prosecution might legitimately be brought against such publications, the state had insufficient interest to warrant a prior restraint. The Court said that the "object of the statute is not punishment, in the ordinary sense, but suppression." The suppression is "accomplished by enjoining publication, and that restraint is the object and effect of the statute." In short, the objectives and means embodied in the statute were the essence of censorship. The Court also pointed out that the statute too seriously limited what might be said about public officials. References to public corruption or malfeasance or neglect of duty create a public scandal by their very nature. Under the statute, however, they are scandalous and defamatory by definition. The Court said that "the recognition of authority to impose previous restraint upon publication in order to protect the community against the circulation of charges of misconduct, and especially of official misconduct, necessarily would carry with it the admission of the authority of the censor against which the constitutional barrier was erected"; although "charges of reprehensible conduct, and in particular official malfeasance, unquestionably create a public scandal, the theory of the constitutional guaranty is that even a more serious public evil would be caused by authority to prevent publication." *See also* *NEBRASKA PRESS ASSOCIATION V. STUART* (427 U.S. 530: 1976), 377; *NEW YORK TIMES V. UNITED STATES* (403 U.S. 713: 1971), 382.

*Significance* *Near v. Minnesota* (283 U.S. 697: 1931) provided the baseline standard in the critical matter of defining prior restraint. *Near* holds such restraint to be heavily suspect but possibly justifiable in the instance of threats to the national security, obscenity, incitements to government overthrow or other violence, or interference with private interests. The prior restraint exceptions set forth in *Near* have remained largely undisturbed. Using this doctrine, the Supreme Court struck down a gag order intended to safeguard jury selection in a criminal trial in *Nebraska Press Association v. Stuart* (427 U.S. 539: 1976). It also freed the publication of the Pentagon Papers in *New York Times v. United States* (403 U.S. 713: 1971).

**_Nebraska Press Association v. Stuart,_ 427 U.S. 539 (1976)** **(377)**

Examined the propriety of a gag order on the media as a way of preventing prejudicial pretrial publicity in violation of the fair trial requirement of the Sixth Amendment. *Sheppard v. Maxwell* (394 U.S. 33: 1966) placed responsibility for maintaining a fair trial environment with the trial judge. In this case, Judge Stuart restrained the media from "publishing or broadcasting accounts of confessions or admissions made by the accused or facts 'strongly implicative' of the accused" until such time as a jury was impaneled. The Supreme Court rejected the gag order, although it noted that the trial judge "acted responsibly, out of a legitimate concern, in an effort to protect the defendant's right to a fair trial." Nonetheless, the Court viewed the restraining order as excessive. It suggested that truly extraordinary prejudicial publicity must be present in order to consider an action as severe as prior restraint. Given that the gag order is a denial of free speech, the Court said it must review carefully whether the record justifies such an "extraordinary remedy." Included in such an examination are certain factors: (1) the "nature and extent" of the coverage; (2) alternative measures and their likely impact on mitigating publicity; and (3) the effectiveness of the gag order in preventing damaging and prejudicial publicity. The Court concluded that, in this instance, the record was not sufficient on the last two factors. Although the Court did not rule out the possibility that a restraining order might be sustained under certain circumstances, Judge Stuart's order was found to be excessive and a denial of the Nebraska Press Association's First Amendment rights. *See also* CHANDLER V. FLORIDA (449 U.S. 560: 1981), 341.

*Significance* *Nebraska Press Association v. Stuart* (427 U.S. 539: 1976) dealt with whether the press should be precluded from publishing what it already knows. This problem differs from that of *Sheppard v. Maxwell* (384 U.S. 333: 1966), which focused on remedies after prejudicial pretrial publicity had already occurred. *Stuart* looked at the gag order as a means of stemming pretrial publicity before the fact. The prior restraint considerations of *Stuart* had been suspect for 25 years before the case was decided. Although *Stuart* stopped short of invalidating the gag rule altogether, the clear thrust of the decision was to impose conditions that are virtually impossible to satisfy. The case becomes an intermediate point between a policy course that stresses after-the-fact remedies and an approach that would close judicial proceedings to the public and the press. It is apparent from *Stuart* that prohibiting the press from reporting what they observe directly in open court is the least favored approach.

**Network** **(378)**

An interconnection or chain of broadcast stations. The broadcast media are dominated by several giant networks, three in television [American Broadcasting Company (ABC), Columbia Broadcasting System (CBS), and National Broadcasting Company (NBC)], and four in radio (the three television networks and the Mutual Radio Network). The networks are privately owned and create heavily concentrated units of power and influence for the broadcast media. Although the networks are limited in the number of actual stations they may own, they link together large numbers of affiliated independent stations. More than 80 percent of the commercial television stations in the country are affiliated with one of the major networks. The affiliates subscribe to the networks for upwards of 70 percent of their radio and television programming, including news programming. Thus, the several networks serve as the principal source of news and political information for the vast majority of U.S. households. *See also* CONCENTRATED OWNERSHIP, 345; MEDIA MARKET, 371.

*Significance* The political impact of the giant broadcasting networks is that they dominate the gathering and communication of news, at least at the national and international levels. This handful of networks typically covers the same events and reports them in highly similar ways. Thus, brief reports shown on network news broadcasts have virtually uniform content. As a consequence, networks tend to have substantial influence on electoral campaigns and the setting of national political agendas. At the same time, independent local stations simply do not have the resources to gather news other than at the local level. The print media have no exact counterpart to the networks. Ownership of newspapers, however, continues to become more concentrated through regional and national chains. In addition, the print media are highly dependent on two dominant wire service sources for national and international news.

**Newsperson's Privilege** **(379)**

A policy that prevents journalists from having to disclose their news sources or the substance of information obtained from news sources. Newsperson's privilege, also known as reporter's or journalist's privilege, means that journalists are free from the obligation to testify about their news sources in court because in testifying, their press function would be impaired. Newspeople contend that many sources would not be available to them without the promise of confidentiality. Loss of such sources would, in turn, seriously impair their newsgathering capacity. *See also* BRANZBURG V. HAYES (408 U.S. 665: 1972), 338; EDITORIAL PRIVILEGE, 350; SHIELD LAW, 401.

*Significance* Newsperson's privilege is a claimed derivative of the First Amendment. It is based on the premise that the press occupies a special or elevated position such that it may operate in a fashion not available to the general public. The contention that newsperson's privilege exists was rejected by the Burger Court in *Branzburg v. Hayes* (408 U.S. 665: 1972). In *Branzburg,* the Supreme Court weighed the newsgathering interests of the press and the interests of those who were investigating criminal conduct and chose the latter. Recognizing the public interest in controlling crime, the Court said that reporters have the same obligations as private citizens to provide information in their possession. Largely in response to this ruling, many states have enacted legislation known as "shield" laws to establish the special privilege of source confidentiality for the media.

**Newsworthiness** **(380)**

Journalistic judgment about the extent to which a news story warrants media coverage. Determination of newsworthiness is largely a subjective judgment that is influenced by many factors. It is a necessary judgment, however, because the media—print as well as broadcast—are unable even at the local level to report all the news that is available. Judgments concerning newsworthiness are, in part, a function of professional values and orientations. At the same time, the media is influenced by political and economic factors. The media are dependent on political figures as sources and are, in turn, vulnerable to manipulation by those figures. Economic pressures are even more substantial in that the media are always competing for a bigger share of the audience. Coverage of news items that may broaden audience appeal is thus a strong motivation. Selection of specific news items depends largely on whether the story is both timely and "hits close to home." In addition, items that receive coverage tend to feature conflict or violence and focus on persons or events that are familiar to the readers or viewers. *See also* BEAT SYSTEM, 336; BIAS, 337; RATINGS, 397.

*Significance* Determination of newsworthiness is complex. It generally involves considerations that go beyond social value per se. The media in the United States are privately owned and profit-seeking, which means that media news operations must be audience sensitive. This fact obviously affects judgments about which items are covered and reported. Judgments on newsworthiness involve not only the threshold issue of what to cover but also the combination of stories to be presented and the substantive emphasis each story will receive. Whatever selections are made are also designed to maximize audience impact as well as report items of obvious importance and value.

***New York Times v. Sullivan*, 376 U.S. 254 (1964)** **(381)**
Held that publications may not be subjected to libel damages for criticism of public officials and their official conduct unless deliberate malice could be shown. *Sullivan* attached stringent conditions to certain libel actions involving speech that attacked public officials. Libel or intentional defamation has not generally been considered a protected expression. A state libel action was brought by a police commissioner in an Alabama court against the *New York Times* for its publication of a paid advertisement that charged police mistreatment of black students who were protesting racial discrimination. It was stipulated that the advertisement contained errors of fact, and the trial judge, finding the statements in the advertisement to be libelous, instructed the jury that injury occurred through publication and that both compensatory and punitive damages could be presumed. Substantial damages were awarded by the jury, which also found malice on the part of the *Times*. The Supreme Court reversed these judgments. The Court's position was that libel law must provide free speech safeguards. To allow unrestricted libel actions "would discourage newspapers from carrying editorial advertisements of this type, and so might shut off an important outlet for the promulgation of information and ideas." Such laws would shackle the First Amendment in its attempt to secure the widest possible dissemination of information from diverse and antagonistic sources. Even the factual errors did not jeopardize the advertisement's protected status. The protection of the advertisement, clearly "an expression of grievance and protest on one of the major public issues of our time," is not contingent on the truth, popularity, or social utility of the ideas that are offered. Mistakes or errors of fact are inevitable in free debate and must be protected if freedom of expression is to have the breathing space it needs. Neither does injury to the reputation of a public official justify limiting expression: "Criticism of their official conduct does not lose its constitutional protection merely because it is effective criticism and hence diminishes their official reputations." Any rule "compelling the critic of official conduct to guarantee the truth of all his factual assertions—and to do so on pain of libel judgments

virtually unlimited in amount—leads to a comparable 'self-censorship.'" Such a rule severely dampens the vigor and limits the variety of public debate. The Court did allow for recovery of damages where it can be proved that statements were made with actual malice—that is, with knowledge that they were false or with reckless disregard of whether they were false or not. *See also* *HERBERT V. LANDO* (441 U.S. 153: 1979), 360; LIBEL, 365.

*Significance* *New York Times v. Sullivan* (376 U.S. 254: 1964) expanded the Supreme Court's experience with seditious libel, a special category of libel that involves defamation of government and its officials. The Court has generally included libel in the category of unprotected speech. *Sullivan* provided the Court an opportunity to refine the classification. Libel laws cannot inhibit debate on public issues even if the debate includes strong and unpleasant attacks on government and its officials. *Sullivan* did hold that public officials could protect themselves through libel actions in situations in which false statements were made with reckless disregard of their untruthfulness and with "actual malice." But the *Sullivan* decision approaches an almost unconditional free press position relative to public officials.

***New York Times v. United States* (Pentagon Papers Case), 403 U.S. 713 (1971)** **(382)**

Dissolved an injunction against the *New York Times* that restrained publication of the Pentagon Papers. The Pentagon Papers cases examined the question of whether a prior restraint upon publication may be warranted if national security is threatened. The *New York Times* and the *Washington Post* had come into possession of copies of Defense Department documents detailing the history of U.S. involvement in the Vietnam War. After failing to prevent publication by direct request to the newspapers, injunctions were sought by Richard Nixon's administration in federal court against the two papers to stop publication of the documents on national security grounds. An injunction was obtained against the *Times* but not against the *Post.* The Supreme Court determined that injunctive restraints against either paper were unwarranted. The Court said there is a "heavy presumption" against prior restraint and that the "heavy burden" had not been carried in these cases. Each member of the Court entered an individual opinion. Justices Hugo Black and William Douglas both categorically rejected prior restraint. Justice Black said that "every moment's continuance of the injunction against these newspapers amounts to a flagrant, indefensible, and continuing violation of the First Amendment." He recited the history of the amendment and noted the essential function assigned to the press. The press, he said, "was to serve the governed, not the governors. The Government's power to censor the press was abolished so that the press would remain forever free to censure the Government." Of all the press functions, "paramount among the responsibilities of the free press is the duty to prevent any part of the government from deceiving the people and sending them off to distant lands to die of foreign fevers and foreign shot and shell." Justice William Brennan allowed that prior restraint might be possible in the most extreme circumstances but found no such circumstances present in these cases. The other members of the majority, Justices Potter Stewart, Byron White, and Thurgood Marshall, focused on the absence of statutory authority for federal courts to issue injunctions such as those sought by government. It was pointed out that Congress had directly rejected such an option in legislative debate. Justices Stewart and White, however, did indicate concern that national security had been compromised. They suggested that the criminal process could be utilized against the newspapers in this instance. *See also* NEAR V. MINNESOTA (283 U.S. 697: 1931), 376; PRIOR RESTRAINT, 393.

*Significance* *New York Times v. United States* (403 U.S. 713: 1971) represented an important free press challenge. The Supreme Court decision in this case was expected to provide a definitive statement on when prior restraint might constitutionally be imposed, but the decision did not produce such a ruling. The Court's judgment actually hinged on the fairly narrow issue of whether government had sufficiently demonstrated that immediate and irreparable harm would result from publication of the documents. Although the *Times* prevailed, the various opinions did not constitute a strong ruling for freedom of the press. The criminal prosecution of Daniel Ellsberg, who had furnished copies of the documents to the *Times* and the *Washington Post* in the first place, was ultimately dismissed. Thus, the Court was precluded from another opportunity to consider the free press issues contained in the Pentagon Papers imbroglio. Similarly, an attempt to prevent publication of an article in *The Progressive* about the manufacture of a hydrogen bomb was resolved before the matter reached the Supreme Court.

**Pack Journalism** **(383)**

Term used to describe a newsgathering approach that resembles "follow the leader." Those who engage in pack journalism watch those who are recognized as being foremost in the field and govern their newsgathering activities accordingly. If one of the media leaders discovers a potentially good news story, the followers are drawn to it as well. Broadcast news presentations in particular reveal how the journalistic judgment of the media leaders influences pack journalists. The event chosen to be featured by the networks produces a pattern of presentation by others. Critics of pack journalism sometimes refer to it as the "jackal syndrome"—the media leaders find the "meat," and the others descend on their find like jackals. Pack journalism also partially explains why there is such similarity of approach to and supply of the news. *See also* NEWSWORTHINESS, 380.

*Significance* Pack journalism portrays newsgathering as many reporters pursuing the same information to extremes. Even when a story is newsworthy, pack journalism suggests that it is subjected to journalistic overkill by large numbers of reporters who arrive on the scene and chase down even the most remote details. This practice encourages, if not fully explains, why news coverage appears almost uniform in character. The phenomenon of pack journalism is readily seen in the way the media cover electoral campaigns, especially at the presidential level with the lengthy nomination process that precedes the general election campaign. Pack journalism may also contribute to erroneous dissemination of news. Information tends to be widely shared among many reporters under these circumstances; as a result, inaccuracies at the source may be widely circulated.

**Pentagon Papers** **(384)**

Documents that discussed why the United States became involved in the Vietnam War. More precisely, the Pentagon Papers described the Defense Department study that examined in detail the history of U.S. entanglement in that conflict. The study, commissioned by Defense Secretary Robert McNamara, was extremely critical of both U.S. motives for engagement and the wisdom of U.S. military strategy. The study was sufficiently volatile that McNamara classified the documents as top secret. Daniel Ellsberg, one of the participants in the study as well as a coauthor of the report, delivered photocopies of the study to the *New York Times* and *Washington Post.* The newspapers began to publish excerpts, an action that Richard Nixon's administration sought to restrain through court order. *See also* *NEW YORK TIMES V. UNITED STATES* (403 U.S. 713: 1971), 382; PRIOR RESTRAINT, 393.

*Significance* The law case that developed out of the attempt to restrain the *New York Times* from publishing the Pentagon Papers had important freedom of the press consequences. The Supreme Court decision in *New York Times v. United States* (403 U.S. 713: 1971) considered the issue of whether prior restraint of publication may be warranted if national security is threatened. In this case, the Supreme Court ruled that government had not shown that sufficient, immediate, and irreparable harm would result from publication of the documents. The policy issue contained in the Pentagon Papers cases focuses on the long-standing and difficult media problem of security censorship. Although this decision allowed publication, it did not break new ground on the broader prior restraint question. Rather, the Court reiterated the position that prior restraint may be justified where truly sensitive information is involved. In such cases, there is a "heavy presumption" against restraint, but it cannot be categorically ruled out.

**_Pittsburgh Press Company v. Human Relations Commission_, 413 U.S. 376 (1973)** **(385)**

Declared that particular kinds of commercial speech may be regulated. The *Pittsburgh Press* was found to be in violation of a Human Relations Commission ordinance because it placed help-wanted advertisements in sex-designated columns. The commission ordered the newspaper to end the gender-referenced layout of the advertisements. The Supreme Court ruled the order was not prior restraint. The Court first determined that the advertisements were commercial speech, not merely because they were advertisements but because of their commercial content. They were, in fact, "classic examples of commercial speech" because of the proposal of possible employment and were therefore unlike political advertising. The *Pittsburgh Press* argued that editorial judgment about where to place the ads should control rather than its commercial content. The Court answered that a "newspaper's editorial judgments in connection with an advertisement take on the character of the advertisement and, in those cases, the scope of the newspaper's First Amendment protection may be affected by the content of the advertisement." The editorial judgment involved in this case did not strip commercial advertising of its commercial character. Even more crucial was the fact that the commercial activity involved was illegal employment discrimination. In the Court's view, advertisements could be forbidden in this instance just as advertisements "proposing a sale of narcotics or soliciting prostitution" could be forbidden. The Court concluded its ruling by saying that the First Amendment interest that applies to an ordinary commercial proposal is "altogether absent when the commercial activity itself is illegal and the restriction on advertising is incidental to a valid limitation on economic activity." *See also* COMMERCIAL SPEECH, 343; PRIOR RESTRAINT, 393.

*Significance* The commercial speech holding in *Pittsburgh Press Company v. Human Relations Commission* (413 U.S. 376: 1973) had its origin in *Valentine v. Chrestensen* (316 U.S. 52: 1942). The latter decision clearly put commercial speech outside First Amendment coverage. *New York Times v. Sullivan* (376 U.S. 254: 1964) substantially narrowed the *Chrestensen* concept of commercial speech, and following *Pittsburgh Press,* the Burger Court narrowed the definition even further. In *Bigelow v. Virginia* (421 U.S. 809: 1975), the Supreme Court protected the publication of an advertisement by an organization that offered services related to legal abortions in another state. The Court held that the advertisement "conveyed information of potential interest and value to a diverse audience," not merely a commercial promotion of services. The next year, in *Virginia State Board of Pharmacy v. Virginia Citizens Consumers Council, Inc.* (425 U.S. 748: 1976), the Court struck down a statute that made advertising of prescription drugs a form of conduct that could possibly lead to a suspension of license. The Court argued that even if the advertiser's interest is a purely economic one, such speech is not necessarily disqualified from protection. Consumers and society in general have a "strong interest in the free flow of commercial information." Such free flow is indispensable in a predominantly free enterprise economy that requires many private economic decisions.

**Pool Reporter** **(386)**

Person who represents other reporters at an event when circumstances prevent the presence of all press members. A pool reporter (or reporters) is selected by the larger group of reporters to access an event on behalf of everyone else. The pool reporter is obligated to share whatever information is obtained with the other reporters at the conclusion of the limited access event. More generally, pooling can occur with resources other than reporters. News agencies such as broadcast networks may share or pool equipment or agree to share production personnel to maximize coverage of a particular event. *See also* MEDIA ACCESS, 369.

*Significance* Use of pool reporters may allow the whole media to access information that would not be available otherwise. A White House press conference will not create the need for pool reporters because the size of the White House press corps is known and adequate facilities are provided. On the other hand, a criminal trial or the carrying out of an execution, for example, will not be moved to special locations simply to accommodate the space needs of the press. In these instances, designation of one or more reporters to witness such an event and share what they observe with those not designated is common practice. Pool coverage also lends itself to coverage of events too large for conventional coverage—for example, coverage of national presidential nominating conventions. Often so much is going on in so many places that a single news agency, even a network or wire service, has difficulty managing. Thus, a combination of individual and pooled coverage is used to allow the broadest coverage of the event.

**Presidential Debates** **(387)**

The discussion of political issues between or among presidential candidates. Presidential debates have only recently become an institutionalized component of the presidential selection process. The first debates occurred in 1960 and featured John Kennedy and Richard Nixon. The televised debates reached millions of viewers and allowed the candidates to exchange views on a wide range of issues. The first debates also had the effect of revealing how important television can be to projecting images to voters. In the four debates between Nixon and Kennedy, Kennedy was able to convey a calm and "presidential" image that appealed to the electorate beyond the substance of his remarks. Between 1960 and 1976, no debates were held because frontrunners did not wish to jeopardize their leads. Debates resumed in 1976 and have occurred ever since. Even incumbent presidents are willing to participate in debates in order to avoid the appearance of "ducking" such an event. Indeed, the practice of jointly appearing in one debate format or another by those seeking major party nominations has established itself as a key element in the primary and caucus processes. *See also* HORSE-RACE JOURNALISM, 361; PRESIDENTIAL ELECTION, 136.

*Significance* Presidential debates do not influence most viewers, but they do sway enough people to be potentially decisive in any given campaign. Those who are already committed or even leaning toward one view or candidate will block out incompatible information through a process of selective perception. The undecideds, however, may ultimately make a decision based on debate performance. John Kennedy's narrow win over Richard Nixon in 1960 is often attributed to the debates. To the extent that these debates put a premium on image over substance, they have a distorting or blurring effect on the electoral process. In addition, media coverage and commentary can influence viewer perception of a debate. For example, surveys taken immediately after the Gerald Ford–Jimmy Carter debate in 1976 revealed that viewers felt Ford had won. After the media pointed out that Ford had erroneously characterized the Soviet role in East Europe during the debate, public perception of who had won changed in Carter's favor. This effect is reinforced by the media tending to engage in "horse-race" journalism wherein reporting who is ahead or who is gaining is of highest priority.

**Press Briefing** **(388)**

Method used to disclose and discuss information. The news briefing is interactive and usually conducted by a staffer serving as official spokesperson. A useful way to understand the function of a press briefing is to look at the release of news from the White House. The most common form is the written press release, a document typically distributed to the press without actual comment. A press briefing is used to allow questions on press releases or to give the official conducting the briefing an opportunity to elaborate on a previous release. In the instance of the White House, such briefings are usually conducted by the president's press secretary. *See also* PRESS CONFERENCE, 389; PRESS RELEASE, 390; PRESS SECRETARY, 391.

*Significance* Press briefings are conducted on a regular basis. Indeed, the White House press secretary conducts them daily. Their utility as a news source is somewhat limited, however. They are conducted in such a way as to permit the press to pose questions, but the content discussed is typically confined to items covered in press releases. As a consequence, reporters have mixed feelings about briefings because they are seldom the place where new information is made available. At the same time, the press attends such briefings to ensure that it will not miss something newsworthy if it does emerge.

**Press Conference** **(389)**

A technique by which information is disclosed to the media. The press or news conference involves the direct questioning of a government official, such as a member of Congress, department head, and, occasionally, even the president. The press is called in by the person to be questioned, and the conference is conducted in such a manner as to allow the official to substantially control the content discussed. Press conferences usually begin with opening statements that allow an official to focus the issues to a degree. From time to time, officials call press conferences that are conducted as off-the-record background. That is, information is discussed, but the newspeople in attendance may not report it or at least not attribute the source. *See also*

BACKGROUNDER, 335; MEDIA EVENT, 370; PRESS BRIEFING, 388; PRESS RELEASE, 390.

*Significance* The press conference offers an opportunity for a particular public figure to be subjected to media questions. Although reporters may ask virtually anything, the items discussed are subject to some control by the person who called the press conference. Some control is exercised through the opening remarks, which, in addition to consuming some of the allotted time, may establish a focus for the questions that follow. Dropping a new piece of information during a conference tends to lead the press to target this item rather than moving to something the speaker would prefer not to discuss. In addition, questions about particular items are anticipated such that preparation or even rehearsal of responses is possible. The designed response is intended to highlight what is favorable. Finally, the person conducting the press conference determines which reporters ask the questions: "friendly" reporters are called upon more often than those who have been difficult or "unfriendly" in the past.

**Press Release** **(390)**

A document that contains particular information that is distributed to newspeople. A press release is the most common source of information to the media. The press or news release is prepared by the issuing official in the hope that the media will use it in its entirety. When a press release is distributed, reporters seldom have the opportunity to pose questions or to further pursue the topic of the release. Questions that reporters have about the content of releases are typically pursued in press briefings that are conducted by an official or agency's press secretary. *See also* PRESS BRIEFING, 388; PRESS SECRETARY, 390.

*Significance* The press release is a highly controlled means of information distribution. A press release may be accompanied by a news briefing conducted by an official spokesperson such as a press secretary. Typically, however, the press release stands alone, thus its content is exactly what the author of the release intends. In other words, the press release is one-way communication and is politically valuable for that reason. Multiple releases may also occur in an effort to occupy press attention by sheer volume. This technique may be intended to distract the media from issues or events with which an official or agency is having difficulty. The press release is also a means by which members of Congress compete for some of the media attention that is usually focused on the president. Releases from individual members or committees often become the basis of news stories and permit those who are skilled in the art of crafting effective releases to represent views that possibly differ from views expressed by the White House.

**Press Secretary** **(391)**
Official spokesperson of a public official or government agency. Use of a press secretary has been a standard practice for the president and a number of other executive agencies. The Office of the Press Secretary is the White House media agency that handles daily contact with the White House press corps. The press secretary meets to brief reporters on particular events and to respond to press questions. The function of the president's press secretary is to represent the official White House interpretation of issues and events. In doing so, the press secretary tries to create favorable press coverage for the president and his positions. *See also* PRESS BRIEFING, 388; WHITE HOUSE PRESS CORPS, 402.

*Significance* The function of a press secretary is to facilitate media access to particular government officials or agencies. As an official spokesperson, press secretaries are also interested in maximizing a favorable image for their respective official or agency. The president's press secretary heads the Office of the Press Secretary and meets regularly with the White House press corps. Further institutionalization of access occurs through the Office of Media Liaison, which links the president to media people other than the regular Washington reporter group. The White House media organization includes a press release office that also provides information associated with previous releases. On a different level, recent presidents have established agencies within the White House to coordinate overall communications strategy. Richard Nixon, for example, established an Office of Telecommunications Policy, whereas Jimmy Carter chose to create a National Telecommunication and Information Agency within the Department of Commerce.

**Print Media** **(392)**
Methods by which written expression is communicated. "Print media" typically refers to daily or weekly newspapers and magazines as components of mass communication. Other print forms such as books seldom reach mass audiences. The first newspapers appeared long before U.S. independence from Britain and served as the principal means of communicating news to the colonists. Most early newspapers were weeklies and as such could not communicate news in a truly timely fashion. Their cost also precluded large circulation. Despite these drawbacks, newspapers served an important function as organs

of the early political parties. Not until the 1830s did newspaper ownership become private and independent of parties. With increased competition for readers, improvements were made in newsgathering and reporting. Wire services, for example, were developed following the invention of the telegraph to transmit news both widely and quickly. It also became common for newspapers to use reporters to gather news and even to assign reporters to specific places or beats where news stories were most likely to occur. Magazines differ from newspapers with respect to how often they are published and in what they choose to feature. Only a small portion of magazines deal with the news, and then in a more selective way. The limited circulation and narrow audiences of many magazines argue against their being regarded as part of the mass media. At the same time, several weekly newsmagazines such as *Time, Newsweek,* and *U.S. News and World Report* have national audiences in excess of 2 million each. *See also* BROADCAST MEDIA, 339; MASS MEDIA, 368.

*Significance* The print media differ in several respects from the electronic or broadcast media. First, they reach smaller audiences. Although weekly newsmagazines circulate upwards of 2 million copies each, many times that number listen to or watch network programming including news reports. Second, with the exception of the several newsmagazines, political information is not nationally circulated in print. Third, the print media are not subject to the same degree of governmental regulation as are the broadcast media. This fact results from the view that the public airwaves are a finite resource requiring close regulation to protect the public interest. Finally, although the print media cannot report news as quickly or with the same visual impact as television, newspapers and newsmagazines have the luxury of length. Reports need not be designed for 30- or 40-second time slots on an evening newscast. As a result, the print media are able to provide information with greater depth and with accompanying analysis in a manner unmatched by broadcasters. Like broadcasters, however, the print media are privately owned, which means they must attend to the economic realities of maximizing sales. This dynamic has direct consequences on coverage decisions and choice of emphasis when stories are reported.

**Prior Restraint** **(393)**

A restriction placed on a publication before it can be published or circulated. Prior restraint typically occurs through licensure or censorship or by a full prohibition on publication. Censorship requirements involve a review of materials by the state for objectionable content. The materials that satisfy the standards of the censor may be distributed or exhibited, whereas materials found unacceptable may be banned. *See also* FREE PRESS CLAUSE, 358; *NEAR V. MINNESOTA* (283 U.S. 697: 1931), 376; *NEW YORK TIMES V. UNITED STATES* (403 U.S. 713: 1971), 382.

*Significance* Prior restraint imposes a greater threat to free expression than after-the-fact prosecution because government restrictions are imposed in a manner that precludes public scrutiny. In this way, prior restraint actually prevents communication. Although subsequent punishment imposes a penalty after the fact, at least the communication has taken place. In addition, prior restraint precludes a trial on the material before a neutral or detached judicial officer. Rather, a prosecutor develops a case and then presumptively declares certain content guilty through imposition of the prior restraint. Prior restraint also prompts people to behave in ways that will avoid regulation. Publishers refrain from content that approaches the margins of protection, thus prior restraint may chill expression by making publishers excessively cautious. The First Amendment therefore prohibits prior restraint in most instances. Prior restraint may be justified if publication threatens national security, incites overthrow of the government, is obscene, or interferes with the private rights of others. Prior restraint is otherwise heavily suspect.

**Public Broadcasting Act of 1967** **(394)**

Federal enactment that created a public broadcasting system. The Public Broadcasting Act was passed in an effort to support public service or noncommercial broadcasting in the United States. The public broadcasting system established under the act draws together a mixture of public and private financing, programming, and radio and television stations. The radio stations composing the system are called National Public Radio (NPR). Under provisions of this act and the Telecommunications Act of 1978, the general administration of the system is handled by the Corporation for Public Broadcasting (CPB). The CPB is a public corporation with some of the characteristics of the British Broadcasting Company (BBC). The CPB provides financial support for the broadcasting system, but because its staff is politically appointed, it has sought to remain separate from programming. NPR is generally responsible for radio program production, whereas the Public Broadcasting Service (PBS) participates in the production of television programming. *See also* PUBLIC TELEVISION, 396.

*Significance* The communications industry in the United States is largely private, but since the passage of the Public Broadcasting Act of

1967, there has also been a public broadcasting component. The primary objective of the legislation was to enable stations that featured educational and public service content to remain viable despite limited audiences and commercial sponsorship. The mix of public financing, program development, and private stations has produced some operational problems. In particular, it has been difficult to keep funding and administration wholly separate from program content. Both the government [through the Corporation for Public Broadcasting (CPB)] and private funding sources have exercised some program influence. This problem is lessened to a degree by revenues that public broadcasting stations can generate from local advertising and viewer subscriptions. Nonetheless, the public broadcasting system is subject to political pressure, if not direct control, and its future remains uncertain as a consequence.

**Public Service Programming** **(395)**

The portion of broadcast time that is devoted to such content as news and local public affairs. The Federal Communications Commission (FCC) requires that every broadcaster use a part of the broadcast day for "nonentertainment" programming. Compliance with this public service programming requirement is a condition of licensure, although the FCC has never closely monitored station compliance with the requirement. Seldom, for example, was programming that was designated as "public service" by a broadcaster ever examined. Rather, inspection of station logs was typically accepted at face value. Since the early 1980s, the percentage levels initially fixed by the FCC have given way to a more general expectation that broadcasters should attend to local public service needs. *See also* FEDERAL COMMUNICATIONS COMMISSION (FCC), 354; LICENSURE, 366.

*Significance* The basis for the public service programming requirement is the premise that the electronic media must be regulated to ensure that certain valuable content is transmitted. Historically, support for public service requirements was also grounded on the scarcity rationale—that the broadcast spectrum was limited and needed access regulation. The advent of cable and satellite technologies created essentially unlimited channel capabilities, thereby eliminating scarcity as a compelling regulatory rationale. As a result, the Federal Communications Commission (FCC) has engaged in some deregulation with respect to public service programming. Even when fixed requirements were in place, it was not difficult for broadcasters to air programs whose content was not locally focused or of a public service character. Nonetheless, most stations continue to devote some fraction of their broadcast time to news and public affairs.

**Public Television** **(396)**
Television broadcasting that is controlled or financed at least in part by government. Television in the United States is largely privately owned, but public television does exist to a limited extent. The rationale for a public component rests on the premise that certain educational and public service content cannot effectively compete in the commercial broadcast market. Government involvement with television occurs at both the federal and local levels. Under provisions of the Public Broadcasting Act of 1967, a public broadcasting system was established, drawing together a combination of private and public funding, programming, and station facilities. The system in its entirety is called the Public Broadcasting System (PBS). General administration and public financing is handled by the Corporation for Public Broadcasting (CPB). Because CPB personnel are chosen for political reasons, efforts have been made to keep management and programming functions separate. Local involvement with public television occurs through the franchising and regulation of cable television. *See also* CABLE TELEVISION, 340; PUBLIC BROADCASTING ACT OF 1967, 394.

*Significance* Public television broadcasting in the United States represents a mixture of private and public influences. A public broadcasting system was established to support the transmission of content that would not attract sufficient audiences to be commercially successful. Public television broadcasting is distinctive in that it carries programs that feature educational, documentary, artistic, public affairs, and public service content. With the possible exception of its children's programming, relatively small audiences avail themselves of public broadcasting. Those supporting public television broadcasting argue that audience size is an inappropriate standard for evaluating its value. Rather, they see public broadcasting as serving needs that are both special and justified on their substantive merits. The levels of support directed toward public broadcasting have increased over the years, but so too has the political pressure on programming. So long as the funding–program content tension exists, the outlook for public television will contain uncertainties.

**Ratings** **(397)**
Estimates of the audience size for broadcast media. Rating measures are taken by private organizations that use various sampling methods to gauge audience appeal. Ratings are directly tied to the commercial

success of the broadcast industry because rates that can be charged for advertising are based on audience size. The larger the audience watching or listening to a particular station, the more advertisers must pay for each 30- or 60-second ad spot they wish to run. The print media are similarly interested in reaching the largest possible audience, but unlike broadcasting, circulation can be directly measured by sales data. *See also* MEDIA MARKET, 371; NEWSWORTHINESS, 380.

*Significance* Ratings competition is a direct consequence of private ownership of the media. Privately owned media must be commercially successful. Such success depends on capturing a large enough audience share to produce advertising revenues that are sufficient to make a profit. Programming is the product that broadcasters sell, so it is imperative that it appeal to the widest possible audience. This fact carries over to news coverage as well. Like other programming, news must be entertaining enough to heighten audience appeal, and this constraint influences, if not governs, decisions about what news stories to cover. Consequently, sensational stories are seen as more newsworthy than those that may actually have more political or social value.

**Rebuttal, Right to** **(398)**

Rule that requires broadcasters to provide reply time to any person or group whose character or integrity is attacked on their station. The right of rebuttal or reply is one of the access rights covered by section 315 of the Communications Act of 1934. The right to rebuttal is founded on the view that maligned persons or groups deserve to access the public airwaves to offer response. It is also argued that the public is entitled to be exposed to competing viewpoints. The principal rationale for the right to rebuttal rule for broadcasters is that public airspace is a scarce commodity, thus regulation in the public interest is required. No equivalent right to reply regulation applies to the print media. *See also* EQUAL TIME PROVISION, 352; FEDERAL COMMUNICATIONS COMMISSION (FCC), 354; *RED LION BROADCASTING COMPANY V. FEDERAL COMMUNICATIONS COMMISSION (FCC)* (395 U.S. 367: 1969), 399.

*Significance* The right to rebuttal rule engages when a station broadcasts content that constitutes a "personal attack." The rebuttal rule requires a broadcaster to inform the attacked person or group that such a broadcast occurred and provide the target with a summary or transcript of the broadcast. The attacked person or group is then entitled to rebuttal time. Claims for equal time that are not voluntarily provided by stations are evaluated by the Federal Communications Commission (FCC). The access rules that apply to the broadcast or electronic media are different from those that apply to print media. Because only so much broadcast "space" is available, the view has been that government needs to regulate broadcasters in the public interest to guarantee access to the virtual monopoly possessed on airwaves by these broadcasters. Government authority to do so has been upheld by the Supreme Court in such cases as *Red Lion Broadcasting Company v. Federal Communications Commission (FCC)* (395 U.S. 367: 1969). Nonetheless, there has been substantial pressure to modify, if not abandon, many regulatory rules. Critics of the regulations point out that the development of cable and satellite technologies, for example, facilitates public access to the electronic media and diminishes the need for regulation. Critics argue that these regulations interfere with the free press right of broadcasters. Many broadcasters, rather than risk being compelled to allow rebuttals, reduce or even eliminate the airing of controversial content.

### *Red Lion Broadcasting Company v. Federal Communications Commission (FCC)*, 395 U.S. 367 (1969) (399)

Upheld an FCC regulation known as the fairness doctrine. A Red Lion broadcast impugned the honesty and character of a third party. The third party demanded free time for a response, but was refused. The FCC ruled that Red Lion had failed to satisfy a requirement of equal access, and the Supreme Court unanimously affirmed the FCC. Although the broadcast media have First Amendment rights, their relative scarcity of access means Congress unquestionably has regulatory authority. Without regulation in the form of such rules as the fairness doctrine, station owners and a few networks would have, said the Court, "unfettered power to make time available only to the highest bidders, to communicate only their views on public issues, people and candidates, and to permit on the air only those with whom they agreed." The Court concluded that no sanctuary exists in the First Amendment for unlimited private censorship that operates in media not open to all. *See also* EQUAL TIME PROVISION, 352; FAIRNESS DOCTRINE, 353; FEDERAL COMMUNICATIONS COMMISSION (FCC), 354.

*Significance* The thrust of *Red Lion Broadcasting Company v. Federal Communications Commission (FCC)* (395 U.S. 367: 1969) is that a balance must be struck between the First Amendment interests of the broadcast media and the need to regulate government-granted channel monopolies. The fairness doctrine at issue in *Red Lion* had not kept the station from expressing its own views. It only required that reply time be provided when a station carries a broadcast that personally attacks an individual. The print media may not be required to do the same thing, however. In *Miami Herald Publishing Company v. Tornillo* (418 U.S. 241: 1974), the Supreme Court overturned a Florida right to reply statute that required reply space in a newspaper for any political candidate who was attacked. Such required space was found to be an affirmative prior restraint. A law such as this, said the Court, authorizes governmental "intrusion into the function of editors in choosing what material goes into a newspaper."

### ***Richmond Newspapers, Inc. v. Virginia*, 448 U.S. 555 (1980)** **(400)**

Determined that the press had a constitutional right of access to criminal trials. In *Richmond Newspapers,* the defendant's counsel requested that a murder trial be closed to the public. The prosecutor expressed no objection, and the trial judge ordered the courtroom cleared. Under Virginia law, a trial judge has the discretion to exclude from a trial any person whose "presence would impair the conduct of a fair trial." The Supreme Court ruled that the closure order violated press right of access. The Court began with a lengthy treatment of the history of the open trial. This "unbroken, uncontradicted history, supported by reasons as valid today as in centuries past," forced the Court to conclude that a "presumption of openness inheres in the very nature of a criminal trial under our system of justice." The Court said the open trial serves a therapeutic purpose for the community, especially in the instance of shocking crimes. Open trials offer protection against abusive or arbitrary behavior. They allow criminal processes to "satisfy the appearance of justice." Although access to trials is not specifically provided in the First Amendment, it is implicit in its guarantees. Without the freedom to attend trials, important aspects of free speech and free press could be eviscerated. In this case, the closure order was defective because the trial judge made no specific finding to support such an order. Alternatives to closure were not explored, there was no recognition of any constitutional right for the press or the public to attend the proceeding, and there was no indication that problems with witnesses could not have been handled otherwise. *See also* *CHANDLER V. FLORIDA* (449 U.S. 560: 1981), 341; MEDIA ACCESS, 369; *NEBRASKA PRESS ASSOCIATION V. STUART* (427 U.S. 539: 1976), 377.

*Significance* *Richmond Newspapers, Inc. v. Virginia* (448 U.S. 555: 1980) clearly distinguished the trial from pretrial hearings and elevated the press interest to prevailing weight in the former. In most instances, the Supreme Court has found a criminal defendant to be entitled to insulation from media coverage as a basic requirement of due process in pretrial hearings. Consistent with the objective of minimizing adverse pretrial publicity, the Court allowed closure of pretrial proceedings in *Gannett Company v. DePasquale* (443 U.S. 368: 1979). The Court held in *Nebraska Press Association v. Stuart* (427 U.S. 539: 1976) that material from a public proceeding or record could not be kept from the public through a court gag order. *Nebraska Press Association* also said that the press cannot be restrained from reporting what it observes. A balance of press and criminal defendant interests was struck in *Chandler v. Florida* (449 U.S. 560: 1981), in which the Court upheld a policy whereby trials might be broadcast so long as broadcast coverage is not disruptive, intrusive, or prejudicial to the outcome of the trial.

**Shield Law** **(401)**

An enactment that conveys the privilege of source confidentiality to journalists. The adoption of shield laws is based on the view that the newsgathering function of the media requires such confidentiality. The claim of this privilege as a direct derivative of the First Amendment was rejected by the Supreme Court in *Branzburg v. Hayes* (408 U.S. 665: 1972). *See also* BRANZBURG V. HAYES (408 U.S. 665: 1972), 338; NEWSPERSON'S PRIVILEGE, 379.

*Significance* Shield laws accept the premise that newspeople occupy a distinctive and elevated position from the public at large. These laws exempt the reporter from the obligation imposed on other citizens to furnish information to the criminal process. The rationale for the protection is that news sources might disappear without the promise of confidentiality and thereby generally impair the newsgathering function. This consequence, in turn, may interfere with the protected right to publish. Furthermore, many people fear that without shield laws the independence of the media is threatened because in effect reporters become part of the investigative arm of government. Shield laws may not absolutely protect confidentiality when that interest conflicts with the fair trial rights of a criminal defendant to access information from a reporter.

**White House Press Corps** **(402)**

A group of reporters who cover the president on a regular basis. Most of the White House press corps, which numbers upwards of 100 persons, represent the large national media and are assigned exclusively to cover the White House beat. Among the media represented are the wire services, radio and television networks, national newsmagazines, and major daily newspapers such as the *New York Times*,

*Washington Post, Chicago Tribune,* and *Los Angeles Times.* The White House press corps is part of the larger Washington press group that generally covers the Washington political scene. Members of the White House press corps are usually highly regarded veteran newspeople. The White House press corps travels with the president both nationally and abroad. Otherwise, these reporters generally operate out of the White House press facilities where they regularly receive press releases and have daily briefings with the White House press secretary. *See also* MANAGED NEWS, 367; NATIONAL MEDIA, 375; NETWORK, 378; WIRE SERVICE, 403.

*Significance* The White House press corps is generally knowledgeable about Washington political life and persistent in its efforts to obtain information about government activities, especially those involving the president. Indeed, their persistence and aggressiveness in newsgathering is often taken for hostility toward one or another administration. At the same time, the White House press corps is vulnerable to having its perspective affected by its closeness to the president. These reporters are also subjected to extensive news management by the White House. The press depends on the administration to provide access to information. Since the 1970s, this access has become institutionalized through such structures as the Office of the Press Secretary. The White House press corps meets on a daily basis with the spokesperson for the White House and receives information from press releases or through briefing sessions. These forms of press contact with the White House allow presidents and their staffs the opportunity to manipulate the content and timing of what is released. Given its dependence on the administration as an ongoing news source, the White House press corps has little choice but to adapt itself.

**Wire Service (403)**

Newsgathering organizations that provide information to subscriber newspapers and broadcast stations. Wire or news services assign reporters to particular beats at the national and international levels. A story filed by a wire-service reporter is carried electronically to subscribers who, in turn, print or broadcast some or all of the story. A wire service allows subscribers to avoid the cost of having as many of their own reporters engaged in newsgathering, especially the cost of covering foreign beats. There are two principal wire services: Associated Press (AP) and United Press International (UPI). In addition, wire services are operated by several larger newspapers, such as the *New York Times,* but the number of subscribers is quite limited when compared with AP or UPI. *See also* BEAT SYSTEM, 336; NETWORK, 378.

*Significance* Wire services are the only national and international news source for many newspapers and broadcast stations. Virtually every paper or station that communicates news on a daily basis subscribes to Associated Press (AP) or United Press International (UPI) or both. Wire-service reports tend to appear substantially unchanged for an overwhelming number of smaller newspapers and stations. The wire services clearly facilitate the gathering and dissemination of news. At the same time, it must be recognized that the two major news services dominate news production. Consequently, local papers and stations have generally similar, if not identical, content. The importance of this source concentration is reinforced by the network organization of the broadcast industry, in which upwards of 90 percent of stations are affiliated with one of the three major networks, which provide newsgathering at the national and international levels for most of their affiliates.

**Yellow Journalism** **(404)**

Publication of newspapers that feature content selected for its sensational or entertainment value. Yellow journalism was common in the late nineteenth and early twentieth centuries and was driven exclusively by a desire to broaden circulation. During this period, far more newspapers existed than do today, and most of the larger metropolitan areas had many daily papers as well. New York, for example, had 29 newspapers in the 1880s. Competition for readership was intense, and publishers turned to a number of devices to expand sales. During this period, comic and sports sections, entertainment columns, and photographic coverage of news became common. In addition, newspapers began to sensationalize news coverage by exploiting aspects that might sell copies. Accuracy in news reporting was clearly not a priority. *See also* INVESTIGATIVE JOURNALISM, 363; MUCKRAKING, 374.

*Significance* Yellow journalism has not disappeared, although the intensity of circulation competition has diminished over the years. Several larger city dailies and national weeklies still pursue mass appeal through sensationalism. Generally, however, the level of professionalism exhibited by newspapers has risen, which, in turn, has diminished the tendency to engage in yellow journalism. One consequence of yellow journalism is the current premium placed on investigative reporting. A central element of yellow journalism was muckraking—newspapers liked to expose scandal and corruption in governmental and corporate sectors. Although the objective of muckraking was to expose for sensationalistic reasons, it was the precursor of investigative journalism.

# *INDEX*

In this index, a reference in **bold** type indicates the entry number where a particular term is defined within the text. Numbers in roman type refer to entries the reader may wish to consult for further information about a term.